Action and Reaction

Action and Reaction

The Life and Adventures of a Couple

Jean Starobinski

Translated by Sophie Hawkes with Jeff Fort

ZONE BOOKS · NEW YORK

2003

The publisher would like to thank the Centre National du Livre at the French Ministry of Culture for its assistance with this translation.

Originally published as *Action et Réaction: Vie et aventures d'un couple* © 1999 Editions de Seuil.

Printed in the United States of America.

Distributed by The MIT Press,
Cambridge, Massachusetts, and London, England

Library of Congress Cataloging-in-Publication Data

Starobinski, Jean.
    [Action et réaction. English]
    Action and reaction : the life and adventures of a couple / [Jean Starobinski].
        p.   cm.
Includes bibliographical references and index.
ISBN 1-890951-20-X (cloth)
1. Act (Philosophy) 2. Reaction (Philosophy) I. Title.

B105.A35 S7313   2002
194—dc21   2002071388

Contents

Preface to the American Edition

The title and subtitle of this work could have been placed in quotation marks. The expressions come from Honoré de Balzac's "Louis Lambert," in which the protagonist, who has a passion for the history of words, speaks of the action and reaction between thought and speech, comparing their relationship to that of a loving couple. Balzac did no more than sketch out a program of linguistic inquiry. But I thought it necessary to refer to this program, since, formulated in these terms, it allows one to see how seductive both the idea of tracing the history of words and the use of the verbal couple "action and reaction" had become in the first flush of modernity.

This conceptual couple is the product of philosophical language. Its use is widespread in Western thought and literature. Now it belongs to so-called ordinary language. How did I come to trace its biography? I will briefly summarize how my work evolved.

My initial questions concerned the adoption of the word "reaction" by Enlightenment thinkers, and then by the medical sciences, psychiatry in particular. My teaching at both the Faculty of Medicine and the Faculty of Letters at the University of Geneva enabled me to put these questions in a larger historical perspective. At what point and for what reasons did people begin to speak of reactive mental disorders? In what circumstances did the word "reaction" gain the political meaning by which we know it today? How did the various specialized uses of a single word come into being? I asked these questions not out of idle curiosity but because I believe that the semantic history of familiar terms — especially those that belong among our intellectual tools — helps us to understand better who we are.

My intention was to situate the new contexts in which the word "reaction" was used. From Aristotelian physics to classical mechanics, a fundamental mutation occurred. Historians of science have recounted and interpreted it many times. Now it is common knowledge. I have focused on the lexical traces this scientific revolution left in its wake. I wanted to note the moment at which scientific language (with its calculations) and ordinary language (with its literary productions) began to diverge. In the first chapter, I am interested in the prestige attached to the couple "action and reaction" by writers and the educated public. These words eventually became representative of the success of mathematical language in other milieus and — at least at first — they were used in debates and speculations outside the fields governed by mathematics. Starting from the specific case of Diderot, the second chapter studies extrapolations from the idea of reaction and the intuitions with which it became associated, particularly in chemistry. In the third chapter, I analyze the free extrapolation and generalization that brought about the first uses of the word in studies of life phenomena and in medicine. The fourth chapter attempts to retrace the elaboration of Freudian theory based on the idea of abreaction, while noting the criticism it encountered.

It was also necessary to take stock of the metaphoric uses of the couple "action and reaction." Balzac's imagination, which vacillated between radical materialism and radical spiritualism, solemnizes reaction within the confines of life and death (discussed in the fifth chapter). Many nineteenth-century poets and philosophers combated mechanistic reduction and "the disenchantment of the world." They attempted to reappropriate the couple "action and reaction" in order to give it a vitalist meaning, associating it with the metaphor of the beating heart. Edgar Allan Poe, in *Eureka*, gives it an impressive scope. My sixth chapter is devoted to this attempt at metaphoric reversal. Finally, the seventh chapter closely studies the introduction of the word "reaction" into political discourse, where it became metaphorically appointed the antonym of "revolution," and then of "progress." Yet, quite independently of these antitheses, "reaction" ended up designating the response of individuals or groups of people to challenges. It henceforth became a common, neutral, almost banal term, applicable to all sorts of responses, signifying a sequence of behaviors and decisions. It is one means by which we interpret links of causality and intelligibility in human history. At a moment when we are obliged to reflect on questions of necessity and nature, on the means and consequences of our reactions, I do not think it a useless luxury to give an account of the semantic history of a word we use so often. Everything that constitutes civilization may have, at one time or another, been considered a useless luxury.

The history of ideas, semantic and philological history, literary history, the history of medicine and biological sciences: representatives from these various fields attended meetings of the History of Ideas Club, in which I participated during my three years of residence (now long past) at Johns Hopkins University in Baltimore. Most of my books bear witness to my memory of that experience, but this one constitutes the clearest proof of it. It is only right that I should mention the people whose example encouraged me: for the history of ideas, Arthur O. Lovejoy and

George Boas; for semantic and philological history, Leo Spitzer and Ludwig Edelstein; for literary history, Georges Poulet; for the history of medicine, Owsei Temkin. Of course, I mention their patronage only to legitimize some aspects of my project, not to justify the result. To their names I must add that of Michael Shepherd, M.D., whom I met at Johns Hopkins Hospital at the same time. Through his research, publications, and teaching at the Maudsley Hospital in London, he was one of the masters of contemporary psychiatry. His friendship, his thought, our conversations (until his premature death in 1995) had a great impact on me during the decades in which this work evolved.

Jean Starobinski
December 15, 2002

Preface

> I would be very happy ... if in your working method
> you began not with a general problem but with a
> singular phenomenon, carefully and decisively chosen,
> something like the history of a word or the interpreta-
> tion of a passage. This singular phenomenon could
> never be too small or too concrete and should never be
> a concept introduced by us or by other scholars, but
> rather something suggested by the object itself.
> — Erich Auerbach[1]

Honoré de Balzac attributes an enthusiasm for linguistic exploration to his hero Louis Lambert:

> Often have I made the most delightful voyage, floating on a word
> down the abyss of the past, like an insect embarked on a blade of
> grass tossing on the ripples of a stream. Starting from Greece, I
> would get to Rome, and traverse the whole extent of modern ages.
> What a fine book might be written of the life and adventures of a
> word! ... But is it not so with every root-word? They all are stamped
> with a living power that comes from the soul, and which they restore
> to the soul through the mysterious and wonderful action and reac-
> tion between thought and speech.[2]

Louis Lambert, whose gaze is drawn toward the East and the Bible, thus includes etymological inquiry within his vast speculative program. He offers examples: the words flight (*vol*) and especially true (*vrai*), in which he discovers, without giving any reasons, "a certain imaginary rectitude." Here lies the program for "an entire science." This project accords with the theory of language Plato attributes to Cratylus. Louis Lambert's conviction is a romanticized version of Cratylism, whereby the secrets of the spiritual world are to be sought in the life of words.

Balzac, through his protagonist, believes he can assert a difference between thought and word that is metaphorically equivalent to the difference between the sexes. He resolves the opposition through the magical effects of a mysterious formula of reciprocity, a formula that sets up between them an "action and reaction" similar to that found in an amorous relationship. "Might we not speak of it as a lover who finds on his mistress's lips as much love as he gives?" These passages from Balzac express the persistent desire to recover a primal speech that would have pronounced the true names of all earthly beings. Balzac (like so many before him) speaks of "the primitive speech of nations," of which our modern languages know but the remnant. As communities grow old, the grandeur and solemnity of this original language decrease.[3]

Louis Lambert presents his project as a *descent*, a drifting downstream, which allows him to imagine the origin that has been left behind. The linguistic "life and adventures" he hopes to retrace unfold in a sorrowful tale, a tale of decline and dispersal, betrayal and oblivion, which the voyager's thought would rectify by rediscovering the first words spoken in the remotest depths of time. By comparing himself to a traveling insect, the young Lambert seems to be engaging in self-mockery. But in this comparison he indulges in an immense privilege, since his "delightful voyage" is supposed to have begun at the source itself.

Most linguists today take a synchronic approach and have no interest in the "true" archaic source of words, which they consider a mirage. But historical semantics (as defined by Michel Bréal in 1897 or as illustrated by the works of Emile Benveniste) has never succumbed to the illusion that the most ancient meaning of a word is a philosophical truth. There was often an underlying etymological fallacy in the practice of historical semantics. But giving up that fallacy should not entail abandoning historical semantics altogether. Indeed, historical semantics has much to gain from a general and formal linguistic theory. The history of language, inseparable as it is from the history of societies, fields of knowledge, and technical advances — and capable, therefore, of indicating significant landmarks — is invaluable for understanding our present age and situation. It helps us to recognize how we differ from our predecessors. In other words, a vocabulary's semantic *variation* is itself a signifier, and by referring back to successive "states of language," it allows us to see more clearly the changes undergone by various "states of culture." In this way, the demands of a differentiated knowledge can be satisfied.[4]

"The mysterious and wonderful action and reaction between thought and speech": Balzac tempts me to take him at his word. True, he did not have a monopoly on the use of the words "action and reaction." He inherited the formula, which appears in many continental European Romantic texts. But the persistent use of this verbal couple, as well as the frequent isolated use of the word "reaction," is characteristic of Balzac's style and demands closer scrutiny.

Since we have been offered the curious image of an insect "embarked on a blade of grass," we may well wonder whether "action and reaction" might not in turn provide our own blades of grass. Might we not expect a few revelations from an exploration of the "life" and "adventures" of these two terms that Balzac uses to link together the sound and the meaning, the flesh and the soul of words? They are instrumental words, and through their good offices Lambert sketches an explanation of the bonds between thought and speech.

As abstract nouns, substantives derived from neutral verbs, "action" and "reaction" are simple, symmetrical, specular notions — almost mirror images of each other — in which the immense variety of everything that acts, "inasmuch as it acts," and everything that reacts, "inasmuch as it reacts," becomes concentrated. There is a certain satisfaction in encountering them as a pair, for they are able both to establish and to reconcile oppositions. They are related to the concepts of the mutual, the reciprocal, and at times the alternative. More often than not, they are used without any observation or interrogation of their provenance, their affinities, or their diffusion. Kant, however, did demonstrate the importance of the category of *relation*, of which they are the recognized representatives.[5] "Reaction" will receive more attention here, because this word bears a mark, its precise directional prefix, that particularly sets it off, and because its history can be more clearly traced.

I began by mentioning the ideas of one of Balzac's visionary heroes, who is also his double. I must confess that my slightly voyeuristic curiosity about the intimate life of the couple "action/reaction" stems from my having come across it a thousand times in the most disparate places. It has by now become part of common knowledge. Since the Middle Ages, it has haunted treatises on physics. Later it transferred onto the geometers' ships, rigged with equations. It navigated under the banner of mechanicalism — the philosophical doctrine that phenomena are mechanically caused — and then reappeared among the faithful followers of vitalism.

"Reaction" soon set off on its own adventures. For vitalism, in fact, "reaction" gave life the means to resist death. Later it was reduced to the response to a stimulus, through motor innervation, in the living body. In political-historical vocabulary, the words "action" and "reaction" were first used to turn the wheel of a cyclic history of revolutions. But then, when the goal of history became the improvement and perfection of humankind, "revolution" and "progress" chose "reaction" as their adversary: political gatherings, newspapers, tracts, and everyday speech have broadcast this fact clearly enough. In the neologism "interaction," the two words have more closely resumed their conjugal existence. Then come their descendants: a little more than a century ago, the good fairy "abreaction" leaned over the cradle of psychoanalysis. Elsewhere (and rather late, around 1890), it was decided that psychic illnesses should be called "reactive" when they arise from external circumstances rather than from an "endogenous" determinism.

Around 1600, "action and reaction" was a chapter heading in the physics of philosophers, and the word "reaction" was scarcely found outside Latin treatises. Today it appears everywhere — and has therefore become banal. This word, a victim of its own success, has moved from a specialized to a general vocabulary. Around 1800, it still had an impact; today it is common coin, and there is no longer anything provocative about it. The only exceptions are the psychiatric and political uses already mentioned. In social-scientific (and journalistic) vocabulary, it takes on psychological overtones and functions implicitly as a term of excuse. It makes even crimes relative, by making them dependent on their socio-historical antecedents. Otherwise, it is a word for all occasions, a ubiquitous word with dozens of uses, depending on the adjective or complement added to it, just as one fits various tools to a single handle, or, more generally, according to the nominal syntagma to which it belongs (thermonuclear reaction, reaction jet, and so on). Whether in physics, chemistry, or medicine, reactions are legion by virtue of the complements attached to this root word. In scientific fields, the word is omnipresent but never considered on its own; only its alliances count. It was used (along with its derivative "reactive" and its acolytes "reflex" and "reagent") to preserve the memory of scientific pioneers. It attracted eponyms and immortalized certain scientists: Bordet and Gengou reaction, Wassermann reaction, Wernicke's reaction, Ehrlich's reagent, Fehling's reaction, and so on. The vocabulary of the daily news is no less rich. Governments or political parties faced with *crises*, stockbrokers, athletes on the playing field, drivers on the road, students in the classroom — who is not obliged to react? Who is not judged by the way in which he or she reacts? This lexical diffusion, in addition to the favor now enjoyed by the more recent term "interaction," is itself symptomatic. Interaction belongs to an almost worldwide "state of language" and makes it possible to speak of a contemporary hyper-reactivism. Whether as a subtext or out in the open, "reaction" intervenes in a great many systems (beginning with the systems theory of Ludwig von Bertalanffy or Niklas Luhmann). And the question asked by our most responsible contemporaries as they face the challenges of the age is commonly formulated in terms of "How to react?" This question is suffused with an anxiety already aware that any reaction can only be a partial event within a much larger interaction that no one can master.

That the couple "action/reaction" could successively pertain to the material universe — in its totality or in the intimacy of its particles — the living body, the events of history, and psychological behavior suggests that observing its movement from one territory to another throughout Western intellectual history would be fruitful. The different values assumed by the word "reaction" since its medieval invention have made it a great indicator, one that could be called, metaphorically, a *tracer* or *marker*. If we return for a moment to Balzac's image of the river, we note that it divides into several branches: the river often becomes ramified and mixes with other waters. Observing a few of the larger branches will provide a more comprehensive account than focusing on a single science or discipline.

In his groundbreaking study, Michel Bréal encouraged a synoptic point of view. In the chapter introducing the idea of polysemy, he aptly remarks:

> A new meaning, whatever it is, does not put an end to the old meaning. They exist together, one beside the other. The same term can be used by turns in the literal and metaphoric sense, in a restricted or general sense, or in an abstract or concrete sense.... As new meanings are given to a word, it seems to multiply and produce new examples, similar in form but differing in value.[6]

Now, in taking on new meanings, the couple "action/reaction" and the word "reaction" changed "domains," transgressing the boundaries between disciplines. Are there not sufficient grounds for closely examining the far-reaching polysemous process just mentioned? This will entail arranging a polyphonic score — or a kind of mosaic. For the case at hand, there is no preestablished method; but there are signposts to be located as precisely as possible, as well as the necessity of meeting them with the most adequate response — or reaction.[7]

CHAPTER ONE

A Word from Physics

A Lately Coined Word

At first glance, the word "reaction" does not seem more difficult to understand than the word "action." One does not usually stop to question its origins. The word does not present an enigma. As for "action," its career and the variety of its semantic functions do catch the historian's eye if he takes the trouble to look into them. How did the value of the word change? How did it penetrate various domains? What intellectual roles did it take on and leave behind? What memory does it awaken? Today it is a rather banal term, but this was not always the case.

Tracing a more remote etymology will help to stimulate reflection. Knowledge of a word's antecedents invites the reader to conceive of it as a *derivative*. Certainly, the deepest "roots" of the words belonging to intellectual language do not necessarily lead to their secret truth, which might just as easily lie in their emergence in concrete gestures at the beginning of a metaphoric transfer. According to etymologists, "act" and "action" (and their homologues in several modern languages) go back to the Latin verb *agere*, meaning "to push forward," "to move a herd forward" — a movement that occupies space on the terrestrial soil and a moment of the day at a time when man was considered in relationship to livestock.[1]

21

One can therefore wonder about this ancient substantive, *actio*, which has been used a great deal to designate the delivery of a speech and may have carried the memory of a more ancient pastoral activity. In its abstract sense, the only one retained today, it appears to be a metaphor that has forgotten its origin. The poet can reflect on it. But this memory does not make us more efficient in our acts and actions. The jurist who "initiates an action" or the "holder of shares [*actions* in seventeenth-century English and in French]" on the stock exchange are not concerned with this echo.

What about *reactio*? History does not allow us to see it as the exact counterpart of "action." It is a much later composite, of scholarly origin, one half of a pair in conceptual abstraction rather than in life. In fact, *reactio* and *reagere* are not part of the ancient Latin lexicon. They are not found in any text from Antiquity. Their components — the prefix *re-*, the verb *agere*, and the substantive *actio* — certainly existed, but they were never combined to form *reagere* or *reactio* in classical language. The antonym of *agere* in classical Latin is *patior* (to suffer, to undergo); the antonym of *actio* is *passio*. Action and passion are much more solidly established conceptual opposites. This couple was present in philosophical Greek (*poieō/paskhō*). Passed on to Latin, it was later transmitted to the European languages. *Reagere* came much later, among the Scholastics, and provided a double for *patior*, while also giving it an active sense. It was formed by being cut from the same cloth as *agere*, of which it became a sort of shadow or a reverse rejoinder. *Reagere* is therefore a derivative (or correlative) term, to which the prefix *re-* added an antagonistic, spatial, and temporal determination: antagonistic because there is no reaction except in opposition to an action; spatial because one thinks spontaneously of a reaction as repelling an action; and temporal because there is no reaction — apparently — that does

22

not follow an action which precedes and provokes it, even if action and reaction can be imagined as infinitely close. Immanuel Kant, as we shall see, denies this consecutive aspect and argues for the simultaneity of action and reaction.

Based on the documents I have consulted, I believe I am able to conjecture that *reactio* was introduced gradually into narrative Latin in the early Middle Ages. Was this indeed the case? I could not find any proof of it.[2] On the other hand, between the twelfth and the thirteenth century, *reagere* and *reactio* appeared in scholarly Latin and never left it. They were specialized words. They enriched the terminology of the natural sciences, that is, of "physics" in its broadest sense — ranging from cosmology to what for the last two hundred years has been called biology — which was the sense this word and this branch of knowledge had in the Aristotelian tradition. My first example is Albertus Magnus, who decisively contributed to the medieval philosophical canon's adoption of Aristotle.

When a Child Does Not Resemble Its Father

In Aristotle's thought, there is much discussion of reciprocal action, in which the "patient" acts upon the "agent." The treatise *On Generation and Corruption* offers a perfect example. Aristotle expounds at length on the opposition between "to act" (*poiein*) and "to suffer" (*paskhein*).[3] This opposition corresponds to the one in the category of motion between "to move" (*kinein*) and "to be moved" (*kineisthai*). But to be moved is to be incited to move in return (*antikinein*). Only one mover is impassive and cannot be moved or move in return: the *prōton kinoun*, the *primum movens*. The "first mover" is unmovable. "And since that which is moved and moves is intermediate, there is a mover which moves without being moved, being eternal, substance, and actuality. And the object of desire and the object of thought move in this way; they move without being moved."[4] In this sense, the first unmovable mover (*prōton kinoun*) is also the final cause, which "produces motion by being loved." Motion in the world proceeds from a sphere lower than God, who is the upper sphere of the heavens and the first mover (*prōton kinēton, primum mobile*). "For motion in space is the first of the kinds of change, and motion in a circle the first kind of spatial motion; and this the first mover *produces*."[5] Motion, beginning with the eternal motion in space of the sky's upper sphere, propagates itself from sphere to sphere toward the sublunary world. But in this lower world inhabited by living creatures, the perennial nature of the local circular motion ends, and death is present: "On such a principle, then, depend the heavens and the world of nature. And it is a life such as the best which we enjoy, and enjoy for but a short time."[6] What is eternal is the succession of generations and corruption, which "imitate circular motion." Indeed, "being...is better than not-being: but not all things can possess being, since they are too far removed from the principle. God therefore adopted the remaining alternative, and fulfilled the perfection of the universe by making coming-to-be uninterrupted: for the greatest possible coherence would thus be secured to existence, because that coming-to-be should itself come-to-be perpetually is the closest approximation to eternal being."[7] The hylomorphic theory of nature makes it "acted upon" (*to paschōn*).[8]

Local motion, or translation (*phora*), is the first motion produced by the cosmos, but it is only one of the four kinds of motion (*kinēseis*) imagined by Aristotelian physics. The other three are increase and diminution (*auxēsis* and *phthisis*); alteration (*alloiōsis*); and generation and destruction (*gēnesis* and *phthora*).[9]

Kinein, "to move": this term comes into play in definitions of the efficient cause, or the very particular motion that through fertilization ensures the generation of living beings. Fertilization is

24

understood as transmitting motion. The same is true for growth and various observable qualitative changes. In fertilization, semen, the addition (or residue, *perissōma*) of nourishment from the paternal body, moves the menstrual matter, which on its part is the residue of the maternal blood. The maternal blood is also considered an addition. The embryo, and later the actual living being, are formed by the consequences of this encounter between the formative agent and the material substratum. That which takes on a form will bear the characteristics of the species and the singular qualities of the individual.

Individual particularities owe a great deal to this "being moved in turn," which prevents the agent from exercising all its formative power. The future *reactio* of medieval Latin terminology will designate that which makes the patient not entirely passive (*patiens*, *paskhōn*) but obliges the agent to be moved and acted upon in turn (*repati*, *antikineisthai*). In *Generation of Animals*, Aristotle expounds on the reasons why children sometimes do not look like their parents. This results from a slackening of the semen's movements; semen, endowed with heat and formative power, acts upon the maternal matter, which is colder and, even while taking on a form, puts up resistance to it, sometimes successfully:

> The reason why the movements relapse is this. The agent is itself acted upon by that on which it acts; thus that which cuts is blunted by that which is cut by it, that which heats is cooled by that which is heated by it, and in general the moving cause (except in the case of the first cause of all) does itself receive some motion in return; e.g. what pushes is itself in a way pushed again and what crushes is itself crushed again. Sometimes it is altogether more acted upon than acting, so that what is heating or cooling something else is itself cooled or heated, sometimes having produced no effect, sometimes less than it has itself received.[10]

Consequently, when the semen's movement is the most energetic, the resemblance to the father (male sex, the father's features) will be greatest. More distant resemblances (with the mother or a grandparent), the formation of a daughter, and the formation of a monster are all results of an increased resistance in the feminine substratum.[11] This theory gives form an active power over matter, just as it privileges the agent over the patient, heat over cold, the male sex over the female. If one subscribes to Aristotle's propositions, then reaction, cold, and femininity are in secondary positions. This aspect of the doctrine lends itself, of course, to the accusation of phallocentrism. Note, however, that there can be action and reaction between the semen and the menstrual residue because their "substratum" is "a single something."[12] What they have in common is what allows one to act upon the other. Heat and cold, along with wetness and dryness, are the primary qualities that form the four elements and are contained within these elements in pairs: fire (hot and dry), air (hot and wet), water (cold and wet), and earth (cold and dry). According to Aristotle, heat and wetness have active powers, cold and dryness have passive powers. These oppositions between qualities enable the elements to act upon each other. Reciprocal action takes place between "tangible" qualities capable of coming together and being mixed. On the other hand, opposites such as lightness and gravity do not exercise a reciprocal action.

Aristotelian thought, as we see, easily accepts the inequality between action and reaction, even while assigning them both to the same genus, within which they differ through contrariety. It also brings the couple *kinein/antikinein* into the realm of perceptions, behaviors, and passions. As proof, one can read this passage from *On Memory*, the interpretation of which is not without its problems: "For a similar reason bursts of anger or fits of terror, when once they have excited such motions, are not at once allayed, even though the angry or terrified persons set up counter motions, but the passions continue to move them on, in the same direction as at first."[13]

Centuries went by before the Latin *reagere* was used as an equivalent to *antikinein*. This occurred in a passage on the reproduction of animals in which Albertus Magnus, directly inspired by Aristotle, introduced *reactio* into scholarly language. In *Quaestiones super De animalibus*, we first read the following lines, which appear like a commentary on the passage from Aristotle I have just cited on the "slackening" (or "remission") of semen:[14] "The more distant any natural agent is from its beginnings, the more continuous its operation, the more it weakens and tends to fail, since the agent, in the realm of nature, must in turn be acted upon when it acts, and in being acted upon, it reacts, as the Philosopher says." This principle is invoked in the same work to explain the shorter length of the upper limbs compared with the lower limbs; their growth encounters a greater resistance: "The closer growth comes to its completion, the more it weakens due to the reaction of the contrary."[15]

In his *Physica*, Albertus Magnus writes, in terms that already appeared in the Latinized Averroës: "It is necessary for the agent to submit in turn to the patient [*Necesse est quod agens repatiatur a passo*]."[16] This time Albertus does not use the word *reactio*, but he gives it the definition that would appear in philosophical dictionaries until the eighteenth century. Purists, attached to classical Latin, accepted this definition, but they concluded, along with Gerardus Johannes Vossius, that *reagere* and *reactio* are incorrect terms that are better avoided or at least restricted to Scholastic debates. Vossius admitted that *reagere* and *reactio* had technical pertinence (*vox idonea rei quam signant*), but he preferred locutions such as *vicissim ager* (to act reciprocally) and *resistere agenti in se* (to resist that which acts upon oneself).[17]

In medieval universities, the teaching of natural philosophy and the arguments between philosophers included propositions on motion, action and passion, and reaction. This teaching and these arguments accompany medieval and Renaissance interpretations of the works of Aristotle and those of his commentators Avicenna and Averroës. In the beginning, there is almost total agreement on the principles of physics set forth by Thomas Aquinas and based on Aristotle: "The fulfillment of what is potentially, as such, is motion"; or, "A thing that is in motion derives its motion from something . . . other than the thing itself."[18] To speak of motion is to speak of nature, for, according to Thomas Aquinas, who appeals to Aristotle on the matter, "nature is the principle of motion and of rest."[19] The Scholastics generally refer to Aristotle to affirm that when a reciprocal action occurs, there is a similarity of genus between agent and patient but a dissimilarity of species.[20] Aristotle postulated both community and difference at the moment of a reciprocal action.[21] One can see here a source or a first formulation of what will become the Kantian notion of community (*Gemeinschaft*).

Intensions and Remissions

The great English universities played an important role in the history of medieval science. The writings and reputations of English philosophers who were active at Oxford, especially at Merton College, are still with us: Thomas Bradwardine, Richard Swineshead, and William Heytesbury.[22] At the beginning of the fourteenth century, they revived and discussed the problems of Aristotelian physics, kinematics, weight, the impact of bodies, and especially heat.[23] Those called the Calculators attempted, speculatively, to quantify reaction. They asked themselves what part of an agent undergoes a reaction (*pars repassa*) and what other part remains unaffected or affected to a lesser degree by the action undergone. They wanted to account for the equal ("uniform") or unequal ("deformed") distribution of qualities in bodies. Depending on the case at hand, some denied a reaction had taken place. These problems were taken up again by the theorists of *impetus* from the Paris school, where Jean Buridan's nominalism had its followers (Albert of Saxony, Marsilius of Inghen, and the brilliant Nicole Oresme).[24] The discussion spread to Italy (Paolo Veneto, Giovanni Marliani). In the course of these debates, a problematic was elaborated that some recent historians have seen as the first glimmer of the rules later imposed by Galileo. Based on the fundamental concepts inherited from Antiquity, the idea of a possible mathematization came to light in an innovative way. It involved a geometry of proportions, a calculation of the "intensions" and "remissions" of moving "forms."

According to the assessment of post-Galilean scientific thought, however, the Calculators' efforts at quantification were applied to inadequate objects. These calculations and "measurements" remained bound to a physics that, despite its principled option in favor of an analytic method, had not yet reduced its object to local motion and had not come to see all of nature as the *experimental* field of application for arithmetic and geometry — that is, a field open to a *possible* experience. It is true that this physics distinguished in principle between "*extensive* magnitudes" (spatial) and "*intensive* qualities." But it did not elaborate on the consequences of this distinction. It granted preeminence to local motion but did not clearly separate it from other types of motion: generation, growth, alteration. And among the intensive qualities of motion it included speed, heat, and cold, as well as tastes and colors insofar as they are perceived by the senses. These qualities were so many "forms," whose increase was known as *intension* and whose diminution was referred to as *remission*. As for "intensive qualities," their calculations remained arbitrary and uncontrollable.

29

Quantitative evaluation remained entirely dependent on sensory intuitions, unaided by disciplined instrumental measurements. As Alain de Libera has said, the Oxford Calculators' project led to "a physics of imaginary reasoning and thought experiments with no empirical aim."[25] Except in the cases of speed and accelerated motion, gradations were attributed to poorly defined phenomena. Numerical transcriptions were imposed on things that cannot be numbered. This physics was therefore incapable of reducing its object to "extensive magnitudes" alone and of squaring its calculations with experimental results. The results obtained were endlessly controvertible. Over three centuries, however, Swineshead's *Liber calculationum* enjoyed surprising success in Europe and was still cited in the seventeenth century.[26]

What phenomena were cited most often up to the eighteenth century? The privileged example of reaction is the red-hot iron immersed in water, such that the iron is cooled and the water is heated. And Aristotle's authority is constantly invoked: "In some of the bodies which are called hot the heat is derived from without, while in others it belongs to the bodies themselves."[27] The type of motion in question is therefore qualitative alteration (*alloiō-sis*). While a distinction was made between them, alteration and mixing, which preoccupied chemistry in its first stages, were often compared. The propagation and dissipation of heat were not understood scientifically and formulated in equations until much later, when they were interpreted in terms of local molecular motion.[28] Medieval thinkers, as seen above, believed they could treat this subject on the basis of the physics of the four elements and according to a scale of substantial qualities — each endowed to varying degrees with activity or resistance. It was supposed in particular that the series of qualities — hot, cold, wet, and dry — were organized along a scale that decreased in *active* properties and increased in *resistant* properties. Degrees of heat (generally eight in number) were not measured but simply attributed, as was the case in the Galenic tradition for the heating or cooling virtues of medicines.[29]

Agreement on the circumstances of its application was far from universal, and almost all of the treatises titled *De reactione* and the dense chapters devoted to this subject in the most general works had a polemical element. And they multiplied; to mention only a few: a work by Giovanni Marliani (around 1482); then those of the Aristotelians of the Padua school, Pietro Pomponazzi (1515) and Jacopo Zabarella (1533–1589).[30] In one of his first writings, Pomponazzi ironically took issue with the English Calculators and with Nicole Oresme and his calculations of forms, that is, of intensive qualities.[31] The *intentio* of these intensive qualities was the result not of an addition of discrete units or supplementary parts but of a qualitative improvement: the form itself can be more intense (*intenditur*) or more attenuated (*remittitur*). One must distinguish, in addition, between the reactions of the inanimate world and those of life. Zabarella, an opponent of Platonic dualism, recognized the omnipresence of natural motion; but he distinguished between an absolute principle, made up of the motion of the heavens, and a motion of terrestrial bodies, which is transmissible ("transient") and is either active or passive.[32] His treatise *On Reaction* defends Pomponazzi and develops a theory of nature that claims to remain faithful to the theories of Aristotelian physics; for example, following Aristotle, he asserts that extreme distance — such as that between the stars and Earth — makes a reciprocal action between elements and lower bodies impossible. In action and reaction, there is a battle (*pugna*) and an effort of self-conservation on the part of each opposite. "When fire acts on water, it acts insofar as it is hot; when fire is acted upon by water, this is not insofar as the fire is hot but insofar as it is potentially cold; for it is through form that it acts and through matter that it is acted upon."[33] Zabarella makes the heavens a corporeal first mover not radically separate from the world in which our life unfolds. Nature is universal, it rules all things, and its goal, through the action and reaction of its elements, is to ensure their conservation and the production of mixed bodies.[34]

A decisive change did not take place until the moment — at the beginning of the seventeenth century — when physics abandoned the metaphoric couple form/matter and when speed and acceleration ceased to be "intensive qualities" and joined the category of "extensive magnitudes." From that moment, geometrized physics, as it established its formulas and turned more and more (though not without difficulty) to measuring instruments in order to verify them, slowly acquired the means to quantify other "intensive qualities" of the medieval doctrine: colors (colorimetry) and heat and cold (thermometry and calorimetry).[35] From the red-hot iron cooled by water (the technique of water tempering) to steam-powered and thermodynamic machines, we find the passage from one era of physics to another.

New Worlds

In seventeenth-century Europe, while Galileo and his first disciples were laying the foundations for what appears today as the great "paradigm shift," scholars remained attached to the Peripatetic definitions of motion, of the different types of motion, of contact (that is, impact), and of mixture. The doctrine was often explained with classic examples and problems: the heated iron and water, the sun acting upon terrestrial bodies without being acted upon in turn. In scholarly works, these examples often use the word *reactio* or the verb *repati*. Such is the case in Johannes Magirus's manual.[36] There is a shared opinion, a common denominator, that simply repeats the formula of Averroës and Albertus Magnus. In his philosophical dictionary, Rudolphus Goclenius the Elder included an entry on *reactio* and defined it as follows:

"Action, in return or reciprocated, of a body that has undergone an action, whereby this body resists the initial agent and changes it, at the same time as it is changed by it."[37] Note that the definition uses the prefix re- in three terms.[38] It thus does not avoid the tautology that threatens so many definitions. Here it establishes a quasi synonym, likening "react" to "resist."

In view of the dates when the new ideas appeared in the great books that marked the first scientific revolution (those of Kepler, Galileo, and Descartes), one might be tempted to believe that important changes took place in the commonly shared worldview. In fact, these ideas at first reached only the small number of minds capable of understanding, discussing, and extending them. The number of "latecomers" was considerable. As late as 1690, Father Jean-Gabriel Boivin, a Minorite, carefully summed up the thought of Duns Scotus for the students at his seminary and repeated the cosmological formulas of Aristotelian provenance: on this earth, there are active and passive powers; but the motion of the earth has its origin in powers that are active and impassive, for universal motion is caused by the perfection of the immobile first mover. This physics abounds in anthropomorphic images: action and reaction imply the "victory" of an "agent" over a "patient." Relationships of power, later analyzed quantitatively by classical mechanics as successive states of equilibrium, are expressed in terms of a dramatized conflict.[39] Boivin raises the usual objection: stars act upon the objects of the lower world without suffering any action in return. The explanation appears simple to him, and it has been formulated countless times: the stars are so distant from sublunary things that they cannot be reached by the latter's reaction, and, furthermore, stars cannot receive "sublunary qualities" (*non sunt capacia qualitatum sublunarium*). Other authors are more influenced by themes from the Stoics' physics, through Hermetism or Paracelsism. They agree that the world is fraught with "influences" or sympathies, through which occult qualities are manifested, causes that the intellect can recognize but are not accessible to the human senses.[40] The sympathies (and antipathies) bring stars, rocks, plants, animals, and the organs of living bodies into contact with each other. Indeed, it was through the interplay of sympathies — which lent the force of reality to metaphoric bonds — that the world could be interpreted as an organism, and the organism as a microcosm. "Sympathetic effects," wrote the Jesuit father Gaspar Schott, "arise from a friendly affection, or coordination and innate relation, of one thing to another ... so that if one is acting, or reacting, or only just present, the other acts or is acted upon."[41]

If this solidarity is not confined to the lower spheres, and if a human being can contain not only all of the heavens but God himself (which Schott takes care not to say, but which the heretics will assert), then there is no imperfection or fall from grace in the lower world. The hierarchies of the organized cosmos disappear, and all condemnation of the disorder of "base" sublunary nature ceases. The consequences of radicalizing the doctrine of sympathies, with its share of poetic magic, paradoxically cleared the path for the new Galilean discipline: the world is one, the powers that govern it are everywhere the same. In the first case, the metaphoric discourse was based on the generality of comparison; in the second, mathematics and successful experiments confirmed the generality of calculation. Good fortune was indeed granted to those who recognized perceptible analogies between different regions of the world, but phenomena can be subjected to calculation. The result of this subjection, for the good Calculators, was technical mastery, which quickly spread. The couple action/reaction found a use in both languages, that is, in an imaginary vitalism that delighted in the divination of sympathies and in a mechanism that applied the rules of geometry to nature.

On the Vernacular

Until this point, I have commented on scholarly texts written in Latin. Many more such texts will be discussed below. Yet one must also ask how the Latin *reactio* gained a foothold in the so-called vernacular languages.

Its entry into French was quite slow. I know of only one use of the word "react" in the sixteenth century, in *La Complainte de nature à l'alchimiste errant* (1516) by the painter Jean Perréal (c. 1455–1530). With Perréal, the term continues to express a process of the most general and most traditional physics. It does not belong to the specialized vocabulary of alchemy, where I have never encountered it, even in much later texts:

> But must I say
> That there is no active element
> That can act with the passive one.
> Just as fire in air acts,
> Air in water reacts,
> And water acts in the air
> When fire wants to wage war.[42]

Perréal paints a picture of a storm, a battle of three elements. One does not, however, find *réagir* (react) or *réaction* (reaction) in the works of the most important sixteenth-century authors, at least if one trusts Edmond Huguet's dictionary or the many indexes that have recently been drawn up. The most likely possibility — until we have more information — is that the term came into circulation in French sporadically and only in works that, popularizing the notions of physics, bore the imprint of Aristotelian and Scholastic thought.[43]

In the Italian of Giordano Bruno, *reazione* is but one of many examples of *contrarietà* that reign in natural phenomena:

Dove è la contrarietade, è la azione e reazione, è il moto, è la diver-
sità, è la multitudine, è l'ordine, son gli gradi, è la successione, è la
vicissitudine.

And where there is contrariety, there is action and reaction, there is
motion, there is diversity, there is number, there is order, there are
degrees, there is succession, there is vicissitude.[44]

Is this idea new? Not at all. Bruno borrowed the notion of contrariety from Aristotle (*enantiotès*: *Metaphysics* 1.3.4; *Categories* 14),
and he follows the Stagirite's text almost word for word; the short
juxtaposed propositions are hurried and breathless, giving a baroque
impression.

What about English? The expressions "to react" and "reaction"
appear in the language as early as the end of the sixteenth century.
In *The Nature of Bodies* (1644), the English Paracelsist Kenelm
Digby remains faithful to the binary Aristotelian formula that had
become canonical: "If fire doth heate water, the water reacteth
againe...upon the fire and cooleth it."[45] Digby is a magician who
likes to call upon astral sympathies. On the other hand, Thomas
Hobbes also used these terms, as we shall see, but within the context of a materialist philosophy that privileged corporeal reality
and attempted to formulate mechanically all natural phenomena,
including mental operations.

In all the languages in which it appears, the word "reaction"
belongs to "physiology" — that is, to natural philosophy. For solid
bodies, it serves as a stand-in for the more recent *contrecoup*
(rebound, repercussion) (which appeared in French in 1560). At
first, it was used solely for natural phenomena, without application to the human world.

Speech and Numbers

It was a good while before the ancient meanings and examples of the word "reaction" were left behind: the hot iron plunged into cold water seemed never to wear out. In Ephraim Chambers's *Cyclopaedia* (1743; "Reaction" entry), then in Diderot and d'Alembert's *Encyclopédie* (1765; "Reaction" entry, translated from Chambers), one reads: "The Peripatetics define re-action to be that which a passive body returns upon the agent by means of some quality contrary to that received from it, in the same part with which the agent acted, and at the same time; as water, while it is heated by fire, does at the same time cool the fire." Nonetheless, Chambers and the *Encyclopédie*, after paying tribute to the Peripatetic school tradition, add a reference to Sir Isaac Newton's third law: "But the equality of the actions was not known. Sir Isaac Newton established it as one of the laws of nature, that action and re-action are equal and contrary." An unusual juxtaposition of Scholastic physics and the new science, in the middle of the eighteenth century, no less. Only now is a line beginning to separate the prevalent philosophical authority of the Peripatetics from modern knowledge, inaugurated by Galileo, in which mathematical precision set forth laws that cleared the way for calculation. The *Cyclopaedia*'s definition does not dismiss the canonical one: it *adds* the notion of equality to it, as if the ancient notion simply needed to be completed. In fact, the ancient definition was not false; but it included too many phenomena, to which it proposed no measurable approach. It is as if the qualified and the quantified definitions could support each other, at least for a while. Thus it was that the Renaissance doctrine of reciprocal action and sympathies could stay in circulation long enough to be reactivated by the Romantics. The word "reaction" did not undergo a radical semantic change in the immediate wake of Newton; rather, it became two-sided, taking on a double connotation.

It could be marshaled under two different banners, as I will often have occasion to note. On the one hand, as soon as the principle of calculable equality was accepted, Newton's third law was interpreted as a valid argument in a mechanistic interpretation of the universe. On the other hand, the word recalled a more ancient idea, less "precise" in the modern sense, which Galileo and Descartes did not use, no doubt in order to distance themselves from Aristotelianism.[46] To be sure, the *Cyclopaedia*'s juxtaposing the ancient conception of reaction with its new quantified status could only be provisional. Before long, the Peripatetic definition became obsolete. Indeed, the favorite examples of ancient physics — notably heat and water — were taken up and treated altogether differently in the new physics.

During its first phase, the new physics set in place a complete theory of mechanics, based on the work of Newton and his immediate successors: more or less explicitly, action and reaction constantly occupied the stage. Then, in the nineteenth century, there was a second phase when modern physics began to reflect on "heat engines" able to produce motion, and this required new laws. Thermodynamics took into consideration heat and its effects on cold bodies "regardless of the substance involved or the way in which one acts upon this substance." Sadi Carnot, who was audacious enough to posit this generalization in the study that opened the thermodynamics era, spoke of "the action of heat" but did not use the word "reaction." He mentioned the "re-establishment of equilibrium," and his successors (Emile Clapeyron, William Thomson, Rudolf Clausius) did a great deal more than refine his thought: they mathematically formulated it, without resorting to Carnot's discursive argumentation. Before returning to the remarks that the Newtonian language calls for here, I want to cite the passage in which Carnot notes the success of classical mechanics, even as he marks the limits of its field of application:

The machines that do not receive their movement from heat; those that are moved by the force of men or animals, by a waterfall, by a current of air, etc., can be studied down to their smallest details by the mechanical theory. Every case can be foreseen, every imaginable movement is subject to firmly established general principles applicable in all circumstances. Such is the nature of a complete theory. A similar theory is obviously lacking for heat engines. We will not possess it until the laws of physics are sufficiently extended and generalized, such that we can know in advance all the effects of heat as it acts in a determinate manner on any body whatever. . . . The production of motion in steam engines is always accompanied by a circumstance that we should carefully note. This circumstance is the reestablishment of the equilibrium of caloric, that is, its passage from a body whose temperature is relatively high to another body whose temperature is lower.[47]

In Newton's *Principia* (1687), the third law of motion is formulated as follows:

To every action there is always opposed an equal reaction: or, the mutual actions of two bodies upon each other are always equal, and directed to contrary parts.

Whatever draws or presses another is as much drawn or pressed by the other. If you press a stone with your finger, the finger is also pressed by the stone. If a horse draws a stone tied to a rope, the horse (if I may say so) will be equally drawn back toward the stone; for the distended stone, by the same endeavor to relax or unbend itself, will draw the horse as much toward the stone as it does the stone toward the horse, and will obstruct the progress of the one as much as it advances that of the other. . . . This law takes place also in attractions.[48]

The law's corollaries, which are just as important, establish the rules of the composition of forces. D'Alembert, without directly citing Newton's third law, declares that all the problems of dynamics can be solved by calculating the composition of forces.

Historians of science have often noted that the inventors of the new physics gave preference to the Platonic notion of a geometer God, as opposed to Aristotle's "naturalism," while at the same time reviving Epicurean atomism and especially the idea that motion becomes no less perfect as it moves away from the first cause. God, or nature, imposes the same law at all levels of the universe.[49] This was therefore the end of the Peripatetic distinction between natural motion and violent motion, as well as the end of the perfection attributed to the circular motion governing the celestial spheres. "Classical" mechanics thus defined itself by postulating relative motion in a homogeneous and isotropic space.

The impact of bodies before Newton formulated his laws of mechanics (particularly the third law) has been the focus of assiduous study. One can trace the idea's successive stages from the fifteenth-century theories of *impetus* to the formulas elaborated by the new physics, from Galileo to Edme Mariotte, by way of Johannes Kepler, Christiaan Huygens, Christopher Wren, and John Wallis. Without using the word "reaction," Descartes saw it as a special case of the transmission of motion.[50] On this point, Newton gave credit to his predecessors in the scholium to the laws of motion. As this debate progressed, it became more and more clear that the idea of motion could not be considered "in different senses," as Aristotle had maintained. Only local motion deserved to be examined and analyzed. The other types of motion proposed by Aristotle (generation and corruption, growth and diminution, alteration) must either be reduced to local motion or cease to be considered. The third law and the notion of reaction

40

allowed Newton decisively to advance ideas he had developed in an earlier manuscript on motion (*De motu*):

> The concept of the internal force of a body transformed itself from a force that carries a body in uniform motion into a force of reaction, a force that a body "exerts only in changes of its state produced by another force impressed upon it," and with this change Newton clarified once and for all his understanding of the concept of inertia as we find [it] in Law 1. Newton was now in a position to perceive the full implication of the notion implicitly present in his concept of centripetal force from the beginning, that uniform circular motion is dynamically equivalent to uniformly accelerated motion in a straight line. This may well be the central insight on which the whole of Newtonian dynamics stands.[51]

The third law makes it possible to dispense with the parallelogram of forces.

The semantic mutation of the word "reaction" is therefore one effect of the scientific revolution. The new scientific mind aspired to translate the laws of nature into a mathematical language, and thus to find the equations through which the physical phenomena could be submitted to precise measurements. It meant abandoning progressively all unverifiable speculation on the four elements, on the substantial qualities (heat, cold, wetness, dryness). It was recognized that one could not speak of changes in inert things the way one speaks of changes in living bodies or appetites. Mathematization succeeded because the variables under consideration were restricted to those that could be measured. Reflection dominated by the model of the living being gave way to a purely mechanical science. Only local motion was retained: henceforth it became necessary to consider only masses in space, distances, speeds, quantities of motion, forces, and kinetic energies.[52] One concept that was profoundly modified was that of the natural agent, which, ceasing to be a power in the process of actualization, became a measurable force. The efficient cause, now calculable, made final causes undesirable and superfluous. Correlatively, the word "passion," which, as we have seen, was the classical antonym of "action," took on an outmoded meaning with respect to natural phenomena and was henceforth used only in matters of the soul. "Reaction" designated the rules and principles that make it possible accurately to predict the speed and direction taken by a body of determinate mass affected by a set of forces. Gravity itself represented a special case in which action and reaction are produced at a distance.

In Newtonian thought, there is no incompatibility, between these exact laws and a recognition of the existence of God. The laws of gravity govern the planetary orbits, but the *regularity* of the position of these orbits is not derived from these same laws. Newton called upon God to guarantee the stability of the universe: the cosmic system is placed in his care. And the famous final "Scholium generale" of the *Principia* carefully defines the attributes that must necessarily belong to the Creator God. This God, without being eternity and space himself, occupies the infinity of space and time, while remaining identical with himself. Although omnipresent, he does not suffer from the action of bodies in motion, nor do these bodies suffer any resistance from the fact of God's existence. One cannot assert any action or reaction between the spirit of God and the matter of the world. "As a blind man has no idea of colors, so we have no idea of the manner by which the all-wise God perceives and understands all things."[53]

In the *Principia*, as in his letters to Richard Bentley, Newton asserts that the force of attraction is not essential to matter.[54] The only force essential to matter, in his opinion, is inertia. He was anxious to counter the reproach of the Cartesians (and of Chris-

tian Wolff in Germany) that he appealed to occult qualities. He
did not believe that the laws of mechanics (by which, it has long
been agreed, he wanted strictly to abide) were capable of explaining everything that can be observed. In the Queries of his *Opticks*,
and in his papers on chemistry (only recently discovered), Newton speculates on various types of ether, on the periodic renewal
of the world, and on cosmic cycles and vital fermentations, without reducing them purely and simply to the laws of motion. This
was one of the points upon which he asserted his disagreement
with Cartesian mechanism. Newton's uneasiness stemmed from
his religious convictions. Some of his first commentators — those
who popularized his works — readily pointed to the equality of
action and reaction as proof of the manner in which God operates
in nature. Thus in his *Account of Sir Isaac Newton's Philosophical
Discoveries*, Colin Maclaurin adopts the idea of absolute space but
also reintroduces the notion of a first mover and appeals to the
pseudo-Aristotelian *De mundo*. Newton himself declared the need
to go back to a Cause superior to pure mechanism, for mechanism
itself attests to a divine intention, a beneficent Providence:

> It is because *action* and *reaction* are always equal, that the mutual
> actions of bodies upon one another have no effect upon the motion
> of the common center of gravity of the system to which they apper-
> tain.... If it was not for this law, the state of the center of gravity
> of the earth would be affected by every action or impulse of every
> power or agent upon it. But by virtue of this law, the state of the
> center of gravity of the earth, and the general course of things, is
> preferred, independent of any motions that can be produced at or
> near its bowels. By the same law, the state of the lesser systems of
> the planets, and the repose of the general system, is preferred, with-
> out any disturbances from the actions of whatever agents there
> may be in them.... And the necessity of this law, for preserving the

regularity and uniformity of nature, well deserved the attention of those who have wrote so fully and usefully of *final causes*, if they had attended to it....

Tho' [God] is the force of all efficacy, yet we find that place is left for causes to act in subordination to him; and mechanism has its share in carrying on the great scheme of nature.

Thus the equality of action and reaction limits and mechanically restricts the forces that are the "instruments" God made "to perform the purposes for which he intended them."[55]

Newton is not the only one to transmit this conceptual tool to the Enlightenment. His great adversary Gottfried Wilhelm Leibniz integrated the same idea into his system, though he developed it in an entirely different way. In "Principles of Nature and of Grace," Leibniz asserts:

Everything is a plenum in nature.... And since everything is connected because of the plenitude of the world, and each body acts on every other one more or less, depending on the distance, and is affected by it *in reaction*, it follows that each monad is a living mirror, or a mirror endowed with an internal action, and that it represents the universe according to its point of view and is regulated as completely as is the universe itself.[56]

Leibniz does not accept Newton's concept of absolute space and time. He could only sanction a cosmology in which God intervenes like a watchmaker who might, from time to time, need to repair his timepiece. An attraction exerted across the void seemed absurd to him. Even when discussing the material realm, Leibniz was preoccupied with not leaving the field wide open for mechanism: "The origin of action cannot be a modification of matter."[57] Speaking of himself in the third person in a text in which Philaretus is in dialogue with Aristes, he introduces the Platonic idea of antitypy:

> Bodies are composed of two natures, that is, the active primitive force...and matter, or the passive primitive force, which seems to be *antitypy*. For this reason, he maintains that everything in material things can be explained mechanically, with the exception of the principles of mechanism themselves, which would never be derived from the consideration of matter alone.[58]

According to Leibniz, the active primitive force could also be called the vital force. Here one finds a hypothesis that Newton did not propose so openly but that enjoyed great success among eighteenth-century physicians and nineteenth-century vitalists.

In making each monad a mirror of the universe, Leibniz gives a logical-mathematical and dynamic expression to the vitalism of sympathies that before him had been expressed in an intuitive and disordered way in "magical" cosmologies. He offers a system — that of a preestablished harmony — that can make room for mechanism, without letting it take up the entire space.

Kant

In his pre-critical writings, Kant addressed the question of the order of the world, but without claiming to find in this order cosmological proof of God's existence. Unlike Maclaurin and even Newton, Kant did not call on God to establish or preserve universal order. The creation of the world could be explained entirely by the laws of mechanics. Kant was satisfied with ontological proof: the world and matter belonged in the category of the *possible*, God alone was *necessary*.[59] For the creation of the solar system, Pierre-Simon Laplace hypothesized an initial nebula (also imagined by Buffon), but without postulating the existence of

God: this was the hypothesis that Laplace, according to the famous anecdote, did not need.

In his *Metaphysical Foundations of Natural Science*, Kant, extending the *Critique of Pure Reason*, no longer examined proofs of the divinity: he elaborated a "philosophy without theology."[60] Having learned from Newton, he then renounced the idea of absolute motion, limiting himself to relative motion instead. In his examination of mechanics, which follows those of phoronomy (our kinematics) and dynamics, the third law of motion is interpreted as establishing the principles of both relation and simultaneity: "This is, then, the *mechanical law* of the equality of action and reaction. This law is based on the fact that no communication of motion takes place except insofar as a community of these motions is presupposed."[61] Jules Vuillemin rightly observes: "We note the reason why simultaneity is for Kant the *sui generis* synthesis of permanence and succession. These two terms are abstractions in relation to which simultaneity reestablishes the concrete character of the real." It follows that "the idea of necessity has no application outside the community of substances, which is to say outside the limits of space and time, the subjective forms of possible experience. While in Leibniz's system this community would require preestablished harmony for its principle, the simple law of the equality of action and reaction suffices as soon as one gives up trying to construct a theory of knowledge of things in themselves."[62] According to Kant's deduction, the judgment of *relation* is at work in the third law of motion, in its *disjunctive* form, and in accordance with the category of *reciprocity*.[63]

It is a matter of mechanics, then, and one must avoid attributing a phantom life to matter. In the third theorem of chapter 3 ("Mechanics") and in an important appended remark, Kant interprets the second law of mechanics (inertia) as the principle according to which "all changes in matter have an external cause." He goes on to say:

> The inertia of matter is and signifies nothing but its lifelessness, as matter in itself. Life means the capacity of a substance to determine itself to act from an internal principle.... Now, we know of no other internal principle of a substance to change its state but desire and no other internal activity whatever but thought, along with what depends upon such desire, namely, feeling of pleasure or displeasure, and appetite as well. But these determining grounds and actions do not at all belong to the representations of the external senses and hence also not to the determinations of matter as matter. Therefore all matter as such is lifeless.[64]

Jules Vuillemin writes in turn:

> Kant does not stop at life: and herein lies the principal difference that sets him apart from the Romantics. Or if, in the *Critique of Judgment*, he makes it the object of meditation, it is by insisting on the purely regulative (reflective) character of judgments that come into play.... Romantic philosophy would contradict this affirmation: in the hylozoism of *Naturphilosophie* — a hylozoism which for Kant was "the death of all philosophy of nature" — it would find again the essential themes that inspired Leibniz's metaphysics insofar as the latter endowed each monad with a representative faculty; it would create a poetic universe of value, but only by substituting reveries and imaginings for exact science — and the only exact science at that time was Newton's.[65]

Kant's philosophy attempted to highlight the discipline of scientific reasoning, to reveal its conditions of possibility and of validity. But the discipline that applied to matter and material bodies had its limits. Without passing directly into a Romanticism of desire, certain eighteenth-century mathematicians attempted at times to go beyond the realm of matter. They proposed their arguments as correctives or supplements to Newton's thought and presented them as propositions submitted to the scholarly community's judgment. Whatever one might reproach them with, it is not with abusing words or wanting to impress the public.

Among those who wished to perfect Newton's theory and find the "causes of gravity" was the very curious Genevan scholar George-Louis Le Sage, author of *Lucrèce newtonien*, which proposed a "system of otherworldly minute particles."[66] More important still was the theory of force and elementary particles proposed by the Jesuit Ruggero Giuseppe Boscovich (1711–1787), with whom Le Sage was in communication. This theory postulates an action-at-a-distance diffused among these particles of matter, which are indivisible, unextended, lacking in mass, and noncontiguous. In announcing his theory of mutual forces (*vires mutuae*), Boscovich invokes both Leibniz and Newton. Why Leibniz? Because he upheld the principle of continuity. Why Newton? Because in the last of the famous Queries of the *Opticks*, he addresses the phenomena of gravity, cohesion, and fermentation conjointly. Boscovich hastens to add that his thought differs as much from one as from the other and that he is answering the questions they left hanging.[67] His system, which is both original and coherent, did not receive full consideration until the end of the nineteenth century. Friedrich Nietzsche, the philosopher of force, praised Boscovich for having definitively substituted force for matter, thereby destroying an apparent truth that had been wrongly accepted, as Copernicus had done before him: "While Copernicus has persuaded us to believe, contrary to all senses, that the earth does *not* stand fast, Boscovich has taught us to abjure the belief in the last part of the earth that 'stood fast' — the belief in 'substance,' in 'matter,' in the earth-residuum and particle-atom." Nietzsche was not alone in recognizing Boscovich's merits. Boscovitch was also given his due by James Clerk Maxwell, who decisively advanced knowledge of electromagnetism.[68] The advent of electromagnetism, which gave rise to the theory of relativity, opened a region of the physical world in which phenomena are not determined according to the gravitational laws of classical mechanics. Add to this the problems concerning the large-scale structure of the universe and the domains in which atomic and subatomic interactions occur, and physicists soon felt the need to formulate a "unified theory" that would gather these various regions together under a single law.

We still lack such a theory. It is nevertheless generally accepted today that classical mechanics is no longer sovereign or fundamental and that Newtonian action and reaction are but a special case in which a symmetrical formula can be favorably applied.[69]

Derivative Fictions

The history of scientific words is not limited to the writings of reputable scholars who use them in good conscience. This history also encompasses those who use scientific terminology without its method and who look to it for easy inspiration or for a way to impress a public unlikely to know the difference. The spread of a vocabulary also takes place through distorted appropriations and illegitimate venues. It is difficult to sort out the naive meanderings from the deliberate impostures. A number of adventurers, passing themselves off as inventors, assumed the oracular tone of assertion to appropriate the third law of Newtonian mechanics without considering whether or not there was the least simultaneity or the least measurable "community" (to use Kant's term) between the bodies or forces they presented as acting and reacting upon each

49

other.[70] A properly established law, such as Newton's third law of mechanics, can be used to legitimate unverifiable propositions. The more a science succeeds through innovative formulas, the more the predators of its vocabulary multiply. It is made to answer for things it never said. It is amalgamated with its opposite. Scientific language, which (since Galileo) was constituted by separating itself from ordinary language, was formed from calculations and equations; but it could not avoid resorting to simple words to designate its operations, and these words, sometimes borrowed from the common language, naturally return to this language or slip back into it. They are available to everyone, and, in the absence of technical competence, they become banal and unremarkable. The word, with its scientific aura, circulates in ordinary conversation, newspapers, and poetry. Since my research is lexical, I will not ignore these displaced uses that, according to rigorous scientific criteria, are considered degraded.

Some catchwords of the newly created mechanical science could thus be adopted independently of the requirement of quantification. Someone was always ready to buy into the most foolhardy speculations, which were presented on the same footing as the most methodical experiments. All kinds of reciprocities and alternations, both verifiable and unverifiable, took on the aspect of universal laws once they were associated with Newton's third law. Inexact or supernatural assumptions took shelter under the auxiliary words used by the exact and natural sciences or by rigorous mathematics. From the inception in the eighteenth century of a scientific language that was both rigorous and prestigious, its vocabulary was abused to enhance confused intuitions. The search for the scientific effect, in order to intimidate adversaries and seduce the public, hardly began in our day. The contemporary cultural phenomenon discussed in Alan Sokal and Jean Bricmont's *Fashionable Nonsense* was already quite evident in the two decades preceding the French Revolution.[71] To excite public opinion — whose reign was established during the eighteenth century — nothing was more profitable to the ambitious than borrowing the terminology of the most admired sciences, which also allowed them to benefit from the margin of doubt that scrupulous scholars grant to both their adversaries and their followers.

Although the physics instituted by Newton conquered the scholarly world, and although the efficacy of its technical applications assured positions of power to its representatives (in the academies under the ancien régime and in the great institutions of learning under the French Republic and the Directory), the swirl of public opinion around this physics and in its wake lacked the homogeneity of an *episteme* (in the particular sense Michel Foucault gave this term). While there was a dominant scientific "discourse," there were also counter-propositions, short-range endeavors, and pseudo discoveries all around it: a concert of discordant voices, each with its season of notoriety. Many of these voices took up old ideas using a new vocabulary. Such diversity is often misunderstood. The reason for this misunderstanding is clear enough: the events of an epoch, as contradictory as they might be, always form a finite whole, and the temptation is great to singularize this whole by reducing it, out of laziness, to a simple formula, a "spirit of the age," as if belonging to the same moment in time produced unity.

For the sake of instruction, let us examine a few examples of the risky use of the formula "action/reaction" in the eighteenth century. The verified mechanical model served as a guarantee in various domains for a great number of speculations by free analogy, inaccessible to precise observation or mathematical formulation.

In 1771, the Methodist minister John Wesley described "a continual action of God upon the Soul, and a re-action of the Soul upon God."[72] An action and a reaction thus seem able to intervene

51

between a God who is entirely spirit and the human soul, which implies that God himself, in his omnipotence, can be passively affected by the reaction of the soul he has touched. The formulas of reciprocity and mutuality are the compensation that dualistic thought takes pleasure in imagining as a way to repair the metaphysical rift separating the reign of the spirit from that of the body.

One of the most ingenious dualists was the abbot John Turberville Needham. He asserted that matter is not the primary elementary principle. It is composed of two simple agents without extension: a principle of motion and a principle of resistance, which act upon each other. Thus: "All the effects produced in the Universe are but the result of action and reaction.... Any sensible point in Nature (that is, any point accessible to our senses) is essentially active and reactive..., the life of the Universe is counterbalanced action." Not only is "my body...a complete system of action and reaction," but "the actual order of our knowledge is such that we cannot conceive of the resisting agent *as resisting* without the motor agent, nor the motor agent *as motor* without the resisting one."[73] Thus the immaterial is the secret insider of all matter. Needham perhaps remembered Ralph Cudworth (a Cambridge Platonist), who a century earlier had imagined immaterial "plastic natures" to which God had assigned the task of moving matter in a regular and orderly fashion.

For their part, the illuminati and the creators of systems at the end of the eighteenth century readily used the language of "natural philosophy" as a resource that might render their speculations credible. Jean-Paul Marat tried it out in his medical theories. Jean-Louis Carra (1743–1793), in his *Système de la raison*, writes: "Universal and perpetual motion is this general oscillation, this continuous *vibration*, that runs through the infinite circle of space and eternity." According to Carra, when energy acts *per ascensum*, it produces the nature of distinct things; when it acts *per descen-*

sum, it results in the destruction of distinct things, or chaos. Such is "the play of the universe, the circulation of matter, space's turning back onto itself, the circle of eternity." He continues:

> In this way we see that the system of action and that of reaction, otherwise [known as] the force of energy and the force of inertia, each merges in turn with the other, obeying now its own law, now the opposite, relative to the calculation of time and the immensity of space, beginning worlds in order to end them and ending them in order to begin them anew.[74]

This peremptory cosmosophy, with its terms borrowed from musical theory (vibration) or a mysticism of neo-Platonic inspiration (*ascensus* and *descensus*), wants to be taken at its word. The image of the circle and circulation belongs both to a world of very ancient symbols and to the modern representation of the circulatory irrigation of the bodies of higher animals.[75] Carra supported the Revolution, but he was not the only revolutionary to propose a cyclic conception of cosmic history. The advocate Jean Delormel, in *La Grande Période*, likewise included the revolutionary event as the basis of the eternally repeated cycle of a Period related to the Platonic "great year" or to the cycles imagined by the Stoics, who doomed the universe to perpetual combustion and rebirth.

The physician and champion of industry Franz Anton Mesmer, in his *Mémoire sur la découverte du magnétisme animal*, which he published in 1784, noted a sudden revelation during a solitary stay in the forest:

> I asserted, according to the familiar principles of universal attraction, ... that these spheres [the sun and the planets] also exert a direct action on all the parts that constitute animal bodies, particularly the nervous system, by means of an all-penetrating fluid. I denoted this

action as INTENSION and the REMISSION of the properties of matter and organic bodies — such as gravity, cohesion, elasticity, irritability, electricity.

In Mesmer's list of terms, one notes the timeworn words "intension" and "remission." They belong, as we have seen, to the vocabulary of Scholastic physics (the Calculators of Merton College) when treating the concept of action and reaction. Mesmer's vocabulary is that of a latter-day seminarian, but he needs all the scholarly and scientific words that express the reciprocal play of the world's forces, which he then applies to the human body. One has only to recall the first propositions in which he summarizes his "doctrine":

1. There exists a mutual influence between the Heavenly bodies, the Earth and Animate bodies.
2. A universally distributed and continuous fluid, which is quite without vacuum and of an incomparably rarefied nature, and which by its nature is capable of receiving, propagating and communicating all the impressions of movement, is the means of this influence.
3. That is, reciprocal action is subordinated to mechanical laws that are hitherto unknown.
4. This action results in alternative effects which may be regarded as Ebb and Flow.[76]

Mesmer interprets illness as a perturbation of one's harmony with the universe and attributes to himself the power to reestablish this harmony.

We find the same initial illumination in Antoine de La Salle, who in 1788 published a book that did not go unnoticed, *La Balance naturelle*.[77] La Salle based his entire system on a vision he had on the night of January 15, 1787. The system he elaborates is perfectly bipolar, a regular succession of expansion and compression ruling the universe. This universe, vibrational and oscillating, undergoes a perpetual alternation of attractive and contractive forces and of repulsive and expansive forces. The world is subject to the law of action and reaction, but La Salle tries to be original with regard to Newton:

> As for me, I think that any action is not merely accompanied by a reaction, or action in the opposite direction, but that it is followed by yet a second reaction once the initial motion has ceased. . . . The Newtonian reaction that is an obstacle to motion is contemporaneous with the action; our reaction, subsequent to the time of the action, is an actual and positive motion, caused by the perpetuity, universality, and equilibrium of the two forces that animate the world.[78]

La Salle understood very well that the Newtonian reaction was exactly contemporaneous with the action. For his part, he wanted to go from simultaneity to rhythm. The result of this coming and going is not merely an oscillating image of the law of the physical world; it is a doctrine of moral equilibrium. "Everything turns, everything circulates," and therefore "everything is *counterbalanced* here below."[79] The life of the world alternates between evil and good influences, and the good ones win out in the end. Among the multiple mechanical considerations, an organic metaphor is inevitably added to the image of circulation: a beating heart is the source of this motion. I find this image extremely revealing:

> The direct action of the sun and, in general, of fire is but a motion of expansion, dilation, and repulsion; that of the opposite force is a motion of tightening, contraction, or attraction; the equal and reciprocal or alternating action of these two forces produces the motion

of vibration and oscillation; hence this universal systole and diastole, of which the heart is but a particular case.[80]

Here it is not merely the gravitational ebb and flow that move the ocean mechanically but the activity of an organ that irrigates the body of the universe and ensures the life of the great All. In this anthropomorphic reverie, the world becomes an organism, and nothing hinders the temptation to imagine it as the single God. Pantheism is one path taken by the desire to restore to the world the "enchantment" stripped from it by the exact calculations of mechanics.

La Salle thought he was providing an intuitive and inspired complement to positive science. He claimed to expound great truths. Some of the philosophers or "magi" of Romanticism produced similar works. Scholars themselves, even today, cannot resist the temptation to extrapolate. Edgar Allan Poe, in *Eureka*, proposed (as will be demonstrated later) a heterodox cosmology in which action and reaction are the inner springs and which he placed under the double insignia of Truth and Poetry. This hypothetical reconciliation of science and poetry was nonetheless situated entirely on the side of literature. In the nineteenth century, it was the poets who wanted, by sheer force of the imagination, to do justice to the vital intuitions that some of the illuminati of the eighteenth century thought they could inscribe within the framework of science. But these poets still protested the loss of meaning that scientific language inflicted on the relation between man and the world. Criticizing a field of knowledge that confined itself to mechanical actions and reactions, they replaced it (in an often intermediate vocabulary) with images of living reciprocity. By taking up terms made popular by science, they tried to substitute warm, affective actions and reactions for the cold relations of quantified action and reaction.

CHAPTER TWO

Diderot and the Chemists

"I, Who Am a Physicist and a Chemist"

Diderot wanted to be called "the philosopher," and his favorite role was that of Socrates. Voltaire called him "brother Plato" in the cryptic language of his letters. But Diderot assumed many other roles as well. In "Philosophic Principles of Matter and Motion" (1770), he writes, "I, who am a physicist and a chemist...." Diderot was both physicist and chemist with regard to his interests and the company he kept, but not in practice or in the laboratory.[1] He nevertheless borrowed various words from the language of physicists and chemists; he knew their presuppositions and their underlying dogmas. He was familiar with the philosophical and theological stakes involved.

In Diderot's time, geometers and metaphysicians spoke of action and reaction. For the most part, professional chemists did not feel they had the right to transport Newtonian mechanics and gravitation into their domain, and they did not adopt the language of these fields. In their scientific writings, the word "reaction" did not become prominent until much later, toward the end of the century, as the preferred term for the analytic procedure involving reagents (for example, in the work of Torbern Bergman and Louis-Bernard Guyton de Morveau). Now, Diderot, who was interested in everything and dabbled in everything, had somewhat preceded them, without giving much thought to analytic chemistry. Did he anticipate this usage? I am not sure. In his own way, he modernized an older physics, which had been set forth in two distinct versions in the previous century, a mechanistic version in Thomas Hobbes's *De homine* and a vitalist version in Francis Glisson's *Tractatus de natura substantiae energetica*. In Diderot, we find traces not only of Leibniz's energetics but also of the theory of matter set forth by John Toland in his 1704 *Letters to Serena*.

In Diderot's works, the word "reaction" is an element in the representation of various systems, combinations, or organisms — whether it is a question of the whole universe, the animal body, society at large, or the nations of the European continent.[2] There can be action and reaction in a system provided that it contains sufficient reciprocity, internal oppositions, conflicts, or collisions among its constituent elements. The play of action and reaction can be considered on every level, from the large-scale to the smaller parcels of matter. Two examples will suffice.

In the first example, from the important entry of the *Encyclopédie* titled "Encyclopédie," Diderot eloquently justifies the central position attributed to man in the universe:

> Why do we not introduce man into our work the way he is placed in the universe? Why do we not make him a common center? Is there some point in infinite space from which we can to greater advantage draw the immense lines we propose to stretch to all other points? What a lively and sweet reaction it would create from all beings toward man and from man toward all beings.[3]

The rhetorical chiasmus that Diderot adopts here at the end of the sentence is the syntagmatic figure of the temporal succession of action and reaction.

The second example will show how Diderot tended to formulate in terms of action and reaction what one would today call the interdependencies (or interactions) of a culture. He perceives concretely — and makes physical — what Montesquieu called the "general spirit of a nation." In Athenian society, Diderot asserts, beliefs, arts, poetry, and living beings were linked by close correspondences. In defending the idea of the organic coherence of the Greek city, his *Notes on Painting* (1766) depicts all forms of artistic invention as acting and reacting:

> It's absolutely necessary, my friend, for me to talk to you here about the action and reaction of the poet to the sculptor or painter, of the sculptor to the poet, and of both to the animate and inanimate objects in nature ... these artists influenced one another ... they influenced nature herself, stamping her with a divine imprint.[4]

Taken together, these mutual influences in the Athenian republic determined the embodiment of the gods as well as of humans, the artistic representations of the flesh, and the figures of living beings. In this way, according to Diderot, a network of incarnated significations and sentient qualities was constituted, one filled with religious meaning. The words of the poets, the great myths, the statues they inspired, the grace of the bodies resembling the statues: all such beauties corresponded to and represented each other in perfect equilibrium. They were elements in a single system, offered through both fiction and reality, for pleasure and for veneration.

And when music is added, the reciprocal actions intensify to the point of enthusiasm and "frenzy":

> In Athens ... since a musician's listeners and judges were also musicians, it was only natural that a sublime piece of music would throw

the whole assembly into the same frenzy that agitates those who execute their works in our concerts. But it is the nature of all enthusiasm to communicate itself and to increase with the number of enthusiasts. Men thus produce a reciprocal action upon each other through the energetic and lively image they offer each other of the passion with which each is transported; hence the mad joy of our public festivals, the fury of our popular riots, and the surprising effects of music among the ancient Greeks.[5]

This time *reciprocal action* does not generate equilibrium. It engenders a collective energy that leads to excess. Once again it is a question of a body, a mass, allowing itself to be overcome by agitation. "To agitate" and "agitation" are the frequentative forms of "to act" and "action." Agitation is the disordered paroxysm of action. Diderot's association of agitation with the phenomenon of action and reaction must be noted; we will see that in his work this formula comes to be used at various levels and with various dimensions — notably on a cosmic scale.

Diderot knew of Newton's writings. He had evidently retained the notion that "an action is always equal to a reaction."[6] He declared, however, that he had "studied Newton with the intention of clarifying him . . . , if not with a great deal of success, at least with quite a bit of energy." Diderot found Newton obscure.[7] He therefore took the liberty of critiquing Newton in the fifth of his *Mémoires sur différents sujets de mathématiques* (1748), in which he studied the resistance of air in the motion of the pendulum. And he distances himself from Newton: "While I was once quite familiar with mathematical subjects, questioning me about Newton today is like asking me about one of last year's dreams."[8] There was, however, one part of physics and its calculations to which Diderot remained attached: acoustics. One can guess why: the vibrating strings and their mathematical expression are not abstract; if need be, they could serve as models of the fibers of which it was believed living beings were composed. Diderot was tempted by the comparison between the human organism and a harpsichord.[9] He was ready to apply acoustic calculations to a larger framework. Sensitive to Leonhard Euler's arguments, Diderot preferred to treat colliding bodies as if they were vibrating strings.[10] To him it seemed that the resistance one mass opposes to another should be treated as a problem of elasticity.

The Origin of Motion

Chemistry, more than geometry, seemed decisive to Diderot, for in chemistry one can test the crucial question of matter and motion. The testimony of chemistry, he thought, would allow one to settle a dispute affecting the foundations of our understanding of the world: it obliged one to accept that matter was "heterogeneous" and that motion was "essential to matter."

As a reader of Lucretius, Diderot was familiar with the feats of language through which particles and molecules are combined. By counting on their infinite divisibility, one could easily make them into rational beings of which we would have but an abstract notion, like mathematical points. But Diderot preferred to imagine that molecular elements are bearers of energy and that in the course of time they come together, in changing circumstances, to form everything in the world, from the most perishable to the most stable, from the tiniest to the most enormous. On this scale, the validity of the Newtonian laws of attraction that governed the "large bodies" of the universe was unverifiable — one had to admit that the attraction of "small bodies" might obey other laws. This is why the philosopher, unable to rely too heavily on mathematics to understand phenomena, had to make himself into a laborer, experimenter, and observer. "The reign of mathematics is over. Tastes have changed."[11] In *Thoughts on the Interpretation of Nature*

(1753), Diderot heralded "a great revolution in the sciences." What he calls an "experimental art" or "experimental physics," which is presented as an inspired empiricism, would, in his opinion, supplant "geometry," which is inseparable from calculation. Geometry produced splendid results, thus reaching its limits. It is henceforth necessary, he argued, to follow other paths whose proof is not based on the rules of calculation. Of course, Diderot was mistaken about the future of science. The idea of sensitive matter that he wished to champion was merely a reworking of an ancient hylozoism. True progress would come, rather, from a mathematized physics. Diderot's dream, as we have seen, was a nostalgic (or premature) extrapolation that took root at a moment when chemistry and, to a greater extent, physiology seemed inaccessible to quantification but when research into life, long delayed by the "spirit of the system," seemed to promise great discoveries.[12]

In a later work, "Philosophic Principles on Matter and Motion," Diderot challenged an adversary who supported Descartes's theory of material inertia. Diderot could not accept the idea that "matter was equally indifferent to motion and rest." He attributed to every molecule an "intimate force," which he declared inexhaustible, immutable, and eternal. This was the occasion he chose to associate the action/reaction couple with the image of agitation. The force that produces agitation eludes geometric law: this law is entirely in the geometer's head, not in reality. One must be a chemist or a physicist (in the "experimental" or "laboring" sense Diderot attributed to him) to be able to account for concrete phenomena. Diderot reproaches the Cartesians in the following terms:

> The molecule endowed with a quality proper to its own nature, is in itself an active force. It exercises its force upon another molecule,

which in turn exercises its force upon the first one.... What does it matter to me whether you regard matter as homogeneous or heterogeneous? What does it matter to me that, abstracting its qualities and only considering its existence, you see it in a state of rest? What does it matter to me that, in consequence, you seek for an external cause to move it? You can concern yourself with geometry and physics as much as you like; but I, who am a physicist and a chemist, I, who consider bodies as they are in nature and not as they are in my head, I see them as existing, differing, having properties and actions, and agitating in the universe as they do in the laboratory, where a spark cannot be placed beside three particles made of saltpeter, carbon, and sulfur without an explosion necessarily following.[13]

One finds an "action [of the molecule] outside itself, action of other molecules on it." We do not know exactly whom Diderot was trying to refute in this polemical text, but one might conjecture that he was thinking of Jean-Jacques Rousseau, who had been his friend and with whom he had had a falling-out in 1758.

Rousseau had asserted the exact opposite of what Diderot was trying to prove. In fact, in a passage inspired by Descartes in "Profession of Faith of a Savoyard Vicar" (1762), Rousseau, taking a stance against the materialism of the *philosophes*, had sought to demonstrate the necessity of a Creator God. In support of his conviction, he, too, put forth the notion of action and reaction in nature; but in his opinion these were only the effects of a motion transmitted by a first cause. Rousseau considered matter passive. There is no motion except transmitted motion, and its source, as Descartes maintained, must be sought in the divine will. The material universe can only conserve the quantity of motion imprinted on it by God, for material motion did not produce itself. Action and reaction can be noted everywhere, but they are only shocks and collisions following upon previous ones. The regressive chain of causes is not infinite. One necessarily comes up against an origin, which is divine omnipotence. The material world, and man in his corporeal existence, *received* motion. One must accept the hypothesis of a God who *willed*, with one and the same act of will, to produce matter (extended substance) and motion. All fleshly beings are made of this same stuff, but the human soul cannot be reduced to it. It has a reserve of moral will and freedom of judgment that are its spiritual share and allow it to act spontaneously:

> The first causes of motion are not to be found in matter; matter receives and transmits motion, but does not produce it. The more I observe the action and reaction of the forces of nature playing on one another, the more I see that we must always go back from one effect to another, till we arrive at a first cause in some will; for to assume an infinite succession of causes is to assume that there is no first cause. In a word, no motion which is not caused by another motion can take place, except by a spontaneous, voluntary action; inanimate bodies have not action but motion, and there is no real action without will. This is my first principle. I believe, therefore, that there is a will which sets the universe in motion and gives life to nature. This is my first dogma, or my first article of faith.[14]

Further on Rousseau adds: "To conceive of matter as producing motion is clearly to conceive of an effect without a cause, which is to conceive nothing at all." Rousseau undoubtedly had in mind (but did not name) Diderot, Paul Henri d'Holbach, and the other Spinozists. The antagonism is blatant.

In any case, Diderot took the opposite stand from Rousseau on this essential point. He intended to undermine this "first dogma" that prolonged the reign of dualist metaphysics. A resolute materialist and monist, Diderot asserted that matter — through the

64

internal *nisus* of the molecule — produces motion and is auto-kinetic: "Force that acts on the molecule exhausts itself; force that is internal to the molecule does not exhaust itself."[15] Thus each of the now antagonistic friends asserted universal action and reaction in support of his own cause. This proves — let me emphasize this point — that these terms were available and ready to serve under the banner of either materialism or deism. Action and reaction are tied to the evidence of phenomena, and contrary doctrines want to be able to assert the phenomena in their favor. We can draw a lesson from this. When words and concepts are too general — and when, logically speaking, extension becomes more important than comprehension — they are easily claimed and manipulated. Used as an explanation, they have the ambiguous status of a fact. They can supply weapons for the arguments of the attack as well as the defense. The breadth of the semantic field, or rather of the possibilities for applying the action-and-reaction model, gives some indication of its possible uses and abuses. Like Carlo Goldoni's Harlequin, action and reaction have served two masters: a Cartesian dualism and a vitalist monism.

For Diderot, everything proceeds from material molecules and their internal reserve of motion, which is potential energy. Proof seemed to be found in the laboratory: after referring to the necessary explosion, he goes on, in the same work, to discuss fermentation. A supplementary proof is provided by the demonstrable *passage* from the inanimate to the animate. Action and reaction, fusion and repulsion are charged with a vital, almost sexual power. Diderot's originality lies in his particular stress on this idea, not in the idea itself, which had wide currency. For Jean Bernoulli, for example, fermentation and effervescence are the same thing, and each could be considered slow-moving explosions.[16] Here is Diderot's act of faith:

I fix my gaze on the general mass of bodies; I see everything in action and reaction, everything destroying itself under one form, recomposing itself under another; sublimations, dissolutions, combinations of all kinds, phenomena incompatible with the homogeneity of matter; and therefore I conclude that matter is heterogeneous, that an infinity of diverse elements exist in nature, that each of these elements, by its diversity, has its own particular force, innate, immutable, eternal, indestructible; and that these forces contained in bodies have their action outside the bodies; whence comes the motion, or rather the general fermentation of the universe.[17]

Motion or fermentation? Diderot seems to hesitate. For him, they are not exactly the same. Motion, in the strict sense of the term, is a matter of geometry and mechanics. Hardly has he set the word down than he corrects it and substitutes another. "Action and reaction" is the intermediary concept conveying the movement toward fermentation. Now, fermentation is a phenomenon of chemistry; it arises from this "laborer's" discipline, which he calls "experimental physics." Diderot opts for fermentation — in other words, for life and sensibility. In the great spatiotemporal intuition of the dying Saunderson (*Letter on the Blind*; 1749), it is "matter in fermentation" that "spawns the universe," beyond which a "new ocean" can be seen, stirred by "irregular agitations."

Dream Words

Diderot was aware that fermentation was a far from universally accepted cause. To make his case, he used his favorite literary forms: discontinuous fragments (*Thoughts on the Interpretation of Nature*), and the dialogue (*D'Alembert's Dream*). The dialogue was particularly suited to this, since it allowed him to stage the doubt and resistance of an adversary, together with the arguments that overcome this resistance and the acquiescence thereby obtained.

Dramatizing thought through dialogue makes it possible to multiply the interrogative turns, to mark progressions, and to shed a brighter light on the triumphant proofs. In the alternation of attack and defense, dialogue places the energy of words under the tension of imminent contradiction.

In using d'Alembert as his imagined interlocutor, Diderot represents himself in a struggle with the strongest conceivable opponent, for d'Alembert was the geometer par excellence, the intellect who yielded only to duly demonstrated theorems. He was the author of the remarkable *Traité de dynamique* (1743 and 1758), in which he declared that he wanted to consider only simple principles: inertia, the equilibrium of bodies, and kinetic energy. In "Discours préliminaire" of this treatise, d'Alembert affirms that he will not engage in the "famous question of *live forces*" and that he has "turned away from *motor causes* to imagine only the motion they produce."[18] Consequently, he adds, he has "entirely proscribed the forces inherent to bodies in motion, those obscure and metaphysical beings that are capable only of spreading shadows over an otherwise clear science." Everything takes place as if, for the sake of clarity, d'Alembert preferred to rely on the "principle of equilibrium" rather than on Newton's third law: in his treatise, he never once uses the word "reaction." Diderot, on the other hand, tends to reason freely about the forces inherent in material elements, which allows him to imagine — in a "wild" speculation — the *passage* from inert sensibility (which he attributes to matter) to active sensibility (the prerogative of the living being). For Diderot, the phenomena of life, and our knowledge of them, were of decisive importance: he saw them as realities and objectives whose philosophical and moral consequences were more illuminating than mathematical truths.

In a vivacious impulse of writing, Diderot first represents himself in dialogue with d'Alembert: this is the moment when the interlocutor resists "A Conversation between Diderot and d'Alembert." Then he presents the geometer speaking and declaiming in his sleep: this is when the latter becomes convinced by the argument he has rejected, taking it up for himself and elaborating it with a neophyte's enthusiasm. The dreamer's words are commented on by Dr. Théophile de Bordeu, who comes running to the sleeper's bedside when summoned by Julie de Lespinasse. Having noted the sleeper's words from the beginning of his dream, she submits them to the physician. The doctor's commentary further develops the materialist-vitalist arguments expounded by Diderot in his first conversation. The victorious philosophical discourse is thus echoed from one person to the next — from Diderot to d'Alembert, from d'Alembert to Julie de Lespinasse, and from Mlle de Lespinasse to Bordeu. This *passage* of speech from one character to another is all the more significant because the contents of the discourse, as we have seen, concern yet other *passages*: from inert sensitivity to active sensitivity, and from the contiguity of molecules to their continuity through fusion. To put the matter very schematically: the words "to pass" and "to continue" belong, in this text, simultaneously to the referential, the discursive, and the metadiscursive register. They say what passage (in nature) is, while at the same time saying that they themselves are words that pass (from one speaker to another) and create linkages.

The fictive dream, the central part of the trilogy of dialogues, thus extends the preceding fictive debate between the geometer and the philosopher concerning the principles animating nature and the uselessness of any spiritualist hypothesis. D'Alembert is presented as skeptical: though he challenged Descartes's dualism and was not inclined to call upon an otherworldly God, he was no more inclined to sanction the materialist dogma. Yet the dream of the geometer who repudiates geometry (a dream reflecting Diderot's own desires, in fact) removes every objection: in imagination, d'Alembert finds himself in the same situation as in the previous dialogue; he repeats all his friend's arguments, but this time he gives in to them, and — drawn on by the inspiration of a second consciousness more susceptible to suggestion — he develops even further the theses of a vitalist materialism to which he is initially opposed. We find here a d'Alembert who is gradually vanquished (at the whim of the trickster controlling his speech) by a philosophy which in reality he rejected. An opponent of systems becomes converted to a materialist system! A closer examination reveals how Diderot's presence and voice haunt the sleeping geometer to the point of taking possession of him. Having become the writer's puppet, d'Alembert completely abandons his intellectual prudence. At the time of his *Letter on the Blind* and of his imprisonment at Vincennes, Diderot learned that it could be dangerous to support such ideas. Why not, twenty years later, grant himself the malicious pleasure of presenting d'Alembert as his accomplice, whereas in reality d'Alembert had broken off his collaboration on the *Encyclopédie* in 1758, at the moment when the danger arose?

The dreamer's remarks, through their discontinuous delivery and the accompanying intermittent commentary, trace the outline of a whole: they begin, as a "preamble," by evoking the first organization of the animal realm, culminate in the successive appearance of the most varied types of living beings (including monsters), and end with images of the dissolution of bodies, whose death undoes the organic bond while leaving the scattered molecules intact. In the text, action and reaction appear at strategic points, that is, at the two extremes: the being in formation ("preamble"), and the being in dissolution (the end of the dreamed "excursion"). Their positions are almost symmetrical. There is an emphasis, however, on the initial affirmation, which is doubled and reasserted in a chiasmus, as if to mimic the formation of a "network" or a "fabric" — the question at hand concerning the

69

unity of the animal organism, constituted by the combination of heterogeneous elements:

> Continuity arises from the contact of two molecules of the same substance, of exactly the same substance.... And this is all that happens in the most perfect case of union, cohesion, combination or identity that can be imagined.... Yes, Philosopher, if only the molecules are simple, elementary substances – but what if they are composed or composite?... Combination will take place all the same, and hence there will be continuity and identity.... And then the usual actions and reactions.... Yet it is certain that contact between two living molecules is quite different from the contiguity of two inert particles.... Well, never mind, never mind; perhaps I could quibble with you about that, but what's the use? I'm not one of those people that always have to have the last word in an argument.... But let's get back to the question. I remember now.... A thread of very pure gold, that was the comparison he used – a homogeneous network in the meshes of which other molecules can be fitted in, forming perhaps a second homogeneous network, a fabric of sensitive matter assimilated to the other one by the contact between them – so you have active sensitivity here, inert matter there, and the sensitivity communicates itself just as motion does. Not to mention, as he very acutely remarked, that there is a difference between the contact of one sensitive molecule with another and the contact between two molecules that are not sensitive – but what can be the nature of this difference?... The usual actions and reactions must be of a very special kind.... Everything concurs therefore to produce the kind of unity that exists only in the living animal.[19]

In this passage, the material fusion of sensitive molecules and the formation of interwoven networks combine to guarantee the continuity of elementary particles, the organicity and the unity of the living body. The brief mention of the "thread of very pure gold" is illuminated in the entry "Thread" in the *Encyclopédie*, which states that "metallic threads are usually so fine that they can be worked with threads of silk, wool, or hemp." Our curiosity will be repaid as well by the *Encyclopédie*'s entry on weaving machines and the illustrations included there. The image of the network in *D'Alembert's Dream* gains another concrete figuration in the example of the spider web, a metaphoric model of the nervous system, with its center (its original *point*) and periphery.

Action and reaction are therefore the great linchpin, the great operative *link*. The formula functions for molecules as well as for aggregates. It is at first proposed as a hypothesis but is used almost immediately to advance the demonstration. During the argument, the couple action/reaction is the perfect binding agent. It is the postulated principle, but then it takes on the role of the crucial experiment. Though it is what needs to be explained, a sleight of hand is enough for it to provide the awaited explanation itself. Thus it satisfies the requirements of a proof: action and reaction are referred to as "the usual actions and reactions." As soon as Diderot summons the evidence for this, the couple can serve him as an *ultima ratio*. Almost magically, they lead to the QED: "Everything concurs *therefore....*" Here we see one of the short circuits of which logic disapproves but that is not forbidden to philosophical rhetoric.

At the culmination of *D'Alembert's Dream*, d'Alembert's ecstatic tirade, which Diderot makes coincide with the dreamer's seminal emission, celebrates the sovereign reign of universal fermentation as the producer of the most marvelous life-forms. The dreamer's body is illuminated by the same flash as his thought:

> You have an infinite succession of little animals inside the fermenting atom, and the infinite succession of animals is called Earth....

Who knows — perhaps the fermentation is complete and its products have all been used up.... But was the elephant, that enormous organized mass, a product of sudden fermentation? Well, why not?... Can I not compare the small number of elements fermenting in the hollow of my hand with the immense reservoir of elements that are to be found everywhere — inside the bowels of the earth, all over its surface, in the depths of the sea, and even in the currents of the air![20]

Then, in a disillusioned address to the "poor philosophers" invited to consider their "first origins" and their "final dissolutions," the tone suddenly plummets. The end of the dream coincides with the downward movement from the organized mass to the elementary minute particles:

And life itself?... Life is a series of actions and reactions.... As long as I am alive, I act and react as a mass; when I am dead I shall act and react in the form of disparate molecules.... Does this mean that I shall never die?... Well, of course, in that sense I shall never die, neither I nor anything else for that matter.... Being born, living, dying — these are only changes in form.... And what difference is there between one form and another? Each form experiences the happiness and unhappiness that belong to it. So it is with the elephant and the flea and all the intermediate beings.... So also with all those between the flea and the living, sensitive molecule, the origin of all the others — there is no *point* in all of nature that does not know suffering and enjoyment.[21]

The decrescendo is perfect and has a perfect inverse symmetry: after the assemblage of elements in the elephant, the dissolution leads from the elephant to the flea, and from the flea to the initial molecule. The molecule and the point are the last *subjects* in the dreamer's discourse, while "suffering" and "enjoyment" are the last *nouns*. Hence the dream has spanned the gap between different worlds: the discourse begins with a first point ("a living point"); rises ecstatically to the spectacle of Saturn, the universe, and millions of centuries; and closes by returning to this last "point" found in "all of nature," a synthesis of the whole and the infinitesimal element. Along the way, d'Alembert himself has formulated the questions and answers, echoing the things Diderot has told him in the first conversation, discarding his own objections one after the other. The geometer has been divided in two before giving in to the philosopher's arguments, which he has at first contradicted. The two thoughts soon become one. In this intellectual fusion, d'Alembert's thought leads to an assurance of immortality. But it is a molecular immortality, impersonal and without memory. Diderot himself had dreamed this image of survival, and had used the very same words, when he wrote to Sophie Volland on October 15, 1759. He imagined his tomb beside Sophie's, so that their two elemental lives could remain merged. Paradoxically, he promised himself the perpetuation of love through the obliteration of corporeal identity.

Once the dream's great solo is completed, Bordeu and Mlle de Lespinasse continue the conversation continues at the geometer's bedside. They speak of the nerves' physiology and its anomalies, and in particular they speak of the dream. Herein lies the key, not to the dream's contents, but to its mechanisms. Any dream — and therefore the one just witnessed, with its erotic culmination — is perfectly explainable by the directional relations between the cerebral center ("the center of the web") and the peripheral organs. The physiology of the dream puts into play the reciprocal relations between the brain and the viscera while the relation to the outside world is interrupted by sleep. Dreams are either "ascending" or "descending," depending on the direction of the movement between the cerebral center and the organs:

Nothing else need occur beyond these actions and reactions. All this is merely the result of the specific property of the center and it all follows from the law of continuity and habit. If the process should begin in one of the voluptuary fibers, destined by nature to serve the pleasures of love and the propagation of the race, then the image evoked will be that of the object of one's passion — this will be the reaction at the center of the web. If, on the other hand, the image should appear initially at the center of the bundle of fibers, then the reaction in the voluptuary fibers will take the form of tension, erection and emission of seminal fluid.[22]

More than once Diderot assigns the diaphragm (seat of the emotions) the status of a peripheral organ in relation and in opposition to the brain.[23] The mechanism he invokes is the same: action and reaction. In modernized terms, Diderot judges that the origin of the dream varies but that this variation is subject to a simple alternative: either cerebral or somatic. The direction taken by the excitation can be either centripetal or centrifugal. In reading *The Interpretation of Dreams* (1900), one finds that in Freud's time dreams were still commonly explained by peripheral somatic excitations; Freud refuted this, granting primacy instead to "dream-thoughts." But he does not deny that the dream-thought can take as its material momentary sensory stimuli, upon which it is able to construct its own interpretations. I shall merely note here that a physiological explanation (proposed by Bordeu) makes d'Alembert's monologue the product of an action and reaction arising within his organism. D'Alembert has dreamed because there has been an action and a reaction between his brain and his nerve "fibers." Now, this dreamed monologue — at once rational and inspired — invokes action and reaction in order to make them the masters of life, from its origin to its dissolution. The field is occupied by action and reaction both in the dreamer's body and in his discourse. In a way not intended to please the protagonist himself, and that necessitated the destruction of the text, Diderot made autoerotic pleasure and pan-erotic ecstasy coincide in d'Alembert.

The Grain of Yeast

To define his hero's originality in *Rameau's Nephew* ("second satire"), Diderot goes through a series of expressions, several of which are derived from the lexicon of chemistry. He uses this language metaphorically to give his protagonist a moral sense: "The fellow is a *compound* of elevation and abjectness, of good sense and lunacy," says the narrator at the beginning of the dialogue. He adds:

> I have no great esteem for such eccentrics.... If such a character makes his appearance in some circle, he is like a grain of yeast that ferments and restores to each of us a portion of his natural individuality. He shakes and stirs us up, makes us praise or blame, brings out the truth.[24]

To ferment, to stir up, it all amounts to the same thing, as we saw in *D'Alembert's Dream*. It is helpful to know what the science of the times said about such phenomena. According to the physician Arnulphe d'Aumont, the author of the entry on fermentation in the *Encyclopédie*: "Modern chemists have made this word into a generic denomination, under which they include all boilings or swellings excited in a natural body by the various *agitations* of its parts." The author, referring to Thomas Willis's *De fermentatione*, continues:

> [The chemists] have consecrated the word fermentation to express the reciprocal action of various principles preexistent together in one and the same sensitively homogeneous natural body, at first

hidden, idle, inert and then developed, awakened, set into play. The movement such a reaction causes is imperceptible, such as the one that constitutes liquidity.... The end or the primary and essential effect of fermentation is the decomposition of the fermenting body, the separation and attenuation of its elements.

Fermentation decomposes, I might add, because it "restores" to the components of the mixture "a portion of [their] natural individuality" (to use Diderot's terms in reference to the Nephew). What is peculiar to the Nephew, writes Diderot, is that he *breaks* "that tedious uniformity which our education, our social conventions, our customary good manners have brought about." Because he is an exceptional individual, his very presence awakens unknown singularities, while he dissipates the neutrality of good manners: he makes clear the polarity of positive and negative, good and evil; in bringing out the truth, "he discloses the worthy and unmasks the rascals." Rameau's scandalous presence destroys soothing mystifications, undoes the fiduciary bonds that make people believe in social cohesion, and reveals contradiction and conflict. The word "reagent" had not yet seen the light of day when Diderot wrote his text, but the terms he uses prefigure it.[25] In another text, he discusses the "luxury of imitation" that characterizes Paris. Using a metaphor derived from chemistry, he denounces "an assimilation that jumbles all the ranks." He finds this a bad assimilation that enforces an illusory resemblance, a hypocritical equality among people. It's precisely this assimilation that the fermenting yeast-man thwarts when he "brings out the truth."

In the entry on fermentation in the *Encyclopédie*, bread and wine are the main examples to which the reader, through cross-references, is directed. Since the Nephew is a "grain of yeast," we will follow the cross-references and ask the *Encyclopédie* how the action of yeast manifests itself. A surprise awaits us. The entry on yeast (written by Paul-Jacques Malouin and appearing in the supplement) speaks not of decomposition but of assimilation:

> [Yeasts] are ... the greatest agents in nature; they have the property of communicating their qualities to whatever is analogous to them, and to assimilate it as they merge. Every body that acts upon another tends to some degree to assimilate it; even simple mixture is a type of assimilation of bodies that have merged.

In his dream, d'Alembert speaks of a "contact that assimilates" the molecules in forming organisms. In a separate fragment, Diderot attributes fermentation to an effect of assimilation; in this case, the terms are used metaphorically: "Two languages mix; but it is only through a long fermentation that they are assimilated."[26]

Should one focus on decomposition or assimilation? How to reconcile such diverse aspects of fermentation? In physiology, this ambivalence would be resolved a generation later, when it was better understood that digestion is carried out by fermenting agents that decompose food in such a way as to make it assimilable. I should also point out here that the Nephew, who is an eccentric, a unique and "bizarre" fellow, aspires above all to enrich himself through roguery "like anyone else," that is, by becoming similar to the most widespread model of success. But he remains poor, because by nature he cannot avoid being "marginal," dissimilar.

In the rest of the explanations concerning yeast, action and reaction are invoked, as we might have expected:

> Everything tends to reproduce itself, everything tends toward its own propagation: it is not only the nature of animals that seeks to engender itself, it also pertains to some degree to plants, and even to minerals: all bodies, being perishable, must reproduce themselves: all those for which a combination of parts is not enough, and which can

77

> only re-create themselves through a combination of principles, re-create themselves through yeasts.... The action of the yeast requires and assumes, in the dough to be risen, a binding or connection among the elements that make up the dough, for otherwise it would not rise; the union of the parts of a body is essential for fermentation, as action is to reaction. This binding of the elements of the dough, this adhesion among them, is necessary for the dough to rise.

The *seminal* value of fermentation is confirmed. Everything that ferments is a vital agent; all that is sperm or seed ferments.[27] Here we encounter one of the "material reveries" that Gaston Bachelard took pleasure in demonstrating in "prescientific" thought.[28] The homogeneity of the dough is presented at times as a condition for the action of the yeast and at times as its result. Is there not a curious crisscrossing between what one seeks to explain and what is considered a presupposition or a means of explanation? Assimilation by the dough will not take place if the elements to which it is to be applied are not already perfectly bound together. What results is the swelling. The dough that "rises" is a growing organism. To knead the dough is to give shape to a living being.

Now, the baker's gesture — kneading — is also the act of a form-giving demiurge, who is evoked in another passage in the text. The Philosopher asks the Nephew why he is a "ne'er-do-well." The Nephew excuses his lack of genius and his roguery through a series of metaphors that plead natural necessity. First, citing hereditary determinism and its consequences, the Nephew blames the "paternal molecule": "The paternal molecule was hard and obtuse, and this accursed primary molecule assimilated all the rest."[29] Then, referring to a mold imposed by the caprice of nature, the Nephew claims he can do nothing about it: nature has formed him such as he is. Nature smiled as she fashioned the great composers, but she grimaced when she kneaded the Nephew, as well as the "idols," the wicked and ridiculous characters from whom he makes a living by making them laugh. The third metaphor is taken from physics: the ineluctable law of attraction. "Lunatics and fools entertain one another," the Nephew explains. "They seek one another out and are mutually attracted."[30]

For Diderot, kneading is a gesture associated with the elementary processes of assimilation and fermentation. To return for a moment to "A Conversation between Diderot and d'Alembert": the Philosopher has applied himself to tracing the stages through which "inert sensitivity" becomes "active sensitivity." The passage from marble to vegetable and the animal's digestion of the vegetable are stages in an "animalization" of consciousness. Just how can a pulverized statue be assimilated? The question has a very simple answer. The plant cannot grow unless the mineral elements it absorbs have been previously *kneaded* and then *putrefied*:

DIDEROT: As soon as the block of marble has been reduced to an impalpable powder I will *mix* the dust with some humus or dirt containing vegetable matter. I will knead the powder into the humus, sprinkle water on the mixture, and then I will let it putrefy for a year, two years, a hundred years. Time means nothing to me.... I'll plant seeds in the humus — peas, beans, cabbages and other garden vegetables. The plants will get their food from the earth and I will get mine from the plants.

D'ALEMBERT: Your notion may or may not be true, but I like the idea of this passage from marble to humus, from humus to vegetables, and from vegetables to animals — to flesh.

DIDEROT: Well, that is how I make of flesh or of the soul — as my daughter says — a kind of matter that is actively sensitive.[31]

Kneading and putrefaction also go into the preparation of manure. If we check the *Encyclopédie*'s entry on *Putrefaction* (written by Antoine Louis, 1723–1792; the guillotine was also called the *louisette*), which supplements the doctrine of fermentation, we find the following:

> Putrefaction is the final stage of fermentation, and is usually regarded as the extreme dissolution of bodies undergoing corruption. Stahl maintains that it is the last stage of the division in which mixtures preserve their combination, and come the closest to being individuals.... Corrupted substances provide the best earth for fertilizing fields; its lightness makes it all the more penetrated by the principles of fecundity, but it does not retain them for very long. Another reason that manure favors fecundity is that it acquires a saline quality, through putrefaction, that makes it alter and conserve the moisture in the air.

This chemistry is still bound to the farmer's age-old experience. Without trying to follow the argument too closely, one can recognize traces of it in the literary discourse that derives from it metaphorically. If the Nephew restores to each "a portion of his natural individuality," isn't it because his fermenting quality is not only that of yeast (which makes dough rise) but also one that leads toward the "final stage," namely putrefaction (which fertilizes the fields and produces new life)? Doesn't the Nephew act in society in the same way that putrefaction (according to Georg Ernst Stahl, cited in the passage above) reduces compounds to little more than "*individuals*." In any case, the Nephew claims to know about such matters. In the tirade in which he gives a positive assessment of all past moments, and of everything that a well-fed individual would eliminate from his "wardrobe," he exclaims, in the Latin of the agronomists, "*O stercus pretiosum!*" (O precious dung!). This interjection is immediately followed by an evocation of death and putrefaction, which annuls the distinction between wealth and poverty: "To rot under marble or to rot in bare earth is still to rot." Putrefaction and fermentation are produced in the very passage between life and death, and between death and life. Immediately after this funeral couplet, the Nephew demonstrates to the Philosopher the resurrection of his violinist's wrist. But it is a simulacrum of playing: a stroke of madness. The most important passage over which fermentation presides is that between wisdom and madness.

Madness and Fermentation

A very sensible statement from the Nephew provokes the Philosopher's astonishment: "'Oh you master crackpot!' I broke out. 'How does it come about that in your silly head some very sound ideas are all muddled up with extravagant ones?'"

The person and the ideas of Jan-Baptista van Helmont (1577–1644) were greeted with a similar digression from Diderot. Diderot certainly had not read the Flemish physician's *Ortus medicinae*. As was his custom, he was content to read and summarize Jakob Brucker, who, in the fourth volume of his *Historia critica philosophiae*, had given an account of the modern chemists, beginning with Paracelsus. The entry on theosophists in the *Encyclopédie*, written by Diderot, briefly reviews van Helmont's doctrine, in which fermentation is omnipresent. Diderot's summary is given as a series of juxtaposed propositions. For example:

> Water is the matter of which everything is made.
> Seminal and generative fermentation is the rudiment by which everything begins and creates itself.
> The rudiment and the seed are the same thing.
> The seminal ferment is the efficient cause of the seed.
> Life begins with the production of the seed.
> The ferment is a created being; it is neither substance nor accident;

its nature is neutral; from the beginning of the world it has occupied the places of its empire; it prepares the seeds; it excites them, it precedes them. Ferments were made by the Creator; they shall last until the end of time; they regenerate themselves; they have their own seeds, which they produce and which are awakened by water....

Foreign ferments introduce corruption, and through them corruption begins, continues, and is completed.[32]

All life is depicted as beginning with the action of a ferment. Any illness would thus be a war of ferments! Such ideas both seduced and exasperated Diderot, who also undoubtedly knew that the Hebraic tradition and the Jansenists had compared original sin to a "bad leavening." In his entry, Diderot attaches great importance to Paracelsus, the "philosopher by fire." Paracelsus had proposed "the first seed of chemical theory; the differences among the elements, the formation of mixtures, the difficulty of their decomposition, the origin of physical qualities, their affinities." But after the account of the doctrine of van Helmont — the prophet of ferment, the aura, the "archeus," "blas," and "gas" — Diderot interrupts himself, as if out of breath.[33] Here he interjects a flight of oratory that is like an effervescent version of the Philosopher's exclamation upon hearing the chaos of the Nephew's "sound ideas" mixed with "extravagant ones." On the tumult of van Helmont's ideas Diderot himself writes a tumultuous passage:

I conjecture that these men of somber and melancholic temperament owe this extraordinary and almost divine penetration that we intermittently note in them, and which leads them to such mad and sublime ideas, to a periodic derangement of the machine. They thought themselves inspired, yet they were mad: their fits were preceded by a type of debasement, which they regarded as the state of man in a depraved natural condition. Drawn from this lethargy by the tumult suffered by the humors rising in them, they imagined that it was the divinity descending, visiting them, working them; that the divine breath, with which they had been first animated, had suddenly come alive again and revived a portion of its ancient and original energy; they formulated precepts for artificially attaining this state of orgasm and drunkenness, in which they found themselves exalted and which they missed; similar to those who have experienced the enchantment and delicious delirium that the use of opium brings to the imagination and the senses; happy in their drunkenness, stupid in rest, tired, over-wrought, bored, they looked at ordinary life with disgust; they sighed after the moment of exaltation, inspiration, alienation. Tranquil or agitated, they fled commerce with men, which was unbearable to themselves and others. How very close genius comes to madness! ... Times of ignorance and great disasters breed them: then men, believing themselves pursued by the divinity, gather around these types of madmen, who take advantage of them. They order sacrifices, which are carried out; they order prayers, and people pray; fasts, and people fast; murders, and throats are slit; songs of happiness and joy, and people crown themselves with flowers and sing and dance; temples, and they are built; the most desperate enterprises, and they succeed; they die, and are adored. Among this class of men we must include Pindar, Aeschylus, Moses, Jesus Christ, Muhammad, Shakespeare, Roger Bacon, and Paracelsus.[34]

These "great men" are altogether different from those cited as exemplary in *The Paradox of Acting* because they are masters of themselves. The tone, with regard to theosophists and their kind, is both admiring and defiant. When it is a question of poetry, Diderot expresses himself in a similar fashion:

Poetry presupposes an exaltation of the mind that comes from an almost divine inspiration. Profound ideas come to the poet, but he is ignorant both of their origin and of their implications. For the philosopher, they are the fruits of long meditation, and thus he cries, "Who could have inspired so much wisdom in this madman?"[35]

The passage on theosophists is animated by an imitative impulse. It speaks of agitated people and abandons itself to a warm exaltation. It evokes drunkenness by exuding an air of intoxication. The colors used by Diderot come from the traditional typology of melancholy, which at the time was being used again in a new debate on genius. Diderot rediscovers the terms Montaigne used to speak of Torquato Tasso's divine inspiration and madness. In comparing genius and madness, Diderot proceeds to a medico-philosophical development that rises gradually to an eloquent solemnity and a contemplation of all the ages of history. The haze of early Romanticism's artificial paradises (since opium is mentioned here) becomes confused with the sacrificial smoke of classical religions.

The distant "sources" of the discussion on madness and inspiration are Plato's *Phaedo* and Aristotle's (or Theophrastus's) famous *Problem* 30.1, in which melancholy is defined by the alternation of opposite states: cheerfulness and sorrow, sovereignty and prostration, mental vigor and overwhelmed stupor. Why these phenomena? The Aristotelian text cites a cause derived from an analogy between the effects of the melancholic humor (black bile) and those of wine. Black bile, like wine, produces froth (*aphros*). Breath or wind (*pneuma*), according to Aristotle, causes drunkenness and the raging phase of melancholy, as well as sexual pleasure.[36] In this respect, Diderot forgets nothing, since he speaks of "divine breath" and associates drunkenness with "orgasm." This last term requires some historical precision, for in Diderot's time it was not restricted to the single banal erotic meaning it has today. In the eighteenth century, the word "orgasm" retained a pathological meaning from the medical tradition, completely forgotten today. It is important to recall it here. In Bartolomeo Castelli's medical dictionary, an entry is devoted to the series of Greek and Latin words: *orgao* (to swell, to be excited), *orgasmos, turgeo* (to swell), *turgescentia, turgentia.* We learn here that in the strict sense it is a matter (according to Hippocrates) of the ardor of sexual pleasure and the evacuation of semen. But the author continues: "This meaning was transposed by Hippocrates and his disciples to designate excessive, superfluous, and unnatural humors that form in the body and that, whether agitated [*agitati*] or unnaturally effervescent and fermented [*fermentati*], must be excreted. Hence: orgasm is the name of the abnormal movement [*pravus*] of the humors and their expulsion through the excretory stimulus [*impetus cum stimulo excretionis*]."[37] Once again we find associated the notions of agitation and fermentation that Diderot so frequently linked together.[38]

Madness and genius, according to Diderot, are compounded in melancholics. From the beginning, I have stressed the chemical value of the notion of the compound: Rameau's Nephew is a "compound ... of good sense and lunacy." In Diderot's medical philosophy, the human being is composed of conscious molecules, but in the molecule consciousness is a "blind quality." "Nothing is as mad as it is. The wise man is but a compound of mad molecules."[39] In his *Réfutation d'Helvétius*, Diderot included an allegorical "gay tale," told in a Rabelaisian spirit and prefiguring the style of Jacques Offenbach (which, in this case, is not in the best taste). There he depicts the first man as a bastard child, conceived in drunkenness, of Minerva and Momus (the god of derision, who is "always mad").[40] "The bastard of Folly and Wisdom, delivered by Truth, and the god-child of Jupiter, suckled by Stupidity; such is man." This child was "all his life truthful and lying, sad and gay, wise and mad, good and wicked, clever and stupid." Man is thus a *compound* par excellence. "His various fortunes" are "a great series of thick tomes" — nothing less than "universal history compiled by a society of men of letters."[41] It is therefore not solely in his conception of matter that Diderot prefers the heterogeneous to the homogeneous, or the complex chemistry of ferments to the simple physics of masses.

From the Chain of Being to the Singular Individual

In *Eléments de physiologie*, his last work, Diderot saw himself as a physician-philosopher as well as a chemist. This unfinished manuscript includes an outline, but its propositions remain sketchy. Diderot would have liked to collect and articulate all the principles of a philosophy of living nature, and thus to found an anthropology that would lead both to a psychology (he does not use the word, but the thing is there) and to a morality. "Beings should be classified beginning with the inert molecule, if there is one, and passing to the living molecule, to the animal-plant, to the microscopic animal, to the animal, to man. The chain of being is not interrupted by the diversity of forms." Diderot begins with the "vegeto-animal": "The vegetal is produced by heat and fermentation."[42] He mentions the "small eels" that Needham had noticed in ergotic rye and fermented wheat. These might be the elementary components of all living bodies. Next the text proceeds to discuss the animalization of "vegetable matter," according to the process Diderot had described in the dialogue in which he expounded his fundamental biology and embryology to d'Alembert. The fermentation that sets life in motion is therefore, primordially, the producer of a "coordination of infinitely active molecules"; innumerable fragile attempts at organization will proceed from there.

At the beginning of the second part of *Eléments de physiologie*

86

— this time concerning the human body — Diderot asserts that man recapitulates the chain of being and that he carries within him the gradation of all natural qualities:

> Man has every kind of existence: inertia, consciousness, vegetable life, polypous life, animal life, human life.
>
> The animal body is a system of actions and reactions: actions and reactions are the causes of the forms of the viscera and the membranes.[43]

Thus man has both behind him and within him this vegetable life that begins with fermentation. He is a theater of action and reaction, even in fulfilling the higher faculties proper to his species. Between the brain (or the cerebellum) and the nerves, there is action and reaction. "The action of the nerves brings to the brain unusual desires, the most bizarre fantasies, affections, and frights." Reciprocally, "the action of the brain on the nerves is infinitely stronger than the reaction of the nerves on the brain." Consequently, the nerves are not always the brain's "despots"; they can also be its "slaves." If one or the other prevails, madness ensues. Beware of circumstances in which inflammation besets the brain, for "delirium, madness, and apoplexy" are its results. Is this not already the case with dreams? "There is indeed an affinity between dreams, delirium, and madness. Whoever persists in one of the first two is mad. Reasoned delirium and sustained dreams are the same thing." Moreover, dreams are the "action and reaction of the fibers upon each other."[44]

We must avoid a misunderstanding here. The explanatory model of action/reaction might seem, in these circumstances, to be reductive and simplistic, a facile way to reduce the unknown to the known: in short, an expeditious procedure of materialist speculation. In fact, although it might be a case of the magic wand lending the appearance of science to a notion that wants to say everything but settles on nothing, Diderot modulates it and puts it to work in order to arrive at qualitative differentiations. This general principle of animal life can be used to recognize the singularity of the living being. In 1773, when he read Helvétius's *De l'Homme*, Diderot was exasperated to find that it was content to summarily mention a few necessary conditions and pass these off as sufficient conditions. He protests: "I could never rest content with such generalities. I am a man, and I require the causes proper to man.... To take conditions for causes is to expose oneself to puerile paralogisms and insignificant consequences."[45] He demanded not only specific knowledge but also a knowledge that made possible an understanding of the individual. Calling upon the fundamental notions of logic, he reproached Helvétius for not respecting the difference between genus and species:

> Because the definition of man and of the man of spirit is not the same, and because every definition contains two ideas, of which one is the proximate genus and the other the specific or essential difference, the man of spirit is essentially different from man — as essentially different from man as man is from beast.

Now, the example Diderot uses to support his argument is not liveliness of spirit but madness: "You haven't said a word about madmen."[46] It is in speaking of them, without abandoning the principles of material determinism, that the most refined physiological considerations ought to lead to a better understanding of the "true cause of the differences between minds." Such "defects of organization" are infinitely varied:

> Can you really believe that in a machine such as man, in which all the organs act and react upon each other, one of the parts, either solid or fluid, could be tainted without bringing harm to the others?[47]

Action and reaction are given free rein in the countless organs and components of the human "machine." The physiological phenomenon of action and reaction remains a general and indeterminate law, which is nonetheless called upon to manifest itself in a differentiated, and thus specific, manner, which allows for the recognition of the distinctive "character" of the individual. The Nephew is thus a "species" in the pejorative sense of the term.[48] The desire to use general laws remains unquestioned. Nonetheless, while taking account of organic causes — that is, of the actions and reactions appropriate to an organization conferred at birth — Diderot wishes to recognize the singular "character" of each individual ("Each individual has his character"[49]) and especially those who bear the stamp of genius. Geniuses are all dissimilar. This means that in taking account of the multiplicity and the quality of the components involved in organic actions and reactions, we would not be left with only a simplifying generality; we would arrive, given certain supplementary research, at the proper formula that makes it such that the individual is himself. The principle of action and reaction is therefore unique, susceptible to various applications in the infinite number of representatives of the human species. Now, there is a human type who "is himself" in a more marked way, because "his character" breaks sharply "with that of other men": he is "the poet," "the artist," the original author. When it comes to the artist, Diderot argues not for fermentation but for the effect of fermentation, an innate intoxication:

> If the artist is not born intoxicated, the finest education will only succeed in teaching him to counterfeit intoxication more or less sullenly. Hence all the flat imitators of Pindar and of all original authors.... In my opinion, an original is a bizarre creature who possesses his own, singular way of seeing, feeling, and expressing his character. Had the original man not been born, one is tempted to

believe that what he did would never have been done, so much do his productions belong to him.[50]

Moreover, what makes an author original is, once again, the heterogeneity of his inventions:

> What is called original is not always beautiful; far from it. The sort of beauty for which there are no previous models is almost nonexistent. If Shakespeare is an original, is this originality found in his sublime passages? Not at all. It is in the extraordinary, incomprehensible, inimitable *mixture* of things in the best and the worst of taste, and it is especially in the bizarre nature of these things. What is sublime, in and of itself, I dare say, is not original. It only becomes so by a sort of singularity that makes it personal to its author; it is necessary to be able to say: it's the sublime according to so-and-so.[51]

To descend into singularity without renouncing a universal principle of explanation and comprehension, both material and physiognomic — such is the imperative Diderot seeks to satisfy.

"Small Bodies": Attraction in Default?

Diderot distinguishes between chemistry, whose object is the relationship among molecules, and physics, whose area of interest concerns the motion of masses. In the first conversation in *D'Alembert's Dream*, he takes up the ideas of the Montpellier physician Gabriel-François Venel, who wrote the entry on chemistry in the *Encyclopédie*. In this article, chemistry is split into organic chemistry and nonorganic chemistry (which was not yet known as "inorganic" or "mineral" chemistry), while the study of masses is considered more properly the task of physics. This subdivision is formulated as follows:

All the changes that take place in bodies, either by nature or by art, can be reduced to the following three classes. The first includes those that make bodies pass from the nonorganic to the organic state, and reciprocally from the latter to the former, and all those that depend on the organic economy or that comprise it. The second includes those belonging to the union and the separation of the constituent principles or the materials of the composition of sensate, nonorganic bodies, all the phenomena of combination and decomposition studied by modern chemists. The third, finally, includes all those that make masses or aggregate bodies pass from rest to motion, or from motion to rest, or that modify motions and tendencies in different ways.... Consequently, the phenomena of organization should be the object of a science essentially distinct from all the other areas of physics.

Physics, according to Venel, is concerned only with masses, and "these exert upon each other actions very distinct from those proper to minute particles." Chemistry is concerned with the tiniest particles. Physics radicalizes the demands of a calculable mechanical intelligibility, whereas chemistry admits — at least provisionally — a kind of matter that is not subject to calculation. The chemist gives himself over to an "experimental presentiment." Diderot, drawing conclusions from these distinctions, speculated on matter in its simplest state, which is to say minute particles. But he imagined transitions. He declared that masses (such as stone) resolve into minute particles and that all minute particles, as Venel put it, are capable of passing "from the nonorganic to the organic state."

Diderot, however, did not share Venel's mistrust of the hypothetical attraction of minute particles. In distinguishing the competence of physics (masses and aggregates) from that of chemistry (minute particles and mixtures), Venel resigned himself to the idea that a unified explanation could not be applied to all natural bodies. He cared little for the summary extrapolations of John Keill and John Freind (*Praelectiones chymicae*), who, using Newton as guarantor, imagined a chemistry subjected to the general laws of motion.[52] According to Venel, one must avoid reducing everything to "our alleged laws of motion." The truth of chemical operations is found not in "the mutual action of certain solid and elastic minute particles," but in "the general laws of affinity," which are "scarcely a mechanical principle." Diderot, on the other hand, did not dismiss the attraction supposedly taking place among minute particles. Despite his hypothesis of the inherent sensitivity of matter, he remained attached to the majesty of a law reigning over all of nature. This law is the law of attraction, with an enlarged field of application. He appreciated it for precisely what the latter-day Cartesians reproached it for: not fitting into the mechanical laws of transmission and motion and resembling an "occult quality." It appeared acceptable to Diderot, as long as certain neglected factors were taken into consideration:

> There are grounds for believing that the attraction which causes planets to orbit and which precipitates heavy bodies toward the center of the earth produces still other natural effects, such as hardness, the adherence of fluid parts, fermentations, and generally all phenomena born of cohesion or relating to it. Indeed: (1) It is sufficiently proved that these various phenomena do not depend on impulsion, at least not as a sole or even principal cause; (2) if attraction is a general property of matter, a notion that, to say nothing more, is quite probable, it is natural to attribute all analogous effects to it; and those of which I have just spoken are certainly among them.
>
> We must admit, however, that a considerable problem arises here. The force with which heavy bodies, notably planets, are carried

toward a center is always reciprocally proportional to the square of the distance; and that with which particles approach and unite with each other in cohesions, etc., is manifestly greater. It seems as if these two forces could not be produced by a single and same cause.[53]

Diderot recalls that certain writers tried to overcome the difficulty by proposing a double law of attraction. This would be the inverse square of the distances for large bodies and the inverse cube of distances for minute particles. This hypothesis did not satisfy him. While declaring that he can "never speak without also doubting," he formulated two explanations that take into account the "extreme smallness of the particles" and the "reciprocity of attraction." This supposition made it possible to recognize a single law in all of nature. In this way, Diderot raised the doubts that Newton left on the subject of "another attractive force" in the famous Query 31 of his *Opticks*:

> And thus nature will be very comfortable to her self and very simple, performing all the great motions of the heavenly bodies by the attraction of gravity which intercedes those bodies, and almost all the small ones of their particles by some other attractive and repelling powers which intercede the particles.[54]

A general law is postulated for the whole of nature. But how to prove this?

A few years later, Buffon pleaded the same case, and this passage of the *Seconde vue de l'histoire naturelle* (1765) was often cited in the last decades of the eighteenth century:

> The laws of affinity by which the constituent parts of these various substances [of the mineral kingdom] separate themselves from others in order to reunite with them and form homogeneous matter are

the same as the general law according to which all celestial bodies act upon each other; they exert themselves equally and in the same relationships of mass and distance; a globule of water, sand, or metal acts upon another globule as Earth's globe acts upon that of the Moon; and if up to now people have regarded the laws of affinity as different from those of weight, it is for want of grasping or understanding them, for want of embracing this object in all its breadth....

Newton was right to suspect that chemical affinities, which are nothing more than the particular attractions about which we have just spoken, occur through laws quite similar to those of gravitation; but he does not seem to have seen that all these particular laws are but simple modifications of the general law, and that they only appear to be different, since from a very short distance the shape of atoms attracting each other creates as much and even more than the mass for the expression of this law, with this shape thereby entering for some into the element of distance.

It is, however, on this theory that the intimate composition of crude bodies depends: the foundation of all matter is the same — mass and volume — which is to say that the form would also be the same if the shape of the constituent parts was the same. A homogeneous substance can differ from another only inasmuch as the shape of its primitive parts is different.

Buffon concludes: "A single force is the cause of all the phenomena of crude matter, and this force combined with that of heat produces living molecules on which depend all the effects of organized substances."[55]

Analysis and Reagents
In the language of specialized chemistry, the word "reaction" was introduced marginally, with little fanfare. It did not attract the attention of historians of this science.[56] They had their hands full

94

with many other subjects: the nomenclature of chemical bodies, the discovery of new elements, the objection to Stahl's theory of the phlogiston. Lavoisier's foundational writings do not contain the word "reaction."

The term only managed to slip into chemical works before the second half of the eighteenth century through temporary borrowings from the general physics inherited from Scholastic or Renaissance Aristotelianism. Seventeenth- and eighteenth-century knowledge assigned chemistry to the "operations" aimed at the separation or the union of elements.[57] The word "operation," like the word "experiment" (*experimentum*), was used in reference to all the chemist's undertakings: mixtures, solutions, calcinations, distillations, sublimations, digestions, precipitations, crystallizations, and so on. The only use of the term "reaction" I have found is in a passage by Johann-Joachim Becher (1635–1682), in which the author goes all the way back to God in order to attest to the presence of life in the universe. This life implies the presence of motion, and thus of action and passion, and thus of reaction. On this basis, one must admit permutation or transmutation. This includes recognizing animal, vegetable, and metallic transmutations, whence Becher concludes that transmutation into gold (the most perfect metal) is the true object of the transmutative art of metals.[58]

The word "reaction" seems not to have appeared until after a precise definition for "*reagent*" was adopted. Such a definition, proposed by Torbern Bergman in his *De analysi aquarum* of 1775 (which inaugurated analytic chemistry), initially came into play in the plural. In Louis-Bernard Guyton de Morveau's very accurate translation, we read:

> There are two principal methods by which to understand the heterogeneous parts of waters: reactions and evaporation. Reagents are the

substances whose addition immediately, or at least very quickly, causes a change in color or transparency, and thus reveals the principles found therein. Reagents save a lot of time, but they do not always allow for a sure evaluation, especially when it is a matter of determining quantities.... The synthesis must confirm the analysis so that no uncertainty remains.[59]

A number of *reagentia* exist, and Bergman soon gives a list: beginning with litmus (*lakmus*), there are twenty-five of them. Reaction is not a general and universal phenomenon, a chemical law in the same sense as the mechanical law of the equality of action and reaction. There are as many reactions as there are analytic operations that reveal the presence of an element or a compound. In other words, all reactions are specifically determined. The word "reaction," in this case, refers to a precise operation performed by the chemist at work — a laboratory exercise — and not to a material regularity found in all of nature. If "reaction" has a general meaning in Bergman's chemistry, it is to designate the procedures that allow for the analytic identification of particular substances. Analytic chemistry, not general chemistry, is the field of reactions. Reactions exist only to make determinate bodies appear.[60]

Bergman attributed great importance to *affinities*, or elective attractions. (The German equivalent is *Wahlverwandtschaften*, which Goethe used as the title of a novel.) Bergman certainly did not invent the term, which seems to have been introduced by Johann Conrad Barchusen (1666–1723) and was used extensively by Hermann Boerhaave. In 1718, Etienne Geoffroy had published a table of affinities. Gabriel-François Venel, in the entry on chemistry in the *Encyclopédie*, praised Geoffroy while also declaring that affinities are not reducible to mechanical explanation. In addressing the notion of affinity, Bergman nonetheless tended to present it as a manifestation of attraction, a universal law in need of a reinterpretation that would apply also to the shapes and dimensions of minute particles.[61] Guyton de Morveau, his translator and French correspondent, congratulated him for this, for, he said, it was necessary to "bring ... to chemistry a mathematical exactitude of which no one beforehand would have thought it susceptible."[62] Despite Venel's fears and criticisms, a reconciliation between physics and chemistry emerged as a possibility:

> Thus this great law of physics that moves the stars has become, in the Uppsala laboratory as in our own, the key to all the operations that our art demands of nature in order to unite or to separate the elements of small bodies; this conformity seems to us to promise at last the reuniting of long shared opinions on so capital a point and gives us confidence that the Physicist and the Chemist will henceforth cease, in the case of the former, to appropriate exclusively for himself the use of mathematical rules and calculation and, in the case of the latter, to be limited to those sympathies that are as sterile as they are imaginary and that appeared to justify this schism in the natural sciences.[63]

While attraction can be referred to Newton, the principle of the *equality* of action and reaction is left aside, for in chemistry, unlike in the mechanics of masses, it does not correspond to any working hypothesis that can be submitted to a rationally devised experiment. It can only be a question of aggregation, composition, fusion, exclusion, or exchange:

> In general, Bergman substitutes the term "attraction" for that of "affinity"; he distinguishes the attraction of aggregation from that of composition, that is, from dissolution or fusion, where the latter produces the union of two bodies; he calls simple elective attraction that which, in the concurrence of three bodies, combines two of

them and excludes the other; it becomes double attraction when there is an exchange between two compounds of two principles each.[64]

In the introduction to his *Essai de statique chimique* (1803), Claude-Louis Berthollet repeats almost verbatim the fundamental formulas of Buffon, Bergman, and Guyton de Morveau, whose numerical expression he hoped to perfect. In fact, the thought closest to his is that of Pierre-Simon Laplace, whose scientific program intended to draw all the conclusions of Newtonian attraction down to the molecular level:

> The powers that produce chemical phenomena are all derived from the mutual attraction of the molecules of bodies, which, to distinguish it from astronomical attraction, is called affinity.
>
> It is probable that they are both the same property; but astronomical attraction only exerts itself between masses placed at a distance, such that the figure, spacing, and particular affections of the molecules have no bearing; its effects, always proportional to the mass and the inverse ratio of the square of the distances, can be rigorously subjected to calculation; the effects of chemical attraction or affinity are, contrariwise, so altered by particular and often indeterminate conditions that they cannot be reduced to a general principle but must be ascertained successively. Only a few of these effects can be isolated enough from all the other phenomena to lend themselves to precise calculation.[65]

Berthollet thus remains persuaded that, to make progress, chemistry must follow the model of the science of mechanics. Although he does not use the word "reaction," he speaks of the "reciprocal action of chemical bodies":[66]

98

Observation alone must be used to ascertain the chemical properties of bodies, the affinities through which they exercise a reciprocal action in a determinate circumstance; however, since it is probable that affinity does not in its origin differ from general attraction, it must also be subjected to the laws determined by mechanics for the phenomena arising from the action of mass, and it is natural to think that the more the principles attained by chemical theory become generalized, the more analogous they will be to those of mechanics.

It is thus necessary to proceed to a rigorous analysis of "chemical action"; it is also necessary to remember physics itself, for physics and chemistry should "illuminate each other."[67] In this way, Berthollet relativizes the list of affinities (according to Bergman), endowing molecules with a mutual power of attraction of a different sort. As a result, the proportions in which two substances combine vary case by case as a function of the physical conditions of the experiment (heat, pressure, and so on). The process leads to a stable system, analogous to a "planetary system in which the sum of the forces exerted between the celestial bodies finds a state of equilibrium."[68] Hence the very idea of chemical statics.

As the investigation of electrical phenomena established a new experimental field, produced new phenomena, and defined new laws in new terms, direct reference to Newton began to wane. But polarity offered reaction an occasion to expand its validity. It is still a matter of *paired terms*. Proof of this can be found in one of the earliest writings by Hans Christian Ørsted (who discovered electromagnetism). His French translation, by Marcel de Serres, bears the title *Recherches sur l'identité des forces chimiques et électriques*. This translation, which appeared in 1813, is dedicated to Berthollet. Ørsted announces a theory of forces:

99

In reducing all motion to its fundamental laws, we have raised the mechanical part of the natural sciences to its current perfection, in which it embraces all the motion of the universe as a great mechanical problem whose solution allows us to calculate in advance an infinite number of particular phenomena. To prepare the chemical part of the natural sciences for a similar degree of perfection, we must try to retrace all chemical actions to the primitive forces that produce them. Then we shall also be in a position to calculate all the chemical properties of the primitive forces and their laws. Now, since chemistry is concerned solely with these properties, this whole science will be converted into a theory of forces — to which mathematics will also be applied — and will perhaps reach a new level, as was the case in their application to motion.[69]

Ørsted's conclusion is that "chemical forces are fundamentally the same as electrical forces, except in a different form of activity":

There are two opposing forces that exist in all bodies and that can never be entirely removed. Each of these forces is an expansive and repulsive action in the area in which it is dominant; but when they react upon each other, they attract each other and produce a contraction. The freest action of these forces produces electrical phenomena. These forces can be condensed, contained within a certain space, and even rendered entirely latent by their attraction to each other.[70]

Ørsted's idea of reaction pertains to laboratory experiments, but also to a metaphysical and religious vision of the universe. It is both experimental and speculative.

Soon the notion of affinity disappeared from the vocabulary of chemistry. It was followed by different fundamental laws: the law of defined proportions (Joseph-Louis Proust, against whom

Berthollet argued); the law of multiple proportions; the definition of elements (so often called "principles" until this point); the
atomic hypothesis, leading to that of atomic weights; the observation of the speed of chemical phenomena, and so on. The word
"reaction" gained a foothold in the vocabulary of this science, but
at a level of generality equaled only by the facility of its use. It
designated any process in which chemical bodies were present
and in which one could ascertain a starting point and an end
point. It often bore the name of those who first observed or
established it. It became an ancillary word, with no pretensions
or stakes, an omnipresent and quasi-invisible word, always an incomplete signifier if it appeared in isolation. It had meaning only
when a supplement specified which well-determined reaction
was being referred to. Chemistry knew hundreds of thousands
of reactions, which prevented this hopelessly *common* term from
acquiring a signification any more precise than that attached, for
example, to the word "phenomenon."

The word "reaction" flowered at a time when the finest minds
(Condorcet, Berthollet, and even Bonaparte) hoped to see Newtonian mechanics and the chemistry of "small bodies" united.
Around 1800, this analogy was imagined as a stage in the realization of a complete continuity between chemistry and physics
within the discourse (or formulas) of a unified science. The attempt to think of the unity of nature made it possible to hope for
a rational transcription of the law expressed in the universality of
phenomena. Gravity seemed so conclusively demonstrated on
the planetary level that only a few optimistic extrapolations were
needed to see it at work on the atomic level. Need we recall that
science today still lacks a unified theory? After the development
of thermodynamics, electromagnetics, and quantum theory, the
quandary of reconciling gravitational theory and quantum theory
— incompatible theories whose validity can be proved in different

contexts — emerged. Their opposition has not yet been overcome. But beginning with Albert Einstein, who did not succeed in solving it, the problem has spurred research in atomic and cosmological physics.[71]

A Chemist Defines the "Great Man"

Early in the twentieth century, the chemist Wilhelm Ostwald proposed a historical overview of his discipline's evolution.[72] The word "reaction" accompanies the conceptual history of all chemistry. Ostwald makes anachronistic use of it, as if chemistry had spoken of reactions from its inception. I do not wish to criticize this use, which is almost a general rule; there is no reason to forbid the application of present-day interpretative codes to the past. I shall merely point out that "chemical kinetics," prefigured by Berthollet's chemical statics and more clearly defined fifty years later, is presented as the true "theory of reactions." Ostwald, a pioneer of physical chemistry and electrochemistry, claims that chemical kinetics emerged with "general chemistry," and he credits Ludwig Ferdinand Wilhelmy (1812–1864) for it. Ostwald wrote a great deal; he was a great propagandist of science, and his ambition was to unite science and philosophy in a unified interpretation of the world — an interpretation that would present itself as a monist energetics. One of his books offers us an unusual surprise. In a series of lectures devoted to "great men," he poses the question raised at the beginning of the conversation between Rameau's Nephew and the Philosopher: What is genius, scientific genius in particular? The answer given by Ostwald (who received the Nobel Prize for his very real scientific accomplishments) is striking for its naïveté and archaic typology. There are, in his opinion, two types of geniuses: the classical and the romantic. Classicals, "phlegmatic" and melancholy, are individuals with *slow reaction*. Romantics are sanguine and choleric, with *quick reaction*.[73] Here is our guiding word used once again, with a most summary neurophysical meaning. It rings like a scientific word, but only to provide an image in a pseudo explanation.

CHAPTER THREE

Life Reacting

To Live Is to React: Hobbes, Glisson, and a Few Others

If the existence of a medical concept is measured by its presence in a dictionary, one must conclude that the word "reaction" took a long time to gain official recognition. There is no trace of it in Bartolomeo Castelli's *Lexicon medicum* (new edition, Geneva, 1746). Nothing in Robert James's *Medicinal Dictionary* (translated and published by Diderot, Paris, 1746–1748), in Ephraim Chambers's *Cyclopaedia* (fifth edition, 1743), or in d'Alembert and Diderot's *Encyclopédie* (1751–1772) documents any medical meaning of the term.[1] To my knowledge, the first French medical dictionary to contain an entry on reaction was by the former Oratorian Joseph Capuron (1806).[2] Dictionaries are always behind the times. There is often a delay between the incidental use of a term, its adoption by a larger group of users, and its ultimate consecration in the reference books.

From the start, then, we can rest assured that by the middle of the eighteenth century, before its confirmation by the dictionaries, "reaction" had occupied a place in the medical vocabulary.

But we must go back even further; it made its first appearance, with an already "modern" twist, in the seventeenth-century language of sensory physiology. Here, rather than in Descartes, where one would have expected to find it — especially in those passages in which, with complete self-assurance, he attempts to explain sensation and motion in terms of mechanics.[3] It is well known that he transferred the realm of simple machines into living bodies, multiplying pulleys and levers, tubes and receptacles. In *L'Homme*, he constructs the organism on the model of hydraulic automatons, using collision and transmitted motion, traction and pressure as models, but he has no use for the words "react" and "reaction," which were perhaps too reminiscent of Scholasticism. Certainly the passions of the soul correspond to the actions of the body, but the soul is a substance distinct from that of the body.[4] Descartes was careful not to establish between them a relation of action and reaction. As for the body's motions, these are caused by the flow, in the muscles, of that subtle fluid known as animal spirits. If the perception is strong enough, it opens the floodgates that ready the nerves and muscles for the influx of these spirits. The motion transmitted is never directly repelled by a reaction.

It is quite a different story with Thomas Hobbes (1588–1679), who readily used the action/reaction couple (*reactio*, or *antitypia*) to explain our perceptions. It is the starting point for many of his works, *Leviathan* in particular. His mistrust of language and his extreme nominalism led him to support the materialist hypothesis alone, which he presents very clearly in the fourth of the sixteen objections he addresses to Descartes on the subject of his *Meditations*: "Reason gives us no conclusion about the nature of things, but only about the terms that designate them."[5] Hobbes proposes an anthropology in which the sense organ fulfills a primary role and sensation is reduced to a simple mechanism. Action and reaction are the products of the physics of local motion and occur successively.[6] Explained at great length, sensation (what Hobbes called "sense" or *sensio*) is defined in such a way that it becomes "a phantasm, made by the reaction and endeavor outward in the organ of sense, caused by an endeavor inward from the object, remaining for some time more or less."[7] Sensation, I should stress, is a motion outward; it is "an effort of resistance on the part of sentient beings against external objects."[8] But this resistance does not imply spontaneity. Hobbes's sensory physiology is an extension of his physics, whose only feature, at every level, is propagated impulse, transmitted motion: "Motion has its cause only in the motion of a contiguous body." Hence, in the perception of a flame:

> First, it is evident that the fire, the only lucid body here upon earth, worketh by motion equally every way.... From such motion in the fire must needs arise a rejection or casting from itself of that part of the medium which is contiguous to it, whereby that part also rejecteth the next, and so successively one part beateth back another to the very eye; and in the same manner the exterior part of the eye presseth the interior.... Now the interior coat of the eye is nothing else but a piece of the optic nerve; and therefore the motion is still continued thereby into the brain, and by resistance or reaction of the brain, is also a rebound into the optic nerve again; which we not conceiving as motion or rebound from within, do think it without, and call it light.[9]

Hobbes found it necessary to add a distinction in order to establish a separation between animate and inanimate bodies:

> But though all sense, as I have said, be made by reaction, nevertheless it is not necessary that every thing that reacteth should have sense. I know there have been philosophers, and those learned men, who have maintained that all bodies are endowed with sense. Nor do I see how they can be refuted, if the nature of sense be placed in reaction only.[10]

Hobbes's argument, as summarized by Arthur Hannequin, is as follows: "It is not enough to react, there must also be a prolongation of the reaction even after it has ceased; and whereas in most bodies the reaction stops at the same time as the action, in sentient beings it persists in the form of imagination or memory."[11] This historian presents Hobbes as a "modern" thinker:

> To reduce . . . all the various forms of physical agents to the unique form of motion, and all organic actions of the various sense organs to a uniform action of the nervous system, and then to claim to find perception not in the direct impression of objects on the mind but in the reaction of the brain and the conscious center on the objects from outside was (1) to glimpse the tremendous import of mechanical explanations of the universe; (2) to look for a cause for the diversity of sensations in the diversity of the dispositions of the nervous system and the reaction of the centers, as the modern physiologists after Johannes Müller were to do; and (3) to recognize the preponderant action of consciousness on the nature of our sensations.[12]

The action of consciousness? Note that Hobbes did not understand consciousness as a separate entity.

The Cambridge Platonist Henry More endeavored to defend — against Hobbes — the idea of an incorporeal and immortal substance, and he centered his polemic precisely on sensation. Even if sensation is the effect of an instantaneous material reaction, the latter cannot account for the operations of which we are conscious within ourselves. More's argument sets out to define and to limit the domain in which the concept of reaction can legitimately be applied. Everything that is not reducible to this domain belongs to the mind. Common sense, free will, and thought are the acts of a substance distinct from matter.[13] The notion of reaction allowed More, albeit negatively, to demarcate a frontier.

Hobbes, in fact, did not recognize this frontier. A reaction, according to Hobbes, produces sensation. But this results from the bodily motion that has provoked it from without. Through the living body's resistance, sensation merely continues a bodily motion. The effort (*conatus*) from the inside toward the outside (that is, the sensation) is not original in relation to the *conatus* from the outside toward the inside (which is the motion of external objects functioning as stimuli). Thus sensation is but a mode of bodily life. And so is thought.

In formulating his objections to Descartes's *Meditations*, Hobbes takes issue with Cartesian dualism and with the proofs given for the thinking substance. Descartes's "I think" leads Hobbes to declare: "The proper inference seems to be that a thinking thing is material rather than immaterial" (Second Objection).[14] The acts of the understanding are a continuation of bodily motion: for the acts of the understanding, as seen above, apply only to terms, that is, to names. "If this be so, as is possible, reasoning will depend on names, names on the imagination, and imagination, perchance, as I think, on the motion of corporeal organs. Thus mind will be nothing but the motions in certain parts of the body" (Fourth Objection).[15] It must be acknowledged that the body is the receptacle of a motion that is not inherent to it. It acts only by received impulse. What makes it susceptible to being put into motion is the fundamental inertia of matter. Of course, when Hobbes speaks of effort (endeavor, *conatus*), he appears to be calling upon an anthropomorphic metaphor. But nothing is more foreign to his thought than the vain desire to endow material bodies with properties other than those of receiving and transmitting motion. Life, sensation, and reasoning are merely their most complex modifications. Hostile to any recourse to final causes, Hobbes does not endow the *conatus* with an aim. In language that anticipates the numerical codifications of mathematics, Hobbes's intuition can be summarized thus: "Force is in a state of *conatus* ... when the motion is evaluated in a space and an instant that are smaller than any given quantity. The *conatus* represents force in a state of tension, and marks the degree of tension in the force; and this is by reason of speed."[16]

"It is not necessary," writes Hobbes, "that every thing that reacteth should have sense." Hobbes is economical in the properties he grants to matter. A rather different meaning of the action/reaction couple was emerging in the seventeenth century. Francis Glisson (1597?–1677) declared that the tiniest particles of matter perceive, desire, and have the spontaneous power to enter into motion, and thus to act and react. Glisson was a physician who studied and taught at Cambridge. His thought and works were sustained by an intuition concerning the life of matter (willed by God), which the whole current of medical vitalism later claimed for itself.

Glisson has not been forgotten. Historians associate him with the idea of irritability, considered a property of the living being. In his first work, *De rachitide* (1650), Glisson introduces the verb "to irritate" and the substantive "irritation," which had already been used by a few of his predecessors. These words helped him to define the property of bile ducts in his *Anatomia hepatis* (1654): "Any part that perceives an external hindrance does its best to get rid of it; this is properly called being irritated. From this fact, when parts that experience injuries [*injurias*] try to rid themselves of them [*iisdem vindicari*], it is correct to say that they are capable of irritation."[17]

Later, in his *Tractatus de ventriculo et intestinis* (1677), Glisson highlights the concept of irritability and explains it at length. The term "irritability" itself was new. It did not gain acceptance immediately. Glisson had hesitated to associate it with nervous excitation; he made it a property inherent to fibers.[18] It had to be

rediscovered. The notion of irritability was taken up again, in citing experimental results, by Albrecht von Haller in *A Dissertation
on the Sensible and Irritable Parts of Animals* (Latin text, 1749;
French text, 1753; English text, 1755). Although Haller did much
to credit Glisson with having invented the word, he himself
received the glory of having discovered "a new division of the
parts of the human body," one that, "being essential to all animals,
and perhaps all plants, would rightly be counted among the first
qualities of organic bodies henceforth."[19]

Glisson interrupted the writing of *De ventriculo* (begun around
1660) to write *Tractatus de natura substantiae energetica, seu, De
vita naturae ejusque tribus primis facultatibus: Perceptiva, appetitiva,
motiva* (1672). This work presents his fundamental physics, and as
such his general physiology. An entire chapter of this treatise is
devoted to reaction (chapter 20). Later, in *De ventriculo*, in treating the irritability of the motor fiber (chapters 5, 6, and 7), Glisson refers repeatedly to his treatise *De vita naturae*. Yet he never
mentions a "reaction" of the fiber; he discusses its action (*actio*),
its "passion" (*passio*), or its motion (*motus*).[20] The intellectual
connection with the concept of reaction is evident, but it is not
engaged. It took a few more decades, and many missed encounters, before "irritation" and "reaction" were put into direct verbal
relation.[21] In fact, Glisson did not introduce reaction in connection with irritability because he saw life, action, passion, reaction,
and motion in all of nature.

All matter is active and reactive. Glisson was a proponent of
the concept of the "motion essential to matter" (as Diderot would
later say) and even of an obscure sensitivity inherent in all the
parts of matter. To Cartesian dualism he opposed a monism in
which the whole universe is a mirror of divine activity. "Whatever
exists must, for that reason, act. For the fundamental principle
of existence and that of action are not really distinct, but rather

incomplete concepts of a single thing. In positing the existence of matter, one posits at the same time its energetic nature."[22] A *naturalis perceptio* and a *naturalis appetitio* are buried within all things, independently of innervation. Thus, since he sees reaction everywhere, Glisson implicitly offers an explanation of the irritability he studied in certain organs (such as the gallbladder and the stomach), without demonstrating that it is a special type of reaction.

In every respect, Glisson bears witness to the anthropomorphic and vital meaning taken on by the notion of reaction before the advent of Newtonian mathematics. His lexicon is still that of the Scholastics and the Aristotelians. He developed his ideas on reaction based on the propositions of Francisco Suárez (1548–1617) and in the Scholastic terminology of the doctor of Coimbra. Through his examples and definitions, Glisson animalized to the utmost the contemporary concepts of pre-Cartesian philosophy. All action is an effort to move (*nisus movendi*, chapter 19). There are "immanent" actions and "transient" actions. Immanent action remains within the agent and has no external goal. ("Immanent action, properly speaking," Suárez had declared, "is found only in vital actions."[23]) "Transient" action goes on to produce a modification in the external body that is acted upon. Glisson specifies: "Although the body that is acted upon makes sure (at least as far as it itself is concerned) that the agent does not produce an actual motion or permanent mutation in it, it is nonetheless impossible to predict that the simple effort of moving will not affect it" (chapter 20, 17). The reaction occupies an intermediate time in a sequence that is not without its dramatic side. "The reaction intervenes between the patient's actual motion and the agent's effort in moving" (chapter 20, 16). He takes up the classic example of the iron in cold water (chapter 19, 10–11), dramatizing it in terms of a relationship between an *aggressor* and a *defender*. Furthermore, he differentiates the cases in which action and reaction take place at a distance from those in which the latter is produced in hand-to-hand combat between the agent and the reagent. There are "pure reactions" in which the first agent is not affected by a reaction. "The pure reaction is the effort of the patient [*passi*] to defend itself from the change it senses the agent is trying to inflict upon it. The agent attempts perpetually to make the patient similar to the agent, and therefore to change it. The patient, in perceiving this, resists and tries to protect itself."[24] It can either repel the action undergone or accept it within itself and try to make it tolerable by softening, correcting, or tempering it. One example Glisson proposes, which is not lacking in beauty, echoes the Scholastic commentators on Aristotle encountered above: the rays of the sun create effects in minerals, plants, and animals, which are transformed and perfected. These entities convert the rays to their own ends, in the interest of their own preservation, but their reaction does not reach the sun. "Since reaction is a species of action, it has an end [*terminus*]. What is the end of this reaction? I assert that the end of this reaction is the preservation of that which is acted upon."[25] As expounded by Glisson, the reaction theory associates reaction with the triple property of perception, desire, and motion that belongs to all matter. Glisson's terms ("aggression," "defense," "preservation") were taken up by medical science in new discursive contexts. Jacques Roger considers Glisson a source of inspiration for the Montpellier school, where his influence compounds that of Stahl. The physicians who collaborated on the *Encyclopédie* (Théophile de Bordeu, Jean-Jacques Ménuret, Henri Fouquet) appealed to his authority. True, his name does not appear in Diderot's work. But the Latin word *nisus*, which Diderot uses to designate the molecule's effort toward motion, is indeed present in Glisson, who speaks in particular of a *nisus movendi* (effort of motion).[26]

With Glisson, as with Hobbes, a doctrine of action and reaction in the living body is thus found before the publication (of Newton's *Principia* in 1687). But neither one foresaw Newton's principle of the *equality* of action and reaction, which was to be so beneficial to mathematized physics and its applications.

In comparing the philosopher Hobbes with the physician Glisson, one might say that the theoretical problem was as follows: Is life the *result* of organization (Hobbes), or does life lie in matter itself, *prior* to all organization (Glisson)? To support either thesis, the modus operandi of action and reaction was a useful argument, though at the price of great semantic imprecision. Yet these pre-Newtonian concepts, as approximate as they were, benefited from the glory and success of Newton's principles. As soon as one invoked Newton's name in the defense of a completely imaginative theory, one was credited with (and spared the necessity of) a demonstration conforming to "mathematical principles." Arguments that revived the ancient verbal antinomy could pass themselves off as corollaries of the exact law; they could appeal to it and in this way renew their legitimacy, without correcting much of their initial imprecision. In eighteenth-century medical and natural sciences, it was not unusual for a scholar to pay homage to Newton (for the success of a method that made predictive calculations possible), all the while using the notion of reaction in a very approximate sense, a sense dating back to the science — or rather the philosophical speculation — before the *Principia mathematica*. As it happens, the vagueness and the verbal abuses of so many superficial Newtonianisms attest both to Newton's prestige and to the survival of a previous way of thinking. Those whose thought owes a great deal to Glisson's vitalism (such as the Montpellier physician Louis de La Caze) proclaimed themselves Newton's disciples — in order to intimidate their adversaries.[27]

Buffon

Metaphysics demanded some explanations. Is there but one substance, or two, as Descartes claimed? Anyone who wanted to have
a book printed in eighteenth-century France was well-advised to
subscribe to the radical opposition between spirit and matter. We
would be well-advised, for our purposes, to reread Buffon's famous
passages, which Jacques Roger and Robert Mauzi in particular
have admirably analyzed from a different perspective.

With his system of "organic molecules," Buffon showed considerable boldness in his attempt to give each side its share while
remaining entirely within the material realm. For him, there is
in the world, on the one hand, inanimate matter and, on the
other, a great reserve of living matter that is finite in quantity and
that circulates among the soil, plants, and animals, taking on individual forms for a lifetime by virtue of what he called "organic
molds." Living matter and inert matter are not the same. By introducing a duality into the material realm, Buffon was able to construct a complete world with matter alone, in its two states, thus
dispensing with spirit. Yet Buffon did not wish to break completely with the Cartesian tradition. He was attempting to draw a
new dividing line, this time between man and animal. According
to him, human nature was not explainable by the play of "organic
molecules" alone; it was necessary to acknowledge a dual nature:
homo duplex.[28] Buffon contrasts a "spiritual principle" with an
"animal principle." Thus man was granted an acceptable theological status.

In the Aristotelian-Thomist tradition, there was nothing scandalous in acknowledging a large share of animal life in man, in
which he is no different from other living beings. In all animals,
the nerves transmit "disturbances" to the brain, and the brain
reacts in determining external motion. The images Buffon uses to
explain muscular motion conform to the "explosive" chemical

theory proposed by Thomas Willis.[29] It is even tempting to conjecture that the "law of all or none" was presaged, long before H.P. Bowditch, by Buffon's acumen.[30] Buffon realized that he could not accept the rule of equality postulated by Newton. The symmetrical model of action and reaction is not respected in living bodies. This model is applicable only if it is transposed into the chemical register of the explosion:

> Objects act upon the animal by means of the senses, and the animal reacts upon objects by external motions; in general, the action is the cause and the reaction the effect.... One will perhaps say that here the effect is not proportionate to the cause; that in solid bodies following the laws of mechanics the reaction is always equal to the action, but that in animal bodies it seems that the external motion or reaction is incomparably larger than the action.... Yet it is easy to respond to this.... With a spark one can ignite a powder storehouse and blow up a citadel.... Consequently, it should not appear extraordinary that a slight impression upon the senses could produce a violent *reaction* in the animal body, which is manifested by external motions.[31]

Most of these external causes escape us, Buffon adds, because "in nature most of the effects depend on several causes combined in different ways, including causes whose action varies, whose degree of activity does not appear to follow any rule or constant law, and which we can therefore neither measure nor even estimate except in the way we estimate probabilities, that is, by seeking to approach truth in terms of what is likely to be true."[32] Buffon continues his demonstration by noting that "the impression of objects on the senses" is the source not only of "progressive motion" in the animal but also of desire in man:

When an object strikes us through any of the senses, and the sensation it produces is pleasurable and gives rise to desire, this desire can only be relative to some of our qualities and some of our ways of experiencing pleasure; we can desire this object only in order to see it, taste it, hear it, feel it, or touch it; we can desire it only to satisfy more fully the sense through which we have perceived it, or to satisfy a few of our other senses at the same time, or to make the first sensation even more pleasurable, or to stimulate another sensation that takes pleasure from this object in a new way; for if, in the very moment when we first perceived it, we could fully take pleasure in it with all our senses at the same time, we would desire nothing. Desire thus occurs because we are poorly positioned with regard to the object we have just perceived: we are either too far or too near; naturally we therefore change our position, because at the same time as we perceived the object, we also perceived the distance or proximity that produces the inconvenience of our position and that prevents us from taking full pleasure in it. The motion we make as a consequence of desire, and the desire itself, come only from the impression this object has made upon our senses.[33]

Desire goes hand in hand with a restricted satisfaction and with the pursuit of a sensation that becomes more rich in being repeated — a sensation that is both different and deferred. Buffon describes the motion that results from desire in a hallucinatory passage in which a mental experience unfolds under the impetus of a reasoning that begins with the schematic evocation of sensory action and motor reaction:

> It is therefore the action of objects upon the senses that gives rise to desire, and it is desire that gives rise to progressive motion. In order to understand this better, imagine a man who, in the instant when he wishes to approach an object, finds himself suddenly deprived of the

limbs necessary for such an action; this man, whose legs we have sev-
ered, will try to walk on his knees. Sever his knees and his thighs, yet
preserve his desire to approach this object, and he will try to walk on
his hands. Deprive him of his arms and his hands and he will creep,
drag himself along, he will use all the strength of his body and help
himself with all the flexibility of his vertebrae to set himself in
motion, fastening himself by his chin or with his teeth to a support
to try to change position; and when we reduce his body to a physical
dot, a globular atom, if the desire remains he will still use all his
strength to change position; but since he will have no other means to
move himself than to act against the plane upon which he is carried,
he will not fail to raise himself more or less high to reach the object.
The external and progressive motion does not therefore depend at
all on the organization and the shape of the body and limbs, since,
no matter how an individual is externally shaped, he cannot fail to
move, provided he has senses and the desire to satisfy them.[34]

To find a text comparable to this we would have to look in Lau-
tréamont or Samuel Beckett! What an itinerary — from the provocative sensation to the sensation pursued by desire, in a body
reduced to the larval state!

Buffon poses the question — as an enigma — of converting sensory stimulation into motion. "Between the *action* of objects and
the *action* of the animal" there must be a "middle term" in which
the "determination of motion" takes place.[35] In the animal, this
middle term, considered "an internal and general sense," resides
in the brain. This allows one to say that in the animal "the determination of motion is a purely mechanical effect." And in man?
"The soul takes part in almost all our motions." However, it is
"very difficult for one to distinguish the effects of the action of
this spiritual substance from those produced by forces of our
material being alone."[36] What do we gain from not being depen-

dent on our material organization, like the animal, if the race to satisfy desire is as imperious and mutilating as the one that Buffon, in the case of the hypothetical man, has just described for us?

Let us listen to Buffon's answers. The soul enables us to compare, form thoughts and judgments, and understand. Herein lies our infinite superiority. But the soul's activity is secondary. It characteristically manifests itself late in the development of one's constitution and late in one's personal history. On the one hand, it does not intervene until after we have been determined by the "animal principle," at the mercy of the mechanical succession of actions and reactions; on the other hand, it does not awaken, does not "exert itself" until later in the life of humans.[37] This latecomer's status jeopardizes the soul's independence in relation to experiences that, themselves dependent on the "internal material sense," enjoy an inevitable precedence. "Therefore, let us distinguish the physical from the moral in the passions of man: one is the cause, the other the effect." The first emotion lies in the internal material sense; the soul can receive it but "does not produce it."[38] The "moral," which is proper to the soul, risks being drawn into the sphere of "physical" action that pertains solely to animal existence. Hence man is plagued by troubles and misfortunes. The mistake is to *divert* the soul from its specific function: "It was given to us only so that we may know, but we want to use it only to feel; if we could stifle its light entirely, we would not miss it, we would envy the fate of the insane."[39]

Whose fault is it if *we* make poor use of our spiritual faculties? The soul's? The intensity of desire's? And who is this *we* given over to wayward distraction? At one point, Buffon questions the soul's dubious complicity with a type of imagination "that depends solely on the bodily organs" and that man shares "with the animals."[40] This is an inferior imagination, with no relation to that of

119

the "superior mind" and "the genius," which have the power "to compare images with ideas, to give color to our thoughts." Our passions always make us unhappy. They spoil the part of our life related to the "physical." It is here that the famous apostrophe to love occurs: "Why is it that you are the happiness of all creatures but the sorrow of man!" The proposition that follows tends to downplay the "physical" and the "moral" aspects of love in favor of the "material principle": "The reason is that only the physical aspect of this passion is good, and despite what those in love might say, the moral aspect counts for nothing."[41] Wisdom consists in giving each side — both body and spirit — its share and in reconciling these two separate "principles": "The man who has gained wisdom is undoubtedly the happiest being in nature; he combines the pleasures of the body, which he shares with the animals, with the pleasures of the spirit, which belong to him alone; he has two means to happiness that mutually complement and strengthen each other."[42] But while the wise man is capable of harmonizing the contradictory demands of these two principles — feeling and knowing — most individuals live this duality as a combat, an opposition, and an inner conflict. They are two people struggling with each other. Since man ceaselessly pursues happiness, and since happiness for him consists of "the unity of his inner being," a last resort would be the temporary eviction of one of the two antagonists. However, subjected to perpetual alternatives, to "simple impulses" that favor one of these two "principles," existence becomes no less unhappy for all that: it leads to indifference, laziness, and boredom.[43] But worse than that is when these two "principles" are both active, when they counterbalance and paralyze each other instead of "mutually . . . strengthen[ing] each other." Then come melancholy and despair, which Buffon describes using terminology from the mechanics (or dynamics) of forces: thus, in a surprising way, he speaks of equilibrium and the equality of opposite forces to discuss not compound motion but a type of violent immobility determining an inner obliteration:

> The most unhappy of all beings is he in whom these two sovereign powers of man's nature are both in motion, yet equally so, which produces equilibrium: here is the source of the most profound boredom, that horrible self-loathing which leaves us with only the desire to cease living and which allows us no action other than what is necessary for self-destruction, by coldly turning the weapons of fury against ourselves.
>
> What an awful state! I have just painted its darkest shade, yet how many other somber shades must precede it! All the situations and positions akin to this one, all the states approaching this state of equilibrium, in which the two opposing principles have difficulty overcoming each other, and *act* at the same time and with almost equal force, are times of trouble, irresolution, and unhappiness. The body itself comes to suffer from this disorder and these inner conflicts: it languishes despondently or consumes itself in the agitation that this state produces.[44]

Thus does Buffon discuss the antagonistic actions turned against the self: suicide, or the inner conflict's somatic reverberation. In speaking of this situation, he uses only the verb "to act." Yet one might guess that the opposition between the physical and the moral, the material and the spiritual principle would provide a wonderfully suitable field of application for the explanatory schema of action and reaction.[45]

Charles Bonnet
The naturalists and the first anthropologists (in the philosophical sense of the term) wasted no time in making ample use of the formula. Charles Bonnet's *Essai de psychologie* (1755) gives some

fine examples, notably in its discussion of the crescendo of passion: "Such is the union of the soul with the body that when certain ideas are presented to the soul, certain motions are stimulated in the body that intensify these ideas. As these ideas intensify, they increase the strength of the motions, and from this type of action and reaction a constantly increasing passion results."[46] The metaphoric use of action and reaction lends an air of normality and naturalness to the relationship between ideas and motion, that is, between the soul and the body. The metaphysical problem of the union of the soul and the body appears to be glossed over or set aside. In any case, it does not hamper the exposition of a psychosomatics. This is not the place to ask how the soul, an immaterial substance, could provoke a material reaction: this question is the shadow cast by Cartesianism over the entire French medico-philosophical tradition. In his embryology, Bonnet has no difficulty harmonizing the relations between material parts and those binding the soul and the body.

In the chapter of *Essai de psychologie* titled "The State of the Soul After Conception," we read: "As the seed develops, the reciprocal action of solids and fluids acquires greater force or intensity. The nerve fibers, which have not yet been made sensitive, begin to become so. The soul's reaction on nerve fibers or on the animal spirits, which is always in proportion to the degree of their motion, consequently increases in intensity."[47] In the developing individual, the soul has occasion to react in many circumstances, in particular in the act of attention: "By itself, the soul may greatly intensify a slight impression. In reacting on the fibers representing a certain object, it can make the motion imprinted on these fibers by the object more intense or more lasting, and this faculty is called attention."[48] Bonnet is not much concerned with the relation between the soul and the body: these "two substances act ... or appear to act reciprocally upon each other."[49] He adds:

"This question seems to come down to this: Does one perceive an action where there is no reaction at all? What idea can we form of the impression made by an active being on an absolutely passive being? But the soul does not react on the body as one body reacts upon another body. On the occasion of the brain's motions, the soul's activity unfolds in a certain way, and the resulting effect is necessarily the formation of an idea or sensation."[50] Bonnet returns to this idea when he outlines an explanation of kinesthesia in terms that anticipate those of Maine de Biran and that propose, in traditional metaphysical terminology, what is known today as feedback: "The soul comes to feel that it moves my arm because of the arm's reaction on the brain."[51]

Similarly, Condillac explains memory and habits by the brain's reaction on the senses. Beginning with the metaphor of the harpsichord made to vibrate by a person's fingers, his explanation ends with the image of motion in return: "Throughout all the time that we are awake ... our memory is always active. The brain ... goes, by habit, from movement to movement, it leaves behind the action of the senses and brings long sequences of ideas to mind again: and it does more still, it vividly reacts upon the senses, sending back to them the sensations which they had previously sent it, and it persuades us that we see what we do not see."[52] This is how one plays long pieces of music from memory.

In Bonnet, the occasionalist or Leibnizian terminology easily conveys the postulate of the reciprocal action of the physical and the moral, henceforth considered a law of nature. Human freedom is not excluded: "This motor force of the soul, this activity it exercises on the organs as it pleases, is *Freedom*. Inner feeling shows us that we are endowed with this force, just as it shows that we are endowed with the faculty of thought."[53]

A lexical use was established and soon became widespread. In speaking of the "reaction of the moral upon the physical," one could adopt and rejuvenate the older idea of the imagination's influence on the life of the body. Such was the case for Rousseau, though he did not make systematic use of this formula. One reads in a fragment, "The moral has a great reaction on the physical and can even alter the features of the face at times."[54]

I'd like to add a last remark: by the time the action/reaction of the physical and the moral was introduced into the anthropological discourse of the Enlightenment, scholars had already acknowledged that the physical (Buffon's "animal principle"), on one level, is governed according to the law of sensory action and motor reaction. There is thus a double action and reaction: first, between the interior and the exterior of the animal and, second, between the "animal" and the "spiritual" life of this exceptional animal, the human being. Some philosophers would be very tempted to make it a single law. Today, one might speak of a sub-system (body-world) within a global system (body-spirit-world).[55] But for the moment, for Buffon, and for Bonnet, a residual metaphysical dualism makes it possible to safeguard the autonomy of the human subject in raising it, so to speak, above nature. Buffon grants the human being the possibility of escaping the generality and anonymity of what is produced according to the universal law of nature. No animal is unique; no animal is a subject with a memory of its past. It is the soul that differentiates every human as a person endowed with singularity:

> It is in our souls that we differ among ourselves: it is through our souls that we are *we*; our souls create the diversity of our characters and the variety of our actions. Animals, on the other hand, who have no soul, also have no *ego*, which is the principle of difference, the cause that constitutes the person: therefore, since they resemble each other through organization or since they are the same species, they must all copy each other, do all the same things in the same way,

and, in a word, imitate each other much more perfectly than men are able to imitate each other.[56]

Using modern terms, one might say that according to Buffon, the id reacts in the animal and similarly in the "material" part of man, whereas man, through his soul, can grasp himself as an *I think*. Animal life is a necessary, but not a sufficient, condition for thought.

Vis Medicatrix *(Bichat)*

The word "reaction" enjoyed great success on the eve of the French Revolution. Its use, which had been limited at the beginning of the century, became more widespread. In 1788, the lexicographer Jean-François Féraud noted the term's diffusion. "Reaction," "to react," he wrote, "are used in relation to all sorts of subject matter."[57] It was a question not just of more frequent use but also of an expanded application into various fields, as one symptom of considerable historic change. At the same time, this change was borne out in redistributions and modifications that were notional as well as lexical. Society had changed, philosophical-scientific discourse was no longer the same, and new myths appeared. The mutation did not take place along a neatly determined course, along one simple line of intellectual evolution. It was made up of related, interdependent phenomena on many levels, and in many changing circumstances.

A Hippocratic saying had come down through the ages: life is assisted by the "healing power of nature" (*vis medicatrix naturae*). The Hippocratic formulation is a simple proposition that dispenses with the use of a verb, "*hē phusis ho iētros*," or literally "nature, doctor." A fine example of an ellipsis, it allows for immediate contact between the subject and the nominal attribute. The foremost agent combating illness is found inside us: nature itself.

Our bodies possess the power of spontaneous resistance to all noxious agents. It was even a considerable argument for those who disputed doctors' claims. It was repeated across the ages without the word "reaction" having been uttered.

But by the eighteenth century, the word had begun to seem perfectly appropriate to this idea. Such is the case with the Scottish physician William Cullen. In his *First Lines of the Practice of Physick* (1775), we find these fundamental propositions:

> In every fever, there is a power applied to the body, which has a tendency to hurt or destroy it.... In consequence of the constitution of animal economy, there are certain motions excited, which have a tendency to obviate the effects of the noxious power, or to correct or remove them. Both these kinds of motion are considered as constituting the disease. But the former is perhaps strictly the morbid state, while the latter is to be considered as the operation of the *vis medicatrix naturae*, or salutary tendency, and which I shall hereafter call the *reaction* of the system.[58]

Here we witness a decidedly Scholastic formula being deliberately replaced by — translated into — a word more appropriate to contemporary scientific language. Indeed, "healing power" belongs to the repertoire of occult (or substantial) qualities that were largely dismissed at the time; "reaction," on the other hand, was related to a great law of nature, one that had become generally accepted. As set forth by Cullen, the word "reaction" synthesizes notions and is accessible to a large audience. In comparison to the ancient saying, which rapidly came to be seen as periphrastic, it was infinitely more manageable. I should also note that Cullen, Robert Whytt's successor as professor of medicine at the University of Edinburgh, was a chemist who was very up-to-date on scientific developments.[59]

Once the reality of a vital principle has been acknowledged, how does one provoke a favorable reaction? How does one determine the resistance of a sick body? On the basis of an extremely limited experimental knowledge, it was possible to argue for an "expectant" medicine that would not impede natural reactions. Most writers on the subject were occupied with constructing speculative systems that, they thought, would be able to evaluate vital forces, the organism's deficits, and the reinforcements and compensations that therapeutics was likely to bring. One such system took the form of Brunonianism, named for its founder, the rowdy John Brown (1736–1788), who had been taught by Cullen (with whom he quarreled) and who enjoyed a fleeting glory in Europe. Brown attributed an important role to variations in irritability (or excitability) and claimed to calculate the necessary doses of tonics or sedatives in proportion to the organism's divergence from the extremes of sthenia and asthenia.[60] His system was an extreme form of allopathy. Brown himself never used the word "reaction." But those who paid attention to him — and there were many in Europe around 1820 — often referred to the production of salutary effects by remedies combating illness as "reaction." An echo of these ideas is discernible among philosophers and writers. Hence in Novalis we find this masochistic idea: "Fatigue and sadness have an agreeable reaction. They are remedies; and this is why men find them so useful and beneficent." Undoubtedly because for him reaction implies a sequence, Novalis notes again: "The idea of reactions is a historically authentic idea."[61]

The same insistence on vital force underlies the homeopathy of Samuel Hahnemann (1755–1843), who adopts the idea of treating an ill with another that resembles it: *similia similibus*. "It is solely the morbidly affected vital principle which brings forth diseases." The guiding principle of homeopathic therapies is that a natural illness must be combated by an artificial illness of a higher energy, which has to be provoked through a more powerful agent. First one has to identify the substances whose effects are analogous to the symptoms of the illness. The dilution of the substance analogous to the ailment is then supposed to increase (potentialize, spiritualize) the "dynamic" action of the medication. The word "re-action" was used by Hahnemann, and in particular by his disciples, to designate the "homeopathic aggravation" of the illness noted after the first administration of the cure.[62] This homeopathic aggravation is considered a sign of efficacy and a portent of healing.

With Xavier Bichat (1771–1802), one enters a new era. He expressed his convictions forcefully and soberly, avoiding the Latin motto *vis medicatrix naturae*.[63] Bichat accepted the vitalist idea as it had been modernized by Cullen, yet he expressed it in a discourse that did not rely on past authorities: his concern was to define a present fact in the language of the present.

In his preface to *Physiological Researches on Life and Death* (1800), he writes:

> The definition of life is usually sought for in abstract considerations; it will be found, if I mistake not, in the following general expression: Life consists in the sum of the functions, by which death is resisted.
>
> In living bodies, such in fact is the mode of existence, that whatever surrounds them, tends to their destruction. They are influenced incessantly by inorganic bodies; they exercise themselves, the ones upon the others, a continuous action; under such circumstances they could not long subsist, were they not possessed in themselves of a permanent principle of reaction. This principle is that of life; unknown in its nature, it can only be appreciated through its phenomena: a habitual alternation of action and reaction between exterior bodies and the living body, an alternation whose proportions

128

vary according to the age of the latter, is the most general of these phenomena.

There is a superabundance of life in the child: In the child, the reaction of the system is superior to the action, which is made upon it from without. In the adult, action and reaction are on a balance; the turgescence of life is gone. In the old man, the reaction of the inward principle is lessened, the action from without remaining unaltered; it is then that life languishes, and insensibly advances towards its natural term, which ensues when all proportion ceases.

The measure, then, of life in general, is the difference which exists between the effort of exterior power, and that of interior resistance. The excess of the former is an indication of its weakness; the predominance of the latter an index of its force.[64]

Here a definition is formulated through a play of opposites. The defensive reaction of which Bichat speaks is global and implicates the entire living body in its response to external aggression. The reaction of the living ensures the independence of an inside confronted with an outside. In speaking of the "permanent principle of reaction," Bichat makes life into a continuous struggle for survival.

The global confrontation discussed in the preface is followed, as early as the first chapter, by new divisions, which are noted when the physiologist carries out a more detailed investigation. Bichat establishes a distinction, which will remain famous, between "two lives." This distinction proceeds from a new opposition between the external and the internal. *Organic* life (also known as "vegetable life") is considered "a habitual succession of assimilation and excretion": within this life, the animal lives only within itself, like vegetable life. In *animal* life (also known as the "life of relation"), on the other hand, the individual animal exists outside itself. It "feels, it perceives, it reflects on its sensations, it moves according to their influence, and frequently is enabled to communicate by its voice its desires and its fears, its pleasures and its pains."

This dichotomous distinction will give rise to a series of new binary, correlative, or secondary distinctions.

Animal life, in fact, is defined as a coupled phenomenon. Sensations that originate from the outside are carried to the brain; in this first order of functions, the brain is "almost passive." But it becomes active through "volition." Beginning in the brain, this volition puts the organs of locomotion and the voice into action, thereby reacting upon external objects. Part of the resistance proper to life considered globally is thus devolved upon the will. The brain is the central organ between sensation and volition.

Another couple, that of assimilation and disassimilation, constitutes organic life, whose "organ" and "middle system" are the "sanguiferous system."

Here we have a nice symmetrical construction, neoclassical in style. The binary system continues in the opposition between the *will*, which is centered on cerebral life (and which, in man, is interdependent with reason), and the *passions*, which have their seat in the organs of organic life. In admitting this visceral localization of passion, Bichat's thought preserves an archaic aspect, which quickly prompted objections and which it is worth commenting on more extensively here. Furthermore, the relation to the external world, which the preface granted globally to "life" in general, becomes specialized in the sensory-motor functions of animal life.

Three types of reaction have thus been formulated. The first results from the interaction between life as such and what was soon known as the "environment." The second occurs specifically within the sensory and motor branches of "animal" activity and is essentially voluntary. The third is manifested in organic contractility or "irritability," through which passion, as well as its consequences, is defined.[65]

How does Bichat conceive of the relations between the two
lives of a single individual? The brain, on the one hand, is excit-
able by means other than the nervous system, and this establishes
an important link between the two lives: the heart is the "natural
stimulant of the brain, by means of the blood which it sends
there." On the other hand, Bichat does not recognize the cerebral
centrality of all sensations. He admits of sensibilities localized in
the viscera yet capable of producing cerebral effects. To account
for this phenomenon, Bichat resorts to the concept of influence
or sympathetic excitation, adding, of course, the mechanism of
reaction. Without speaking of reflex, he discusses muscular
movements whose first origin belongs solely to vegetable life. In
this case, the organs react upon the brain, which sets the muscles
into action without willing the motions it imprints on them. Involuntary contractions are the result of cerebral automatism,
which is the result of a visceral affection. Bichat, faithful to tradition, still considered certain passions purely organic. Clearly,
he does not possess a completely modern and systematized representation of the nervous system. However, his explanations,
though in a vocabulary that today seems antiquated, are worth
reading:

> The most numerous sympathies unite all the internal viscera to the
> brain or to its different parts. Every step which we make in practice
> presents us with affections of the brain originating sympathetically
> from those of the liver, stomach and intestines. Now as the effect of
> every kind of passion is to produce a change of power in one or the
> other of these viscera, such change will sympathetically excite either
> the whole of the brain or some of its parts, whose re-action upon
> the muscles, which receive from thence their nerves, will produce
> the motions, which are then observed. In the production of these
> motions, the cerebral organ is so to speak almost passive, whereas it

is active when the will presides over its efforts.... Such is the manner in which they appropriate, if I may so express myself, the phenomena of animal life, though they have their seat essentially in organic life.[66]

Thus an action (Bichat also says reaction) is exercised by the organs and passively undergone by the brain when it is subjected to the law governing the life of the passions. The passional life does not intervene in animal life except as usurper or antagonist. Bichat specifies:

> Although the brain is not the only terminus for the re-action of inter-nal viscera affected by the passions, it is nevertheless the principal one, and in this respect may always be considered a central source at all times in opposition to that represented by the internal organs.[67]

This reaction, a type of alienation and madness, makes the individual into the plaything of his organic life and contributes to the creation of his "character" and "temperament." But the will, which in Bichat's terminology originates in animal life, is always ready to recover "its empire" and become master of its "moral acts" once again.[68] This allows Bichat to distinguish between two types of individuals: the passionate, in whom organic law and the "epigastric center" prevail; and the willful, whose movements are directed by the cerebral center. Equilibrium is rare. There is more commonly an "alternating predominance of the two lives." This doctrine is in keeping, once again, with neoclassical aesthetics, since it compares the superiority of the will over the passions to that of composition over color.[69] It is thus a doctrine perfectly suited to the age of energy and will in the early nineteenth century, and Bonaparte's career soon gave his contemporaries a legendary expression of it. Stendhal's writings — in particular the figure of Julien Sorel—bear witness to this fact, which is no less pertinent for being so often noted.

Bichat does not consider the phenomena he speaks of accessible to measurement. He holds the vital forces to be irreducible to the regular laws of mechanics, challenging the Newtonian analogy that had been so appealing in the previous century. At the same time, Bichat discourages the endeavors of an organic chemistry in which physiological experimentation would calibrate excitation and measure responses. His method, which remains that of Haller and fundamentally that of Galen, consists in observing the results of sectionings, lesions, irritations, and excisions and raising questions about how to maintain or eliminate the great vital forces, without subjecting them to quantitative analysis. These procedures had certainly not been exhausted: in the proper, deft hands and with improved equipment, including the use of anatomic verification, the results were not disappointing. Nonetheless, the experimental method in physiology and the "numerical method" in the clinic could not take full flight until they had confronted the interdictions thus propounded by Bichat:

> Attraction is a physical power; it is always in proportion to the mass of brute matter in which it is observed; sensibility is a vital power, but in the same mass of matter, in the same organic part its quantity is perpetually changing.
>
> The invariability of the laws which preside over the phenomena of physics enables us to apply the formula of calculation to all the sciences which have them for their object. Applied to the action of the living body, mathematics can never give us general formulas. The return of a comet, the resistance of a fluid in traversing an inert canal, the rapidity of a projectile may be calculated; but to calculate with Borelli the force of a muscle, with Keill the velocity of the blood, with Jurine and Lavoisier the quantity of air entering into the

133

lungs, is to build upon quicksand an edifice that is solid of itself but that will soon fall for want of a sure foundation.

This instability of the vital powers, this tendency they have to vary and fluctuate at every instant, impress upon all the physiological phenomena a character of irregularity which particularly distinguishes them from those of physics.[70]

Bichat, who made the great mistake — as his adversaries saw it — of not recognizing an essential difference between animal and man, makes a great deal of the difference between the living and the nonliving.[71] In so doing, and in defining life by the faculty to *react* against the hostility of the external world, Bichat, like some of his predecessors at Montpellier, reassigned to life a term from Aristotelian physics (so stamped with "biologism") that eighteenth-century geometers had used to designate an order of mechanical and quantifiable phenomena. The originality of Bichat's position lies in its implicit challenge to the mind/body duality while transporting a dualism between animal and organic life into the very center of life. The perplexity he evinces when he attempts to depict action and reaction between animal life and organic life is very similar to the difficulty that metaphysics, since Descartes, has had establishing a relation between thinking substance and extended substance. Bichat's complete opposition to the Cartesian system bears on two essential points: he does not believe the living body can be reduced to a mechanism; and he shifts will and thought onto the side of animal life.

The defensive meaning that Cullen and Bichat had attributed to reaction was finally confirmed in Joseph Capuron's *Nouveau Dictionnaire*:

Reaction: Type of motion that tends to prevent or destroy the effects of a noxious omnipotence applied to the animal economy and that some physicians have attributed to what they call the healing power of nature, the vegetal principle, the soul, the organism, and so on.[72]

This definition would be authoritative for the rest of the century.

Claude Bernard

In the legacy from his predecessors, Claude Bernard found and accepted the notion of reaction. He proclaims its validity throughout all of nature. He generalizes the principle, to the point of making it the password of his "physical vitalism":

> The most superficial examination of everything taking place around us shows us that all natural phenomena are the result of the reaction of bodies upon each other. The *body* in which the phenomenon takes place must always be considered, as well as the external circumstances or the *environment* that *determines* the body or provokes it to manifest its properties. The combination of these properties is indispensable to the manifestation of the phenomenon. If one takes away the environment, the phenomenon disappears, just as if the body had been removed. The phenomena of life, as well as the phenomena of inorganic bodies, present us with this double condition of existence. We have on the one hand the organism, in which the phenomena of life take place, and on the other hand the cosmic environment, in which living bodies, as well as inorganic bodies, find the conditions indispensable for the manifestation of their phenomena. The conditions of life are neither solely in the organism nor solely in the external environment, but rather in both at the same time. In fact, if one removes or alters the organism, life ceases, while the environment remains intact; if on the other hand one removes or corrupts the environment, life disappears as well, even if the organism has not itself been destroyed.[73]

Bernard is trying to prove the need for a dual relation in the production of a phenomenon, be it organic or inorganic; however prudent this might be, and however far removed from the idea of polarity so dear to the Romantics, we see that he proposes a dual universal schema:

> Since a natural phenomenon is only the expression of connections or relationships, there must be at least two bodies for it to become manifest. Hence we must always consider (1) a body that reacts or that manifests the phenomenon; (2) another body that acts and plays the role of environment in relation to the first.[74]

Bernard explains this proposition very carefully:

> Phenomena therefore appear to us as simple effects of the contact or *relationship* between a body and its *environment*. In fact, if in our minds we completely isolate a body, we obliterate it at the same time; and if, on the other hand, we multiply its relationships with the external environment, we multiply its properties.
>
> Phenomena are thus the relationships of determined bodies; we always conceive of these relationships as the result of *forces* external to matter, because we cannot locate them absolutely within a single body. For the physicist, universal attraction is merely an abstract idea: the manifestation of this force demands the presence of two bodies; if there is but one body, we can no longer imagine attraction.... Similarly, life is the result of the contact between the organism and its environment; we cannot understand life with the organism alone, nor with the environment alone. It is therefore also an abstraction, or a force that appears to us to be outside of matter.[75]

Bernard considers the relationship of the living organism with the external environment to be coupled with the modifications of the organism's internal environment. Essential bodily regulations and "vital phenomena" in general "are but the results of the contact between a body's organic elements and the *internal physiological environment*." This is so much the case that experimental medicine, Bernard says, should consider "the reciprocal and simultaneous reactions of the internal environment of the organism on the organs, and that of the organs on the internal environment."[76]

In the texts just cited, the italics highlight not "reaction" but the words "body," "environment," "internal environment," and "forces" and the verb "to determine." The word "reaction," although used for the demonstration, designates something that is more important than it. It leads to an understanding of something other than the mere idea of reaction. In this passage from Bernard, it is associated with *relation*, in the name of which the scientist invites his reader to adopt a scientific reserve that renounces grasping "the essence of things." Bernard uses the word "reaction" to set his readers on the path leading away from "literary expressions" such as "life," "death," "health," "illness," since these lack "objective reality"; we use these expressions "because in our minds they represent the appearance of certain phenomena." The experimental method, on the other hand, deals with "elicited observations"; the physiologist acts in such a way as to obtain reactions, that is, regularly verifiable and predictable "relations." This is what allowed Bernard to adopt the idea of an "absolute determinism in the conditions of existence of natural phenomena."[77]

Bernard paid homage to Bichat, while contesting his form of vitalism, which he considered "metaphysical":

There are, in a word, only physical conditions at the basis of all phenomenal manifestations. Only this is tangible. And yet the interpretations we give to these physical phenomena are always

metaphysical because our minds cannot conceive of things or express them otherwise.[78]

Bernard adds a nuance both to his praise and to his critique:

> Bichat, in founding general anatomy and in relating the phenomena
> of living bodies to the elementary properties of tissues as effect
> and cause, established the true solid base on which general physi-
> ology rests; not that Bichat considered the tissues' vital properties
> special physicochemical properties leaving no room for the mys-
> terious agents of animism and vitalism: his work consisted uniquely
> in decentralizing the vital principle. He localized the phenomena
> of life in tissues: yet he did not embark on the path of their true
> explanation.[79]

As Georges Canguilhem has noted, Bernard did not renounce giving "theoretical" shape to the "general conception of life" that he
derived from his experiments as a physiologist. In *Leçons sur les
phénomènes de la vie communs aux animaux et aux végétaux*, which
marks the last phase of his thought, Bernard's theory culminates
in a powerful formula: "Life is creation." Were anyone to reproach
Bernard for offering a "literary" formula, he would have retorted
that it is not a postulate but a result, as demonstrated by his many
experimental proofs. In substituting "creation" for Bichat's "reaction," Bernard invites the consideration of an evolutionary phenomenon, one that unfolds over a long time, whereas Bichat's
"reaction" was but an alarm set off from moment to moment and
an act accomplished in the here and now.

In many respects, however, despite the repudiation of Bichat's
"vital principle," Bernard's agonistic conception of life is not
without similarities to his predecessor's. Bernard asserts:

The phenomena of life are not spontaneous manifestations of an
inner vital principle; they are, on the contrary, ... the result of a conflict between living matter and external conditions. Life is the constant result of the reciprocal relation between these two factors, as
much in the manifestations of sensibility and motion — which are
usually considered of a higher order — as in those related to physicochemical phenomena.[80]

This is what makes him say that poisons are "life's reagents."[81]

Such considerations lead the great physiologist to continue
using the word "reaction," not to make it the key to a more general definition of life, but to characterize the different types of
irritability and sensibility across the entire gamut of living beings:

In a general way, irritability is the property, possessed by any anatomic part (which is to say the protoplasm that enters into its constitution), of being prompted into acting and reacting in a certain way
under the influence of external stimuli.[82]

Countering the philosophers who restrict *sensibility* to the psychic realm, Bernard defends a broader physiological meaning:

Since a reaction can be imagined in the cell, in the organ, or in the
system responding to excitations, *sensibility will be considered the
reactive aptitude of the whole organism — the whole nervous system — of
one of its parts, or of a simple cell.*[83]

Thus reaction is taken for granted, but questions remain: Which
reaction? On what level, what scale? Today's molecular biology
goes well beyond the cellular level and has demonstrated that
for many of the decisive questions played out at this level, the
notion of sensibility is no more than metaphoric. This has only

accentuated the idea of a hierarchy — from the "total organism" to its smallest parts. For Bernard, it was important to define the nature of this "reactive aptitude" on different planes. It is essential to specify this. In the text immediately following the passage just cited, other, more descriptive terms appear that, depending on the organism in question, characterize the "reactive aptitude" in three different ways:

> The reactive aptitude of the cell lies in its irritability or sensibility. Similarly, the reactive aptitude of the nervous system or *conscious sensibility* can be considered the irritability of the whole system. *Unconscious sensibility* is the reaction of a part of this system, a secondary sensibility.[84]

The text goes on to explain that cellular or protoplasmic irritability has the paradoxical synonym "insensible sensibility." Certainly, it is important to have made "reactive aptitude" a common priority. It is no less important, however, to have recognized the differentiated categories of sensibility, qualified by their conscious or unconscious aspect. This will make it possible to retrace one's states of consciousness or unconsciousness back to modalities of physiological reaction.

The definition of "reflex" in Bernard's *Leçons sur la physiologie et la pathologie du système nerveux* (1857) is particularly interesting.[85] It is a definition by opposition: reflexive movement versus voluntary movement. At the same time, it is a definition by localization: the opposition is based on the distinctions between the nervous passageways involved and on the experimental proofs of this difference:

> Sensibility, which is transmitted from the posterior roots through the medulla, can take two forms: it can lack consciousness or have perception.

In the case of perceived sensibility, the impression is conducted to the brain, and, after the perception, transformed by the intelligence into a conscious reaction. Volition, in this case, is the last stage preceding movement.

In other cases, sensibility is not perceived; there is nonetheless a movement or reaction in which intelligence or volition has played no part. This is what Magendie called sensibility without consciousness and has since been termed reflex movement.[86]

Bernard demonstrates very clearly that adopting a new term corresponded to crossing a threshold in conceptualizing the tasks of physiology.

Is there any need to insist further? In the development of modern physiology, the notion of reaction fostered two important fields of research: that on the *reflex*, and that on various bodily *regulations*. This notion was useful in formulating theories and experiments, but it quickly proved too indeterminate and too general and was used simply as a sort of shorthand and in the popularization of science.

Reflex Actions

We have reached the point in physiology where the questions related to reaction lead (through the creation of an appropriate instrumental apparatus) to a search for the laws of reflex — that is, to one of the most fruitful scientific undertakings of the nineteenth century. From the start, the word "reaction" competed with other terms designating the object of the resolvent investigation into the phenomena of life, since the words "response," "contraction," and "motion" were also being used by researchers for similar purposes. "Reaction" is the most general term, and therefore the most easy to use when one remains at the level of generalities; but when the scientific message becomes specific, it must be refined (by complements) or replaced (by curves on a graph). The words of common language can serve as a temporary covering for observed or elicited phenomena, which they represent only imperfectly. By the end of the nineteenth century, the semantic function of the word "reaction" in this domain had run its course, despite the diverse notions with which it found itself associated. Its triumph rendered it obsolete. It was relieved of most of its tasks when its functions became the models for cybernetics and feedback, which it follows around like a ghost.

As for reflex, I shall restrict myself to generalities here, since I am outlining the history not of science itself but of a conceptual tool that was operative over a long period. I have not set out to review experimental ideas and practices. The main stages of this history cover more than a century, from the precursor Georg Prochaska (1749–1820), to Charles Bell (1774–1842) and François Magendie (1783–1855), up to Ivan Petrovitch Pavlov (1849–1936) and his "conditioned reflexes." A decisive development came from the genius of Johannes Müller (1801–1858), who freed himself from the Romantic philosophy of nature and inculcated a large group of students with his rigorous scientific standards. To go no further than mentioning a few names, we should recall Carl Ludwig (1816–1895), Hermann Helmholtz (1821–1894), Emil Du Bois-Reymond (1818–1896), Eduard Pflüger (1829–1910), Ewald Hering (1834–1918), and Ernst Brücke (1819–1892), who was Freud's teacher.[87] One must not forget the machines they invented and the instruments they used, which elicited and transcribed reactions and objectified them in graphs, the most precise images possible of the variations caused by the stimuli. We should also recall the extraordinarily varied panoply of mechanical, electrical, and thermal stimuli that the physiologists imagined; the thresholds of intensity, the frequency, and the summation of excitations; the "preparation" of animals, the use of pincers, scissors, electrodes;

the sectionings of afferent and/or efferent nerves at various levels
and sectionings of the medulla, the most important of which was
decerebration; the chemical interruptions or modifications intervening in the path of excitation; the means of recording and in-
scription, the most efficient of which was the kymograph, with its
rotating recording drum coated with lampblack, upon which the
traces of everything that palpitated or contracted were inscribed
(students practiced in laboratories on the heart and gastrocnemius
muscles of the frog); the measures of the amplitude and duration
of currents of action produced by successive generations of electrical recording devices; the study of tissue receptors, the anatomic verifications that mobilize microtomes, dyes, optical devices,
electron bundles, or wave sequences.[88] The investigation was pursued down to the tiniest structures: membranes, synapses, cellular
protoplasm, mitochondria, nuclei, chromosomes, genes, ferments.
Such were the illustrious avenues traveled by the investigation of
reaction — or of its absence, or of its alterations. The result of the
(quantifiable) Stimulus is translated into a (measurable) path, the
Response or Reaction. S determines R. The result, transcribed by
science, is sometimes called the S/R system, situated in the immense chain within which it is preceded, accompanied, and followed by other S/R systems. Relatively recently, the binary model
of stimulus/response was supplanted by a less conspicuous model
in "neuronal networks."[89]

The nineteenth century inaugurated the era in which reaction
became universally implied as the term lost any specific meaning
unless accompanied by a qualifier. From that point on, the qualifier added to "reaction" counted for more than the word itself,
which was then overlooked completely. Since chemistry and biology are the realms of reaction, it was better to omit the term
"reaction" — to syncopate it the way a syllable is syncopated or
contracted in the evolution of a word. It was necessary to choose

a *distinctive* part for the whole and to drop the unimportant part. Most often, the proper name used to specify the reaction displaces or rather erases the word "reaction," according to a linguistic law identical with that which, in the medical language of today, dispenses with explicit groups of words and abridges them with eponyms or acronyms. When a laboratory does "an agglutination" or "a Noguchi," when a patient's clinical chart mentions "a Pirquet" or a "Bence-Jones," the words "reaction" or "test" are dropped. In textbooks, they appear as chapter headings but not in the body of the text. It goes without saying that an inflammation is a reaction, but it is not necessary to repeat it every time. Whoever speaks of immune reaction is usually content with the words "immunity" or "resistance."[90] Allergy manages on its own, as does anaphylaxis: the crutch provided by the word "reaction" is optional. All the adaptations, bodily regulations, and operations of life undergo physicochemical reactions, yet the object of interest is not the common denominator "reaction." As if the scientific lexicon were a struggle for the survival of the fittest, the terms with the best-defined referents marginalize and tend to eliminate those encumbered by a polysemy that renders them obsolete. Terminological refinement follows accessible levels and parameters, all the way to the molecule: we have now reached a moment when reality is translated into images produced by highly complex instruments and filters into ordinary language only through neologisms, acronyms, abbreviations, and graphics. The rift widens between the designated phenomenon and the word in the so-called natural language that refers to it. The word becomes supercharged with mutable signifieds as its context ceaselessly modifies it. Standing alone, "reaction" is so equivocal and polysemous, and often so subordinate, that it is almost never included among the ideas and subjects listed in the indexes of "serious" books.

The development of reflex theory at the end of the nineteenth century included important anthropomorphic considerations. We might well speak of reductionism to characterize the doctrine that made the reflex the elementary unit from which all mental life was constructed. From this point of view, the prerogatives granted to the willing subject, the free consciousness, and the "I" all disappear. When it appeared among twentieth-century philosophers, this contestation acknowledged its origins in the works of Nietzsche and Freud, but without always being aware that these two writers were preceded by physicians and physiologists such as Thomas Laycock, William Carpenter, Henry Maudsley, Wilhelm Griesinger, Moritz Schiff, Alexandre Herzen, and Théodule Ribot. It is from their works that Nietzsche and Freud derived their arguments demystifying the spiritual powers upon which man prided himself. In addition to directly borrowing from these earlier writers, Nietzsche and Freud both subscribed to a specific "scientific" train of thought: the recognition of the human being's integral belonging to natural reality, but without continuing a "grammatical habit" (Nietzsche) in which the "I" considers itself responsible for its own thought.[91] In analyzing the historical context of this evolution of ideas, Marcel Gauchet writes: "The advent of the society of emancipated individuals translates at a profound level into the ruin of self-possession. The man released from subjection to the collective is a man who will discover himself to be internally subjugated."[92] Reflexive mechanisms, described as objective phenomena or as regulating forces governing the universe of things, were henceforth seen as the most adequate explanation and best approximation of psychic phenomena. Whether one takes up the mechanistic thesis that, in the seventeenth century, denied souls to animals or adopts the form of vitalism that, in the nineteenth century, acknowledged the existence of a "medullary soul," the result is the same:

the processes that can be observed in the spinal cord take place in the cerebral mass as well. Then action and reaction as manifested in the reflex arc become the fundamental material of the individual, whose every moment of existence is involved in integrating a variable sum of elementary processes, both sensory and motor. These processes unfold "in the third person," and this third person comes to supplant the first person "I." The concept of reaction proved to be the active operator of this removal. One might say that the concept of reaction became — paradoxically — the agent of a revolution that deprived the thinker of the possibility of declaring himself active.

A single example should suffice. In 1873, the physiologist Alexandre Herzen published *Physiologie de la volonté* (original text in Italian; French translation published in 1874). Its aim was to challenge the doctrines of free will scientifically. Herzen supported his claims with the works of his teacher Moritz Schiff (1823–1896), the physiologist Ivan Sechenov (1829–1905), and the psychiatrist Wilhelm Griesinger (1817–1868):

> Images, according to the famous Griesinger, become tendencies and volitions according to an internal necessity in which, among the most intimate operations of psychic life, we find the fundamental laws of the reflex arc.

Herzen continues:

> Voluntary movements are therefore *reactions* as necessary as simple reflex movements: only the latter are immediate *reactions* of direct peripheral impressions, while the former are mediate *reactions* of indirect central sensations or images and ideas among which those of movement itself must necessarily be found.[93]

146

In contesting the illusion of free will, Herzen calls upon Hobbes, Hume, d'Holbach, and even Luther. One must, he proclaims, set aside the notion of freedom and seek definitions more in keeping with the teachings of science. In speaking of individuality, Herzen asserts that it is "the *positive or real* concept that must replace that of freedom":

> The word "freedom," when applied to individual activity, means precisely the absence of external or internal, physical or moral obstacles that might prevent the individual from acting in full conformity with the tendencies inherent to his physical or moral constitution, that is, in conformity with the result of the conditions within which he has developed. In other words, the individual's freedom consists of the faculty *of being able to react in one's own way and without constraint*, according to the volitions or desires awakened in him by circumstances.[94]

Herzen defends himself against the accusation of disintegrating or destroying the individual and "the unity of the self." Anticipating his adversaries' arguments, he fine-tunes his thought: it is not difficult, he claims, to conceive of bodily individuality, even though the living organism is "a workshop of material and dynamic transformations, maintaining its physical and chemical constitution through a perpetual exchange of matter and force with the outside world." Can one not likewise conceive of the "inalterability of psychic individuality despite the continual outward radiation of various organic forces and the perpetual arrival of new external impulses and the transmutation of these impulses into organic energies reacting in turn upon the outside world?" While preserving the basic schema of stimulus and reaction, Herzen reassures his readers: he is not contesting the continuity of consciousness. "Millions" of medullar and cerebral "cells" occupy the intermediate space between the promptings of the outside world and the individual's reaction, creating an immense "labyrinth" in which impressions and images circulate:

> The labyrinth about which we are speaking is the special sphere of psychic life, and this sphere intervenes between the action of the outside world upon the individual and the individual's reaction upon the outside world.[95]

Among this "mobile multitude of representations," a "more constant, more persistent, more compact phalanx" may be created, "which does not allow itself to be easily repelled, approving or criticizing, welcoming or rejecting all newcomers: this is the *psychic self* in the larger sense of the term." But that is not all. Apparently concerned with giving a material base to the individual, Herzen adds a spatial and quasi-political image (evoking a government or central committee) with no relation to any anatomic localization:

> Now, at the heart of this phalanx, there is a most compact, impregnable, indelible nucleus, which, except under exceptional conditions, remains ever identical with itself and does not allow for the elimination of any of its components, except to replace them on the spot with something equivalent or identical. This nucleus is of internal origin: it is the *psychic self* in the restricted sense of the word, that is, that sentiment of persistent unity which, once formed and in its normal state, accompanies us almost unaltered over the course of our lives.[96]

This "psychic self" that resists decomposition is both dependent and permanent. The permanence this author acknowledges is not always found in psychological models based on the reflex arc, often by authors, such as Théodule Ribot, inspired by Herzen's own writings. In Ribot's *Diseases of Personality*, the self, when sensorially and physiologically conditioned, is but an ephemeral configuration varying according to the unpredictable fluctuations of coenesthetic sensitivity.

Herzen's attempt to reconcile determinism and individual initiative deserves our attention. It is as if, after having subjected the individual to the law of impersonal reactions and the indefinite series of phenomena produced by causality in the third person, Herzen recognizes the possibility that the individual might react in the first person. The condition he posits is that external constraints are lifted. "The freedom of such a self consists simply in following the laws of its own being."[97] This displacement of the sense of freedom — which is no longer a spiritual decision but the elimination of external constraint — is symptomatic, and it will undoubtedly be possible to find examples of this in his contemporaries, especially Nietzsche.[98] It is important to underline the ambiguous functions of the word "reaction." On the one hand, it is used in the service of a reductive analytic procedure that goes back to the elementary mechanical or quasi-mechanical process; it refers back to the simplest partial phenomenon; it calls for an "atomization" of biological fact. On the other hand, when reacting "individuality" is discussed, it does not refuse its services in the creation of a "holistic" vision of the relation between the organism as a whole — or the person — and the surrounding world. The notion of integration, first used in 1862 by Herbert Spencer (in his *First Principles*), is not yet mentioned explicitly by Herzen. It will be enriched in neurophysiology by the major contributions of John Hughlings Jackson (1835–1911) and Charles Scott Sherrington (1857–1952) and will make it possible to understand how partial reactions, spread out over different anatomic levels of the nervous system, can be ordered into a totality. The notion of integration thus goes hand in hand with that of the "dynamic" hierarchy of the nervous functions, between medullar automatisms and cerebral associations. This hierarchization was itself considered a product of the evolution of species. From a Darwinian perspective, the higher animals are those in which elementary reactions are controlled by a more complex reactive system farther up on the nerve stem. Intellectual activity — including awareness of reality — is thus defined as a reaction.

Such ideas were widely disseminated in the second half of the nineteenth century, spread through teaching and scientific reviews. We can hear an echo of them in one of Anton Chekhov's characters. In the magnificent story "Ward Number Six," Doctor Ragin, speaking with the patient Gromov, who suffers from a persecution mania, extols the virtues of stoic indifference and refuge in an impregnable interiority: "If you meditate more you will appreciate the insignificance of all those externals that so excite us. One must seek the meaning of life, for therein lies true happiness." The enraged patient answers:

> "Externals, internals ... This makes no sense to me, sorry. I know only one thing," he said, standing up and looking angrily at the doctor. "I know God made me of warm blood and nerves, that I do know, sir. Now, organic tissue with any spark of vitality must react to every stimulus. So react I do! To pain I respond with shouts and tears, meanness makes me indignant, revolting behavior sickens me. This is what life means, actually, or so I think. The lower the organism the less sensitive it is and the weaker its response to stimuli, whereas the higher it is the more receptively and forcefully does it react to reality. Why, it's so obvious! ... A Stoic once sold himself into slavery to ransom a neighbor. So even a Stoic reacted to a stimulus, you see, since so generous a deed as self-denial for one's neighbor's sake presupposes feelings of outraged sympathy.... Well, take

Christ. He reacted to the external world with tears, smiles, grief, wrath — with anguish, even."[99]

Truth, at the beginning of the twentieth century, speaks through the mouth of the paranoid Gromov: he believes himself the target of a police conspiracy, and he reduces the whole of moral life to physiological reaction.

CHAPTER FOUR

Reactive Pathologies

Science of Man

Faced with the duo the soul *and* the body, with its remarkable philosophical longevity, the question became whether the relationship was one of subordination (master and slave) or of an equitable partnership and conjugality (Montaigne). If there is action *and* reaction between the soul and the body, the "and" is situated at an eminently sensitive point: for many centuries, this was a locus of ontological disparity that both revealed and concealed this disparity. The conjunction "and" has disjunctive value, while also binding the terms and thereby coupling them. In a dualist regime, morality *and* physicality, "spiritual" life *and* "animal" life, occupy distinct levels.

The problem was taken over by philosophical anthropology, that is, by a "science of man" that acquired its particular status in the eighteenth century.[1] It sought to unite a physics and a psychology of the human species within a descriptive corpus. It wanted to gather together what people thought they knew about human physiology and what had been compiled on the intellectual faculties and the passions of the soul (memory, imagination, psychology of the human species within a descriptive corpus medicine and in the natural sciences, which had been enriched by travelers' and geographers' accounts, sustained this philosophical inquiry, which prided itself on its empiricism. Naturalists, physicians, and historians could all claim to contribute to it. As I have stressed, the project of an anthropology, in tandem with that of a psychology, took off at the moment when the various philosophical doctrines were emancipated from the theology-inspired metaphysical tradition, in which there had been no question of treating man as an object in the physical world and subjecting him to the laws of an experimental and mathematized natural science. "Between the epoch of recourse to God and the one in which people called for limitless personal freedom in the name of *dignitas hominis*, people looked toward Nature."[2]

I have already discussed one example from anthropology, Buffon's *Histoire naturelle de l'homme*, which took its place in a *Histoire naturelle* that encompassed all the kingdoms of nature. The initiative goes back to late-sixteenth-century authors: the public's expectation was a result of previous great discoveries.[3] Physicians saw themselves as *naturally* involved. *The Natural History of the Soul* (1745) and *Man, a Machine* (1748) by the physician Julien Offray de La Mettrie and *Idée de l'homme physique et moral* (1755) by the physician Louis de La Caze are typical productions of this new kind of work. Diderot dreamed of a medically inspired anthropology when he undertook his *Eléments de physiologie*, which remained unfinished. Thus, on the basis of a medical knowledge that was transforming itself and gaining authority, scholarly Europe sustained a debate, in many voices, concerning the "relations between the physical and the moral." Based on data from experiments that would make a tabula rasa of the "novelistic" propositions of Descartes, Hobbes, Malebranche, and Leibniz, anthropological reflection reconsidered the ties between the soul and the body. In this debate, writers constantly appealed to the results of "empirical" research, citing the introspective wisdom of the normal individual as well as the lessons gleaned from all the aberrations and alienations of the natural and mental order. In the preceding chapter, I traced the protohistory and genealogy of Western biology, based on the lexical usage of the action/reaction couple. Now, in the same manner, I shall follow the protohistory and genealogy of modern psychology and psychiatry to verify that at first the two histories are closely linked and that an appeal to the action/reaction verbal couple is as frequent in the mainly somatic as in the mainly psychological interpretations of mental disturbances. My commentary is based on a few pointed examples.

The Physical and the Moral

Pierre-Jean-Georges Cabanis was a doctor. His twelve memoirs in *On the Relations Between the Physical and Moral Aspects of Man* (1802) articulate a materialist anthropology. Thus, at the end of the eighteenth century, the path seemed open for a reduction of the moral to the physical in terms of a modernized atomism and mechanism that displaced Epicureanism. Was it not tempting to consider "morality" no longer as a different substance but as another order of reaction? To put it very schematically: Was it not tempting to replace the difficult union of the soul and the body with the easy transition from action to reaction? Morality certainly did not have priority in theory: it was a point of culmination. Cabanis focuses on "emotions" and "moral habits," and he devotes eight of his twelve memoirs to them.

His argument is unequivocal. If there is a circle of cause and effect, can we not deduce that it progresses in a common substance and a single world, in which the material cause might produce a direct effect and the effect might occur *naturally* from the cause? This is what Cabanis proposes in postulating the general principle of an elementary sensibility liable to transform itself into thought and will. Sensibility is a primary given from which everything is explained in terms of transformation and derivation. But how to explain sensibility itself? Cabanis does not seek its cause. In his refusal, he invokes a predecessor, Newton, who refused to posit an ultimate cause of attraction: "In a word, general facts *are* because they *are*, and one must no more, today, wish to explain *sensibility* in the animal physique and in rational philosophy than one must wish to explain attraction in mass physics."[4] Cabanis presents a monist thought, which finds in the conceptual couple action/reaction the means to produce all the derivative by-products of what he takes to be the primordial element; these by-products are called desire, attention, and reflection:

> One must therefore not be surprised that the operations which, together, bear the name of moral are related to those other operations that are more particularly designated by the term physical, nor that they act and react upon one another....
>
> The organs are capable of entering into action and of executing certain movements only insofar as they are endowed with life or feeling. It is the sensibility that animates them; it is by virtue of its laws that they receive impressions and that they are forced to move. The impressions received by their sentient extremities are transmitted to the center of reaction; and this partial or general center sends to the corresponding organ the impulses that together constitute the functions proper to this organ....
>
> Whether these impressions have been received by the external or internal sentient extremities, or whether their cause has acted within the cerebral mass, they will always end in a center of reaction that reflects them in tendencies, movements, and functions in regard to the parts to which each of these operations is assigned. This action and this reaction can often take place without the individual having any consciousness of it.[5]

In the triple contingencies he imagines, Cabanis accounts for the categories of perception customarily distinguished by medieval Aristotelianism and upheld by Descartes in the treatise *The Passions of the Soul.* These three orders of sensibility are the external sense (perception of objects delivered by the five senses), the corporeal sense (perception of the organs of the body), and the internal sense (perception and comparison of mental images). In Cabanis, one encounters a speculative physiology that resolves its problems by referring to various "centers of reaction" (peripheral ganglia, the spinal cord, and the brain). Based on a still conjectural knowledge of the nerve networks, Cabanis's system is quick to posit the differential relationship between "periphery" and "center."[6] This was a spatial arrangement perfectly open to the trajectory of action and reaction, as well as a simple model that lent itself easily to the image of the "reflection" of the flow of sensation in short (local or ganglionated) circuits or in long (cerebral) circuits. The system is rudimentary, but it includes a minimum of elements necessary to create subsystems. Without being based on a clear idea of what was later called the reflex, it paves the way for a reflexological interpretation of the psychic activities of the living. What, in particular, is instinct for Cabanis? It is a deferred reflex constituted on the basis of "internal impressions" — described as "confused and vague" — which the fetus receives in the uterus.[7]

Once Cabanis has established that sensations can be reflected, these elementary "reflections" become the material with which he constructs his representation of psychic life. Hence the "cerebral center of reaction" is defined as the site where sensation becomes modified into "ideas," "volitions," and "attention"; the same energy spreads in two directions, centripetally and centrifugally. By virtue of a common prefix, the verb "to reflect" seems to lend itself spontaneously to the dynamic image of reaction. Quite often Cabanis uses the prefix *re-* to express a similar intuition:

The operations of the sensibility may thus be considered as occurring in two stages. First, the nerve extremities receive and transmit the first warning to the entire sensitive organ or only ... to one of its isolated systems. Next the sensitive organ reacts to these to put them in a state to receive the entire impression. Thus the sensibility that at first seems to have fled from the periphery to the center, in the second stage returns from the center to the periphery. In a word, the nerves exert on themselves a veritable reaction for feeling, as they exert another on the muscular parts for movement. Daily observation shows that this obviously occurs this way, in relation to external impressions; it can prove that it does not happen differently in relation to those of the internal organs.... This reaction of the sensitive organ on itself to produce feelings and on the other parts to produce movements happens in all the operations of life. It follows simple impressions, on the one hand to complete them, and on the other to bring in all the characteristics that are related to them.[8]

The anatomy of the nervous system was still imprecise. The schema of the trajectory of excitation that later led to the definition of reflex channels is rather vague here. Cabanis's physiology is founded on macroscopic anatomy, not on laboratory work and experimentation.[9] Yet some of his intuitions had a long life. Continuing his argument, he said that "sensibility behaves like a fluid of a determined total quantity, which, each time it flows more abundantly into one of its canals, decreases proportionally in the others."[10] The image of a shock (of an "impression"), by which a body arouses a reaction in another body, does not preclude the metaphor of fluid and its derivatives. Elsewhere I have pointed out that Freud readily used the same images in describing emotional energy, or the libido.[11] Of course, between Cabanis and Freud lies a century in which research into nerve *impulse* provided experimental content for what, in 1800, was merely conjecture.

In *The Interpretation of Dreams*, Freud mentions Cabanis in passing among writers who linked dreams and mental illness; it is possible that Freud knew of Cabanis's statement that "sleep is not a passive function, and that to produce it the cerebral organ enters into real activity."[12] The reader is free to compare the following passage, in which Cabanis speaks of the nightmare accompanied by "nocturnal emissions," with Diderot in *D'Alembert's Dream* or with Freud — or with both:

> Men of letters, thinkers, artists, in a word all the men whose nerves and brains receive many impressions or combine many ideas, are very much subject to nocturnal emissions that are very disturbing to them. This accident is almost always related to dreams, and these dreams sometimes take on the nature of nightmares before producing their final effect. I have treated many patients of this type, for it is not rare for their state to become a true illness. I have met two in whom the event was preceded by a long and detailed dream: they saw a woman, they heard her approaching their bed, they felt her lean with all her body's weight on their chest; and it was after having endured the anguish of a real nightmare for several minutes that, the genital organs having become excited by the presence of this imaginary object, the catastrophe of the dream ordinarily led to the end of sleep.

These are "movements that begin in one part and end in another, or which pass from the first to the second, without one finding a cause in the known organic sympathies. Such transitions obviously depend on the determinations conceived in the very depths of the nervous system."[13] Like Bordeu (or Diderot) in *D'Alembert's Dream*, Cabanis asserts a mechanism of reaction, but the "transitions" he refers to are already "displacements":

The conclusion that may be drawn from this is undoubtedly remarkable; but it results no less clearly, in fact, from all the activities of the memory or the imagination, whose original impressions belong to one organ, whereas the determinations appear to react on it in passing, in order to direct themselves entirely toward another organ.... I shall only observe that if the power of the imagination is more extensive; if its reaction upon certain organs, for example, on those of generation, is more complete during sleep than during the waking state, the reason for this is very simple, and can be found without difficulty. During the waking state, some external impressions are in fact always arriving at the brain, and they modify to a greater or lesser extent its operations and to a certain extent rectify the errors of the imagination. In sleep, however, everything happens in the interior; the internal impressions consequently become livelier or more dominant. Illusions are complete, and the determinations related to them encounter no obstacle from opposite impressions received by the senses.[14]

The passages devoted to sympathy speak of imitation and its transformative power. Cabanis also discusses the means by which the moral influences the physical, as well as the educational and therapeutic effects that can result from these means.

Based on a critique of the physiological system propounded by Cabanis, a restoration of metaphysical dualism seemed conceivable.[15] Seeking to found his philosophical reflection on a "science of man," Maine de Biran initially considered the theses of the ideologues (Cabanis, Destutt de Tracy), as well as those of Bichat, valid. He brought to them an important corrective: the human condition is essentially active.[16] It is impossible to reconstruct it on the basis of sensation, which is passive. The primary fact is motor initiative and awareness. This involves the sense of effort, which is in turn subdued by its contact with the nonself. At the beginning of his book, Bichat discussed the "functions *resisting death*." In speaking of resistance, Maine de Biran claims:

> We cannot know ourselves as individual beings without feeling ourselves to be causes relative to certain effects or movements produced in the organic body. The cause or force actually applied to moving bodies is an active force called will: the self completely identifies with this active force. But the existence of the force is only relevant to the self inasmuch as it exerts itself, and it only exerts itself inasmuch as it can be applied to a resistant or inert point. Force is therefore only determined or actualized in relation to its point of application, just as the latter is only determined as resistant or inert in relation to the actual force that moves it or tends to set it in motion. This tendency is what we call *effort* or *willed action* or *volition*, and I maintain that this effort is the true primary fact of the inner sense.[17]

Motor initiative needs muscular resistance in order to perceive itself:

> The soul begins to move by acting spontaneously on the organic center to which it is united or that serves as its immediate point of application. It transmits action to the motor nerves, which immediately transmit the contractile influence to the muscles.... Once the contraction takes place in the muscle under the immediate influence of the motor nerves and the mediate influence of the soul, the muscular organ reacts by contracting; the product of this reaction is transmitted to the soul, according to an inverse progression from that of the initial action, namely: from the contracted muscle to the nerves, the nerves to the organic center, and the organic center to the soul, which perceives or feels the contraction and the movement as the result of the preceding action or as the *effect* of which it is the *cause*.[18]

This perception of muscular effort is known today as kinesthesia. Maine de Biran considers it "the immediate sensation of existence itself" and makes it a source attesting to a "hyper-organic force," which ensures the superiority of the human soul in relation to matter and all simple animal life. In his concern to base a spirit/matter dualism on something other than the Cartesian distinction of substances, Maine de Biran makes a "science of man" his founding principle, or at least the obligatory passageway of philosophical knowledge. For him, certainty originates in "I try" rather than "I think," and "moral" consciousness originates in the resistance to "the physical." The soul discovers itself and grasps itself by perceiving the obstacle to its motor initiative. Later, in speaking of this psychology that attempted to go beyond the sensory-motor schema constantly referred to by Cabanis, some would argue that it represented "a *reaction* against the philosophy of sensation."[19] It is odd to find a word from sensualist physiology used to designate a reply to sensualism.

Maine de Biran listened to physicians, and physicians closely followed his thought. In volume 47 of *Le Dictionnaire des sciences médicales* (1819–1820), known by the name of its editor, Panckoucke, the entry on reaction is signed by the physician Jean-François Delpit, a friend of Maine de Biran's; it is a remarkable summary of this subject.[20]

Delpit identifies two types of reaction: physical and moral. As for physical reaction, he readily adopts the principle postulated by Bichat: defensive energy "acts against all destructive causes, draws its means from the more or less constituted elements of the organization, and is essentially bound to the vital properties that, presiding over all functions, direct the preservative acts of the individual or the species." But is "physical reaction" always protective? If it consists in an "uninterrupted circle of reciprocal influences," could it not become excessive and harmful? Would not the mechanism that defends life also produce disease? One cannot, Delpit warns, attribute an infallibly favorable effect to it:

> This physical reaction cannot always be determined by preservative concerns or always restrict itself to reasonable limits. Hence the reaction of the organs of generation, if too strongly exerted in response to stimulating substances, can reverberate in the cerebral organ and determine all the phenomena of aphrodisiac neuroses. The reaction of the blood system against obstacles presented to the circulation, by defects of structure or momentary constraints of the organs, can cause ruptures in the vessels or equally harmful effusions of blood. The physical reaction of the organs therefore has its aberrations and excesses; to be useful it must remain under the influence of a salutary medication, with which it can create a barrier against harmful deviations.

As the physician Isidore Bricheteau, who also wrote encyclopedia entries, said a few years later, there is such a thing as a "pathological reaction."[21] The danger of letting nature take its course in every case justified medical intervention. One can confine oneself to "expectant medicine," which relies on spontaneous forces to effect a cure. Hence this theory, which at first applies to the single individual, also gives the physician a role. Knowing how to discriminate between a good and a bad reaction, the physician becomes the arbiter of "salutary medication" (Delpit) or the creator of a favorable reaction (Bricheteau). Through appropriate medications, he can produce beneficial "counterreactions."[22] This conception systematized a number of very approximate elements. It postulated physical relationships whose *paths* remained conjectural. It provided an answer to everything, in complete ignorance of major metabolic processes, minute innervations, stimuli, and specific mediators and responses. Yet this language speaks to us. To accept it, we need only remind ourselves that it is discussing not organs but our representations of organs. It speaks — figuratively — of the relations between organs in the way the language of psychoanalysis, to which we are now accustomed, speaks of the sites and energies of the psychic apparatus.

Once the distinction between the somatic and the psychic was accepted in principle, the desire to surmount this division created reciprocal relationships between terms belonging to one or the other register. Thus the ground was broken for a theory with two approaches, psychosomatic and somatopsychic, in which dispensing medication was not the only possible recourse. The beginning of the nineteenth century witnessed a flowering of praise for moral reaction, as well as a discourse that placed the physician at the controls of the operation.

On this point, Delpit and Bricheteau completely agree. First of all, they both are faithful to the tradition that attributes humoral and behavioral troubles to "alterations" in the organs. Galen's lesson had not been forgotten, in particular the famous treatise that declares, "The ways of the soul follow the temperaments of the body." Thus Delpit states:

> The exercise of physical reaction is not limited to the systems or the organs which make up our organism, for in some cases it bears upon our moral constitution: any alteration in an organ thus reacts vehemently upon the faculties of the mind or the affections of the soul. Hence, the stomach excited by wine or spirits reacts upon the mind, which becomes more lively, sharp, and prone to boisterous outbursts. Congestion of the liver or spleen brings sadness, discouragement, melancholy, and so on.[23]

But these authors willingly imagine the opposite effect, *ad majorem gloriam medici*. The physician who can modify the dispositions of the soul can alleviate the illnesses of the body. The *affections of the soul* once figured among the six "things" enumerated by the hygiene inspired by Galen. These "things," oddly called "nonnatural," consisted of those acts of bodily existence that individuals (especially if they were free) had the power to modify and regulate through careful effort. The passions were thus listed alongside air, food, repletion and evacuation, exercise and rest, waking and sleeping. The old "medicine of the passions" still had great importance in the Romantic era. And it maintained the spectacles, voyages, and dramatic stagings prescribed since Antiquity for drawing melancholics from their torpors. Bricheteau lists many examples in which the physician plays a major role:

> Like the organs, man's physical and moral aspects, considered abstractly, react upon each other: a man who is falling ill will have difficulty healing if he is under the sway of sad thoughts and biting sorrows, just as it is difficult for a suffering man to exercise his faculties successfully. In the first case, make the moral affliction cease and you will react upon the illness; in the second case, make the suffering cease and you will reestablish the free exercise of intellectual faculties; which means that physical forces can be depressed and relieved suddenly through the influence of a great and profound impression. Both joy and terror can cause death, just as great excitation of another kind seems to renew the thread of life or restore the exercise of functions that had seemed forever abolished. A mountain dweller far from his native land falls into nostalgia, loses all his strength, and can barely take a few steps in the hospital that seems destined to serve as his tomb; kindle the hope of seeing his mountains again, and everything changes for this individual; he recovers his strength, his appetite, and the use of his legs. Do you want to cause a reaction in the moral condition of an unhappy soul who is quietly undermined by a deep grief caused by a reversal of fortune? Instead of giving

him drugs, imitate, if you can, the great practitioner from the last century who, after having unsuccessfully treated a merchant having trouble in business, cured him almost instantaneously by writing him a prescription for thirty thousand francs to collect from his notary.

What an odd variety of things capable of eliciting a moral reaction! The image of a shock reverberating in the organs often recurs. In many nineteenth-century writings, the medical act and the patient's response are equally sudden. For the physician, it was enough to make a few gestures or utter a few words using the performative functions of language; the response, symmetrically, fulfills his expectations. Of course, the "patient" remains passive; a surprise has been arranged for him, as for a child to whom a present is given. In this case, medicine dreams of possessing an instantaneous power over souls and often admits that it is competing with the miracles once attributed to supernatural causes. However, it claims to rely on nothing other than nature and the judicious calculation of what will trigger a favorable response. For a long time, and especially in the treatment of mental illness, people believed that an unexpected word, or an overwhelming emotion, could provide a jolt to the deranged mind that would bring it back to reason. Why couldn't emotion produce sudden cures, just as it produced sudden deaths? It was hoped that through such simulacra and promises the patient would be duped by facile theatrical stunts. The immediate effect attributed to emotional reaction makes it possible to explain the success of magnetic treatments, the laying on of hands, homeopathy, and such. The public, furthermore, scarcely distinguished between the physicians of magnetism and those who, like Delpit, confined themselves to words alone.

Yet in other circumstances, and with Delpit in particular,

moral treatment was a long-term undertaking; it involved listening to the patient, ongoing conversations, an insinuating pedagogy, and all the right gestures. The method of calling upon the
patient's own resources was not yet known as psychotherapy, but
it already bore all the characteristics. One has a clear sense in the
lines that follow (from Delpit's entry on reaction in *Dictionnaire
des sciences médicales*) that the physician is assuming the delicate
task of directing conscience:

> All ailments do not derive from an alteration in the organs or from a
> disorder in their functions; neither do all ailments yield to purga-
> tives, narcotics, tonics, or bloodletting. A physician confronted with
> the sorry ravages of boredom, ambition, grief, or love needs a differ-
> ent sort of medicine from the one consisting of potions and pills.
> When courage is weakened by a reversal of fortune, the torment of
> the passions, a great and profound pain, the fear of a pressing danger,
> can the artful man entrust himself to the resources of material ther-
> apy alone? Must he not raise himself to the hidden wellsprings that
> motivate our passions and that can develop spiritual courage, the
> source of so many heroic acts and marvelous cures? Should he not, in
> certain cases, give to the impressions of the soul a direction that
> would successfully react upon their physical impressions and modify
> them completely?
>
> ... Joy, hope, all sweet and pleasant sentiments fortify the soul
> and provide it with the means of successfully reacting upon the mus-
> cular forces and upon the organs that carry out the vital functions.
> Seneca said that everything that exalts the soul fortifies the body; but
> what sentiment can exalt the soul of someone overwhelmed with
> pain, consumed by evil, whose constitution is threatened with com-
> plete dissolution? Where will he find the courage necessary to react
> upon the material causes of destruction and arrest or suspend their
> course? Ah! if there still exists a means to restore the hope that each

instant seems to destroy, it is found only in the confidence inspired by the physician. How powerful is this tool when wielded by a deft hand! How many tempests raised by moral emotions have been calmed by the physician's voice, whose duty here is linked with that of the most sensitive friendship. The unfortunate patient needs to unburden his soul: who more than the physician is used to lending an attentive ear to a long account of suffering? The patient believes in him, and this confidence is already a healing balm, a sweet stimulant to the whole constitution. In turn, the physician should do everything in his power to inspire or fortify this constitution, since it can so felicitously enhance the workings of medication and so efficaciously stimulate the reaction of the moral on the physical. A calm and serene air, affectionate care, easily understood explanations, unexaggerated promises, a wide range of insight brought to bear on the consultations, conversations in which science has brushed aside everything that is obscure or severe and whose language borrows the expressions of concern and of the heart, in short, everything in the physician's manners, speech, and actions must combine to strengthen this confidence, in which there lies a powerful means to stimulate the constitution and prepare favorable solutions of the illness.

A voice to calm the storms! Just like the operatic gods. Convinced that the relationship between the physician and the patient is by nature emotional, Delpit, in the language of his times, adds a remark that easily translates into the language of ours:

> More than anything else, men need to be loved, and this sentiment is all the more paternal and sweet when offered by those who are already charged with the care of watching over their waking hours.[24]

This time the moral reaction is not thaumaturgic: it is conceived as the long-term result of a relationship based on confidence, confession, and positive "transference." Here I intentionally use a contemporary word that, despite its technical aspect, is not at all inappropriate in defining Delpit's recommendations. No doubt, it is a question here of a method that today would be denounced as encouragement, the consolation that takes the patient's complaint at face value without seeking hidden sources. The role proposed for the physician is that of a benevolent father, and the patients are invited to indulge in filial outpourings of the heart. In return, they gradually recover the will to live. Delpit inscribes moral treatment within the parameters of friendship, without suspecting the ambiguous (we would say Oedipal) character of the relationship with the father.

Hippolyte Bernheim

In truth, given their writings, there is not so great a distance between Delpit and Hippolyte Bernheim (1840–1919), the master of the Nancy school. Sigmund Freud spent a few weeks with Bernheim in 1889 and translated two of his works in 1888 and 1892.[25]

In the entry on reaction that Bernheim wrote for *Dictionnaire encyclopédique des sciences médicales*, he recognized that "the word 'reaction' has assumed ... such a broad meaning that it can no longer be defined and no longer has any precise meaning."[26] With a prudence that bears witness to the advent of positive knowledge, the entry notes the omnipresence of reaction. We are far from possessing the knowledge that will allow us to exercise the art of healing conscientiously:

> By this word we designate any act following from any kind of influence affecting a part of the living being, whether this act is useful, harmful, or neutral to this being. Reaction conceived in these terms includes all the phenomena of life.... The history of reactions is that of pathology in its entirety.... To provoke or favor useful reactions,

to predict or prevent dangerous ones, such is the physician's role.... The art of healing is included within the science of reactions. It is an especially difficult art, for it presupposes that one knows, on the one hand, the pathology of each illness and the role that each symptom plays in its morbid evolution and, on the other, the intimate action of each therapeutic agent on the parts and the functions of the organism.

This expanded definition of reaction deprives it of the defensive privilege that Bichat and the physicians of the Montpellier school had given to it. Bernheim's entry on reaction rings like a farewell to "vital reaction," to the "vital force," to "mediating nature." In recalling these formulas, he wants to see them at best as "an idealized and abstract representation of a fact of observation.... Those who would like seriously to admit the existence of a vital principle that oversees the organism like a vigilant sentinel blocking all that is harmful, those who actually assert that all reaction is a curative effect of this vital principle, adhere to an outdated doctrine going back to the infancy of our science and at odds with the progress made by modern anatomy, physiology, and biology." There are certainly "reactions appropriate to a defensive goal," and there are certainly "adapted reflexive movements." But "is it necessary to refer to a special principle in charge of our defense"? Basically, there are too many reactions, and in too many different senses, for a single term to be used without causing confusion.

However, one meaning does justify maintaining this word in the vocabulary of medicine. Bernheim retains the principle of the "moral reaction," in which he sees the "phenomena of cerebral activity, causes or effects of the phenomena taking place in the other organs." In terms that recall those of his predecessors, he insists on the role played by the physician's person and voice. At first glance, it is the same argument. Yet a new idea is introduced:

the notion of *functional* disturbance, as opposed to *organic* lesion. The functional aspect of so many of the symptoms presented to the internist prompts him to consider psychological treatment:

> Often the moral aspect, that is, the activity of psychic functions, brings about salutary reactions. To console someone who is ill, to support his flagging spirit, free his soul from the terrifying anxieties that beset him, is often to produce a healthy reaction in the patient. Upon hearing the soft and persuasive voice of the physician, the patient, restored as if by a salutary balm, feels his confidence return and his illness dissipate despite all moral influences. Yet the very numerous *functional* disturbances — precordial anxiety, nervous palpitations, and panting — can be ameliorated by a new modality imprinted on the nerve centers. Hence we find the explanation, or rather the conception, of the immense influence a sensitive and tactful physician can exercise over a patient using this moral medicine, a true neurasthenic reaction, which is not the least powerful among therapeutic agents.[27]

The opposition between functional disturbance and organic illness survives today: the category of the functional opens and delineates the field in which psychological intervention ("moral medicine" or consoling words) is both efficacious and legitimate.[28] This intervention acts through "commotion" (joy, fright, and so on) or "diversion." One might expect to hear Bernheim discuss the power of suggestion, whose doctrine and implementation would make him famous, but he does not do so here. At the time he wrote the entry on reaction (prior to 1875), he undoubtedly had not yet met Ambroise-Auguste Liébeault, the Nancy practitioner who would introduce him to hypnosis and suggestion. In the final pages of his book *De la suggestion et de ses applications à la thérapeutique* (1886), Bernheim acknowledged that he had been unaware of this type of treatment when writing his 1875 entry on reaction. But he does cite the paragraph transcribed above (which can be read in Freud's German).[29] Of course, once he adopted the word "suggestion," Bernheim focused all his attention on it. The notion of moral reaction, which was more vague, faded away, reappearing only rarely.

Thus, as soon as the young Bernheim wrote his entry on reaction, hysteria took center stage in his work, although he was not a trained psychiatrist:

> The physician threatens a convulsive hysteric with douching and spraying or actual cautery, and in some cases he will succeed in preventing further attacks through this intimidation. He stops the attacks of hysterical convulsions and demonomania through the suppression of the moral causes that produced them, by communicating other emotions to a brain inflamed with unhealthy passions. Nervous complaints in which the brain seems to play no part can "suddenly heal" under the influence of a strong emotion, even though they had resisted all therapeutic agents.... The hysterical contraction of limbs, after having resisted all medication for months and years, and even though one might have thought the marrow had become sclerotic, can sometimes "suddenly heal" under the influence of an event that makes a strong impression on the imagination.

Threats can have a therapeutic effect: in this instance, Bernheim is not speaking any differently from whole libraries of medical treatises. Threats were still one of the favorite resources of the psychiatrist François Leuret.[30] In the generations that preceded Bernheim, it was the penultimate measure by which one tried to avoid the physically "extreme measures": douching and spraying, gyrations, or (as here) cauterizations.

A fantasy of medical omnipotence, upheld by a myth of heroic liberation, constantly resorted to these extreme constraints. "Authoritarian personalities" had never been so assured of their success, whether legitimate or illegitimate, as when they were promising liberation. All the "energetic" measures — and some quite brutal ones — were justified for provoking "a salutary reaction." Countless documents could be cited here. In examining them, one finds a few constant characteristics in the therapeutic methods. Most of the procedures consist in persuading the patient and sometimes in giving him a surprise, such as very intense joy or fright. According to a model inspired by the physics of the impact of bodies, psychological reaction was conceived as a precise event that, by reversing the course of an illness, suddenly gave the upper hand to psychic or vital forces combating the illness: it is a dramatic turn of events, a theatrical effect, a miracle arising from nothing other than nature itself, but a nature masterfully directed. False ideas, illusions, and somatic complaints are suddenly dispelled: the patient speaks again only to declare himself cured, brought back to himself, delivered. The words exchanged between patient and doctor are few. Usually a single gesture or short sentence is enough, and there is a sudden turnaround. Rarely is there any question of relapse; but in that case one would intervene as needed.

Suggestive therapy, tempered by caution about overly imperative injunctions, was the more gentle variation. The attempt at instantaneous healing through words was the secular equivalent of exorcism, whose heir it openly claimed to be. It was a utopian image of medical intervention, at that point where the person of the physician, in and of itself, counted for more than medication. (The placebo is its latest avatar.)

Bernheim calls on Thomas Laycock and Jean-Martin Charcot as witnesses to the effects of reaction.[31] He cites them not only to

bless the possibility of instantaneous healings with their unques-
tionable authority but also to join them, along with the positivist
Emile Littré, in the struggle against "the therapeutic supernatural," that is, magical or superstitious methods. The concept of
reaction — a natural nervous phenomenon — provides a sufficient
explanation.

Breuer and Freud: Trauma, Abreaction, Catharsis

In Bernheim's later works, the notion of reaction is generally no
longer applied to the mechanisms of healing. It survives almost
exclusively in reference to the genesis of hysteria. Contrary to
what Charcot and several of his collaborators and students had
maintained, hysteria, according to Bernheim, has no organic substratum and has nothing to do with an attack of the uterus or the
ovaries; nor is it an ailment of the brain; it is not confirmed by
any bodily indications. In the preface to the work he published in
1913, Bernheim declared that "hysteria is not an illness but a reactive emotive psycho-nervous syndrome." This definition is ceaselessly repeated: "The hysteric is a subject who exaggcrates certain
psychodynamic reactions and translates them into crises." No
doubt one had to have a "hysterical constitution" to have a hysterical crisis. "Each organism reacts with its diathesis."[32] The crisis
represents a dynamic functional element, at times superimposed
on a totally distinct organic state. Treatment by suggestion makes
it possible to separate "the dynamic from the organic."

Bernheim knew Josef Breuer and Sigmund Freud's *Studies on
Hysteria* (1895), and what drew his attention in this work was that
the authors attribute the ailment to "insufficiency of reaction."[33]
In 1913, Bernheim's definition of psychoanalysis refers to *Studies
on Hysteria* alone. Psychoanalysis "is curative because it allows the
patient, through a verbal reaction, to disengage the emotionality
of the hysterogenic shock, which was not originally disengaged by

a sufficient reaction; it also makes it possible to correct, through other associations, the hysterogenic mental representation, by provoking it in a state of normal consciousness, in which these other associations can be produced." Nonetheless, Bernheim expresses disagreement. He is willing to concede that the emotive memory "creates hysterogenic suggestibility," but he does not agree "that these memories persist because the original reaction was insufficient."[34] Reaction, for Bernheim, is illness itself: more reaction means more hysteria. The principal misunderstanding stems from Bernheim's not taking into account the mental topography later adopted by Freud. Bernheim was attentive to amnesia and to the different degrees of sleep, but one searches his writings in vain for a conceptualization of the unconscious that recognizes it as part of the territory of psychic life. Certainly, he admits the existence of events that escape consciousness. He speaks, for example, of a "reflexive ideomotor excitability" stimulated in the hypnotic state, resulting in an "unconscious transformation of the idea into movement, of which the will is unaware."[35] But the passage into consciousness never seems to have been a problem for Bernheim. His therapeutic goal, using hypnosis and suggestion, is summarized in terms borrowed from the physiologist Edouard Brown-Séquard: the idea is to exert an *inhibition* on the excessive reaction of hysteria and to inspire a benevolent *dynamogeny* in order to reestablish the nervous forces. Suggestion, the voluntary effort of the therapist, aims to reawaken the will and self-mastery. As opposed to Breuer and Freud, Bernheim proposes a method involving the calm clarification of memory and a controlled inhibition of emotion in a confidential relationship in which the physician firmly exercises an active and benevolent pedagogy. The dynamic schemata are extremely simple compared with those that Freud would propose. One thinks of Delpit when reading the following lines from Bernheim:

Slow, measured, rational, explanatory speech is a diversion, a safety valve that disciplines emotion, preventing it from escaping in a violent torrent, but disengaging it progressively, in small doses; it obliges the subject to inhibit it to some extent, out of the necessity of translating these memories into words rather than into emotions. Great sorrows and great passions are relieved when confessed to a physician, a confessor, a friend.[36]

At the end of the preface to his 1888 translation of Bernheim's *De la suggestion et de ses applications à la thérapeutique*, Freud still uses the language of neurology, even while arguing for an unconscious buried in the nervous system. Let me cite a few examples from this little-known text. Freud proposes not a form of therapy different from Bernheim's but rather another interpretation of the phenomena. For him, it is above all a matter of recognizing the role of "indirect suggestions" (or "autosuggestions") and of the unconscious:

> Indirect suggestions, in which a series of intermediate links arising from the subject's own activity are inserted between the external stimulus and the result, are none the less psychical processes; but they are no longer exposed to the full light of consciousness which falls upon direct suggestions. For we are far more accustomed to bring our attention to bear upon external perceptions than upon internal processes. Indirect suggestions or autosuggestions can accordingly be described as physiological or as psychical phenomena, and the term "suggestion" has the same meaning as the reciprocal arousing of psychical states according to the laws of association.... There is no justification for making such a contrast as is here made between the cerebral cortex and the rest of the nervous system: it is improbable that so profound a functional change in the cerebral cortex would occur unaccompanied by significant changes in the

176

excitability of the other parts of the brain. We possess no criterion which enables us to distinguish exactly between a psychical process and a physiological one, between an act occurring in the cerebral cortex and one occurring in the sub-cortical substance; for "consciousness," whatever that may be, is not attached to every activity of the cerebral cortex, nor is it always attached in an equal degree to any particular one of its activities; it is not a thing which is bound up with any locality in the nervous system.[37]

The criticism is directed against the myth of cerebral localizations. Freud followed up this critique rigorously, notably in his 1891 book on aphasia and in the article written in French for *Revue de neurologie* on motor and hysterical paralyses (1893).[38] In the preface to his translation of Bernheim, Freud is still struggling with the dichotomy between the moral and the physical, which had become that between psychology and physiology.[39] After having pushed physiological hypotheses quite far in "Project for a Scientific Psychology," sent to his friend Wilhelm Fliess in 1895, Freud put all his thought into elaborating a psychology (and first of all a psychology "for the neurologist") that would consider the *satisfactions* pursued, missed, buried, deferred, and sidetracked by neurosis and not the *innervations* involved. The correspondence between Freud and Fliess shows clearly that the two friends immediately divided up the labor, with Fliess settling into the realm of scientific biology and the rhythms of life and Freud setting himself up, not without torment, in the territory of empirical psychology, where his only predecessors were poets and connoisseurs of the human heart (*Menschenkenner*). A physicochemical process has no sentiment and is not an emotion, and hence Freud did not concern himself with it. By the time of *The Interpretation of Dreams*, "nervous associations" — which the preface to Bernheim's book and "Project for a Scientific Psychology" already conjectured — had made way for associations of a different sort, in conformity with a purely psychological "topography" and "economy." The emotions are displaced and transformed outside of any anatomic reference but — and this is obviously a point that will lead to controversy — under cover of a claim to scientific legitimacy equal to that of physiology. Freud certainly never challenged the principle of a physiological approach, except to postpone it to a more distant future in which biochemistry will have made sufficient progress. Later, in the second topography — in which Freud formulated his metapsychology — we see a return to biology, but in the style of a Romantic philosophy of nature, of which Fliess had given both a typical and a dismaying example. Physiology, abandoned on this side of psychology, reappeared beyond it, in the mythic figures of Eros and Thanatos.

In his *Autobiographical Study*, Freud attributes a twofold terminological innovation to Breuer. This innovation, he says, was the governing principle behind *Studies on Hysteria*:

> Breuer spoke of our method as *cathartic*; its therapeutic aim was explained as being to provide that the quota of affect used for maintaining the symptom, which had got on to the wrong lines and had, as it were, become strangulated there, should be directed on to the normal path along which it could obtain discharge (or *abreaction*).[40]

Two words, "catharsis" and "abreaction," thus make up the lexical index used by Breuer and Freud to define a therapeutic procedure and to indicate its originality. The following remarks are devoted to the writings that constitute the very significant point of departure for Freud's psychoanalytic works. This point of departure was decisive with regard to the lexical questions that concern us here.

"Catharsis" was not a new word. But this was the first time it had been used in psychology. It was vouchsafed by its Greek origin, and yet it was innovative. Its effect was reinforced by its being accompanied by the neologism "abreaction."

The neologistic character of "abreaction" comes from its supplemental prefix. The word *reactio* already had a prefix (*re-*), indicating return, response, secondariness. In adding the Latin-Germanic *ab-*, Breuer and Freud doubled the prefix and reactivated, for a very well defined use, a term that had become exhausted through too many different meanings. "Reaction" needed to be specified by a determining adjunct term or by forming a compound in German. German, of course, has great possibilities for creating prefixes. "Abreaction" is a good example. In his later terminology, Freud could only follow the usage of his language, which led to compound words formed through accretion (for example, *Unlustreaktion*, a reaction of displeasure), whereas French or English translates Freudian compound words into groups of words that remain separate or sometimes exploits the resources of Greek terminology."[41]

The lexical innovations of Breuer and Freud's book were effective, for they gave a verbal figure to their theory. This would become Freud's talent in the rest of his works, as he constantly linked his thought to unforgettable words. "Catharsis" and "abreaction" had the power to materialize emotion, to embody it, without going into the details of the old nomenclature that tried to specify various emotions. These two words suggest all the qualitative potentialities of emotion, making it almost quantifiable, while still escaping any objective measure. Implicated in these two terms are both the individual (in whom the *emotion* is contained) and movement (which *mobilizes* the contents).

In *The Birth of Tragedy* (1871), Nietzsche mentioned in passing "the pathological discharge, the *catharsis* of Aristotle, of which philologists are not sure whether it should be included among medical or moral phenomena."[42] He was calling attention to a vacillation between the physical and the psychic realm. Indeed, the idea of catharsis as it appeared in Aristotle's *Poetics* (1449b26) had divided interpreters. The moral interpretation was developed by Gotthold Ephraim Lessing, who understood catharsis as an ennobling of the passions. The philologist Jakob Bernays, the uncle of Freud's wife, criticized this moral interpretation and proposed an understanding of the word based on the concrete meaning attributed to it by Greek medicine from the time of the Hippocratic collection: it designated the elimination and evacuation of humors or excrement.[43] Aristotle, according to Bernays, would have been aware of this when he gave it a metaphoric meaning: through terror and pity, tragedy provokes the expulsion of these passions. Bernays was right, but, it seems to me, he merely rediscovered a tradition of reading the *Poetics*.

In the seventeenth and eighteenth centuries, to define the effects of tragedy and to translate *catharsis*, French authors discussed the "purging of the passions" and recognized the medical value of the Aristotelian expression: "It seems," wrote André Dacier, "that to purge in this sense can signify nothing other than to uproot and drive out the passions from the soul." But once recognized, this sense of the word was the object of reservations and attenuations. The same author adds: "Since it is not true that tragedy can fully purge the passions in this rigorous sense, it is claimed that we must understand something else here, namely that it represses their excesses and moderates them. It purges terror and compassion by means of themselves and thereby teaches us to tolerate all setbacks courageously."[44] As we see, the meaning hovers among expulsion, repression, and a treatment of evil with evil. Thus for Father Pierre Brumoy, purging passions consists in "preserving what is useful in fear and pity" and separating out what is harmful: "Poetry corrects fear through fear, pity through pity, which is all the more pleasant because the human heart loves its sentiments and weaknesses. Therefore it imagines that it is being flattered and finds itself unwittingly cured by the very pleasure it takes in seducing itself. A happy mistake, whose results are all the more certain in that the cure is born of the very ailment that is cherished."[45] Let me add that for Aristotle the "purging of the passions" concerns the *spectator* of the tragedy, not the tragic character himself, beset by the sudden twists of his fate and led to a belated recognition of his own faults.

Whatever meaning was retained by the theorists of tragedy, "catharsis" and the adjective "cathartic" in particular were firmly rooted in the medical lexicon up to the nineteenth century, and they were justified by references to the schools of Hippocrates and Galen.[46] Most pharmacopoeias contained a chapter on cathartic drugs (also known as "purgatives" or "evacuants"). Did one need to refer to Aristotle and his use of a term derived from medical language when this term itself remained present in nineteenth-century medical practice? In a series of material metaphors, it was perfectly suitable for expressing the expulsion of an affect that remains trapped (*eingeklemmt*) like a foreign body (*Fremdkörper*).[47] In the lines already cited, Freud established a quasi synonymy among "evacuation" (*Abfuhr*), "catharsis," and "abreaction." These words accumulate a sense of deviation, elimination, discharge, with an obvious connotation of intestinal expulsion.

Freud and Breuer investigated the blockage caused by abreaction, to which they attributed a pathogenic effect, just as Freud, at the same time, attributed a pathogenic effect to coitus interruptus. They both imagined — each in his own way — the mechanisms by which the "emotions" were retained or deflected, later to generate hysterical symptoms. In their theory, any aspect of a sudden emotion not immediately evacuated becomes pathogenic.

Has it been sufficiently noted that their conception of the

"foreign body" is very similar to the idea expressed by Nietzsche in 1887 in *On the Genealogy of Morals* (essay 1, section 10)? Nietzsche begins with the distinction between "noble souls" and "men of *ressentiment*" — a distinction that covers quite neatly that of health and illness. "Noble" beings are not restrained by prudence; they are carried away by "enthusiastic impulsiveness in anger, love, reverence, gratitude, and revenge." For them, revenge and resentment are expressed without delay. "*Ressentiment* itself, if it should appear in the noble man, consummates and exhausts itself in an immediate reaction, and therefore does not *poison.*... Such a man shakes off with a *single* shrug many vermin that eat deep into others."[48]

Shortly after the publication of *Studies on Hysteria*, Freud substituted the term "psychoanalysis" for "cathartic method," and he did not return to the word "catharsis" until writing the history of his ideas. Practically the same goes for "abreaction." This word lasted in Freud's writing only as long as catharsis, to which it was closely tied, was part of his theory. Added to his intellectual reasons for distancing himself from them was the fact that these terms were closely associated with their co-inventor, Josef Breuer, whom Freud quickly suspected of being hostile to him.

Later, in "Remembering, Repeating, and Working Through" (1914), Freud said "abreaction" faded into the background, whereas "working through" (*Durcharbeiten*) came to the fore.[49] Experience, he says, had taught him that the analyst's attention must be focused on lifting resistance, which occurs in stages. This takes some time. These differences are inscribed in the words themselves. Inasmuch as it resembles a nervous crisis, abreaction is produced almost suddenly, whereas working through (as indicated by the prefix *durch-*, or "through," in *Durcharbeiten*) takes a long time. In the entry on abreaction in *The Language of Psycho-Analysis*, Jean Laplanche and J.-B. Pontalis correctly wrote:

The exclusive emphasis on abreaction as the key to psychotherapeutic effectiveness is above all typical of the period in Freud's work which is known as the period of the cathartic method. Yet the notion is retained in the later theory of psycho-analytic treatment. There are empirical reasons for its survival, for every cure involves manifest emotional discharge, though to varying degrees according to the type of patient. There are theoretical reasons too, in so far as every theory of the cure must take into account *repetition* as well as *recollection*. Concepts such as transference, working through and acting out all imply some reference to the theory of abreaction, even though they also lead us to more complex conceptions of treatment than the idea of a pure and simple elimination of the traumatizing affect.[50]

The word *Durcharbeiten* is not a Freudian neologism. It has been in the German language since the eighteenth century. It appears to have been created under the influence of Pietist thought, and Goethe uses it in a very significant way in *Elective Affinities* (part 2, chapter 3): "Charlotte went back into her room ... to work through thoughts and concerns [*um ihre Betrachtungen und Sorgen ... durchzuarbeiten*] that she could not communicate to anyone." The deployment of the prefixal possibilities of German accompanied (or guided) the rise of psychoanalysis. It is primarily not the unconscious but psychoanalysis that is constituted as a language. Later it would be easy to find in the unconscious what had been attributed to it when it was first conceived.

Freud's language is a mixture of narrative and scientific languages. From the very beginning of his psychological work, the notion of abreaction was defined by opposition: the retention of affect, conversion, defense, resistance, repression, and so on. Not only did later therapeutic experience lead Freud to differentiate the various mechanisms hindering abreaction, but some of them

183

took on the word "reaction," such as "reaction formation" and "negative therapeutic reaction." In the notion of reaction formation (*Reaktionsbildung*), Freud designates that which stops or hinders excitation, and no longer its "flowing off." It is more or less the same for negative therapeutic reaction (*negative therapeutische Reaktion*).[51] Here one finds the emergence — in opposition to the "unconscious investment" — of an entity Freud used in his first works under the word "counter-will" (*Gegenwille*), which had also appeared as "resistance" (*Widerstand*). Things have thus become quite complicated, since the word "reaction" was used to designate both catharsis and its opposite. In following the verbal track of "reaction" in Freud, which is often merely an auxiliary and a smallest common denominator, one risks being led down unexpected paths.

Hence repression and reaction are closely bound. Shortly after the publication of *The Interpretation of Dreams*, Freud, speaking of repression as his "core problem," explained in an important letter that repression "is possible only through reaction between two sexual currents."[52] Ernst Kris, recalling the introduction of the concept of "infantile sexuality," finds it revealed in childhood experiences, in which "it is always a matter of sexual excitations and the reactions they provoke."[53]

"Repression" and "reaction": these two terms, and the dynamic model connecting them, had appeared more than one hundred years earlier. It is a question here of an intuitive schema, supported by a hydraulic analogy, available for many figurative uses. In this case, Freud's intuitions used preformed verbal devices, which had already manifested themselves. The images of repression and reaction, as we have seen, had been used by Cabanis to explain fevers.[54] One also finds, in Balzac and his contemporaries, a number of examples of the literary use of the verb "to repress" applied to feelings that cannot be revealed. Another example in which "repression" and "reaction" are part of a reflection on mental illness, but without being directly linked to each other, appears in Wilhelm Griesinger's remarkable treatise of 1845. In speaking of the "first beginnings of mental illness," Griesinger writes:

> The diminished power and energy of the "*I*," the contraction of its sphere of ideas, produces an indefinite state of mental pain, and, from its vagueness, great irritation of the feelings.... The mental pain discovers itself in some of the familiar forms of agitation, anxiety, sadness, and entails all the aforementioned ... consequences of a radically charged reaction towards the external world, and of a disturbance in the motor function of the mind.[55]

The same notion of an energy of the "I" or "ego" (to use the term adopted by Freud's English translators), the same sensory-motor model is also used by Freud, notably when he discusses trauma.[56] Which trauma? Freud speaks of accidents but also of aggression and "early seduction." Later he renounced this hypothesis, arguing instead for infantile sexuality and instinctual conflict, which somewhat attenuated the importance given to trauma.

This idea nevertheless played a determining role. The characteristic disturbance in hysteria consists of a perturbation of the motor response, which, when delayed or deviated, cannot function properly. In adopting this conception of hysterical behavior, Freud subscribed to the widespread theory that explained cerebral functions according to a model based on physiological experiments involving the sensory-motor spinal reflex.[57] At the time, the reflex schema was a guarantee of scientificity. Having accepted it, Freud imagined its dysfunctioning, which was soon known as "repression." On this point, we can consult the article he published in French in *Archives de neurologie* in 1893. There

Freud recalls that Charcot pursued the notion of a "lesion ... that is purely functional or dynamic" and that he had been the first to "teach us that to explain the hysterical neurosis we must apply to psychology." Freud asked permission to abandon neurological considerations and "move on to psychological ground." As for traumatic hysteria, he interposed the production of the mental *representation*, which complicated the two-stage schema of the reflexes. Rallying to Pierre Janet, he declares that "the lesion in hysterical paralysis" is "a lesion of the conception — of the idea — of the arm, for example." Freud remarks — in a now-famous statement — that "in its paralyses and other manifestations hysteria behaves as though anatomy did not exist or as though it had no knowledge of it."[58] One might also recall the example given by Freud in 1893 at a conference at the Vienna Medical Club: a worker is struck on the shoulder by a piece of wood and returns home with a simple contusion.[59] Several weeks later, he awakens with a paralyzed arm. What has happened? When the accident took place, that is, at the moment of his strongest emotional state, the worker had thought to himself, "My arm is paralyzed." This inner voice served, with some delay, as a hypnotic suggestion. A traumatic hysteria developed. The stimulus aroused an erroneous representation, which later provoked the paralysis. Through a physical trauma, psychic excitation increased, but the reaction deviated into a muscular symptom (paralysis). To combat this unfortunate reflex, a second reflex arc must be engaged, in which the favorable stimulus will be the suggestive voice of the physician. Thanks to this intervention, the surplus excitation could "be abreacted." Freud postulated that the model of traumatic hysteria is valid for all forms of hysteria. His definition of "trauma" is not restricted to accidental injuries. "Any impression which the nervous system has difficulty in disposing of by means of associative thinking or of motor reaction becomes a psychical trauma."[60] In these hypotheses, one finds a mixture of quantitative *mechanical* elements (such as shock, the quantity of nervous energy) and representations charged with *meaning* (what the victim imagines, the sense he gives to the physician's words, and so on). Such ideas are still quite close to those of Bernheim but presage Freud's great originality with respect to his contemporaries, who were content with short-term reactions defined case by case. Hence Wilhelm Fliess treated nasal mucus in order to cure the "reflexive nasal neurosis" that he had "discovered." But Freud was not satisfied with identifying a stimulus and an immediate, regular, and stereotyped physiopathological consequence. He multiplied the conjectured psychic consequences, considered intermediate formations, and saw them intervening at various stages and on successive levels. He opted for a reflexology *at intervals*, which soon became something other than reflexology. The reactions organized themselves into a history of episodes — "a history of sufferings" (*Leidensgeschichte*) — that might take another route if the subject succeeded in grasping its origin and in reliving the decisive moments in a different way.[61]

"Reaction" and "abreaction" benefit from an extremely valuable ambiguity. They can be understood as designating a *mechanism*, a phenomenon tied to the nervous system and the amount of excitation flowing from it. But they can also be understood as designating a transitive, voluntary *act* charged with intention. From the very beginning of Freud's psychoanalytic writings, the verb "to abreact" is conjugated as much in the active as in the passive voice: sometimes the subject (the ego) abreacts an emotion, other times a "quota of affect" (*Affektbetrag*) is abreacted. Uncertainty reigns regarding the possible responsibility of a subject. It is not the admission of an unconscious part of psychic life that abolishes the uncertainty: the spinal reflexes are unconscious and mechanical! In fact, the double possibility — active or passive voice — in conjugating "to abreact" allows the phenomenon to be situated alternately on the terrain of physiology or of behavior; this means also that it alternates between a causal "scientific" explanation and a sympathetic comprehension. (Karl Jaspers criticized psychoanalysis for this confusion between the two approaches — causal explanation and comprehension.)

Freud, as we have seen, understood that in mental life, representations (*Vorstellungen*) come between the stimulus and the response. These representations are charged with a "quota of affect" (*Affektbetrag*) that must be "disposed of." A proper abreaction immediately takes the verbal and motor paths; failing this, neurosis is not inevitable, for the representation charged with affect can participate in other representations that attenuate, disperse, and rectify its traumatic effect. The harmful effect can thus be attenuated. Freud thought that the representation following on an event can be made inoffensive either by its exteriorized expression (abreaction properly speaking) or through the work of thought. In both cases, we are dealing with a behavior on the part of the subject. Even if physiological mechanisms are involved, they cannot be apprehended as such. Only a psychological approach, which lends intention and volition to a subject (or to agencies within him), is operative. The *ab-* in "abreaction" is not merely a distancing spatial prefix; it indicates an intentional externalization. As early as Breuer's and Freud's first writings, it found an equivalent in the *aus-* of *ausdrücken*, analogous to the *ex-* in "expression."

Freud plays freely with the opposition between active and passive, voluntary and involuntary. According to one of Breuer's hypotheses, "retention" and "conversion" are produced by the "hypnotic state"; then the diversion of representation and affect supposedly takes place passively. Disarmed and vulnerable, the individual cannot abreact. How can this inability to abreact be

188

distinguished from the case in which the individual forbids himself to abreact, in which he actively represses the fright, offense, or humiliation? In both cases, a foreign-body memory is ultimately formed in a "second consciousness," on a subterranean level. Certain "groups of representations" would have been separated from consciousness through an "act of will." Such are the terms Freud uses in various texts from 1892 to 1895, notably in the article "The Neuro-Psychoses of Defense":

> In the first of these forms [of extreme hysteria] I was repeatedly able to show that the splitting of the content of consciousness is the result of an act of will on the part of the patient; that is to say, it is initiated by an effort of will whose motive can be specified. By this I do not, of course, mean that the patient intends to bring about a splitting of his consciousness. His intention is a different one; but, instead of attaining its aim, it produces a splitting of consciousness.[62]

As a result, the representation and the "quota of affect" that have been repressed will be manifested in the form of a symptom. One might recall the conditions that Breuer and especially Freud considered necessary for a cure: the patient, with the help of the physician, must be able to retranslate (*rückübersetzen*) into the speech of emotion what has been fixed in the language or symbols of the symptom.[63] Verbalization is therefore assigned a decisive role. The psychoanalytic procedure of the cathartic method confidently sets out to suppress "the operative force of the idea which was not abreacted in the first instance, by allowing the trapped affect to flow off through speech."[64] Whereas the initial model could rely on the simple schema of the reflex arc, with its excitation and response, its sensory and motor branches, here we see something other than the flowing of excitation from cell to cell. We see the unfolding and recounting of stories.[65] The theory has learned from treatments and intuitions (*Einfälle*); it attempts to translate experience into knowledge and "technique"; it is configured to allow one to accompany the patient (the analysand) through an indefinite period of his existence. This is the great advantage of a theory that sets itself in motion and becomes a *method*, as if in search of itself. Having been elaborated on the basis of the empirical revelations of a few key cases, it subjects itself to reality testing upon contact with new cases. Theoretical conjecture is thus transformed into a code of reading, which, in its application, expects to be transformed by the resistances it must overcome.

Stories

At this point, the coupling of "catharsis" and "abreaction" raises further questions. What orders of reality are brought together in these terms? The word "abreaction," as we have seen, is grafted onto neurological language and makes one think of the mechanism of a flow of excitation, without excluding the possibility that it might also designate a kind of behavior. If one recalls the Aristotelian version of the word "catharsis," one thinks of a chain of events, sentiments, and sufferings similar to those of tragic characters. When brought together, "catharsis" and "abreaction" form a hybrid in which the tragic (with its individual nature) blends with the general law of living organisms. Thus, as I have just noted, the nervous trajectory — from trauma to abreaction — breaks down into a series of singular events and behaviors that are not amenable to scientific description: they call for a story. The neurological *model* has been supplanted by a *matrix* of possible narrations. What Freud offers to his disciples is not merely a new nomenclature but a typology of potential histories of affective life. While appealing to the facts of a fundamental reflexology, the theory of the formation and liquidation of the hysterical symptom

190

or the instinctual conflict is laid out as the framework for a *story* or a *scenario*. What reflex accomplished in two schematic stages is drawn out in Freud's conjectures into a series of episodes: bifurcations, fixations, and substitutions become possible. In theory, one is dealing merely with forces acting on the psyche; the actors are called "excitation," "drive," "libido," and so on. The neurologists' neutral stimulus has become sexualized. These dramatis personae of the psyche have no faces, but they trace the lines of destiny, evolving on a stage whose principal dimensions (high and low, foreground and background) are visibly indicated. Furthermore, the theory mobilizes an additional dramatic cast around the representatives of the subject; it anticipates the roles that the various "real" characters will inevitably play in their different ways. We are familiar with these essential partners: father and mother, brothers and sisters, suitors or lovers, and, for a while at least, the confused shadows of very ancient, perverse seducers. The theoretical apparatus put into place in *Studies on Hysteria* — but especially the one Freud developed subsequently — takes account of a previous history; it anticipates the vicissitudes of the treatment and is not disconcerted by failure, which is expected to appear in the form of resistance. In analysis, the theoretical story goes back to the subject's antecedents, just as classical French tragedy begins with an expository scene evoking the protagonists' past.

Based on a theory that emerged as a history that produces other histories, the analytic exploration of individual suffering set its sights on illuminating the origins of this suffering. As is often the case in medicine, the theoretically established doctrine generated corresponding "facts." The "material" consisted of everything that the attentive seeker was able to glean: memories, attitudes, complaints, dreams, and so on. The goal of the different techniques — hypnosis, hand pressed to the forehead, free association — was to gather words and signs from which would emerge, through *interpretation*, the power to link the symptoms to a series of previous events by means of a narrative.[66] What a difference, especially at the end of the nineteenth century, from the "positive" study of organic nervous ailments! The latter objectified deficits and anomalies, noting (hammer in hand) the absence or presence of tendinous reflexes, cataloging the anesthetic zones, observing the reaction of the pupils to light, measuring various sensitivities and muscular strength, and so on. It focused on processes, lesions, compressions, inflammations, and tumors — not truly personal histories but the "natural history" of afflictions poorly identified up to that point. In this type of medicine, nothing obliged the patients to remember (except in the study of amnesia); nothing pushed them to relate their emotions. As a general rule, the physician could only see the implacable progress of organic afflictions. As long as he relied on an organically oriented medicine, his relationship with the patient, even in chronic ailments, remained distant and formal. The physician might dispense some sound advice; he might even add a consoling word. His arsenal, devoid of a specific method, would then put into play biological actions and reactions that had very short-term effects or fell within a very narrow range. In Freud's day, the therapeutic orthodoxy was limited to the monotonous resources of electroshock, baths, rest, restorative diet, and so on. The enterprise of healing was reduced to a successive employment of all the physical tools available. Undoubtedly, in more than a few cases psychotherapy would have proved just as vain. Freud tells of his disappointment when he tried to apply the recipes from Wilhelm Erb's *Handbook of Electro-Therapeutics* (1883), which, in his opinion, "had no more relation to reality than some 'Egyptian' dreambook, such as is sold in cheap book-shops."[67] Therapeutic nihilism could have set in, yet the cathartic method and what followed filled this void. In passages that are now famous, Freud legitimized the use of a quasi-literary narration in order to understand hysteria:

> I have not always been a psychotherapist. Like other neuro-pathologists, I was trained to employ local diagnoses and electro-prognosis, and it still strikes me myself as strange that the case histories I write should read like short stories and that, as one might say, they lack the serious stamp of science. I must console myself with the reflection that the nature of the subject is evidently responsible for this, rather than any preference of my own. The fact is that local diagnosis and electrical reactions lead nowhere in the study of hysteria, whereas a detailed description of mental processes such as we are accustomed to find in the works of imaginative writers enables me, with the use of a few psychological formulas, to obtain at least some kind of insight into the course of that affection. Case histories of this kind are intended to be judged like psychiatric ones; they have, however, one advantage over the latter, namely an intimate connection between the story of the patient's sufferings and the symptoms of his illness — a connection for which we still search in vain in the biographies of other psychoses.[68]

> The procedure is laborious and time-consuming for the physician. It presupposes great interest in psychological happenings, but personal concern for the patients as well. I cannot imagine bringing myself to delve into the psychical mechanism of a hysteria in anyone who struck me as low-minded and repellent, and who, on closer acquaintance, would not be capable of arousing human sympathy; whereas I can keep the treatment of a tabetic or rheumatic patient apart from personal approval of this kind.[69]

Ever since Hippocrates's *Epidemics*, medical observations have frequently been presented in narrative form. This was especially necessary when the affliction and its successful treatment were more striking. After Mesmer, propagandists of animal magnetism — and later those of mediumistic clairvoyance — had a predilection for stories of illness and healing full of circumstantial details. In nineteenth-century European psychiatry, the tradition of ancient "observations" was alive and well. A nosological entity can emerge from the symptoms and signs observed in the course of a history. The stories sometimes contain fragments of the patients' conversations, letters, or autobiographical writings. They expand and develop as alterations of the personality become more spectacular. A single character can give rise to a great monograph. As Henri F. Ellenberger reminds us, "the Seer of Prevorst," to whom the poet-physician Justinus Kerner devoted a book in 1829, set a precedent for an entire scientific-mystical literature that heroized female figures (she also played a role for Carl Jung). In the last decades of the century, dual consciousness and the interest it afforded to doctors and their readers became, as it were, the mother of all stories. Thus began the era of illustrious patients — lending a hand to female mystics and mediums — who became heroines through the mediation of psychiatrists or experimenters. At the Salpêtrière Hospital, Charcot cultivated a few of these women, almost all of whom confirmed the master's theories with their attacks. Félida, Etienne-Eugène Azam's patient, was one of the first to play a solo role as the diva of dual consciousness.[70] Breuer's Anna O. and Freud's four female cases (in *Studies on Hysteria*) came next, and all bore witness to the traumatic etiology of hysteria; their stories proved that a great relief, even a cure, could be obtained through verbalization and emotional discharge. These patients were the guarantors of abreaction and catharsis.[71]

Freud was tremendously gifted as a writer. His famous cases (and that of Dora in particular) could have been presented on the stage, since he had already staged them in his narratives. The four principal female cases described by Freud in *Studies on Hysteria* are masterfully narrated. One notes the multiplicity of narrative voices. It is first and foremost the physician who is writing, as an author of case histories intended for a qualified reader. He establishes various levels of speech. In his narrative, the author represents himself as speaking to the patient. The scientific speech intended for the reader thus echoes the simpler words addressed to the patients. Furthermore, the observation collects and communicates — through direct or indirect discourse — the patients' remarks, the stories they manage to put together concerning their suffering, and the nonverbal signs they substitute for words. The patient is unwittingly transformed from the object of investigation into a co-author of the text. The study of "Katharina" (chapter 2, case 4) is the story of a single session; it is almost indistinguishable from a short story. This account of an encounter with a mountain innkeeper's daughter includes a dialogue that takes place when Freud stops to rest during a hike and that leads to evidence of the cause of the young woman's suffocations: sexual trauma, the rape by an "uncle" (in reality her father, Freud would specify). Much of Emmy von N.'s treatment is related in the form of a dated journal.

While the symptom requires a staging of the past in order to be interpreted and eliminated if possible, the "discussion" that Freud includes at the end of these case histories is a metanarrative, spoken, as it were, in front of the curtain. It is at once a critical return to the recounted story, a consideration of the treatment's progress, and a reevaluation of the method and its results. From the beginning, Freud made very good use of a procedure practiced at the time by a medicine that was eager to prove that it verified its claims and did not lose sight of the later evolution of its cases.[72]

This leads me to note that the "discussion" — the recapitulation of a patient's story, but also of the therapist's hypotheses — is an independent genre. It constitutes the last type of history and form of writing in which Freud proved his mastery: the history of his own ideas. Although he only partially disclosed the results of his self-analysis, he returned on several occasions to the successive stages of his thought. In light of the commentary and paraphrases they have provoked, his multiple intellectual autobiographies have been remarkably persuasive.

Each of Freud's historical recapitulations is a "discourse on method." In all of them, Freud mentions the prelude with Breuer, the "cathartic treatment," and the English terms invented by the inaugural patient, Anna O.: "talking cure," "chimney sweeping." The lectures given in 1909 at Clark University begin with a long recollection of the famous first patient. Her story, as Freud recapitulates it, remains paradigmatic, because it teaches that hysterics "suffer from reminiscences."[73] But as of 1909, "abreaction" is no longer the master word of therapy. A new word, in the fifth, and last, lecture, takes its place: "transference" (*Uebertragung*). Remarkably, "reaction" does not exit the scene; Freud uses the word in referring to an idea of Sándor Ferenczi's.[74] But in Freud's imagistic definition of transference, "reaction" is linked, as with Diderot, to images of fermentation in chemical processes:

> His symptoms, to take an analogy from chemistry, are precipitates of earlier experiences in the sphere of love (in the widest sense of the word), and it is only in the raised temperature of his experience of the transference that they can be resolved and reduced to other psychical products. In this reaction the physician, if I may borrow an apt phrase from Ferenczi, plays the part of a catalytic ferment, which temporarily attracts to itself the affects liberated in the process.[75]

The great advantage of the notion of transference, which remains an essential tool, is that it invites an approach based on a present reaction to a present emotion, independent of any effort at "truly" locating the distant source of this emotion. Knowing that reminiscence is always formulated today, in today's situation, the therapist and his patient (who can be called the analysand if one grants him some initiative) establish themselves on a terrain that is both safer and more dangerous — that of a relationship.

Associations

Eugen Bleuler (1857–1939), the director of the Zurich psychiatric clinic, attached great importance to the psychology of associations. He sponsored a collective work that appeared as *Diagnostische Assoziationsstudien*, which Jung edited from 1906 to 1910. (Six of the twelve works in the collection are by Jung.) In his preface, Bleuler takes the reflex arc as his model:

> All active psychic functioning is based on action and reaction (*Wechselwirkung*), on the associations between the material given by sensation and mnestic traces.... All psychic activity is unthinkable without association.... Association is a fundamental phenomenon of psychic activity. Once association is hampered, perception, thought, and action are interrupted.... The passage from a sensory excitation to the motor part of the reflex pathway is already, in principle, a process identical with the one we must acknowledge in the parallel physiological processes of psychic development.... Most psychic association involves links between actual processes and mnemonic traces, which are revived through the associative process.[76]

The experimental method calls upon a procedure already used by Wilhelm Wundt and Emil Kraepelin: "The reaction was produced by the articulation of the first word that came into the mind of the subject of the experiment upon hearing the stimulus word. Of course, this word response is but a small part of the complex of free association."[77] The term "reaction" here designates a well-defined object: the word that comes to mind after hearing the stimulus word. It refers not to the *symptom* itself, spontaneously produced by the patient, but to a *sign* provoked by the physician and seen as a symbol that can reveal a constitutive element in the "complex." The result consists of responses given to a fixed series of one hundred to two hundred words. In this sense, we are dealing with a diagnostic procedure — a test — that attempts to be as precise as possible. On the one hand, it notes measurable parameters, in particular recording the time elapsed between the stimulus and the response. Thus the young Ludwig Binswanger (1881–1966) was engaged to observe the modifications of the psycho-galvanic reflex during the experiments in association! (Here one has the makings of a career as a phenomenologist — as a result of fleeing in the opposite direction.) On the other hand, the procedure implies an important coefficient of interpretation: the physician relied on it to spur on conversations with his patients. In the same collective work, Jung relates these studies in association directly to psychoanalysis.[78] Around this time, he adopts Freud's views on the sexual nature of the pathogenic complex and on the role of repression in the genesis of psychic troubles. For the reading of symbols, he still largely depends on the lexicon proposed in *The Interpretation of Dreams*, which he cites respectfully.

During the period in which he was friends with Bleuler and Jung, Freud became interested in the ideas (*Einfälle*) generated by stimulus words and was especially attentive to delays in this reaction. Resistance prolonged the time between the stimulus word and the response. Freud returned to these experiments in some of his later works, notably in the sixth lecture in *Introductory Lectures on Psychoanalysis*.[79] There he points out that he had used free association before Bleuler and Jung. He also remarks that in the Zurich experiments, the stimulus word was chosen arbitrarily, which makes the reaction an intermediary product (*eine Ver-*

mittlung) between the stimulus word launched from the outside and the "complex" thus awakened in the experimental subject. In dreams, on the other hand, the stimulus word emanates from the subject's psychic life and is an offshoot of it. "It is therefore not precisely fantastic to suppose that the further associations linked to the dream-elements will be determined by the same complex as that of the element itself and will lead to its discovery."[80] Freud thus recommends *free* association: made of the same stuff as dreams, it is not a reaction to an external stimulus. As for Jung, after *Diagnostische Assoziationsstudien*, he expressed doubts concerning the efficacy of abreaction, though he acknowledged the importance of Freud's theses. In the case of an obsessional neurosis, to master the morbid representations — which are "a State within a State" and "a person within a person" — one must summon a "strong effort" and undertake a veritable "energy-cure." "With a certain ruthlessness," Jung considered it necessary to constrain patients to expel and uncover "these unbearable separate existences [*Sonderexistenzen*]," which are complexes and repressed representations:

> The split-off contents of the mind are destroyed by being released from repression through an effort of the will. So they lose a great deal of their authority [*Nimbus*] and therefore of their horror, and simultaneously the patient regains the feeling of being master of his representations. I therefore put the emphasis on arousing and strengthening the will and not on mere "abreacting" [*das blosse "Abreagieren"*], as Freud originally did.[81]

Psychogenesis

In the twentieth century, in medicine as in other sciences, "reaction" became a general term, a blunted term, facile and vague, with no differentiating power. It had to be supplemented; it

required a qualifier or complement to designate a class of phenomena or a specific biological fact (a few examples among many:
immune reaction, defensive reaction, allergic reaction, vagal reaction). In other cases, it is made into a complement (reaction time,
reaction amplitude). It is a popular item in an accessory store. In
most cases, the word "phenomenon" or "disorder" can be substituted for "reaction," which can only function — like those handles
with multiple uses — when one inserts a finer tool. The historian
of ideas or of science has no reason to pay attention to the recent
history of a global concept of reaction as such, neither in physics
and chemistry nor in internal medicine and neurobiology. There
is, however, one great exception: reaction and the reactive in psychology and psychopathology.

The word "reactive" (*réactionnel*) did not appear in French
until quite late in the nineteenth century. The meaning attached to
it makes it the opposite of "organic." In the language of psychopathology, it is the counterpart of what — around the same time —
is meant by "functional" in internal medicine. It is still very much
alive today (parallel to the English "reactive" and the German *reak-
tiv*). "Reactive" and "functional" ailments are those without any
discernible lesion, *sine materia*. Physicians of somatic disorders at
the time of positivism's triumph tended, however, to make them
material in the hypothetical form of circulatory problems.[82]

In the theoretical realm, and without excessive play on the
meaning of the word, we might say that the notion of the reactive
in medicine took off as a result of an intellectual reaction against
a dominant tendency.[83] On the one hand, while many psychiatrists believed they had to isolate a lesion or impairment in every
case, a few dissenters (including Bernheim) retorted that unusual
behavior should be considered not the result of a localized lesion
or impairment but a response by the cerebral apparatus to a solic-
itation or a lived situation. On the other hand, while many psy-

chiatrists did their best to isolate and classify nosological entities, and thereby construct a repertoire of morbid essences, others refused to subject themselves to such classificatory constraints. Recourse to the notion of the reactive represented a protest against an abusive or at least premature systematization. The protest was directed at times against organicism and at times against what could have been considered ontologism, and often against the two combined. In fact, organicism and ontologism could reinforce each other. To the extent that it sought to identify a specific organic affliction, organicism pursued the cataloging of lesion-related ailments; and psychiatric ontologism posited more or less invariable "clinical pictures" that included a predictable clinical evolution whose cellular or psychochemical bases could remain provisionally unknown.

Many voices spoke out for the necessity of considering the individual as a whole. One of the most noteworthy interventions came from the psychiatrist Adolf Meyer (1866–1950), who had considerable influence in the United States during the first half of the twentieth century.[84] His point of departure was a critique of the "noumenal" attitude, which considers mental illness as a thing in itself. The "meta-neurology" of Carl Wernicke and the classifications proposed by Emil Kraepelin seemed valid to him only in a provisional and indicatory way. As Henri Ey has noted, Meyer cast his lot for an "anti-nosological" point of view.[85] Instead of the practice of labeling mental illnesses, Meyer wanted to see the creation of a "dynamic psychology." What did he mean by this? He meant, certainly, a consideration of all the biological ("infrapsychic") aspects revealed in mental disorders, based on a perception that considers the "illness" as a reaction "of the whole person." From shock, which could be interpreted as a brief event occurring in the interface between the "affective" and the "physiological," to behaviors in which the individual is engaged in a constant struggle with his circumstances, all transitions are conceivable. Reflex is *already* a behavior, and conduct is *always* attributed to a living body. If there is a disorder, it is because the reaction is not adequate; then one is dealing with a failure of adjustment — or a *substitutive* reaction. It is impossible, according to Meyer, to speak in neurological terms about substitutive activity. Meyer helped to introduce the notion of adjustment into American psychiatry, but he saw it as a conduct rather than a mechanism: "It proved to be much more satisfactory to speak in terms of situation, reaction, and final adjustment, and to describe all the facts of interaction according to their weight."[86] This is called a "response to a demand."

Meyer's thought is also part of the current of pragmatism, and it was in the name of pragmatism that in 1908 he defended the theory of hysteria advanced by Freud and Jung. Some complained that this theory did not make it possible to establish the "essence of hysteria." But Meyer notes that "knowledge and words do not aim to become a complete duplication of the concrete facts and events, ... they aim merely to be sufficient for the purposes of a system of action or analysis."[87] From this perspective, and in the absence of the organic signature of an ailment such as dementia praecox, Meyer the practitioner prefers to consider the symptoms of this illness as a chain of inadequate responses; there he finds grounds for action that an ontological conception of illness would not have allowed. Consequently, the clinician's task is to recognize "types of reaction," without worrying about establishing a *fixed* diagnosis or locating the somatic alterations sought by those concerned with the "sham problems of psychophysical parallelism."[88] The psychiatrist should consider particular situations and personal factors. Henceforth, symptoms should not prompt the physician to search at all costs for a specific underlying ailment. The very word "symptom" (etymologically, the symptom is "that which falls with") becomes inadequate. The manifested behavior is not a sign of something else: it is the reaction itself. It is important simply to understand it as such and to undertake the appropriate therapeutic action. One can see in Meyer's thought a psychological neo-Lamarckism that is in some respects quite close to that found in some of Freud's early works. Thus, once again, one concept of reaction supplants another. Just as George Herbert Mead distanced himself from the theory of reflexive functions that John B. Watson made the sole material of his behaviorism, Meyer calls for abandoning the language of neurology (which speaks of reaction without leaving the realm of reflex mechanism) in order to take up the language of psychology (which speaks of reaction as a response and a behavior of the individual as a whole). The "substitutive reactions" that interest Meyer resemble the German psychiatrists' "failed reactions" (*Fehlreaktionen*). They presuppose norms of conduct. We pass from a concept in which reactions (considered reflexes) result mechanically from an unexpected *shock* to another concept in which reactions (considered intentional responses or behaviors) differ according to the degree of *mastery* over a situation. This allows one to take into consideration a larger biographical and social context.

Simultaneously, in European psychiatry, particularly with Bleuler and his students in Switzerland, a theoretical distinction was established between reactions and "evolutive processes." A reaction results from an acute psycho-traumatic injury and takes place in a restricted time frame (from a few hours to a few months); a disorder translates, as it were, the impossibility of mastering an isolated event. In situations in which the individual undergoes repeated injuries (humiliations, excessive labor), there ensue unfavorable alterations and structural modifications, which can be seen as a chain of successive reactions: one must consider the entire evolutive chain of events, as well as initial psychic dispositions. It is clearly implied that such distinctions can only be established through sustained observation in a psychiatric institution.

Not only the words "reaction" and "reactive" took on new functions at the beginning of the twentieth century. Several other terms were created at the same time that made their way in tandem with "reaction." Among the most notable is "psychogenesis." The word was introduced by Robert Sommer (1864–1937) in a work devoted to psychiatric diagnosis.[89] The author wished to argue for a notion that would make it possible to stop using the collective term "hysteria," which he considered inappropriate:

> Even for a specific morbid unity, it is not possible to keep the word "hysteria," for the states [*Zustände*] gathered together under this name are by nature completely dissimilar.... Does the word I have chosen, "psychogenesis," meet all linguistic and scientific requirements? I doubt it.... These states are provoked by representations [*Vorstellungen*] and can be influenced by representations. Furthermore, it is clear that organic morbid states can provoke representations in the same individual which in turn can, through the psychogenic pathway, provoke morbid phenomena that will conceal to some extent the image of the organic affection.[90]

In his only concession to the traditional doctrine of hysteria, Sommer claims that these representations can be provoked by parts of the body, such as the uterus. The notion of psychogenesis (as in the opposition psychogenesis/somatogenesis) endured, but some interference began to occur when there appeared, in Germany and the Anglo-American world, the coupled notions of the endogenous and the exogenous, of which I shall soon speak again in presenting the problems encountered by Karl Jaspers.

Karl Jaspers's General Psychopathology

When brutally separated from their families, and in positions of great dependence, adolescents or young servants sometimes commit terrible crimes: intentionally setting fires, murdering the children entrusted to their care, and so on. The psychiatrist is then called upon to assess these unusual criminals, that is, to evaluate the degree of their responsibility. They suffer from home-sickness or nostalgia (*Heimweh*).[91] Karl Jaspers (1883–1969), a young psychiatrist, devoted his 1909 thesis to such cases: he traced the history of the problem and evaluated its psychological and medicolegal aspects. In the conclusion of his study, titled "Nostalgia and Crime," he defined such behavior as "characteristic reactions," comparable to "prison psychoses." In many such cases, he specified, there is a "psychopathic constitution," a slight "deficiency," or an element of "degeneration" (a word that has fortunately fallen out of use). What is called "reaction" here is not a particular illness (*eine besondere Krankheit*). In this area, Jaspers declares, there are no clearly delimited morbid or clinical pictures, only "personality types or types of reaction to external influences."[92]

Jaspers devoted his great work *General Psychopathology* (first published in 1913) to psychiatric method. His thought must still be reckoned with, even though the book, after four editions, has come to seem repetitive and prolix. I shall spend some time with it, for despite what has become obsolete, and despite what one cannot help criticizing — such as its occasionally didactic and solemn tone — the book is the only true "monument" of twentieth-century psychiatry. Through the revised and augmented editions, Jaspers not only recapitulated the psychiatric knowledge of the first forty years of the century but also opened the philosophical debate on approaches to the ailing individual and to mental illness. The work proposes to illuminate every method that was practiced, without forgoing the right to denounce errors and dead ends. In an examination that often reads like an in-depth inventory, Jaspers analyzes the presuppositions and legitimate expectations of the different disciplines applied to psychiatry: biology, phenomenology, psychoanalysis, and so on. His objective is first to demonstrate that psychopathology has no exclusive method and that an informed pluralism is indispensable. Various approaches can be adopted, on the condition that they declare their principles and recognize the limits of their relevance without demanding hegemonic authority. Research is movement and should never give in to the temptation of "dogmatizing about Being":

> Either we think every piece of knowledge gives us the thing in itself, reality as such, Being in its totality, or we think that there can be no more than an approximate appreciation of context, which implies that our knowledge is rooted in our methods and limited by them.... We have to remember that methods become creative only when we use them, not when we reflect [nachdenken] upon them.... All categories and methods have their own specific meaning. It is nonsense to play off one against the other.[93]

The project announced from the beginning of *General Psychopathology* consists in recognizing two types of approach. After giving an inventory of the numerous "factual data" (*Tatbestände*) and "meaningful objective phenomena" (*sinnhafte Objektivitäten*) encountered by the doctor, Jaspers, following Wilhelm Dilthey (1833–1911), opposes intuitive comprehension and causal explanation.[94] The first interprets behaviors, gestures, and statements as they appear when a sympathetic relationship is established with them. The second looks for causes in organic structures and their functioning: it identifies and analyzes objective sets of events; it submits them to the most precise measurements; it transcribes them into diagrams; it is able to follow step by step the evolution of physiological disorders. Thought as understanding proceeds by way of empathy (*Einfühlung*); it interprets signs and expressions and transports itself (*sich hineinversetzt*) into the psychic life of another. Causal thought attempts to objectify data, which it measures, controls, and coordinates onto graphs; it applies itself to reproducing the data experimentally. In the distinction he draws between thought as understanding and causal thought, Jaspers recognizes his debt to Johann Gustav Droysen (1808–1884) and Wilhelm Dilthey: these cultural historians and philosophers maintained that the method of the natural sciences (whose desire is to explain, *erklären*) was inadequate in the areas of culture and the human sciences, where only a comprehensive method is valid.[95] To aim at understanding (*verstehen*), according to Dilthey, requires an interpretative, or hermeneutical, relationship, one that uses analysis (*Zergliederung*) and description.[96] Beginning in 1912, Jaspers set out to demonstrate, using the "concrete case" of schizophrenia, how causal relations and comprehensible relations could be articulated:

> We understand behavior on the basis of its motives, and we explain causally a movement occurring through nervous excitations. We understand how moods [*Stimmungen*] are the result of emotions and how certain hopes, imaginings, or fears flow out of the moods; we explain the appearance or disappearance of certain dispositions of memory, fatigue, or recuperation, and so on. The name *causality from within* has also been given to comprehensible relations in psychic life [*des Seelischen*], and in this way we have designated the impassable abyss that exists between these relations (which can be called causal only metaphorically) and those which are true relations of causality, *causality from without*.[97]

Despite the "abyss" separating them, one approach does not exclude the other. It would be a mistake to believe, wrote Jaspers, "that the psyche is the domain of understanding while the physical world is that of causal explanation." Scientific exploration has carte blanche and knows no limitation:

> There is no real psychic process [*Vorgang*] ... that would be, in principle, inaccessible to a causal explanation; psychic events can also be subjected to a causal explanation. There is no limit [*Grenze*] to the discovery of causes, and with every psychic event [*bei seelischen Vorgängen*] we always look for cause and effect. *But with understanding there are limits everywhere.* The existence of special psychic dispositions [*Anlagen*], the rules governing the acquisition and loss of memory-traces, the total psychic constitution in its sequence of different age-levels and everything else that may be termed the substratum of the psyche, all constitute the limits to our understanding. Each limitation is a fresh stimulus to formulate the problem of cause anew.[98]

Jaspers is wary, however, of the pitfalls of causal thinking in psychopathology, for knowledge is not increased by multiplying mechanical causes. One must take the many "intermediate causes" into account, and it is difficult to locate them. Is one ever in a position to identify a direct cause? One speaks of causes, Jaspers continues, without knowing whether one is designating a condition (*Bedingung*) or an occasion (*Veranlassung*) or a force (*Kraft*). Jaspers is convinced that a knowledge of causal relations must be established within the framework of a biological, not mechanical, representation. He thus appears eager to maintain the old line of demarcation (found notably in Bichat) between the living and the mechanical. However, almost immediately, through the intervention of action and reaction (*Wechselwirkung*), Jaspers introduces a principle of self-regulation that seems to foreshadow the more recent theories of self-organization:

> One-way causality is an inevitable category of causal apperception, but it does not exhaust life's possibilities. The living event is an infinite action-and-reaction of *cycles* of events, which morphologically, physiologically and genetically are complex configurational unities [*Ganzheiten*]. Life, it is true, makes use of mechanisms (and causal knowledge of living things must grasp these mechanisms) but the mechanisms themselves are created by life, conditioned by life and are transformable. Compared with the automatism of a machine, life is a running self-regulation of the machinery itself, in such a way that we find the final regulating center nowhere else but in the infiniteness of everything living, and then we only find it in the form of an idea.[99]

Note that in raising life above pure mechanisms, Jaspers simultaneously places it outside and beyond the laws of transmitted motion or chemical exchanges. Can one henceforth shun reaction? Not at all, since according to Jaspers there exists a vital action and reaction (*Wechselwirkung*) capable of arising in productive "cycles." In such moments, Jaspers seems to be drawing on the tradition of Romantic vitalism as it was expressed by Carl Gustav Carus (1789–1869). Yet just as he was opposed to absolutizing mechanical causality, he is wary of absolutizing the living totality: the latter can only be sensed or anticipated by an *idea*, which cannot and should not ever be made into an object.[100] On this point, Jaspers remains faithful to the Kantian notion of "reflective judgment."

The importance Jaspers grants to understanding in no way disqualifies the exercise of objectivizing thought. Where understanding reaches its limits, one can always try to establish causal

correlations. Jaspers thus acknowledges a complementarity between the two approaches. In most instances of psychosis, he
believes, the causal explanation must take up where psychological
understanding leaves off: one must therefore consider objective
"processes," and not comprehensible "developments." In this way,
Jaspers, in the last revision of his book (1946–1948), reserves in
advance to neurobiology and genetics the role of reviving causal
explanations (which it is no longer possible to disregard today).
Of course, causal correlations are not easy to establish: they can
be reconsidered at any moment and should not be made absolute.[101] When one tries to establish a link of biological causality,
one must allow for factors that are not present in the subject's
consciousness; such factors are not contained in what he expresses
and can be termed extra-conscious (ausserbewusst).[102] These elements, on the other hand, are not readily accessible to human
knowledge. They must be established or constructed. Given that
causal factors are objectified in a similar way to those in natural
history, they can be generalized and lead to therapeutic "mass-
effects."[103] In this way, the ill can be helped without their active
participation — and there is no reason to take offense at this. In
extending causal thought's field of application, Jaspers clearly
delimits its scope: "Causal thinking impinges on what is alien,
non-understandable and on what can be manipulated (or what is
feasible, machbar)." Causal thinking opens perspectives both ex-
citing and fraught with difficulty. This type of thought must be
aware that "however far it advances, it will never be able to know
or to reproduce the event in itself [das Geschehen an sich]. It will
always remain at a distance from something that is only accessible
if we know that the well-being of man depends decisively on
something in himself which we can approach only by way of
understanding." Concrete understanding is also not easy to apply:
it is not derived from a general law and remains in the realm of

singularity; it can never be anything more than a perpetual starting over according to the particular figure (*Gestalt*) of *this* patient
and *this* physician. Its application is "the most intense presenta-
tion [*Gegenwärtigkeit*] of what is entirely individual."[104] One must
understand man as "within a situation," confronting his conflicts
and reacting to the situation: he must be followed into the most
extreme situations in which the individual, encountering defeat,
threatened to his "very being" (*Dasein*), awakens to existence.[105]
Understanding "impinges on myself in the other and on what is
closest to me in the other."[106] It carries before it the goal of a
totality that will never be attained or objectified, which Jaspers,
in a term that plays a large role in his philosophy, calls "the en-
compassing" (*das Umgreifende*). Certainly, one must respect the
totality of being, while also thinking of it as out of our reach and
ungraspable. One can only try to illuminate it. Jaspers reproaches
Heideggerian-inspired psychology with ontologizing its assertions, and thus of practicing an unavowed objectivization. He
criticizes psychiatrists who follow this tendency for engaging in
"a short-winded attempt at theology and philosophy which mis-
apprehends itself as some supposed piece of knowledge." At the
same time, he deplores the lack of "decisive *reaction* to ideas and
methods which in a philosophical sense conceal [*verdecken*], destroy and indeed exclude human life; in short, any reaction to the
'devil' in psychology."[107] Jaspers, to say the least, is speaking in
veiled references here.[108] What is the lack of "reaction" he is referring to? Is this a reproach addressed to Heidegger for not having openly protested against National Socialist pseudo biologism?
Note that here the term "reaction" no longer designates an object
of study or a conceptual tool: it applies to the attitude that the
philosopher (or the physician) is intellectually obligated to assume
with respect to any misapprehension of the human condition.
Experience had taught Jaspers that psychotherapists, because of

their close contact with their patients' inner being and because they intrude into an individual's most vulnerable regions, can do great harm through a lack of consideration and in particular through excessive confidence in their preconceived schemata.

As noted above, Jaspers had a predilection for inventories. He was drawn to large groupings, and he gave them order through classifications. The detailed subdivision of his book into parts, chapters, sections, and paragraphs is the formal sign of this. But here it was a matter more of methodical research than of a system.

The definition of understanding unfolds as a list of types of understanding. This list proceeds in various ways depending on the aim of understanding. There are three types (*Arten*) of under-standing: cultural, existential, and metaphysical.[109] Understand-ing can be rational, empathic, or interpretative. It manifests itself as static understanding when, in the manner of phenomenology, it is attached to an isolated "psychic state." It becomes genetic understanding when applied to the passage from one state to another. Sometimes the effort of "inner" understanding comes up against the incomprehensible and must accept such a limit.

Psychological interiority is never entirely accessible: it always takes place within a body and depends on the bodily condition (*Leibhaftigkeit*). Jaspers omits nothing, particularly in his dis-cussion of the comprehensible relations resulting from "specific mechanisms."[110] These mechanisms are extra-conscious (suscepti-ble only to causal explanation), but they give rise to manifes-tations that link together comprehensibly. The same is true for instinctual drives, resistances, and sublimations. Jaspers borrows examples from Nietzsche, whom he prefers to Freud. (Some of Freud's concepts in fact have Nietzschean antecedents; repression, for Freud, takes the place occupied by "reactive thought" in *The Genealogy of Morals*.) In Jaspers's eyes, Freudian psychoanalysis simply "popularized" Nietzsche's non-systematized ideas "in a cruder form."[111] Jaspers's severity with regard to Freud, whom he certainly had not read extensively, deepened throughout the subsequent editions of his work. He took exception to Freud's spirit of conquest, his sociohistorical conjectures (*Totem and Taboo*), and especially his style in recruiting disciples. Jaspers's principal complaint is that Freud passes off as causal knowledge (or as scientific, and thus potentially universal, knowledge) relations of meaning that, in his analysands, are valid only on the level of understanding. Freud's true merit is to have developed comprehensive observation and brought it to bear on lived history (*Lebensgeschichte*).[112] But he was mistaken in constructing a worldview (*Weltanschauung*) that demands unconditional adherence, the "sectarian" aspect of which Jaspers criticizes. Most Freudians at the end of the twentieth century seem at least partially to agree with Jaspers, downplaying Freud's scientific myths while retaining his emphasis on the operations of language and his modifications to the understanding of the analyst and the analysand in transference.

Once this methodological model is established, will there be a privileged field for reaction? In fact, Jaspers finds a use for it in the sequence of relations of understanding as well as in the series of causal relations established by explanatory procedures. There is a reaction pertinent to the thought that seeks meaning through empathy, just as there are reactions observed by the gaze that establishes objective causal relations. The word "reaction" is an instrumental concept: it helps in formulating the problems encountered as much by the will to understand as by the exercise of causal thought. It is also a mobile auxiliary force capable of supporting either side. In fact, to use another image, "reaction" is a lexical unit with a low molecular weight; it enjoys great mobility and can aggregate in many compounds. Jaspers mentions the reactions of the individual (when it is a matter of understanding) and the reactions of systems, organs, and cells (when it is a matter of constructing causal explanations). But he does not stop there. Clarifications are necessary, and Jaspers sets to making them.

Any normal life, he reminds us, has its share of reactions to exceptional events. By this he means intense, sudden, strongly felt emotions (*Erlebnisreaktionen*). Any normal life also has its share of reactions to prolonged ordeals. There are also pathological mechanisms. In his consideration of these "abnormal mechanisms," Jaspers inserts some extended remarks on the word "reaction." The word calls for terminological clarification, in the form, so dear to Jaspers, of a classificatory enumeration. Here the enumeration is rapid and precise:

> The term "reaction" has a number of different meanings. We speak of the reaction of the physical organism to the influences and conditions of the external world; of the reaction of an organ, for instance the brain, to events within the organism; of a reaction of the individual psyche to a psychotic disease process; and finally of a reaction to a psychic experience.... The concept of pathological reaction has an aspect relevant to understanding (lived experience and content) and a causal aspect (a change in what is extra-conscious [*im Ausserbewussten*]).[113]

Reaction is thus ubiquitous and lends itself equally well, depending on the situation, to causal explanation and to understanding. Clearly, the first two reactions mentioned above ("of the physical organism" and "of an organ") belong to the causal domain and occur outside consciousness; in the next two examples, the psychological aspect of reaction predominates: one sees the psychic reaction in its comprehensible relation to an event or a group of factors that trigger it. Included in this category are the ailments known as psychogenic, and it is here that one finds hysteria as well as nostalgia and prison psychosis. Jaspers alerts the reader once again that understanding remains incomplete. And he acknowledges that all manifestations of emotion are accompanied by extra-conscious mechanisms, or "physiological phenomena." Without turning to a "parallelist" doctrine, Jaspers admits that a causal sequence comes simultaneously into play, calling for "explanations" it is not easy to establish given the contemporary state of neurophysiological knowledge. What resists psychological comprehension is first and foremost an excess of reaction, the "actual passage [*Umsetzung*] into the pathological." Some types of reaction have no relation, in terms of content, to the event that precipitates them: "For instance, bereavement may precipitate a catatonic illness, a manic episode, or a circular depression. The type of psychosis need not correspond to the experience at all." The "phases" and the "surges" of psychosis often manifest themselves at the slightest pretext. Opposed to this are "true reactions in which the content is in a comprehensible relation to the original event — reactions that would not have arisen without this event and whose evolution depends on the event and their relations to it."[114] This is why it is often difficult to distinguish a true reaction from the surge or phase of an underlying process that has no relation to the individual's fate (*Schicksal*). In a development that appeared in the fourth edition (1948), Jaspers clarifies his thought on "the three ways in which reactions become meaningful."[115] First, there is the intensity (*Mass*) of a trauma, which causes a breakdown. Then there is the overall meaning of the reactive psychosis. Last, there are the "contents" of the reactive psychosis, with their particular characteristics. The more intense the reaction, the greater the extra-conscious (that is, the physiological and somatic) effects. Jaspers recognizes that this represents a modernized version of earlier theories concerning the effects on the body of disturbances and passions of the soul. He considers the role — still partly hypothetical — of neurochemical mediators. This area will be occupied, especially in British and American psychiatry, by shock, stress, "alarm-reaction," and the "general adaptation syndrome."[116] Another threefold subdivision is introduced: reactive states can be classified according to the *circumstances* that provoke them (catastrophe, accident, war, earthquake, exile, imprisonment, foreign linguistic milieu, poverty, and so on); they can be distinguished according to their *psychological configuration* (flight into illness, hysteria, paranoid or confused reactions, and so on); finally, it is possible to orient oneself according to the *type of psychic constitution* and the character traits that condition the comprehensible reaction. Each individual has sensitive "limits": there are irritable characters, constitutional psychopaths, manic-depressives, and individuals going through a phase of exhaustion.[117]

When, in the third part of his book, Jaspers turns to the causal structures of psychic life — that is, to explanatory science — he deals with reaction once again. Recognizing that a mechanical "one-way causality" cannot be reconciled with the phenomena of life, he resorts to the image of actions and reactions (or interactions, *Wechselwirkungen*) that develop in successive cycles. In an entirely Romantic fashion, he calls life an "infinite web." But there are also cycles of interactions that destroy life.[118] The study of the relationship between organism and environment must be inscribed within a causal order that is subject to scientific verification. Jaspers, who remains attached to the distinction between the endogenous and the exogenous, recalls some primary truths:

> Illness is a reaction of the physical predisposition or constitution [*Anlage*] to the influences of the environment.... No psychic event is conditioned purely by the constitution, but there is always the interaction of a particular constitution with specific external conditions and events. The change in the external conditions can be grasped directly but the constitution is always something that we approach

216

through an intellectual operation [*etwas Erschlossenes*]. Only too often when the concept is used in quite a general sense it is simply a cover for ignorance.[119]

With Jaspers, the taste for oppositions is balanced by a taste for the reconciliation of opposites. The antinomies opposing two paths of knowledge (understanding/explanation) or the distinctions made between spaces (inside/outside) establish separations in order to lay out more clearly the conditions for positing a relation. From the very start, in his 1912 article on schizophrenia, Jaspers had indicated that comprehensive psychology and explanatory causal analysis *interpenetrate* (*ineinandergreifen*) in a way that is "certainly complicated" but that would be made manageable and clear by rigorous reflection.[120] An interaction must therefore be established, a relationship of action and reaction between the methods themselves, even if each one must respect its own rules. The philosophical reflection that enacts this coupling of methods discovers first and foremost that man is a living being in an environment. "In abstract physiological terms, we say stimulus causes reaction." But the "abstract physiological terms" are only an arbitrarily limited perspective. The environment in which the individual's real life takes place is the situation. If we consider "the whole of life," then "the activities, accomplishments and experiences triggered or provoked by the situation impose themselves on the individual as tasks [*Aufgaben*]."[121] The task — that is, the response — is much more than a physiological reaction. Jaspers adds a little further on:

All life, in its finitude, has a double character. It *reacts* to situations, facts and people and in its reactions it also becomes *active and creative* in the concrete reality of the confronting situation. Action and reaction are wrongly conceived as opposed and it is a mistake to imagine the possibility of an absolute creativity engaged in objectless activity. It is equally wrong to take reaction as the fundamental feature of life.[122]

When Jaspers criticizes a psychology that relies on the reductive theory of reflex, he has in mind the neurological constructivism of Carl Wernicke (1848–1905), and in some respects his criticism is similar to the one formulated by the neurologist Kurt Goldstein (1878–1965), which in turn inspired Maurice Merleau-Ponty.[123] Here we encounter the persistent reproach, often found in reflections concerned with the whole individual, against analytic procedures that endeavor to construct the entire psychic apparatus on the basis of the elementary couple stimulus/reaction.[124] Paul Ricoeur, in his dialogue with the neurologist Jean-Pierre Changeux, raises the possibility of a "third discourse" that would overcome the opposition between the language of philosophy and that of neurobiology. Hoping to reconcile — but not fuse — scientific objectivity with an acknowledgment of lived experience, Ricoeur takes up Jaspers's idea of the complementarity between the two approaches: "I have always argued in favor of a coordination between (experienced) understanding and (objective) explanation. I want to explain in order to better understand."[125] These recent remarks can be seen as a direct continuation of the thought of Jaspers the psychopathologist and indicate its persistence.

Helmuth Plessner's famous book *Laughing and Crying* takes up Jaspers's notion of the limit situation. Laughing and crying are reactions to limit situations:

One thing at least the analysis has established: what is reflected in the contrast of laughing and crying is not the superficial duality of joy and sorrow, pleasure and pain, but a twofold limitation of human behavior as such. As *reactions* to a limit situation, they reveal typical common properties which, to be sure, cause difficulties for the interpretation of their differences.... If the pleasure principle thus breaks down with regard to laughing and crying, what then gives assurance of their contrariety? On this point, our analysis replies: their character as reactions to a crisis in human behavior as such. Contrast is possible only between things which share common features. What is common to laughing and crying is that they are answers to a limit situation.[126]

Although Plessner uses the words "reaction" and "response" almost interchangeably here, he clearly prefers the latter, since for him it is a question not of a simple biological mechanism but of a form of conduct.

A Note on "Interaction"
In clinical psychology, the word "interaction" currently enjoys great favor. It suggests more agents and moments than does the elementary couple action/reaction. It recovers the notion of a complex montage of feedbacks. Anyone using this term in contemporary language can avoid appearing backward in a world where calculating the composition of forces has been taken over by computers. Many sociologists and psychiatrists use the word "interaction," in part to avoid assigning a direction to the causal relationship. As Ludwig Wittgenstein has noted: "We react to the cause. Calling something 'the cause' is like pointing and saying, 'He's to blame!'"[127] When one speaks of an interactive relationship, a designated culprit disappears. The interactionist perspective is relativistic. It postulates a relationship among coexisting and co-responsible factors. The word "interaction" thus enables one to discuss systems or organizations whose elements are reciprocally and simultaneously causes and effects, means and ends.

This word was also created by adding a prefix to the root

"action." In the 1877 supplement to his dictionary, Littré introduced "interaction" as a neologism. His definition reads: "Action between two or more objects upon each other." He draws his example from an 1872 article in *Revue scientifique*: "Through a series of interactions and adjustments, the three surfaces were made to coincide." The article is signed by the English scholar John Tyndall (1820–1893). The original language was therefore English, and the translator readily carried over into French the English "interaction," whose constituent elements, which come from Latin, were easily integrated into a series of homologous French terms that could be accepted by the reader. Adopting the term did not present any problems to purists. The word maintained itself all the better in French in that it constituted a linguistic entity common to several languages.

It had been preceded in French by *interdépendance*, which Littré included in the 1867 edition of his dictionary as a neologism. The English term preceded the French term by some thirty years. The *Oxford English Dictionary* gives the date 1832 for the noun "interaction" and 1839 for the verb "to interact" ("to act reciprocally"). The prefix *inter-* would be used many times. It was a well-tolerated and permanent agent of lexical innovation: "interdisciplinary," "interbreed" (1864); "intercontinental" (1855); "interface" (1882); "interrelation" (1848).

Under what circumstances was this term introduced into the English language? As in France, the mechanical law of the composition of forces (which d'Alembert made one of his great principles in *Traité de dynamique*) had already been accepted for some time without causing any immediate innovations in everyday language. Yet it certainly paved the way for later innovations.

What is certain is that the word has no direct antecedents in classical, medieval, or philosophical Latin. We find *interagere* in medieval Latin, but in the very precise sense of "to serve as mediator."[128] The word was greatly supported by its nearness to the Latin *interesse* (to interest), but this same kinship existed in French without hastening the emergence of "interaction" and "to interact." In his Latin writings, Kant uses the expression *mutuum commercium*.[129] The German word *Wechselwirkung* corresponds to it in part. It appeared much more frequently in the second half of the eighteenth century. Kant's and Goethe's use of it is particularly significant.

The word "interaction" was first used by English writers to satisfy a need in scientific and philosophical language. These writers were very attentive to the works of German thinkers. One might wonder if the precedent of the German *Wechselwirkung* prompted the invention of the English word.

In the first uses of the word "interaction," physical objects interact, or possibly the body and mind of an individual. Applying the term to the realms of society and to relations among individuals seems to have come later, according to a common form of metaphoric extension. At every moment, the notion of interaction leaves open the possibility of a physico-mathematical model, even if the latter is not expressed in a formalized system. In following the semantic evolution of the English term, one must examine the history of the "interactionist" philosophies and sociologies that emerged in the United States at the beginning of the twentieth century, from James Mark Baldwin and Charles Horton Cooley to George Herbert Mead and Talcott Parsons. Today, "interaction" is useful for designating affective and verbal exchange and every type of change resulting from social ties. In contemporary psychology, it is generally believed that an individual's socialization begins thanks to the *interactive* relationship between the mother and the infant and continues in familial and school relationships. With the help of mass communication, the phrase "interactive games" has entered everyday speech. However, strict reciprocity is not found in such games, since the *user* — regardless of how many options he is presented with — is always captive to the *programmer* who prepared the system. The user makes the choices that the programmer has put into the system. However many options are possible, they are always under surveillance. The question is whether a simulacrum of choice is better than an absence of choice.

Thanks to their dynamic connotations and their forming a large lexical group, "to interact," "interaction," "interactivity," and "interactive" have in many cases supplanted the words "interdependence" and "interdependent," which the defective verb "to interdepend," being too neutral, cannot sustain. One need simply recall that "to interdepend" is used only rarely, in the third-person plural.

Interdépendance has had a century-and-a-half-long career in French. I have noted that in Littré's 1867 edition, *interdépendance* was designated a neologism. The term had been accepted by philosophers because it allowed for the expression of a solidarity among the various parts of a whole, without using such older terms as "reciprocal influence" or "sympathy," which are strongly marked by their use in the Stoic tradition. For *interdépendant*, *Trésor de la langue française* borrows its historical language from Ferdinand de Saussure's *Course in General Linguistics* (1916) and cites the expression "interdependent phonemes," where the adjective conveys what had just been said about "reciprocal relations," or "relations of internal dependence," among phonemes.

The prefix *entre-* in Old French was the vernacular doublet of *inter-*. It was widely used in the language of the late Middle Ages and of the Renaissance. Leo Spitzer sees this phenomenon as an indication of the importance of communal life: banquets, public disputes, popular festivals, debates among courtiers, and so on. In the seventeenth century, the purists of "classical" French elimi-

222

nated many terms with this type of prefix. In some cases, when there were two terms, the "learned" form survived (*interlocuteurs*, for example) to the detriment of the vernacular form (*entreparleurs*, for example). Spitzer claims that the disappearance of this category of words coincides with a loss of the sentiment of reciprocity and conviviality.[130]

English, in which the same sort of doubling did not occur (with the exception of *enter-*: "enterprise," "entertain," and so on), more easily conserved words with the prefix *inter-*. Hence the word "intercourse," whose homologue in Old French, *entrecours*, has disappeared. When Saussure, in defining one of the two forces that contributed to the creation of linguistic or dialectal areas, uses the English notion of intercourse, it is because there is no French equivalent. This appeal to English perfectly demonstrates a lacuna in French, one whose origin the historians of the French language can seek in lexical diachrony. Saussure had at his disposal *interdépendance* and *interaction*, but he did not use them. "Intercourse" — with its erotic connotation — seemed more appropriate to him to designate verbal exchange, commerce, and "communications among men," that is, actions carried out in *speech*.[131]

Dialogue in the Margins

A: I am struck by a light that is much too bright. I close my eyes immediately, irresistibly. I might purposely accentuate the closing of the lids. It is a reaction that I feel and that becomes an expressive act. When an observer shines a less bright light on my pupil, he sees it contract: it is a reaction that he notes, which I barely feel and in which I express nothing. What is taking place in the movement of the lids, in the contraction of the pupil, can be explained by physiologists. They are familiar with every part of the nervous system — the exchanges, the centers, the excitations, the subtle workings of enzymes that link sensations to these more or less visible movements. This familiarity is based on knowledge established by generations of experimenters, on countless living subjects, mostly animals. It is a knowledge that can be universalized: my reactions could have been predicted. With the exception of the movement by which I accentuated the closing of my eyelids, I am not responsible for these movements. If, to believe the voices of authority, all my movements are reactions of the same order, I am an irresponsible automaton. Whatever happens, I am excused. This is based on the absence, in the maze of reactions, of *someone* who could be held accountable and who can assume this accountability. Reactions have taken over everything I thought to be *my* place. I no longer matter. Reactions have snuffed out what I thought was freedom.

B: You might be deluding yourself: you only grant such dominion to reactions to avoid occupying your true place, to shirk your responsibility. These invasive reactions weave themselves together only to give you an alibi. You constructed them in order to subtract yourself from yourself. In a situation that you judge to be inadmissible, in a circumstance that provokes you, do you remain inactive? You decide to respond to it. You make a reply, a riposte. Language has a great reserve of words beginning with *re-* for you to use. You *decide* to react. The "no" you utter makes you a subject. At that moment, you are not thinking like an irresponsible automaton. You give yourself a task and you take responsibility for it. If it succeeds, do you not demand acknowledgment and recompense? An "I," whose name you learned when other people say "you," is thus the agent of your reaction.

A: Maybe you are also deluding yourself. Where does my will fit in? The one I'm familiar with — I suspect it's merely the result, the ultimate effect, of something that happens in me without me. The final flowering, intermittent and quickly fading, of the successively occurring events of my body. If I happen to lose my way, or perform bizarre acts in the course of my reaction, this plea can always be made. I have had nothing but good intentions. But I was overcome, taken by surprise by something I could neither know nor master. A gesture, the moment it is produced, always follows another gesture, the child of another instant, itself consecutive to its impersonal ancestor ... Everything began with this past that was not me, and which I no longer am. I can therefore trace my responsibility back to a rung — for only the first step counts — on the ladder of time, and thus there is no longer any fault that could be my own ...

B: You let yourself off too easily with the good old phrase "post hoc, ergo propter hoc." Using this phrase, one can always mitigate active responsibility with a touch of mechanical causality. In trials, defense lawyers typically assert that the murderer is the primary victim. It's true that the young homesick criminals described by Jaspers deserve pity, due to their constitution — mental weakness — and to the uprooting they had suffered. Can their case, where the excuse is justified, serve as a model for all others — and for yours in particular, where it is not applicable? Do you believe in these subterfuges? You would be like those, so numerous, who maintain two lines of thought. They are ready to receive praise, but they disappear when it's time to repair the damage: "I am *someone*, acknowledge my great merits; there is *no one*, excuse this mechanical drive."

A: I see: between the whiplash of the call "Do not fail to react" and the *a posteriori* excuse "I merely reacted," large spaces are opened up to me.

B: Come talk to me when it becomes a question of politics ...

CHAPTER FIVE

Raphael, Louis, Balthazar

The Wild Ass's Skin

Balzac never lost sight of the poetry of contemporary life: he wanted to be modern, and in his epic undertaking he neglected none of the sources of the language of his time, including the various languages instituted by new areas of knowledge. "New ideas require new words, or a new and expanded use of old words, extended and defined in their meaning."[1] On many occasions, Balzac showed an interest in etymology, historical linguistics (whose birth he witnessed), and semantic history. I must cite once again the passage that provides the title of this book:

> Often have I made the most delightful voyage, floating on a word down the abyss of the past, like an insect embarked on a blade of grass tossing on the ripples of a stream. Starting from Greece, I would get to Rome, and traverse the whole extent of modern ages. What a fine book might be written of the life and adventures of a word! ... But is it not so with every root-word? They all are stamped with a living power that comes from the soul, and which they restore to the soul through the mysterious and wonderful *action and reaction* between thought and speech.[2]

227

Later in this passage, Balzac cites as examples the words "true" (*vrai*) and "flight" (*vol*). His commentary is, of course, related more to the Cratylian rectitude of these words than to their etymology. The words "action" and "reaction" in this quotation are not examined and explained as linguistic objects; they are explanatory means, but they resist being reductive because they are charged with mystery and wonder. These words do not call for the effort of understanding. They belong to the category of concepts one uses *to make things understood*.

Balzac is one of the first French writers to embrace and work with the verb "to react" and the noun "reaction." He undoubtedly used these terms, along with others, to produce an effect of modernity in the novel. Most often, Balzac uses the verb "to react" and the noun "reaction" as words from the everyday vocabulary of his time. He uses them for high points in the narration, for emotional upheavals, for medical situations, and to indicate relationships among parties within a group:

> A terrible struggle overwhelmed his soul, reacting on his external form; and as powerful as he might have appeared, he bent like a blade of grass flattened by the storm's courier winds.[3]

> The eyes of Balthazar Claes were deeply set and surrounded by dark circles, which seemed to tell of long vigils and of terrible prostration of mind in reaction to repeated disappointments.[4]

> In the midst of the infinite joy which his triumph over justice caused him ... Jacques Collin was struck by a reaction which would have killed another man....
> "Lucien arrested!" he said to himself.[5]

> The vagaries of a woman react upon the State.[6]

228

The reaction set in after the terrible throes of fear, and joy almost overcame Diane.[7]

A stomach educated in this manner necessarily reacts on the moral sense, and corrupts it.[8]

Pierette was awakened ... by the intense suffering the moral reaction of her struggle caused in her head.[9]

The desire for gain develops a spirit of ambition, which has ever since impelled our manufacturers to react from the township to the canton, and from the canton to the department, so as to increase their profits by increasing their sales.[10]

Less often, Balzac speaks of reaction in the political sense:

I am one of the thousand victims of political reaction.[11]

This poet [Lamartine] perished miserably through political miscalculation and through a cowardice of character; at the moment when the *Chambre* wanted him to turn against anarchy by becoming reactionary again, he entered the Assembly arm in arm with Ledru-Rollin, with anarchy itself, participating in all the red plots.[12]

Clearly, Balzac readily uses "action" and "reaction" without quotation marks or italics, which would have flagged them as strange. He does not designate them as scientific, political, or medical neologisms. These new meanings were already widely accepted. But there were a few exceptions, as we will see; these relatively new terms gave rise to derivatives (*actionnel, réactionnel*, written deliberately in italics), which were not absorbed into the hodge-podge of novelistic speech and authorial commentary.

Balzac was not satisfied with borrowing from the scholars' lexicon. He dreamed of teaching them a thing or two and even of surpassing them, promoting his own philosophical-scientific views on the soul, the body, the physical world, and the destinies of men. Immodest and arrogant, he saw himself as an *inventor*. Thus he attempted to put together (almost always through fictional characters) a theory of his own invention in which action and reaction played a large part. This theory crops up in all of his work and is developed more explicitly in *Etudes philosophiques*.

The Wild Ass's Skin (1831), which the author placed at the beginning of his philosophical studies, constitutes the portal to *The Human Comedy* and can be considered the great exposition of Balzac's "system." The central motif is the depletion of vital forces, life consumed by desire, will, and thought. The wild ass's skin, a talisman that ensures the realization of desire, symbolizes an existence that shrinks as the desires of its possessor are satisfied, culminating in death. The theme of action and reaction is present as an underpinning, discreet but very obvious once some attention is given to it. The theme initially appears at the decisive moment when the hero, ready to commit suicide, heads toward a curiosity shop, where he discovers the talisman:

> Prey to that maleficent force whose solvent *action* finds a vehicle in the fluid that circulates in our nerves, he felt his frame imperceptibly invaded by the phenomenon of fluidity. The tempestuous blasts of this death-agony seemed to toss him hither and thither as waves toss a boat, so that he saw buildings and men through a haze in which everything was swaying. Wishing to shake free of the titillation produced in his mind by the reactions of his physical nature, he walked towards an old curiosity shop with the intention of finding something to occupy his senses, or else to pass the time before nightfall bargaining over the price of *objets d'art*.[13]

The milieu, the external "nature," "the heavy grey sky" *act* upon the young man's nerves, plunging him into "a painful kind of ecstasy" before producing the *reactions* that reach his soul.[14] Action and reaction represent the tie that binds the milieu to the individual. Here, at the beginning of the novel, Balzac uses these concepts by copying from the doctors of his time. The same is true when the hero notices that he has imprudently expressed a benevolent desire toward his old professor of rhetoric — and thus irremediably lost a portion of his energies:

> Raphael was white with anger; a thin line of foam showed between his quivering lips and there was a bloodthirsty expression in his eyes.... The young man sank back into his armchair. Then a sort of mental reaction set in and tears streamed from his burning eyes.[15]

"Reaction" is the word attributed to the cause of his sudden psychological transformation. But later, as the fateful denouement approaches, Balzac distances himself from the positive sciences. He implies that their notions are irrelevant to the profound psychic forces symbolized by the magic skin. "Science saddens man," he says through a character in "Seraphita."[16] In the part of the novel titled "The Agony," Raphael de Valentin, in deteriorating health and disturbed over the shrinking of the talisman, consults a series of scientific authorities who might know how to prevent the magic skin from shrinking. The zoologist knows only classifications and terms. Planchette, the professor of mechanics, explains at great length the principles and workings of the hydraulic press in terms of action and reaction.[17] But this press breaks during the decisive experiment. The "reagents" of the chemist Japhet are no more helpful.[18] Medical science, in turn, has nothing to say about what caused the physical deterioration of the hero or about what might save him. Balzac takes an ironic distance from the favorite

231

motifs of medical discourse, which he dramatizes as verbiage. In passages reminiscent of Molière, at once comical and moving, he compares and contrasts the contradictory theories of contemporary medicine, dividing them among the three figures consulted, who are at once fictive and easily recognizable: the materialist Brisset (Broussais), the spiritualist Cameristus (Récamier), and the skeptic Maugredie (Magendie).[19] The first speaks of the irritation of the stomach, where "the disorder has reached the brain." He suggests putting "leeches... on the epigastrum." The second suggests a disorder in the "vital principle": in the pathological movement, "the brain affects the epigastric region." He recommends "treating his morals." The third declares: "As for knowing if his epigastrum has reacted on his brain or *vice versa*, we might be able to know that after he's dead."[20] Condescendingly, Maugredie accepts both therapeutic propositions simultaneously, without much faith in either one. Balzac is perfectly well informed on medical matters, schematizing them in his caricatures. We may assume that he was familiar with *Le Dictionnaire des sciences médicales*, which his father owned and in which, as we have seen, reaction was the subject of a long entry by Jean-François Delpit.[21]

"Louis Lambert"

Balzac, so familiar with the vocabulary of medicine and physiology, so inclined to put his confidence in the speculations of magnetizers, dreamed of a great personal synthesis and delegated this ambition to fictional beings. Before the action of the novel begins, Raphael de Valentin has shut himself up to write a *Theory of the Will*; Louis Lambert also undertakes a *Treatise on the Will*. Balzac does not relate Raphael's ideas; rather, it is through the character's fate that the novelist's theory is symbolically enacted. The work attributed to Raphael is but the frame of an absent mirror — the empty and allusive mirror of the novel itself. Yet among the facts described about Louis Lambert's life, the narrator also expounds (ostensibly from memory) the main features of a doctrine whose manuscript has been confiscated — clearly a vestige of many a musing from Balzac's youth. For Louis Lambert, the doctrine of will is closely bound to the idea of reaction: Lambert, the narrator explains, sees our Will as a substance "spontaneously reacting."[22]

Reaction, for Balzac, is a turbulence or a reversal affecting the distribution of a substance that is life, thought, or will. The metaphor of fluid plays a large role here. It allows for the representation of a hypothetical material phenomenon and lends itself, by extension, to the expression of an active spiritual presence that sustains and surpasses the material order. Whether it is a question of an electrical flow, an ethereal substance, thought, or feeling, Balzac delights in images of concentration followed by outpouring, spurting, spouting, or projection.

Beyond the phenomena palpably taking place in measurable time and space are forces *of another order*. The hypotheses Balzac develops (that is, recounts) at times suggest an extension of the material forces that a calculating science is about to conquer, while at other times it is a question of purely spiritual powers, bearers of love and visionary insight. Balzac sees this as both a philosophical dilemma and a double manifestation of a unitary principle to be reached through "mediation."[23] In "Les Proscrits," the theologian Sigier "wedded the whole universe with his gaze and described the substance of God Himself, overflowing like an immense river, from the center to the edges and from the edges to the center."[24] On a narrative level, it is simply a play on the literal and metaphoric meanings of the word "river." One finds in Balzac an assurance concerning the irrefutable superiority of "Spiritual Worlds" over "human science," as well as the desire to establish a reciprocity between spirit and matter by spiritualizing matter and materializing spirit.[25] We find ourselves wavering

233

between a grand materialism (along the lines of Diderot) and a pan-psychism proclaiming the universal reign of spirit.

This double philosophical slant is evident in the fine tale — with a distinctly autobiographical component — titled first "Biographical Information on Louis Lambert," then "Louis Lambert" (which, along with "Les Proscrits" and "Seraphita," appears in *Le Livre mystique* of 1835):

> Louis, at first purely Spiritualist, had been irresistibly led to recognise the Material conditions of Mind. Confounded by the facts of analysis at the moment when his heart still gazed with yearning at the clouds that floated in Swedenborg's heaven, he had not yet acquired the necessary powers to produce a coherent system, compactly cast in a piece, as it were.[26]

When Louis Lambert's doctrine becomes "materialist," all observable phenomena are traced back to an omnipresent "ethereal substance." In the human being, this is transmuted by the brain (which plays the role of a matrass or distiller) before becoming will. Then, in projecting itself into external things, the human will comes to penetrate and dominate the primitive substance it finds in animate and inanimate beings. According to the system related by the narrator from memory, it is here that considerations of action and reaction play their part:

> Having set forth these principles, he proposed to class the phenomena of human life in two series of distinct results, demanding, with the ardent insistency of conviction, a special analysis for each. In fact, having observed in almost every type of created thing two separate motions, he assumed, nay, he asserted, their existence in our human nature, and designated this vital antithesis *Action* and *Reaction*. "A desire," he said, "is a fact completely accomplished in our will before

234

it is accomplished externally." Hence the sum-total of our Volitions and our Ideas constitutes *Action*,[27] and the sum-total of our external acts he called *Reaction*.... The inner Being, the Being of Action — the word he used to designate an unknown specialisation — the mysterious nexus of fibrils to which we owe the inadequately investigated powers of thought and will — in short, the nameless entity which sees, acts, foresees the end, and accomplishes everything before expressing itself in any physical phenomenon — must, in conformity with its nature, be free from the physical conditions by which the external Being of Reaction, the visible man, is fettered in its manifestation.[28]

The doctrine is far from clear. One can understand that the Being of Action, according to Balzac, performs its operations in pure interiority. It is angelic in nature.[29] It has, in particular, the privilege of moving around in a region that lies beyond the obstacles and resistances of the external world. The Being of Action "sees." When transported at a distance, it is in a state of ecstasy. The narrator remembers Louis Lambert's remarks:

> Certain men, having had a glimpse of some phenomena of the natural working of the Being of Action, were, like Swedenborg, carried away above this world by their ardent soul, thirsting for poetry, and filled with the Divine spirit.... [T]he Being of Action ... can abstract itself completely from the Being of Reaction, bursting its envelope, and piercing walls by its potent vision.[30]

Thus he is able to see other angels. The path is cleared for all the telepathies and transmigrations that Balzac, in his excesses of enthusiasm, believed possible. The individual may remain motionless: he travels purely in thought. The Being of Reaction, on the other hand, intervenes in the world, attempts to take hold of it and effect changes in it. In the doctrine the narrator attributes to Louis

Lambert, all transformative activity and practical effectiveness are the effects of the Being of Reaction. The same holds true for magnetism, which Balzac, in his support of universal fluidity, firmly believed in. How is magnetic attraction exercised over others?

> [T]he will might be accumulated by a contractile effort of the inner man, and then, by another effort, projected, or even imparted, to material objects. Thus, the whole force of a man must have the property of reacting on other men, and of infusing into them an essence foreign to their own, if they did not protect themselves against such an aggression.[31]

By defining reaction in terms of a conflict triggering a dramatic story, Balzac remains close to Bichat's "agonistic" conception. But Bichat (whose name Balzac occasionally mentions) had seen the capacity for reaction as a general property in life, before finding it more specifically in the brain's locomotive "animal" response to sensations. Balzac restricts reaction to the "external" being and reserves a different role for the actional being, which does not compromise itself outside its own thought, except to perform sudden acts of clairvoyance and contemplation at a distance. This represents an unusual reworking of Bichat's notion of "two lives." Whereas classical physics and medical physiology thought of action and reaction as inseparable, attributing reaction as much to inorganic matter as to vegetable or animal life, Balzac dissociates them, creates a theoretical schism, and attributes two distinct lives to the actional being and the reactional being, thus reestablishing a duality that elsewhere he would have liked to overcome. The opposition of the outside and the inside reinstalls dualism within a system governed initially by the postulate of a single substance. The tragedy of division supplants a monism of principle.

The individual's attempt to focus exclusively on his actional being is both admirable and fatal. Balzac leaves open the question of whether this focus produces knowledge, madness, or both. The images of reflection and reflux through which he explains the fate of his hero, Louis Lambert, evoke the withdrawal and shoring up of psychic energy. In this regard, Balzac's theories make one think of the concept of introversion that Carl Jung (so well informed about Romantic thought) proposed at the beginning of the twentieth century, making it a tool for the understanding of psychosis. The onset of adolescence (the "second age") marks the beginning of Louis Lambert's introversion: "Checked in his career, and not yet strong enough to contemplate the higher spheres, he contemplated his inmost self. I then perceived in him the struggle of the Mind reacting on itself, and trying to detect the secrets of its own nature, like a physician who watches the course of his own disease."[32] What I have just called psychic energy, Balzac, on the previous page, calls "nerve-fluid," the more common name of which, at the beginning of the twentieth century, would be "libido" (from Albert Moll to Freud and Jung). In any case, the schism between the actional being and the reactional being is closely tied, as we will see, to the madness of Balzac's hero, who, at the end of the story, presents some symptoms of what today is called schizophrenia. This schism is a *schizis*, in the sense of the word used in 1911 by Eugen Bleuler, who coined the term "schizophrenia."

The story of the brilliant child, told by his only friend, begins with a series of separations. To satisfy his appetite for learning, Louis agrees to leave his father and mother; he is educated by an ecclesiastical uncle who has an impressive library. A new separation, for which Mme de Staël is responsible, tears him from this rural world and allows him to benefit — a fatal favor — from instruction at the Collège de Vendôme (where Balzac studied). There Lambert finds a prison world. The condition of the captive

child in this setting is similar to that found in religious confine-
ment and military barracks. Lambert will be deprived of his previous freedom and the natural world of the countryside to which he
has been so close.[33] An "uprooted" flower, subsisting on the pesti-
lential air of the boarding school, he suffers from the devastating
illness of "homesickness" or "nostalgia" — which, according to the
medical doctrine of the day, usually attacks individuals who have
lost their native air. Everything overwhelms him: subjected to the
miasma of communal life and continual punishments, Louis Lambert develops the most characteristic type of melancholy: "With
his elbow on his desk and his head supported on his left hand,
he spent the hours of study gazing at the trees in the court or
the clouds in the sky." Although the superiority of his precocious
spirit makes him more knowledgeable than his masters, he must
obey their rules. He thus takes refuge in a "life of purely inward
emotions." His face shows clearly that his psychic energy is wan-
ing; he turns pale, and his eyes lose their spark: "At one moment
astonishingly clear and piercing, at another full of heavenly sweet-
ness, those eyes became dull, almost colourless, as it seemed, when
he was lost in meditation. They then looked like a window from
which the sun had suddenly vanished after lighting it up." What
remains of the Being of Action in Louis Lambert is expended on
his friendship — a "conjugal regard" — with the schoolmate who
becomes the narrator: "How delightful it was to me to feel his
soul reacting on my own!" The more Louis retreats into interiority, the paler he becomes, until he turns as white as the angels he
contemplates. In class, while the forces of the Being of Action and
of pure clairvoyance overtake him, he appears to be daydreaming
and idle. As punishment, extra work rains down upon him. "You
are doing nothing!" the supervisors scold him. He has fled the
penitentiary constraints of the boarding school to take refuge in
his own inner space, which brings him closer to the "celestial"

spaces. He thus becomes all action (according to the meaning adopted by Balzac), although he appears unoccupied. In this flight, he repatriates himself.

The religious model is clear. In the narrator's words, Lambert becomes "like the martyrs who smiled in the midst of suffering." The hypothesized separation between the body and the inner being, which is applicable to dreams, is radicalized to the point of becoming a mode of existence in itself, a waking dissociation. In the story, one finds an extremely indicative symbolic translation of this hermetism: the retreat into interiority is depicted in the image of the casket into which Lambert locks the *Treatise on the Will* he is working on. Malicious schoolmates betray the secret. The professors confiscate the box, obtain the key, and take possession of the manuscript, which they can see as nothing but rubbish. They are insensitive to the genius's discoveries. Thus Lambert's words have been received by no one, except the friend in whom he confides and who must rely on his own memory to explain Lambert's philosophy. A new and unfortunate separation then occurs, this time between the two friends, when after a long fever the narrator is taken out of the boarding school by his mother. This breaks the bond that has been consecrated by the "coupling" of the two nicknames into a single name: "Poet-and-Pythagoras." At this point, Lambert prophesies his own death: "You will live, . . . but I shall die. . . . I shall be left alone in this desert!"[35] With the exception of befriending the narrator, Louis has not participated in any sort of community. His disappointing excursion to Paris is marked by a surprising event. The scene takes place in the theater, where Louis is overwhelmed to the point of paroxysm by the beauty of a woman he notices in the box next to his speaking affectionately with her lover. Lambert barely resists the "almost overpowering desire" to kill this man. When he sees the woman glancing at another man, his sanity reaches the breaking point. At the furthest extremes of solitude, his murderous impulses — the destructive raptus — have almost reached their goal. But it will be himself that Louis puts to death.

In the lyrical and chaotic systematization of his brilliant hero's doctrine (which is certainly his own), Balzac added an opposition between motion and resistance. In a series of fragments attributed to Louis's visionary wisdom, Balzac writes:

> Motion is the product of a force generated by the Word and by Resistance, which is Matter. But for Resistance, Motion would have had no results; its action would have been infinite. Newton's gravitation is not a law, but an effect of the general law of universal motion. . . . Motion, acting in proportion to Resistance, produces a result which is Life. As soon as one or the other is the stronger, Life ceases. . . . No portion of Motion is wasted; it always produces number; still, it can be neutralised by disproportionate resistance, as in minerals.[36]

Louis Lambert's downfall is due to the disproportion between his spiritual capacity for motion and the material resistance he is incapable of overcoming. His body, weakened by the brutalities he endures and by his nostalgia, is no longer able to produce motion by combining force with the "word." The boarding school, and later the money-dominated society of Paris, form the obstacles against which Louis Lambert renounces opposing any "reactional" effort. Faced with these obstacles, he regresses to a vegetable state, becoming no more than an unknown flower:

> [W]hat name can I give to the power that ties my hands and shuts my mouth, and drags me in a direction opposite to my vocation? . . . If my suffering could serve as an example, I could understand it; but no, I suffer unknown. This is perhaps as much the act of Providence as the fate of the flower that dies unseen in the heart of

the virgin forest, where no one can enjoy its perfume or admire its splendour. Just as that blossom vainly sheds its fragrance to the solitude, so do I, here in a garret, give birth to ideas that no one can grasp.[37]

The more his inhibition grows, the more immobilized and mineralized he becomes, while the inner faculty of his so-called Being of Action remains intact.

In the great "Letter to His Uncle" acknowledging his defeat, the hero's description of himself appears (to the reader today) to re-create a psychotic episode yet merely pushes to extremes the affirmation of the Being of Action and the negativity of the Being of Reaction:

> I am by no means in love with the two syllables *Lam* and *bert*; whether spoken with respect or with contempt over my grave, they can make no change in my ultimate destiny. I feel myself strong and energetic; I might become a power; I feel in myself a life so luminous that it might enlighten a world, and yet I am shut up in a sort of mineral as perhaps are the colours you admire on the neck of an Indian bird.[38]

Pauline's admirable devotion does not save the hero. He writes passionate letters to her, confessions of a mind that, according to the narrator, is "feeding on itself." Balzac attributes to Lambert the following self-analysis: "Thus, when I first met you, I felt the presence of an angelic nature.... At once I felt the awful reaction which casts my expansive soul back on itself; the smile you had brought to my lips suddenly turned to a bitter grimace." To this feeling of repression is added that of a subtraction, a draining of energy: "There are moments when the spirit of vitality seems to abandon me. I feel bereft of all strength." Complete madness comes shortly before his marriage to Pauline: it manifests itself first in a cataleptic state, in which Lambert remains "motionless for fifty-nine hours, his eyes staring, neither speaking nor eating."[39] Next comes a state of "extreme terror," an incurable "melancholy." "He thought himself unfit for marriage." He then attempts to castrate himself.[40] In the letters to his uncle and Pauline, the image of a pitiless demon who *mows down* flowers, and the splitting of Lambert's name into two syllables anticipate this attempt at self-mutilation.[41] The best doctors are consulted: "The Paris physicians pronounced him incurable, and unanimously advised his being left in perfect solitude, with nothing to break the silence that was needful for his very improbable recovery."[42] The final image of the story represents both a triumph of the "inner life" and the worst defeat of the Being of Reaction. In the dark, low-ceilinged room where he is secluded, Louis Lambert does not react to the appearance of the narrator, who was once his closest friend in school. Nothing remains of the bond of action and reaction they had shared. Now Louis does not even notice his visitor's presence:

> He made no reply.... He was standing, his elbows resting on the cornice of the low wainscot, which threw his body forward, so that it seemed bowed under the weight of his bent head. His hair was as long as a woman's, falling over his shoulders and hanging about his face, giving him a resemblance to the busts of the great men of the time of Louis XIV. His face was perfectly white. He constantly rubbed one leg against the other, with a mechanical action that nothing could have checked, and the incessant friction of the bones made a doleful sound.... I opened the shutters a little way, and could see the expression of Lambert's countenance. Alas! he was wrinkled, white-headed, his eyes dull and lifeless as those of the blind. His features seemed all drawn upwards to the top of his head. I made several attempts to talk to him, but he did not hear me. He was a wreck snatched from the grave, a conquest of life from death — or of death from life!

242

> I stayed for about an hour, sunk in unaccountable dreams, and
> lost in painful thought. I listened to Mademoiselle de Villenoix, who
> told me every detail of this life — that of a child in arms.
>
> Suddenly Louis ceased rubbing his legs together, and said slowly
> — *"The angels are white."*[43]

The once graceful body is no more than a living skeleton. His long
hair is the only vestige of his boyish femininity. In Lambert's pos-
ture, monotonous movement, and lack of physical contact, twentieth-century readers believed they recognized the stereotypical
symptoms of schizophrenia as defined by Bleuler (itself the heir,
in psychiatric nomenclature, of K.L. Kahlbaum's catatonia). The
ambivalence that characterizes the illness as it is known today, and
which is found already in some of Louis Lambert's remarks, is seen
again in the contradiction between the horrible spectacle of this
downfall and the hypothesis of a clairvoyance accepted by the narrator and Pauline. Words and gestures that, on the one hand, indicate automatism and hallucination could also, on the other hand,
represent simply the remains left behind by a life absorbed in the
contemplation of a higher truth. Such is the dilemma Romanticism
granted to madness, and its star has not yet fallen:

> An involuntary instinct warned me, making me doubt whether Louis
> had really lost his reason. I was indeed well assured that he neither
> saw nor heard me; but the sweetness of his tone, which seemed to
> reveal heavenly happiness, gave his speech an amazing effect. These
> words, the incomplete revelation of an unknown world, rang in our
> souls like some glorious distant bells in the depth of a dark night. I
> was no longer surprised that Mademoiselle de Villenoix considered
> Lambert to be perfectly sane. The life of the soul had perhaps sub-
> dued that of the body....
>
> "Louis must, no doubt, appear to be mad," said she. "But he is

not, if the term mad ought only to be used in speaking of those whose brain is for some unknown cause diseased, and who can show no reason in their actions. Everything in my husband is perfectly balanced. Though he did not actively recognise you, it is not that he did not see you. He has succeeded in detaching himself from his body, and discerns us under some other aspect — what that is, I know not.[44]

This being with "eyes dull and lifeless as those of the blind" is thus capable of *another* sort of vision. This living-dead man may have gained access to the contemplation of the highest truth. Balzac plays with the uncertainty. Could it be that what I have called ambivalence is simply another version of what, in other passages of the story, appears as a fusion of opposites? Louis Lambert is a child with the ideas of an adult, an adolescent with a woman's charms.[45] He is both an androgyne and a *puer senex*. Could he not also be both madman and genius, defeated and triumphant all at once? Balzac cannot articulate his defeat without mirroring it in a secret victory. In this way, Louis Lambert proves to have a mind powerful enough to conceive of a great system of human powers that could explain and predict the very adversity to which he succumbs. The narrator remarks: "This disorder, a mystery as deep as that of sleep, was connected with the scheme of evidence which Lambert had set forth in his *Treatise on the Will*."[46] Does Lambert grasp the law governing the world as a whole? The question remains unanswered. The book one reads is not the *Treatise* (destroyed by the Fathers) but the "intellectual history" composed much later by a witness who is not sure he has understood his brilliant friend or is able to communicate the full scope of his thought.[47] Hence the composite aspect of the work that Balzac strove to write. It is a broken book, composed, or de-composed, in fragments, a book filled with lacunae, made up of remainders, in which Lambert's ideas appear only in tatters: a few recovered letters, a few sentences gathered by

Pauline, a few conversations preserved in the narrator's memory. This is both because Louis Lambert's fate is *incomplete* and because those who speak of him profess themselves incapable of fully understanding him. Balzac structures the narrative voice in such a way as to keep his hero beyond our grasp and to produce an effect of superiority in his favor. Louis Lambert is the *representation* of an intellectual hero who encapsulates scientific knowledge going back to the most ancient tradition and begins it anew.

The Death of Balthazar

In "The Quest for the Absolute," when a passion for chemistry overtakes Balthazar Claes and he begins to squander his fortune on scientific equipment and costly "reagents,"[48] his wife notices a great change in him:

> Before very long there set in a *reaction of the mental on the physical* existence. The havoc this wrought was scarcely visible at first, save to the eyes of a loving woman, who watched for a clue to her husband's inmost thoughts in their slightest manifestations. She could often scarcely keep back the tears as she saw him fling himself down after dinner into an easy-chair by the fireside, and sit there with his eyes fixed on one of the dark panels, gloomy, abstracted, utterly heedless of the dead silence about him. She watched with terror the gradual changes for the worse in the face that love had made sublime for her; it seemed as if the life of the soul was day by day withdrawing itself and leaving an expressionless mask. At times his eyes took on a glassy color, as if the faculty of sight in them had been converted to a power of inner vision.[49]

Physical destruction has been wrought by the inner tyranny of the idea. This transformation is progressive and slow and is but one modality of reaction. There is another one, brutally sudden, when

Balthazar is impoverished, aged, and tormented by children in the town who throw mud at him: "His decrepit body could not bear the terrible reaction it was undergoing in the higher region of his feelings; he fell, struck down by an attack of paralysis."[50] No less sudden is the old man's last awakening, in which he throws off the "paralysis that bound his limbs": the flash of intuition concerning the truth he sought. On the last page of the story, three events occur in rapid succession: a newspaper's announcement of the discovery and sale of the Absolute by the "Polish mathematician" (M. de Wierzchownia); the sudden solution of the enigma by the paralyzed scholar, who briefly recovers movement and speech; and the scholar's instantaneous death, which makes his ultimate knowledge useless. Thus the shock that activates thought is fatal. This chain of events verifies the extraordinary "influence of the moral on the physical." Balzac narrates these events without repeating the word "reaction" each time, which would have obscured the *scene* in favor of the *explanation*. Yet the absence of the term I am tracing does not alter the fact that the arrangement of the fatal denouement is conditioned by a knowledge of the medical theory that Balzac shares with his readers:

> Suddenly the dying man raised himself on his elbows; his glance seemed like lightning to his terror-stricken children, the hair that fringed his temples rose, every wrinkle in his face quivered with a fiery spirit, a breath of inspiration passed over his face and made it sublime. He raised a hand, clenched in frenzy, with the cry of Archimedes — EUREKA! (*I have found it!*) he called in piercing tones, then he fell back on his bed with the heavy sound of an inert body, and died with an awful moan. And up until the moment when the doctor closed them, his contorted eyes expressed his regret at being unable to leave to Science the solution of the great enigma revealed to him too late, as the veil was torn away by the fleshless fingers of Death.[51]

246

The precipitating event is a newspaper article, read softly at Balthazar's bedside. Although on the verge of death, Balthazar understands the news and realizes that someone else has discovered the Absolute, or, to use his phrase, the "one element common to all substances."[52] In a last effort of thought, Balthazar reaches (or thinks he reaches) the truth that until this point has obstinately eluded him. This illumination, overshadowed by rage, is unbearable. The formula, so dear to Balzac, of the fatal thought puts into play both the response to a stimulus (a mechanical schema) and the dissipation of the resources of vital force (a quantitative energy schema). Balzac simply reveals the ambiguities of the results expected from reaction: the most intense awakening or annihilation.

A similar ending is found in the story "Adieu." Balzac's final classification placed this story among the philosophical studies to which *The Wild Ass's Skin* and "The Quest for the Absolute" also belong. In this story, Stephanie de Vandières goes mad at the crossing of the Berezina when she is separated from her lover, Colonel Philippe de Sucy, who is taken prisoner by the Russians. When he returns to France, he finds her in a state of complete mental deterioration in a country house, where she is looked after by a doting uncle who is a doctor. She has become like an uncivilized creature, incapable of pronouncing any word other than "Adieu." Philippe de Sucy imagines he can make Stephanie relive the exact moment in which she lost her reason. In winter, in the French countryside, he organizes an immense reconstruction of the battle of the Berezina. This time — for such is his plan — instead of being separated from the lover to whom she cried "Adieu!" on the battlefield, she will see him at her side, reassuring her of his presence. Might not this jar her from her madness, restoring her to her life prior to its interruption by the sudden separation? This is the very sort of reenactment recommended by doctors who counted on reaction. The plan succeeds, the wall of madness is broken, thought returns, and with it comes an unforeseen and irremediable disaster:

> For a moment quick as a flash, her eyes shone with the unintelligent lucidity we admire in the bright eyes of birds; then she brushed her hand over her forehead with the keen expression of someone meditating, contemplating this living memory, this past life enacted before her eyes; turning her head toward Philippe, she *saw him*. A terrible silence came over the crowd. The colonel was breathless and dared not speak; the doctor cried. Stephanie's handsome face colored faintly, then deepened, until she beamed with a young girl's sparkling freshness. Her face turned crimson. Life and happiness, animated by a burning intelligence, spread over her like flames. A convulsive shaking rocked her from her feet to her heart. Then these phenomena, which broke forth in a moment, were as if brought together as Stephanie's eyes darted a celestial ray, an animated flame. She was living; she was thinking! She shuddered, perhaps from terror! God himself unbound her dead tongue once more, and again injected his fire into this spent soul. *Human will* came with its electrical torrents and revived this body from which she had so long been absent.
>
> "Stephanie," cried the colonel.
>
> "Oh, Philippe, it's you," said the poor countess.
>
> She threw herself into the colonel's outstretched, trembling arms, and the lovers' embrace frightened the onlookers. Stephanie began to weep. Suddenly her tears were dry, she stiffened as if struck by lightning, and in a faint voice whispered, "Adieu Philippe. I love you. Adieu!"
>
> "She's dead," cried the colonel, opening his arms.[53]

Here, instead of speaking of "reaction," Balzac invokes the surge of human will, that singular substance combining the "celestial" and the "electric." In "Louis Lambert," Balzac described our Will as a substance "spontaneously reacting." And according to the physician Jean-François Delpit, the culmination of "moral reaction" lies precisely in the will: "Moral reaction originates in courage, in the strong determination of the soul that rises above its suffering, masters the impressions caused by this suffering, and replaces them with acts of will."[54]

Provoked by thought, reaction, for the inventor as for the lover, revives life, brings blood to the face, rekindles the fire in the eyes — and brings death.

According to the system sketched by Balzac, the paroxysm of reaction is always marked, as it is with Stephanie, by a substantial rise in heat and a reddening of the face, by fire in the eyes. For Balzac, the ancient doctrine of the rays projected by the eyes is still in full force. These are the vital energies that, long repressed — a term he often uses — suddenly surge forth, at the risk of mortal loss. We saw this phenomenon in the scene of Balthazar's death. And we see it again in Raphael de Valentin's final hour, in his sleep, just before his last wish kills him: "His white cheeks had a lively pink flush on them.... His sleep was an easy one, a pure and even breath was issuing from his red lips." Upon awakening, he looks at Pauline, and she is frightened: "Your eyes are blazing."[55]

CHAPTER SIX

Dead World, Beating Hearts

Senancour

Rêveries sur la nature primitive de l'homme is an important book from the turn of the nineteenth century. In it, Senancour sketches an image of the world that conforms to the scientific thought of his time. It is a disenchanted image, one that acknowledges the omnipotence of mechanical necessity. The distinction between good and evil is no longer operable. God did not create the world, and no safeguard can be expected. One must accept an implacable law:

> All bodies are compounds: every durable aggregation is necessarily organized; every organized being receives the action of other compounds, and reacts upon them: it is therefore sensitive and active. It knows by feeling; it wills by acting. If its organization is more complicated, it retains the imprint of past sensations; hence it has the ability to enact several different reactions; it deliberates, it exercises choice. This series of received and returned impulses makes up the *self* of each organized being....
>
> While man, in imprinting a movement, is simply a secondary and reactive cause, he believes himself to be a primary cause because he does not have the distinct feeling of the prior cause.[1]

251

The material fact reigns supreme. The values to which humans might be attached disappear and become no more than subjective illusions:

> Everything in nature is indifferent, for everything is necessary: everything is beautiful, for everything is determined. The individual is nothing as an isolated being: his cause, his fate are beyond him. Everything exists absolutely, invincibly, with no other cause, with no fate other than itself, no laws other than those of nature, no product other than its permanence.... Beauty, truth, justice, evil, and chaos exist only for the weakness of mortals.... The same earth contains prosperous orchards and destructive volcanoes. The scoundrel triumphs, the hero dies; the orchard becomes barren, the volcano burns out; one same ruin consumes both the animate and the inanimate, buried by the same oblivion; and in a renewed world, no trace remains of what was abhorred or worshiped in a world that has been obliterated.[2]

Nature creates and destroys indifferently: "One same fecundity will produce the insect that will live one day, and the star that will last a thousand centuries; one same necessity will forever decompose the ephemeral worm and the equally transitory sun." One simple law of action and reaction governs the world through and through, from inanimate matter to the higher forms of life. All these phenomena result in "received and returned impulses":

> All compound beings therefore sense their existence, but only the more organized ones are aware of the *self* or the succession of sensations produced by the impulses they have received, and which produce the impulses they exert. This sole difference indicates the degrees of animality, from the least organized compound possible to the most organized possible. The *self* of any organized being

is therefore nothing more than this succession of impulses which must necessarily end in the decomposition of the organs, just as it necessarily began with their formation.[3]

As Senancour sees it at this point in his life, the world is but matter in the process of becoming, ruled according to the principles established by Laplace's mechanics, the philosophy of sensualism, and the human science that knows only organs and secretions. According to this absolute determinism, man's thought and will are the products of physical motions and disappear according to these same motions. But while outside us one order of things is replaced by another, never, in our hearts, will new worlds come to replace those we have lost. We remain dispossessed. All the rest is a dream from which it is impossible to tear ourselves away. It is true that much later, in speaking of flowers, Senancour will claim that they manifest "a thought which is veiled and guarded as a secret by the material world."[4] Senancour — like Mallarmé, and almost as radically — is also one of the first to take cognizance of an inner death: "But in me, . . . barren winter still remains . . . and at the age when life should really begin my only mood was one of life-weariness."[5] A reader today might be tempted to associate this confession with Obermann's decision to be a writer: "[T]here is nothing for me but writing."[6] The project of writing asserts itself like a posthumous vocation. Senancour writes in order to capture a few moments of improbable happiness, to deplore their loss, to replace them with dreams, and not, as Mallarmé would wish, to "endow our stay here with authenticity." It is not easy for Senancour to resign himself; the best he can offer is the unreconciled injunction: "[L]et us perish resisting, and if annihilation must be our portion, let us not make it a just one."[7]

Goethe, Wordsworth, Novalis, Keats

The image of a world traversed by necessity and destruction appeared irrevocable to Senancour. But in his time, other writers did not resign themselves to this. They wanted to recall enchantments, angels, the spirit of God — or, more simply, meaning.

First consider the evidence offered by Goethe. He was a poet who used the language of science, with the notable exception of mathematics. Yet he opted for an organicist and vitalist orientation in science. It was a polemical choice, one that made him sensitive to the stakes associated with scientific words. He understood that adopting a conceptual tool can decide in advance the response to any question. Hence, in a late writing on natural history, Goethe deplored the fact that the vocabulary of mechanistic thought, developed in France by eighteenth-century science, had imposed itself to the point of hampering the manner in which scholars who had a less simplistic nature of nature and life expressed their ideas: "The nation, having adopted sensualist philosophy, became accustomed to using materialistic, mechanistic, and atomistic expressions; and since linguistic usage is inherited and imposed even upon everyday conversation, as soon as it rises into the spiritual realm, the language resists those eminent men seeking to express their views."[8]

In criticizing the vocabulary of mechanistic science, Goethe also considered the problems of art and of the language used in relation to art. He was the first to understand that the terms applied to the living being also apply to the work of art. In his lexical considerations, he thus quickly moved from the representation of nature to aesthetics. Condemning the use of the word "composition" by the French naturalists (as in "unity of composition"), Goethe recalls that he likes it no more in the realm of art: he finds it "degrading" (*herabwürdigend*); one should not say that the painter "composes" or designate the musician as a "composer."

254

"If one or the other truly deserves the name artist, he does not assemble the parts of his works but rather develops a certain internal image, a higher note [*Anklang*], in accord with nature and art."[9] In fact, etymologically, "to compose" is to place side by side, to juxtapose, and to this idea Goethe prefers that of organic growth. This opposition between composition and organic growth is similar to the one established by Coleridge (who was inspired by Goethe) between fancy and imagination. Fancy gathers together elements that remain external to each other. It is a power of aggregation and simple recombination, whereas imagination fashions new and living beings through an organic power of unification and totalization. Coleridge even ventures a neologism, speaking of an esemplastic power — constructed "from the Greek words, *eis hen plattein*, i.e. to shape into one." But the opposition between two approaches (the analytic and the synthetic, the rational and the intuitive, fancy and imagination) is itself a juxtaposition, which demands to be surmounted in a higher synthesis that reconciles them to the benefit of a higher organicity. In chapter 13 of *Biographia Literaria*, Coleridge writes: "[G]rant me a nature having two contrary forces, the one of which tends to expand infinitely, while the other strives to apprehend or find itself in this infinity, and I will cause the world of intelligences with the whole system of their representations to rise up before you." Counteracting forces and the interpenetrations of these forces give "existence to the living principle and to the process of our own self-consciousness."[10] Concerning the power of metamorphosis animating nature, Goethe (who no doubt provided Coleridge with the image) writes, "It is like a centrifugal force and would lose itself in the infinite if it lacked a counterweight: I want to speak of the power of specification, the headstrong capacity to persist, which is inherent to all beings who come to exist, a centripetal force that cannot ultimately be touched by anything outside itself."[11]

255

Desiring above all to affirm the bonds uniting all natural phenomena, Goethe sees the world as a field of multiple actions and
reactions, but he does not use the terms in the mechanical sense
they had for Laplace or Senancour; he gives them the meaning
they had in the vocabulary of the qualitative physics of the medieval Peripatetics or the Renaissance neo-Stoics, for whom the
world was an *animans*, a great animated being. He seeks his sources
in the vitalist intuition that preceded the geometrization of the
universe. He sees nature as a great Weaver and feels that the concrete relationships traversing universal life are irreducible and
cannot be translated into mathematical formulas. Their meaning
reveals itself only to the mind's eye, which, full of fire, is no less
a fleshly eye. Goethe is thus horrified by the calculations of the
mechanism adepts, who want to subject life to the equations of
physics. Like William Blake, he made Newton his bête noire
(without being familiar with his alchemical speculations, with
which he would undoubtedly have sympathized). He opposed
Newton's optics with another theory of light, an objectified theory of the visual experience:

> Light and darkness engage each other in continuous contest. Action
> and reaction of both cannot be denied. Light hastens from sun to
> earth with enormous flexibility and speed and represses darkness.
> Any artificial light acts in a similar manner within a defined space.
> But as soon as this indescribable action ceases, darkness demon-
> strates its power by quickly reasserting itself in shadow, twilight and
> night.[12]

The repressed night gains the upper hand. These sentences recall
the Freudian "return of the repressed." I do not think this is a
coincidence: many elements of Freud's vocabulary are found in
Goethe. Goethe vitalizes the relationship between light and dark-

256

ness. His theory of light represents a visionary optics, fascinated by images of struggling forces. Here, as on many other occasions, he seeks to express the forces and forms of nature with an ambition that has nothing to do with analyzing and calculating its components or parameters. As practiced by Goethe, scientific inquiry proceeds by degrees, through analogical contiguity, from one type of phenomenon to the next. He announces its methodology in his important essay "The Experiment as Mediator Between Object and Subject":

> All things in nature, especially the commoner forces and elements, exist in a perpetual relation of action and reaction; we can say that each phenomenon is connected with countless others just as we can say that a point of light floating in space sends its rays in all directions. Thus when we have done an experiment of this type, found this or that piece of empirical evidence, we can never be careful enough in studying what lies next to it or derives directly from it. This investigation should concern us more than the discovery of what is related to it. To multiply every single experiment through its variations is the real task of the scientific researcher.[13]

The opposition between action and reaction is a generalized principle, of which the antagonism between darkness and light is but a specific case. Action and reaction are at work in all the bipolar couples of which nature as a whole is the theater. Hence, in his reflections on color, Goethe inserts this universalizing remark:

> True observers of nature, however they may differ in opinion in other respects, will agree that all which presents itself as appearance, all that we meet with as phenomenon, must either indicate an original division which is capable of union, or an original unity which admits of division, and that the phenomenon will present itself

257

accordingly. To divide the united, to unite the divided, is the life of nature; this is the eternal systole and diastole, the eternal collapse and expansion, the inspiration and expiration of the world in which we live and move.[14]

This passage echoes the famous words of the apostle Paul concerning the spirit of God: "In ipso enim vivimus, et movemur, et sumus" (For in him we live, and move, and have our being; Acts 17.28). This phrase from the apostolic sermon, so close to certain ideas of ancient Stoicism (Aratus), is interpreted by Goethe pantheistically.[15]

Goethe is not satisfied with attributing to nature alone the great alternating or pulsating rhythms of the human organism. He also attributes them to the activities of the mind and to scientific research in particular. To divide and unite, such are the operations of analysis and synthesis. These operations are radically opposed but must remain connected and alternate like the systole and diastole, or like the two movements of the rhythm of breathing: "A century has taken the wrong road if it applies itself exclusively to analysis while exhibiting an apparent fear of synthesis: the sciences come to life only when the two exist side by side like exhaling and inhaling."[16] It is important for Goethe that the law governing the world's phenomena also be the law commanding acts of knowledge. There must be, in us, action and reaction — an interaction of the powers of discrimination and assemblage — for the world to be faithfully illuminated in its active and reactive life.

Goethe is hardly alone in this stance. A similar appropriation of the apostle Paul's (or Aratus's) words appears in William Wordsworth's preface to *Lyrical Ballads* (1802) regarding the "principle of pleasure" that poetry must satisfy in assuming the action and reaction between man and the objects surrounding him:

Nor let this necessity of producing immediate pleasure be considered as a degradation of the Poet's art. It is far otherwise.... It is a
homage paid to the native and naked dignity of man, to the grand
elementary principle of pleasure, by which he knows, and feels, and
lives and moves.... What then does the Poet? He considers man and
the objects that surround him as acting and reacting upon each other,
so as to produce an infinite complexity of pain and pleasure ... he
considers him as looking upon this complex scene of ideas and sensations, and finding everywhere objects that immediately excite in
him sympathies which, from the necessities of his nature, are accompanied by an overbalance of enjoyment.[17]

What Wordsworth asserts here in a programmatic text he will later
repeat in a beautiful fragment from the first version of "The Ruined
Cottage." There he calls for the interpenetration of the world and
the human subject: such would be the dawn of a new age — a life
regained, where no faculty, no being would remain in isolation:

> Thus disciplined
> All things shall live in us and we shall live
> In all things that surround us ...
> For thus the sense and the intellect
> Shall each to each supply a mutual aid ...
> And forms and feelings acting thus, and thus
> Reacting, they shall each acquire
> A living spirit and a character
> Till then unfelt.[18]

John Keats, in the same spirit as Goethe's polemic against
Newton, took a stand, in some often quoted lines, in favor of the
old world from which the new science had chased away all supernatural creatures. He takes issue with *cold philosophy*, which is, of

course, the science of nature, *natural philosophy*. The damage has been done, the world is disenchanted:

> Do not all charms fly
> At the mere touch of cold philosophy?
> There was an awful rainbow once in heaven:
> We know her woof, her texture; she is given
> In the dull catalogue of common things.
> Philosophy will clip an Angel's wings,
> Conquer all mysterie by rule and line,
> Empty the haunted air, and gnomed mine —
> Unweave a rainbow.[19]

Blake launches a similar anathema against Newton, whom he associates with Locke and Voltaire. The accusation is the same in Novalis's writings, especially *Die Christenheit oder Europa*:

> Man has just been placed at the top of the ladder of beings, and the eternal and inexhaustible music of the universe has been turned into the monotonous ticktock of an immense windmill, driven and carried away by the torrents of chance, a windmill alone, without architect or miller, a veritable *perpetuum mobile*, a windmill that mills itself.

Novalis sees a counter-Church at work, a Church of destruction: "The members of this new Church have relentlessly occupied themselves with the task of stripping all poetry from nature, the terrestrial earth, the human soul, and the sciences."[20] But, Keats asks himself, why not attempt a poetic reconquering of reality, and why should philosophy not aspire to speak with the voice of poetry? It would administer its proofs through *pulsation*: "Axioms in philosophy are not axioms until they are proved upon our pulses."[21] The internal experience of pulsation, even if it is not transferred to the whole universe, as with Goethe, attests to a philosophical truth. Otherwise, in a world become uninhabitable, consciousness could beat a retreat into the world that it is for itself: "The soul is a world of itself."[22] Life would be safeguarded in the depths of a protected solitude, not perhaps without some guilty pride.

Of course, the idea of a return to true life could also assume political guises. This will be examined later. For now, note that the idea of this return, which in 1789 was tied to the notion of revolution, was also associated with a hope for restoration, which in certain circles meant a religious restoration. Hence Novalis, by using the image of the beating heart, maintains the illusion of a secret society and a providential man who would reestablish a Church's authority. He salutes "a new, higher religious life that is beginning to beat [*pulsieren*] in the nations of Europe," and he invites his contemporaries to become apostles, grouped around a "Brother," whom he considers "the heartbeat [*der Herzschlag*] of the new era."[23] Novalis, in his pietistic exaltation, merged the poetic cause with a messianic enthusiasm. It is hard not to read in this a hazy anticipation of the much more disturbing movements of the terrible century that just ended.

Philosophical Versions

It is interesting to recall — for the record — a few textual sources. In Chapter 12 of the moral treatise "Concerning the Face Which Appears in the Orb of the Moon," Plutarch discusses "the analogy and correspondence between the world and the principal parts of the human body":

> The rational principle is in control; and that is why the stars revolve
> fixed like "radiant eyes" in the countenance of the universe, the sun

in the heart's capacity transmits and disperses out of himself heat and light as [if] it were blood and breath, and earth and sea "naturally" serve the cosmos to the ends that bowels and bladder do an animal."[24]

The idea is taken up again and amplified by Marsilio Ficino in *Liber de arte chemica*:

What remains of our weak body once the soul leaves it? No pulsating vein contracts, no sensation is felt. No vital breath resides therein, nor any breathing. This is why some have thought the sun should be called the *world's heart*. For just as a single source of blood is found in the heart, wetting and irrigating all the other parts of the human body, spreading vital movement, so does the sun oversee the vegetation and conservation of all lower and higher things. For with its light it inspires, so to speak, life and warmth in the lower things. In fact, light is a simple act converting all things to itself through its life-giving heat, traversing all beings [*entia*], bringing to all things their properties and virtues, and dispersing the shadows and dark clouds. This is why Phoebus reigns in the middle with his flaming hair, like a king or emperor, holding the world's scepter and helm. All the virtues of the celestial beings are found in him: Iamblichus said this, and many others have confirmed it. And Proclus said that with the sun all forces and all celestial bodies are gathered together and unified. And we believe that these forces descend and disseminate themselves in this lower world by its fiery rays. You will find great proof of this in the fact that when the sun approaches us, the earth is covered with vegetation and becomes pubescent, whereas it loses its bloom when the sun moves farther away.[25]

This great metaphor was not directly refuted by the Copernican revolution. It persevered in various theosophies, which were little inclined to rewrite their mythic systems.[26] It had been set forth in poetic works of the Renaissance and the seventeenth century. It was not necessary to go back to Ficino to find it. People had not stopped reading Plotinus and Proclus.[27] It was the common language of Romantic authors and was more generally part of a widespread organicist conviction which held that the parts and the whole are thoroughly linked, interdependent, and interactive.

An almost uninterrupted philosophical tradition appealed to images of organic coherence, growth, and concrete, pulsing life. In his *Lectures on the History of Philosophy*, Hegel uses these images to express the very unity of philosophical thought: "Philosophy, once formed, is created from within itself; it is a single idea within a whole and in all its parts, just as within an individual there lives a single life, a single heartbeat pulsating through all his limbs."[28] In Hegel, reciprocal action (*Wechselwirkung*) is the stage of logic that brings actuality (*Wirklichkeit*) to its term and prepares the advent of the subjective logic of the concept (*Begriff*). Reciprocal action is the path from necessity to freedom.[29]

The same image of pulsation appears in Friedrich Schelling's *Ages of the World*.[30] It is used to express the process by which the real produces itself. Schelling begins by including negation within God. He makes this the starting point for the circle of nature, from which freedom and redemption should arise:

> The antithesis eternally produces itself, in order always again to be consumed by the unity, and the antithesis is eternally consumed by the unity in order always to revive itself anew.... This movement can be represented as a systole and a diastole. This is a completely involuntary movement that, once begun, makes itself from itself. The new beginning, the re-ascending is the systole, the tension that reaches its acme in the third potency. The retreat to the first potency is the diastole, the slackening upon which a new contraction immediately follows. Hence, this is the first pulse, the beginning of

that alternating movement that goes through the entirety of visible
nature, of the eternal contraction and the eternal re-expansion, of
the universal ebb and flow.

Schelling adds: "Were life to remain at a standstill here, it would
be nothing other than an eternal exhaling and inhaling, a constant
interchange between life and death, that is, not a true existence
but only an eternal drive and zeal to be, without actual Being."[31]
As Karl Löwith notes: "Left to its own devices, primeval nature is
something that 'does not know where to turn,' a life of 'anxiety'
and 'repulsiveness,' that longs for a steadfast Being. The same
applies to man, whose innermost constituent is likewise that
wheel of nature, but from which he wants to be redeemed."[32]
Such is the vital aspect of the interaction and polarity governing
the material world. A new potentialization will make it possible
to surpass it. Schelling elaborates these ideas in his early writings,
and reworks them in some later works, without ever giving them
a definitive systematic shape. The universe is considered "a Totality of systems formed around a pulsating point."[33] We recognize
here, reformulated in the language of speculative physics, the theory of the central mass found in Maclaurin and Kant-Laplace.[34]
One might suspect that Schelling, who knew Jakob Böhme and
the Gnostics, might have been familiar with the theory of the
withdrawal of God (tsimtsum) formulated in the Lurianic Kabbalah.[35] He follows their lead when he affirms that the world-
soul, which is infinite productivity, contains inhibition (Hemmung)
within itself. Then action and reaction come into play, manifest-
ing themselves in all the productions of inorganic nature. It is
appropriate, however, to superimpose a principle upon them,
which, not being a material force, is not accessible to empirical
research: spirit, freedom. In this way, Schelling introduces the idea
of an evolution in nature, while affirming that "the immediate

effect of restrained productivity is an alternation of expansion and contraction."[36] The world-soul (*Weltseele*) is first and foremost Unity, unfolding in the hierarchical diversity of the objects of the finite world and the activities of consciousness. Nonetheless, finite multiplicity is a place of fragmentation and exile, which man must leave in order to make decisive progress, and it is not beyond his power to do so: this step forward should lead him to regain the primordial One. The path of return will lead him to the union of the subject (*productivity*) and the object (*natura naturata*), a process that Schelling, at one stage of his reflections, believed to have been accomplished by mythology and that he hoped to confide to Art and the creative faculties of Genius. In the "created natures" that men are, imagination (some would say dreaming) is the faculty that leads back to the "fatherland."[37]

The terms "action" and "reaction," as well as "interaction," make it possible to recover and reinterpret all the antithetical couples joined — often in archaic expressions — in relations of antagonism, exchange, or reciprocity: sky and earth, male and female, spirit and matter, attraction and repulsion, positive and negative, reason and imagination, life and death, being and nothingness, being and appearing, good and evil, war and peace, yin and yang, and so on. Action and reaction could be used to confirm ontological oppositions, even while proposing their reconciliation and complementarity — as well as what would be called their dialectical surpassing.

The seductiveness of this type of thinking was great, but it also encountered much opposition. Scientific positivism had a greater and more far-reaching influence. And unbelievers also protested. I cannot resist the temptation to let Heinrich Heine's mocking and dissatisfied voice be heard. In *Religion and Philosophy in Germany*, he recognizes that Schelling's philosophy of nature represents a poetic conversion, through which it escaped the abstractions of the "philosophy of spirit" that had preceded it. This was certainly a "liberating reaction," but Heine treats his subject ironically. Contrasting Schelling with Johann Gottlieb Fichte, whose strength lies in his demonstrations, Heine writes:

> [Schelling] lives in a world of intuition; he does not feel at home on the cold heights of logic; he stretches forth eager hands towards the flowery valleys of symbolism, and his philosophical strength lies in the art of construction. But this is an intellectual aptitude found as frequently amongst mediocre poets as amongst the best philosophers. From this last indication it becomes clear that Schelling, in so much of his philosophy as is pure transcendental idealism, remained, and could not but remain, a mere echoer of Fichte; whilst in the philosophy of nature, where he has to deal with flowers and stars, he cannot help blossoming and shining radiantly. Not only he himself, but also like-minded friends attached themselves by preference to this side of his philosophy, and the commotion thereby aroused was only a kind of reaction of the poetasters against the former abstract philosophy of the spirit.... [Schelling] might also have said that he wished to found a school of prophets, where the inspired should begin to prophesy as fancy moved them, and in whatever dialect they pleased. This, indeed, was done by those disciples whom the master's spirit had deeply moved; the most shallow-brained began to prophesy each in a different tongue, and philosophy had its great day of Pentecost.[38]

Heine takes his comparison even further:

> But at this point Schelling leaves the philosophical route, and seeks by a kind of mystical intuition to arrive at the contemplation of the absolute itself; he seeks to contemplate it in its central point, in its essence, where it is neither ideal nor real, neither thought nor

266

extension, neither subject nor object, neither mind nor matter, but
...I know not what!

Here philosophy ceases with Schelling, and poetry — I may say
folly — commences. But it is here that he meets with the greatest
sympathy from a number of silly admirers whom it suits admirably
to abandon calm reflection, and who, as if in imitation of the dancing
dervishes described by our friend Jules David, continue spinning
round in a circle until objective and subjective worlds become lost to
them — until both worlds melt into a colorless nothingness, that is
neither real nor ideal, until they see things invisible, hear what is
inaudible, until they hear colors and see tones, until the absolute
reveals itself to them.[39]

Moreover, according to Heine, the poets' reaction against abstraction will lead to "political reaction," at least with the later Schelling:

[T]he former Schelling, like Kant and Fichte, represents one of the
great phases of our philosophical revolution, compared by me in
these pages to the political revolution in France. In truth, while in
Kant we see the terrorist Convention, and in Fichte the Napoleonic
Empire, in Schelling we behold the reaction of the Restoration
which followed the Empire. But it was at first a restoration in a better sense. Schelling re-established nature in its legitimate rights; he
aimed at a reconciliation between spirit and nature; he sought to
reunite them in the eternal world-soul.... Alas! he ended by restoring things whereby he may in the worst sense be compared with the
French Restoration.[40]

In tirelessly applying the schema of action and reaction, Romantic philosophy could proclaim the common destiny of the
cosmos, of nature, of human societies, and of individual consciousness as determined in philosophical thought and the poetic

imagination. A binary and antagonistic formula such as action *and* reaction admits duality in order to raise it up into a dynamic unity. A thought enamored of dialectics finds resources in this formula. And the living unity — the acting-reacting unity — can therefore appear in the guise of the sexual couple no less than that of respiration or the heartbeat. The images of this symbolic configuration are interchangeable as a whole and susceptible to infinite combinations.

It would be impossible to mention all those who, among Goethe's and Schelling's successors, revived the "cardiac" image of the systole and diastole or proposed variations on this theme. I shall confine myself to a few names and to a few typical statements.

The most radical in the imaginative development of the organic analogy is Gotthilf Heinrich Schubert (1780–1860) in *Ansichten von der Nachtseite der Naturwissenschaft* (1808). Schubert sees comets as the veins and arteries in the body of the universe: they represent the fluid element as compared with the stable and solid parts of the great All. "Bringing new vital material to some, bearing spent material away from others, this strange family [*Geschlecht*) plays its shadowy game in the eternal ether." In his later *Geschichte der Seele* (1840), Schubert has the soul draw a breath of "universal life," as distinguished from the atmospheric air, which comes into play only to maintain the life of the body.[41]

Hans Christian Ørsted, on the other hand, was a remarkable scholar who nevertheless remained attached to the idea of a philosophy of nature even after distancing himself from Schelling, Henrik Steffens, Franz Von Baader, and Joachim Ritter, for whom he had felt an initial enthusiasm. There is hardly an inanimate object that is not the seat of some force and not in a relation of action and reaction with its surroundings. This is all the more the case for organized beings. Their constituent parts are in a state of action and reaction, an uninterrupted activity:

> If breathing did not nurture an incessant flame in your chest, if the heart did not at every moment send blood to all your arteries, including the most minute capillaries, if at every instant new nutritive substances did not reach all parts of your body — in truth, you would cease to be what you are, a living being.... An organization is a world of forces and effects, and if activity perished, it would fall back into chaos.[42]

If the stone is in interaction (*Wechselwirkung*) with all of nature, this is true for the whole earth, with its change of seasons and the "pulsating throb of the sea." The same is true in the great All. "What creates a world is the uninterrupted chain of effects." The German version says *Wirkungen*, which can be understood as the sequence of actions and reactions (*Wechselwirkungen*). Ørsted sees in nature a reason that is intensified in human reason and a circulation that ascends to God. Jacob Moleschott defended an entirely different idea of circulation in his major work, *Der Kreislauf des Lebens* (1852), in which Marx saw the perfect expression of "vulgar materialism."

The physician Carl Gustav Carus (1789–1869) was also a fine landscape painter — close to Caspar David Friedrich — who wanted to be faithful to the spirit of Goethe and Schelling. The systole and diastole are reworked in a related image: the circulation of the Idea in its union with the first-created Substance, which he calls ether, the fundamental material of all material constituents.[43] Carus clearly embraces speculative audacity:

> The same idea continually comes to life in new ether. Every idea lives in continually fresh metamorphoses, in ever different and new substances. Thus we see an eternal drawing in and fleeing away of the elements [*ein ewiges Ziehen und Fliehen der Elemente*].[44]

In a later work, which develops a "comparative psychology," Carus speaks — a bit more soberly — of the soul as a relation (*Beziehung*) that a sentient and reacting being (*Gegenwirkendes*) — at times passive (*leidend*), at times active — establishes with an external world for the purpose of its internal formation and development. This soul is what develops and expands outward from a primordial "center of life" (*Lebensmitte*). Carus insists on evolutionary degrees of the psyche. In a perspective he calls "genetic," he establishes a parallel between the development of psychic faculties up the ladder of living beings and the stages of human psychogenesis.[45] He was among the first to support the idea of a recapitulation of phylogenesis in ontogenesis.

Adolf Trendelenburg (1802–1872) was considered a right-wing Hegelian. His *Logische Untersuchungen* (1840) is based dialectically on the principle of motion, which is "the act [*Tat*] that originarily traverses all Thought and all Being."[46] Interaction (as well as inherence, a complementary category) takes place in the development of the categories of motion:

> Action and reaction [*Wechselwirkung*] are the most secret power of nature, through which the necessary All manifests itself, down to the play of the flakes of its finest particles. This speech exchanged [*Wechselsprache*] by things is the living opposite of mute isolation. When a constraining power suppresses the natural action and reaction, things sigh and, in destitution or ruin, still proclaim their aspiration to totality.[47]

Referring to a "speech exchanged by things," Trendelenburg gives in to a metaphoric and anthropomorphic temptation. His dialectic is established in the alternation between the "energy of the Being" and the "energy of Thought." He is convinced that a single principle of motion confers animation on grammar and on logic.

What was language at the time of its blossoming (*die hervor-brechende Sprache*)? Speech must be defined as "the first *living reaction* of the individual spirit to the chaotic influx of impressions from the outside."[48]

Trendelenburg adds in a note the great formula — almost a motto — contained in section 23 of the Hippocratic treatise *On Nutriment*, to which vitalist thought repeatedly referred: "Conflux one, conspiration one, all things in sympathy."[49] It would be interesting to trace the fate in Western culture of this trinity in which *physis* is manifested. Beginning in the Renaissance, the image of confluence is akin (as seen in the examples above) to the ancient theory of universal circulation, which, according to the Stoics, was ensured by the omnipresence of the *pneuma*. The metaphor of "conspiration" — or communal respiration — will be maintained by its poetic force, to the point of serving as a model for Paul Claudel's play on words *co-naître* (co-birth, a play on *con-naître*, to know — I will return to this). As for the word "sympathy," which plays a major role in Stoic cosmology and Renaissance astrology, its wide circulation gave it a more diffuse and slightly more attenuated meaning, although the concept was still passed on to us in a somewhat bastardized form.

In his metaphysical presuppositions, Félix Ravaisson was indebted to Schelling as well as to Bichat and Maine de Biran. His memoir, *De l'habitude* (1839), considers the ladder of beings in a spectrum that ranges from the inorganic world to human life. Without exalting a vitality that manifests itself like a heartbeat, he nonetheless remarks that animal life is characterized by intermittence: "All its functions alternate between rest and motion; all are intermittent, at least in the succession of waking and sleep; the intermediary functions whose immediate goal is the preparation for vegetable life are subject to shorter and more

regular periods."[50] No doubt, with the term "intermediary functions," he is referring to circulation and respiration. What is
of interest here in Ravaisson's short, dense text is the idea of a
change that modifies the type of reaction as one goes up the hierarchy of beings:

> In the inorganic world, reaction is exactly equal to action, or rather,
> in this entirely external and superficial existence, action and reac-
> tion merge: they are one and the same act from two different points
> of view. In life, the action of the external world and the reaction of
> life itself become more and more different and appear to be more
> and more independent of each other. In vegetable life, they are more
> similar to each other and closely intertwined. Beginning at the first
> level of animal life, they move apart and differentiate themselves,
> and the more or less great agitations in space correspond to the im-
> perceptible states of receptivity.
>
> But if the reaction is more and more distant or independent of
> the action to which it corresponds, it appears more and more neces-
> sary for there to be a center serving as a common limit, where one
> arrives and the other departs; a center that regulates more and more
> by itself — in its fashion, at its own pace — the relationship between
> the less and less immediate and necessary reaction it produces and
> the action it has undergone. It is not enough to imagine an indiffer-
> ent medium term such as the center of opposite forces of the lever; it
> is more and more necessary for there to be a center that, by its own
> means, measures and disperses the energy.[51]

Ravaisson readily calls this center the "soul." And he continues:

> Thus does the reign of knowledge and foresight seem to appear in
> the empire of Nature and cast the first light of Freedom.... Being,
> which originally emerged from the fatality of the mechanical world,

manifests itself, in the mechanical world, in the accomplished form of the freest activity.[52]

Ravaisson thus uses the same term — "reaction" — to designate a phenomenon of the "mechanical world" and a *deferred* response given by man's "freest activity." He does not seem to want to restrict action and reaction to the simultaneity so strongly asserted by Kant in *Metaphysical Foundations of Natural Science*. Does this indicate a lack of rigor in Ravaisson? Or a desire, following Schelling's example, to reconcile nature (*natura naturata*) and the generative idea (*natura naturans*) into a unity? Between the elementary forms of existence and reflective life, there is an ascending progression and a descending slope. Nature rises toward freedom, and freedom returns to nature. Ravaisson pays great homage to habit by making it the path of return:

> In all things, the Necessity of nature is the warp upon which Freedom is woven.... Between the lowest depths of nature and the highest point of reflective freedom, there is an infinite number of degrees measuring the developments of a single power, and as one rises there is an increase in distinction and in the interval between opposites, as well as in the extension of this power, which is the condition of science. It is like a spiral whose principle lies in the depths of nature and which succeeds in opening out into consciousness. It is this spiral that habit descends again and whose generation and origin it teaches us.[53]

Telltale Hearts

The pulse of universal life, the rhythm of respiration — recurring motifs in Romantic poetry. At the beginning of the second part of *Faust*, Goethe's hero says upon awakening:

273

Enlivened once again, life's pulses waken
To greet the kindly dawn's ethereal vision;
You, earth, outlasted this night, too, unshaken,
And at my feet you breathe, renewed Elysian,
Surrounding me with pleasure-scented flowers,
And deep within you prompt a stern decision:
To strive for highest life with all my powers.[54]

Maurice de Guérin's lilting prose also inscribes an alternating movement — that of breathing — into life itself, and in this movement the limits of the individual and the world are blurred:

> Sweet breath, ebb and flow of universal life in man's breast, continual recapturing of a maternal embrace between nature and the life it created and hid in us, I mistrusted you! . . . Today I immerse myself, as if in the choir of the Muses who called the poets of Antiquity onto the heights of mountains, in these moral and physical laws from whose embrace I once recoiled in terror.[55]

Wordsworth compares the pulse to the starry sky: "The pulse of being everywhere was felt. . . / One galaxy of life and joy."[56]

In the final vision in "Seraphita," Balzac opens for the clairvoyant a luminous and sonorous space animated by respiration and pulsation:

> They heard the various parts of the Infinite forming a living melody; and at each beat, when the concord made itself felt as a deep expiration, the Worlds, carried on by this unanimous motion, bowed toward the immense Being, who in his unapproachable center made all things issue from him and return to him.
>
> This ceaseless alternation of voices and silence seemed to be the rhythm of the holy hymn that was echoed and sustained from age to age.[57]

Gottfried Keller associates the pulsation of life and the stellar world, but he includes the motif of failure. In terms that recall Goethe, the poet evokes the beginning of a day in which he hopes a poem will be born to him:

> The sky was clear, soon suffused with the light of day.
> The beating of life pulsed through the world's fullness.[58]

Keller's poem recounts the story of a day that passes without the song's being born. Once night comes, the only song is that of the stars consoling the poet for not having produced the song. The beating of life has not been communicated to speech, and speech can only murmur in mourning for the passing day.

Edgar Allan Poe: Eureka

No one more than Edgar Allan Poe so closely associated the physical laws of action and reaction with the image of the beating heart — systole and diastole — in the widest possible cosmic dimensions. Was Poe influenced by Schelling when he composed *Eureka* in 1848? It is legitimate to ask this question — imagining as many intermediaries as one likes — or at least to admit that the similarities proceed from a common attraction to ancient cyclic cosmologies and a common penchant for "speculative physics," based on the cosmogonic theory of Kant and Laplace.[59] The similarities are striking.[60] *Eureka*, a "fable" (Paul Valéry) or a "cosmological novel" (Georges Poulet), declares its poetic intentions in its dedication:

> To the few who love me and whom I love — to those who feel rather than to those who think — to the dreamers and those who put faith in dreams as in the only realities — I offer this book of Truths, not in its character of Truth-Teller, but for the Beauty that abounds in its Truth, constituting it true. To these I present the composition as an

Art-Product alone, — let us say as a Romance; or, if I be not urging too lofty a claim, as a Poem.

What I here propound is true: — therefore it cannot die; or if by any means it be now trodden down so that it die, it will "rise again to the Life Everlasting."

Nevertheless, it is as a Poem only that I wish this work to be judged after I am dead.[61]

The duality that Poe establishes in the universality of things — as we will see later — is reflected in a duality in consciousness: both dream and rigorous thought, poem and knowledge. The promise that intellectual truth will be reestablished in "Life Everlasting" is but one aspect of the reintegration of all created matter into an original immaterial unity, which is God in a state of extreme concentration. Consequently, the duality so strongly affirmed is only provisional. Poe's argument leads to a syllogism: to know God and the universe, "we should have to be God ourselves." However, we can hope one day to understand God and the universe. Thus our consciousness could one day be merged with that of God: "I . . . venture to demand if this our present ignorance of the deity is an ignorance to which the soul is *everlastingly* condemned."[62]

Poe strongly insists on the idea of proof by *consistency*, which ensures the coincidence of aesthetic value with scientific truth: "[A] perfect consistency can be nothing but an absolute truth." "[T]he Universe . . . in the supremeness of its symmetry, is but the most sublime of poems. Now, symmetry and consistency are convertible terms; thus Poetry and Truth are one. A thing is consistent in the ratio of its truth, true in the ratio of its consistency. A perfect consistency, I repeat, can be nothing but an absolute truth."[63] Poe gives his text a double legitimation, both aesthetic and epistemological. He uses the chiasmus (*a-b-b-a*) to affirm authoritatively the "reciprocal" convertibility of scientific truth and beauty. One is absorbed into the other; each is expressed through the other. Far from positing a separation between the poetic imagination and the rigors of calculating thought, Poe decrees their complete reconciliation. The "poetic" approach to the totality does not exclude the analytic dismembering of observed phenomena. The separation of the two languages, which characterizes modernity since the rise of mathematical physics, is thus declared curable.

Eureka at first proposes the will of a Creator God, who draws matter from his own absolute spiritual essence. In the beginning, matter exists in a state of "concentrated" unity and simplicity. Again it is God's will that provokes the explosion, diffusion, fragmentation, and radiating dispersion of matter, henceforth given over to difference and multiplicity. Such is the first *action*, the big bang before it was called that, producing space and time at a single stroke, launching a great cosmic cycle. But matter is not limitless, any more than space or divine action. Hence dissipation cannot be prolonged infinitely. Poe declares that "the immediate and perpetual tendency of ... disunited atoms" is "to return into their normal Unity." They seek "the principle, Unity," which is "their lost parent."[64] The image of the creative action and the diffusive explosion of the first atom is accompanied by an imperious assertion:

> An action of this character implies reaction. A diffusion from Unity, under the conditions, involves a tendency to return into Unity — a tendency ineradicable until satisfied. ...
>
> Now Reaction, as far as we know anything of it, is Action conversed. The general principle of Gravity being, in the first place, understood as the reaction of an act — as the expression of a desire on the part of Matter, while existing in a state of diffusion, to return into the Unity whence it was diffused; and, in the second place, the

mind being called on to determine the *character* of the desire — the manner in which it would, naturally, be manifested; in other words, being called on to conceive a probable law, or *modus operandi*, for the return — could not well help arriving at the conclusion that this law of return would be precisely the converse of the law of departure.[65]

Using a deliberately anthropomorphic expression, Poe asserts that matter experiences the *desire* to return; this desire is manifested by a Newtonian force of attraction, that is, by gravity. But at the same time, this return should not take place too rapidly, for the world was created in order "that the utmost possible Relation" be developed — for a period of its existence.[66] To this end, and to check the return, God interposed another force: repulsion, which we observe in electrical phenomena. Poe proclaims his "intuitive conviction" that "the principle in question is strictly spiritual." It is God himself who interposes himself between the discrete parts of matter! Nothing is impossible if it is possible to believe that in the world we can observe, "the Body and the Soul walk hand in hand."[67] Nonetheless, the law of reaction is irrevocable: an inevitable catastrophe awaits the created world in its totality, for matter will ineluctably return to its center and compact unity, then to the immaterial purity of God. Reaction is the motor power of a great return. The image of the end of the world — the symmetrical inverse of "the originating Act" — is inscribed in a series of catastrophes in which Poe's imagination takes great delight.[68] He predicts a "chaotic precipitation ... of the moons upon the planets, of the planets upon the suns, and of the suns upon the nuclei. ... While undergoing consolidation, the clusters themselves with a speed prodigiously accumulative, have been rushing towards their own general center."[69] For the symmetry of the end and the beginning to be complete, matter is engulfed in the void from which it was drawn: "Matter, created for an end, would unquestionably, on fulfillment of that end, be Matter no longer. Let us endeavor to understand that it would disappear, and that God would remain all in all."[70] The cosmic suicide none-theless indicates a rebirth. From this end a new creation is desired by absolute Volition. God begins his work anew according to the "law of periodicity":

> Are we not, indeed, more than justified in entertaining a belief... that the processes we have here ventured to contemplate will be renewed forever, and forever, and forever; a novel Universe swelling into existence, and then subsiding into Nothingness, at every throb of the Divine Heart?
> And now — this Heart Divine — what is it? It is our own.[71]

The vital rhythm, the beating of the universal heart, supplants the mechanical model of action and reaction. The world is the mani-festation of a "pulsatory God."[72] Now, if God drew from nothing the substance that forms us, then he is present in us.

The wheel of life and death in the world will turn sempiter-nally. The consistency Poe dreamed of in *Eureka* thus represents the fusion of the myth of the soul's return to a primitive One and the fable of the cyclic eternal return of universal matter. He estab-lishes not only a great analogy between the large bodies and the most minute parts of nature but also a theo-cosmo-anthropo-logical correspondence through superimposed cycles. In "The Island of the Fay," Poe imagined a universal order in which circu-lar motion, exerting itself on every level, does not involve God: "As we find cycle within cycle without end, yet all revolving around one far-distant center which is the Godhead, may we not analogically suppose, in the same manner, life within life, the less within the greater, and all within the Spirit Divine?"[73] In *Eureka,* this fine concentric order is deprived of its stable center, since the divinity itself is manifested by the cycle of its expansion and contraction.[74]

Is the eternal repetition of pulsation really life? Poe proclaims this in one of the last lines of his "poem." But we might wonder whether this ever-renewed pulsation does not attest, rather, to the hopeless impossibility of dying? This God who is reborn only to disappear once again in his creation, does he not resemble Sisyphus? He is constrained by a double limit, for he knows neither the infinity of rest nor the infinity of expansion. Recall that for Schelling the eternal return was but a first level of nature, still subjected to necessity. In certain respects, is this first level not the one where Freud, in his later thought, inscribes the "death drive," a "tendency towards stability"?

This question arises especially when we recall that the motif of the uninterrupted beating heart reappears in Poe's work in a demonized and grotesque form. In "The Tell-Tale Heart," it is the heart of a hideous old man, gratuitously murdered by the narrator because of one of his eyes: "a pale blue eye, with a film over it." The narrator-murderer has hidden the pieces of the dismembered corpse beneath the floor. But while the police officers detect nothing, the pulsation, in an agonizing crescendo, is heard by the guilty man, who himself prefers to be *arrested*:

> I paced the floor to and fro with heavy strides, as if excited to fury by the observations of the men — but the noise steadily increased. Oh God! what could I do? I foamed — I raved — I swore! I swung the chair upon which I had been sitting, and grated it upon the boards, but the noise arose over all and continually increased. It grew louder — louder — louder! And still the men chatted pleasantly, and smiled. Was it possible they heard not? Almighty God! — no, no! They heard! — they suspected! — they knew! — they were making a mockery of my horror! — this I thought, and this I think. But anything was

280

better than this agony! Anything was more tolerable than this derision! I could bear those hypocritical smiles no longer! I felt that I
must scream or die! and now — again! — hark! louder! louder! louder!
louder!

"Villains!" I shrieked, "dissemble no more! I admit the deed! —
tear up the planks! here, here! — it is the beating of the hideous
heart!"[75]

The beating here no longer belongs to the order governing the
succession of cosmogonies; rather, born of crime, it is the unbearable hallucination following the dismemberment of a derisory
Osiris. "Consistency," far from being the accord between Truth
and Beauty, establishes a symmetrical relationship between the
madness of a guilty man and the fable of the victim's survival. The
guilty heart is ultimately the single heart that beats in the dismembered victim and in the murderer's conscience.

Mallarmé's Scintillations

In 1852, Baudelaire presented *Eureka* as a work in which the law
of the creation of the world is simultaneously that of its "destruction" and of its "final dissolution" and therefore of its death.[76]
Baudelaire does not acknowledge the sempiternal alternation of
concentration and expansion that Poe had attributed to his God-
world when he wrote that the "Divine Being . . . passes His Eternity
in perpetual variation of Concentrated Self and almost Infinite
Self-Diffusion."[77] One might think, however, that Baudelaire
adopted Poe's cosmology as his own, although in doing so he
transposed it onto the psychological plane. In "Mon coeur mis à
nu," he writes: "Everything lies . . . in the vaporization and the
centralization of the Self." This image has been rightly compared
to a passage by Ralph Waldo Emerson, who, in "The Conduct of
Life" (1860), contrasts the concentration and the dissipation of

the self.[78] But Baudelaire must certainly have noted that the same image was available to him previously in Poe's work.

For Mallarmé, so quick to "be satisfied with the earth," so attentive to the sensory world (as Yves Bonnefoy has noted), cosmology is not a primary concern. A passionate admirer of Poe, and a translator of his poems, Mallarmé is especially heedful of Poe's "Poetic Principle," which reassures him in his desire "creuser le vers" (to hollow out or thoroughly exhaust the possibilities of the poetic line). The unsurpassable evidence of the "gardens of that star" assigns the poet an "ideal duty," which is to name them ("A Funeral Toast").[79]

If there is a beating in Mallarmé's work, it is first of all the beating of a fan; the alternation is that of the breeze born of an artificial wing in feminine hands — God being, for his part, but a fallen "plumage." The fan, generator of this inspiration, is captive, just as the "sidereal universe" is expressly declared by Poe to be "limited."

First I will indicate, hypothetically, a *literal* trace of *Eureka* in Mallarmé. For this, we must return to the passage where Poe discusses the resemblance between "our Galaxy" and a "capital Y." Poe does not contest the idea that "our Galaxy" might be compared to this letter of the alphabet. But he wishes that the directions of the width and length of the letter were better distinguished: "An inhabitant of the Earth, when looking, as we commonly express ourselves, at the Galaxy, is then beholding it in some of the directions of its length — is looking along the lines of the Y; but when, looking out into the general Heaven, he turns his eyes from the Galaxy, he is then surveying it in the direction of the letter's thickness."[80] Fleetingly, then, one can dream of the *y*'s ("onyx," "ptyx," "Styx") in the sonnet "Her pure nails on high displaying their onyx." One can also look toward the "Constellation" and the "total account in the making" on the last page of "A

Throw of the Dice." Bonnefoy notes: "'A Throw of the Dice' . . . enlarges the room of the sonnet 'in yx' to the proportions of the universe."[81]

While the sonnet "in yx" proclaims itself "allegorical," it is allegorical "of itself," according to the title of its first version. Through its elaborate void, it wants to *respond* to the universe over which no God watches. It does not attempt to *participate* in the divine act, to imitate it in poetic knowledge and in a truthful poetry, as was Poe's ambition in *Eureka*. The poet — having gone "to draw tears from the Styx" — is absent from the poem. In the brief commentary that accompanied the first version of the sonnet, Mallarmé evokes an empty room, an "open nocturnal window," a mirror hanging on the wall inside, and the "stellar and incomprehensible reflection of the Great Bear, binding this lodging abandoned by the world to the sky alone."[82] For the careful reader, the night sky reflected in the mirror of the empty room is a figure in the poem, like the room itself. Nonetheless, in taking responsibility for itself alone, the poem takes responsibility for the world, representing "the Universe as best it can."[83] Speech takes on the task of reflecting an "uncanny mystery" in the depths of the void.[84] In this way, a recentering on the human takes place, such that everything balances on the fine point of the letter traced by the poet's hand. Mallarmé composed this sonnet, and especially "A Throw of the Dice," as if the internal infinity of the poem had nothing to envy the physical infinity of the universe.

No heartbeat, as I have noted, animates Mallarmé's universe. The signal he receives from it consists of "cold sparks," the inhuman glimmer, piercing and intermittent.[85] The rapid alternation of daylight and night is substituted for the systole and diastole of those authors who perceived the cosmos as a great Life. The "one-and-six" of the "scintillations" with which the sonnet "in yx" concludes designates both the constellation of the Great Bear and the seven pairs of identical rhymes of which the poem is composed. A different sort of beating becomes perceptible, that of an incessant alternation between a meaning in the poem that refers illusorily to the world and a meaning that refers allegorically only to the poem. In this way, one witnesses a call to order of the microcosm and a recentering on the human, on the gesture that sets down the signs of the poem.

"I Feel My Heart Within Me" (Paul Claudel)

The image of a world animated by the beating of a single heart continued into the twentieth century, and Poe's work echoes still in the writings of numerous French authors.

Today it is easier to assess the profound influence Baudelaire's translation of *Eureka* had on the generation of poets born around 1870 — Claudel and Valéry in particular.[86] Paul Claudel's use, in 1903–1904, of the action/reaction system and the image of pulsation is particularly striking in *Art poétique*. But in these pages, with their Thomist inspiration, Claudel does not adopt Poe's Gnostic cosmology (which lends itself to a pantheistic interpretation, as Baudelaire noted): he transfers aspects of it to man. In this way, he, too, effects a recentering on the human. In Claudel's texts, man is restored to his place at the center of a world created by the fiat of the biblical Genesis: a world that, oriented toward its supernatural end, escapes the torment of perpetual cycles.

Claudel presents the human creature as a *closed* universe, inhabited by the action and reaction of nervous vibration, and thus similar, in its particular life, to Poe's universe, which was also finite and given over to the alternation of centrifugal and centripetal movement. Here one might speak of a reduction and microscopic refashioning of the vital pulsation that Poe developed on the scale of the universe:

The vibration by which we are aware of the existence and limits of our person is the very thing that built it and that continues to maintain it. The essential creative act is the emission of a wave. The wave can schematically define a motion that, moving outward from a center, reaches all the points of an area circumscribed by the boundary it traces in ceasing. A local displacement is determined on all these points, followed by a reaction, or a tendency to regain the first site, which, to be overcome, requires the accumulation of a new effort, a push from a second wave. Hence there are two movements, one eccentric from the motor, the other concentric from the subject, and these are the two *time frames* of the vibration. The effect of the wave is an *information* or extension of a certain form to the area it determines. All form is a variation of the circle.... Thus the source and workshop of this creative vibration remain the sacred primordial shiver, the cerebral and nervous substance, the cranial and spinal marrow with its so disparate elements — akin to the stars with retractile rays and to notes that might play themselves by stretching their fingers in all directions. It is this essential repulsion, this *necessity not to be* That which gives us life and subsequently to be another thing, which weaves our substance, gives us breath and limb. We live only to resist, to begin anew this mysterious struggle of Israel.[87]

This physiology, which gives such a large role to the relation of opposition, leads to the theory of knowledge (*connaissance*) (or co-birth, *co-naissance*) developed in *Traité de la co-naissance au monde et de soi-même*:

We can now represent man as a body in a permanent state of vibration or, to use terms we have recognized as congeneric, in a state of birth and information. But this body is surrounded by other bodies; it is not born alone; in each moment of its duration it is *co-born* [*co-naît*].... All things, we have said, can be reduced to the constitution

285

of a certain equilibrium or vibration. I have termed knowledge [*con-naissance*] the relations each maintains with the others, based on the resistance it offers, from the action it exerts and the reaction it undergoes. No thing was created once and for all; it has never stopped; it continues to be produced; it expresses the permanent state of tension contained in the effort of which it is the actualization.[88]

What is particularly striking — and may be considered an inheritance of Poe's images — is the anthropo-cosmic conjunction, the positing of a homologous relation between the "nervous" pulsation and the cosmic circuits. Whatever abrupt formulas Claudel uses to express himself — often as if he had entered into the confidence of the Creator — the accent has clearly shifted to the presence of the human subject. Without completely renouncing the ambition to explain the functioning of the universe and the philosophical-scientific laws governing it, the poet takes another tack. Beginning with the conscious creature, he attempts to define its sensory relation to the world by basing it in a direct experience of the body:

I feel my heart within me and the clock at the center of the house.

    I am. I feel, I hear in me the beating of this machine encased within my bones and through which I continue to exist.... At each beat, the pump collects my blood and presses it onward, inflamed by the respiratory sun, to the four corners of my body.... The beating of our heart brings the time that we indicate and that we are.... Man alone marks no other hour than his own. He feels within him, he possesses within himself the very movement of which the successive horizons opening up around him are the circumferential reflections. The appearance of the skies and the earth, the sun setting in the foliage and this foliage with it, the moon on the chrysanthemums are no less the consequence and effect of the *beating of his heart* than his own face, childish or bearded. New astrology! it is not the stars that fix our fates with horoscopic arrest; they themselves obey the hereditary throbbing delegated to this vessel of life within my ribs.[89]

Claudel breathes new life into the Stoic doctrine of "sympathies" with which the life of the world is woven, but he takes man as his focus. He begins with an "I feel" and an "I hear," which are the linguistic propellers of universal motion. The beating that animates this passage has neither the impersonality of the one that moves the system of the worlds in *Eureka* nor the spectral tonality of the one that resounds in "The Tell-Tale Heart." It is the sound of simple life, with its echo carried to the most distant limits, and from there it will receive that which constitutes its form: its "information."

"I Am a Reaction to What I Am" (Paul Valéry)
Paul Valéry, a passionate reader of *Eureka* in his youth, wrote one of his finest essays about it. What interested him was less the alternation of action and reaction on a universal scale than the mutual dependence of the "successive states of the system," the symmetry implied in the notion of consistency. He sees this as an anticipation of "general relativity." He admires Poe's universe for being "formed on a plan the profound symmetry of which is present, to some degree, in the inner structure of our minds."[90] But it is significant that, like Claudel, he is intent on recentering the world on the sentient subject. Thus he gives the physicist priority over physics. Valéry, like a phenomenologist, inquires into the genesis of the idea of the universe in the mind of an individual: this idea is constructed upon the simple act of looking and in the unity of "motor consciousness." The question of the world (and of all possible cosmology) is thus reworked on the basis of the perceiving "I":

I acquire the general and constant impression of a sphere of simultaneity attached to my presence. It moves with me, its contents are
indefinitely variable, but it retains its plenitude through all the substitutions it can undergo. If I move from one point to another, or if
the bodies surrounding me are modified, the unity of the total representation, the quality of enclosing me that it possesses, is not altered.
I can try to flee, to shake myself in all directions, I am still enveloped
in all the *seeing-movements* of my body, which are all transformed into
each other and lead me invincibly to the same central situation....

But this unity... communicates to me the first idea, the model,
and as it were the germ of the total universe that I believe to exist
around my sensation, and that is masked and revealed by this sensation. I imagine invincibly that an immense hidden system supports,
penetrates, nurtures and reabsorbs each actual and sensate element
of my duration, pressuring it into being and into resolution.[91]

The recentering on the human occurs once Valéry returns cosmic
space — as knowledge represents it — to its subjective basis: perceived space, man's relation to the external. In having his human
spectator give birth to the very idea of the cosmos, Valéry explicitly relegates Poe's God to the status of fable — that God who
manifested himself through his desire rhythmically to produce the
universe, which is always the same universe perpetually dying and
being reborn. "In the beginning was the fable," he writes at the
end of his essay. According to the "phenomenological reduction"
he carries out there — as in the notes in his *Cahiers* — Valéry brings
back to earthly life alone, and finally to ourselves, the rhythm of
the systole and diastole in which Goethe, Schelling, and Poe had
found a law for the entire universe. Valéry does not create a cosmogonic theory; his purpose is to maintain awareness about the
physicists's debates; he knows their perplexities, their changing
ideas on ether, and so on. He understands that the doctrines are

288

subject to revision. But he has learned from the physiologists that life is cyclic, and he attributes the greatest importance to this characteristic. From here, by exploiting his full waking attention, during the morning hours when he returns to his notebook, he undertakes to establish both the quantified formula and the poetic expression of the "body-spirit-world system." Isn't he himself a body and a mind? Isn't the world within his reach, in each thing that gives itself to be perceived? And don't the cycles, in their vast generality, bear this out?

> I was struck and exasperated very early on by the periodic nature of "life," in its orbital and seasonal structures, its redundancies, in life itself or in thought — the embroidery on a ground of respiration, circulation, ingestions, eliminations, and cycles.[92]

It is a mental cycle that "Manuscript Found in a Brain" (begun in 1898), which would become *Agatha*, attempts to represent. The original title echoes Poe's "MS. Found in a Bottle." Whereas Poe inscribes the cycle of new beginnings within the total universe, Valéry inscribes it in a sleeping being in order to analyze it using means inspired by Poe and his hyper-lucid detective Dupin:

> A person falls asleep — I will assume it's a cataleptic sleep — I mean indefinitely long — I will assume (not without danger) that all the excitations of the senses are abolished. I will assume finally that he dreams and the succession of his representations are such that the nth = the 1st.
>
> Thus this person turns in the circle *n*, which is closed.
>
> If one limits oneself to hypotheses — it all ends there. If one introduces a new condition — the progressive *alteration* of perception in this cycle due to its repetition — habit — the increasing rapidity of *rotation* — what then? Then, perhaps, this cycle would become

something stable, a world governed by a simple and certain law, an object that is more and more strange — and in relation to which the person in question will be tempted to *think* — and wake up.[93]

Here one again finds the circularity of the cosmos of *Eureka* and even the reaction that brings all things back to their beginning. True, the word "reaction" does not appear in the note I've just cited. On closer examination, however, and in recalling other remarks in the *Cahiers*, I discover that reaction, for Valéry, is implicit in all thought and that it belongs to the wakefulness which would bring *Agatha* to a conclusion: "The notions of thought, knowledge, and so on should be — rejected. That of act and reaction and so on should replace them."[94] To think is to exclude oneself from what one is thinking about; it is to exercise an indefinite power of negation with regard to external alterity, as well as to the other that one is to oneself. To define defensive vigilance, the attitude of deliberate opposition resulting from the "Genoa night" (October 1892), Valéry writes:

> I made myself a *Principle of the Finite* ... which consisted of a reaction of my mind against all expression or impression that came from itself or from *elsewhere* and that introduced things or values that were *inseparable from insoluble terms.*[95]

Valéry endowed his fictional character Monsieur Teste with an analogous heroism:

Monsieur Teste is the witness.

That in us which causes *everything* and therefore nothing — reaction itself, pure recoil.

This is what makes Teste an infinitely separate consciousness and at the same time an infinitely reacting mind:

> In him psychic activity occurs when internal exchanges are at the furthest point from *values*.
>
> Thought is equally free (when he is HIMSELF) of its similarities and confusions with the *World*, and, on the other hand, of its affective values. He considers it as pure chance.

> Or rather he is that one who is a reaction to a certain spectacle that requires at least Someone.[96]

Now, in fact, Teste is only the *proper name* Valéry attributes to the sovereign impersonality that he himself wishes to attain and that on other occasions he calls "the pure me." With regard to Teste, Valéry notes: "God is not far. He is what is nearest." Similarly, he writes in one of his notebooks: "The true God is in intimate union with the me. But the person or personality is nothing to him: he is like the sun that lights up all things.... The pure me is like the formula for the God."[97]

In the voice of Monsieur Teste, Valéry remarks, in a notebook from 1944–1945: "I am a reaction to what I am.... 'What I am' is what appears to that which will be 'what I am.'"[98] It is a matter not simply of a reflection in a mirror but of a production of the self in time — in the immanence of a perpetual transformation that both reinstates and conceals one's presence to oneself. This is what "The Graveyard by the Sea" poetically terms the "grandeur within," "ringing in the soul a still future void."[99] Among the changing metaphors used by Valéry to define the "me," the formulas of the classic dynamic (action, reaction) certainly remain constant. But they are replaceable with borrowings from more modern forms of knowledge. Thus Valéry writes in 1941:

The Me is perhaps the nucleus of the atom Man. Or the center of repulsive forces.... Its essential equinegation, its nature as a universal reaction, RESPONSE TO EVERYTHING — but the first and last response — which creates a *cycle*.[100]

"Universal reaction": the formula is very revealing, but we must note its equivalent as well, "response to everything." Valéry sought to refine his thought by varying it with quasi synonyms, which in some contexts are interchangeable. Many times he resumed the task of sketching a system of question-response. This personal "system" is superimposed on a more generally accepted terminology: that of *reflex action*, in which the stimulus/response couple is operative. Valéry turned reflex into a trump, for he saw no reason not to trust contemporary psychophysiology's favorite notion. On the many occasions in which he discusses the reflex model, he replaces an overly general term — "reaction" — with its best-qualified representative (a kind of delegate) in the realm of animal life. Marcel Gauchet has insisted that Valéry should be given his proper place as a "reflexologist."[101] Having adopted the theory of those scholars who reduced the phenomena of mental life to a set of impersonal reflexes (Laycock, Herzen, Ribot), Valéry understood, as did Nietzsche before him, that this doctrine was the most effective weapon for disarming the conscious subject of the immutable central role attributed to it by the Cartesian tradition. The "I" or the "me," according to Valéry, is the changing and anonymous product of a changing and anonymous corporeal causality. "I strive only to differ — to become different":

Oh, I tell my Self: "It is not you who hunt up your ideas; quite otherwise, it is the idea that tracks you down and makes its home in you.
"What you call 'I,' your 'I,' is not embedded deep down in your

vital system. There is no 'I' in your brain matter; but it generates 'I-ness' as it generates ideas. And in the sudden light of an idea the 'I' is stimulated reciprocally and reveals itself."[102]

"Reflex," "reaction," "response" are *explanatory* words for Valéry. They are precise instruments with which he attempts to simplify and purify our ideas, too long attached to troublesome and illusory philosophical words.[103] These purifying notions, he thought, were immediately transposable to a personal "algebra," in which he wanted to determine the functions that seemed most certain to him.[104] "The idea of function has dominated me. I have thought that the Reflex-act type of function was the fundamental fact." He finds it so fundamental that he expects from it — by way of *reaction*! — a radical change in man's whole system of values and knowledge:

> Functional understanding of the nervous system should *react* on the ideas we have of the value of knowledge in general, on our concepts of certainty, of the Universe, of Man — and all the rest. [In the margin: But this knowledge remains in limbo.]

> Reflex is the central idea, common to both physiological and psychological observation. — It is the Δs.
> Intus et extra, this figure is found everywhere. It is the universal form.[105]

Even if the distinction is maintained between physiology and psychology, Valéry is convinced that "thought and knowledge depend on a mental quasi mechanics — mental, but also vital,... consciousness itself is a product of it." Yet he mistrusts this reduction to "physiologism," upheld by so many of his contemporaries, just as he mistrusts psychologism, which is a "vicious circle."

As Gauchet has noted, Valéry's originality, in the persevering reflection of the *Cahiers*, lay in his not adhering to the usual reflexological construction, which merely accumulated causal stimulus-response series. Valéry introduces a second system, reflexivity. He defines it as a "psychic bi-reflex — with a two-way entry," which produces language and opens onto "possibility."[106] Thus is the mind born of the body and functioning in the reflexive mode. Ultimately, the first *me* detaches itself from a *me* that has become secondary, and the representation of the generating process gives rise to a cosmogonic image:

> Since consciousness distinguishes itself indefinitely from its objects, it tends to believe in itself, in its being as separable from all objects. I think invincibly of a rotating mass, which would feel its own efforts, would distinguish between an acceleration distancing it from its axis and another that brings it back to it. Each instant subjects it to virtual division — it is indivisible, but its state is only conceivable to it as composite. The axis believes it exists.
>
> It is like the perpetual formation of the universe through centrifugation, analogous to the gigantic centrifugation of the Kant-Laplace nebula.
>
> Consciousness perishes either through a slowing down of this rotation — which is sleep — or through an acceleration to the point of rupture.
>
> *Everything takes place* as if the living being centrifuged something that is its universe.
>
> After all — *I am* a terribly simple system, found or formed in 1892 — through an unbearable irritation, which stimulated a *me* no. 2 to detach itself from a first *me*, like an overly centrifuged millstone or a *nebulous mass* in rotation.[107]

The pure me would therefore be in a central, axial situation, which, according to a note from 1936, constitutes a return to the first attempts at formulating the "heterogeneous":

> I did not know (and still do not know) how to express the relation among the heterogeneous, incomparable, and irreducible things that populate our senses and mind, and whose real incoherence is opposed by the CONTRARY — the "Me" — the Constant, Producer of series and continuities, the Eternal, the Central.[108]

The image of the rotating nebula recalls Poe and *Eureka*, which drew from the same source.[109] This time it is a matter not only of a simple cycle but of a veritable cosmogonic model applied to the individual. The pure me attributes a fabulous genesis to itself, although Valéry does not renounce conferring on it the status of a "reflex-response to the heterogeneous."[110] According to an idea that often occurs in Valéry, the changing personality is made up of a multiplicity of impersonal, molecular reflexes, whereas the "me" is an undecomposable *invariant*: it is a remainder (or confronts a remainder in a reciprocal relationship), close to nothingness, and in a perpetual relation of opposition or negation. At times, Valéry makes it a Whole: "The Me is the All of which the personality is a part"; at times, he makes it "what is opposed to the All."[111]

What is important to Valéry, as I have mentioned, is not the general circulation of the cosmos but the circuit of a single being's states. This is where Valéry, in his poetry, encountered the experience of respiration and the beating heart, which is, according to his "system," the organic ground on which the states of consciousness are produced. "At the end of the mind, the body. But at the end of the body, the mind."[112] Thus the neoclassical rhetoric of "The Young Fate" — a text that Valéry saw as the poetic elaboration of a circuit of bodily and conscious states over a twenty-four-hour period — gives rise at opportune moments to the words "blood," "heart," and "beating": the sensation of the body is always linked to the cosmic event and to the perception of mortal limits. One reads in the section Valéry titled "Primavera":

> You hear... Wait no longer... The newborn year
> To all my blood foretells secret impulses:
> Rueful, the frost relinquishes its last diamonds...
> My heart beats! It beats! My burning breast impels me!

Valéry even takes pleasure in conjoining the heart and exhalation:

> Immense being invades me, the burning incense
> Of my divine heart breathes a shape without end....
> All the radiant bodies tremble in my essence![113]

Then, at the end of the poem, in an unusual inversion of roles, the Sun breathes the Fate. She finds her identity in submitting herself to him. "I am still she whom you breathe." The Sun again, at the end, takes possession of the beating heart, beneath the blowing wind:

> If I come in windswept garments
> To this edge, unafraid, inhaling the high foam,
> My eyes drinking in the immense salt laughter...
>
> Then, even against my will, I must, oh Sun,
> Worship this heart where you seek to know yourself,
> Sweet and powerful return of birth's delights,
>
> Fire to which a virgin of blood uplifts herself
> Beneath the gold coinage of a grateful breast![114]

With the "return of birth's delights," a cycle is completed. In the poem's finale, the Sun and the "intense soul" that raises the sea are the triumphant actors. The voice of the lyrical subject makes a gesture of submission: it goes out to meet these powers of the world, accepting them in the space in which they reign and welcoming them into its own bodily existence. The respiratory rhythm, the beating hearts of a whole era of Romanticism are still present beneath the neoclassical rhetoric of this invocation.

Valéry had read and reread *Eureka*. Eugenio Montale, as far as I know, was not captivated in the same way. Nonetheless, when I read "Stanzas," one of the most famous poems in *The Occasions*, I cannot help but think of the cosmogony of *Eureka*. The poem begins with the question of an original *point* from which flows the life that pulses in the wrists and temples of the beloved. The poem evokes the "shock / of the world's gears":

> I seek in vain that point from which
> the blood you're nourished by began, circles pushing
> each other on into infinite space, on
> beyond the tiny span
> of human days.[115]

To use this as an occasion to think of Poe would perhaps be a case of "mistaken recognition," or the effect of a retinal persistence, which often happens when one has stared too long at a luminous image.[116]

Paul Klee beautifully addressed the image of the beating heart in his 1924 Jena lecture. In it, he speaks of the circulation (*Kreislauf*) of the life forces and invites the artist to see not completed forms in the world but a creative process that has not yet reached completion. Nature is always changing. Art must follow this movement; we should renounce the image-as-model (*Vorbild*) and move toward the primal image (*Urbild*)!

> ...Chosen are those artists who penetrate to the region of that secret place where primeval power nurtures all evolution. There, where the power-house of all time and space — call it brain or heart of creation — activates every function; who is the artist who would not dwell there? In the womb of nature, at the source of creation, where the secret key to all lies guarded. But not all can enter. Each should follow where the pulse of his own heart leads.

Klee adds that the Impressionists dwelled "within the matted undergrowth of every-day vision." And they were right to do so. "But our pounding heart drives us down, deep down to the source (*Urgrund*) of all."[117]

CHAPTER SEVEN

Reaction and Progress

Morality and Calculation in the Age of Enlightenment

To extend to the "moral world" the principles reigning over the "physical world" — how not to be tempted by this possibility, especially if one is persuaded that God's benevolence is not limited to material bodies? Newton himself, in his "Scholium generale," had affirmed that "He governs all things." A quarter of a century after the publication of the *Principia*, the following lines could be read in an English periodical:

> The mutual gravitation of bodies cannot be explained any other way than by resolving it into the immediate operation of God, who never ceases to dispose and actuate his creatures in a manner suitable to their respective beings. So neither can that reciprocal attraction in the minds of men be accounted for by any other cause. It is not the result of education, law, or fashion: but is a principle originally ingrafted in the very first formation of the soul by the Author of our nature.
>
> And as the attractive power in bodies is the most universal principle which produceth innumerable effects, so the corresponding social appetite in human souls is the great mechanism and source of human actions.[1]

These lines were written by George Berkeley, who titled his article "Moral Attraction." Here the system of the world becomes the model for the system of minds, both of which have the same theological guarantee. Clearly, this is not an inference drawn from the difficult texts of the *Principia* but rather the echo of a vulgarized Newtonianism. Analogous propositions can be found in the works of another eighteenth-century Irish philosopher, Francis Hutcheson (1694–1746): "The universal Benevolence toward all Men, we may compare to that Principle of Gravitation, which perhaps extends to all Bodys in the Universe."[2] Of course, it is the image, not the rule, of the calculation of forces that carries the point. Furthermore, it was easy to transport the idea of attraction into the moral realm, in part because the terms "attraction" and "attractive faculty" had long been used to define the properties of the magnet. Now, the magnet — as mannerist poetry attests — was the natural model for amorous sympathies and inclinations. The rhetoric of attraction could easily be adapted to the "attractant" motion of the great heavenly bodies, and vice versa. When Newton's system was popularized, people affirmed a universal equilibrium involving attraction and repulsion, which was then associated with the attraction of magnetism, static electricity, and chemical compounds.[3]

The reference to Newtonianism as well as to Petrarchan rhetoric is evident in the letter Rousseau's heroine in *La Nouvelle Héloïse* sends from Clarens to her lover in Paris. She tells him that despite the physical distance, their closeness is in no way compromised: "It is the union of hearts that provides their true felicity; their attraction knows not the law of distances, and our hearts would touch at opposite ends of the earth."[4] Love outdoes the mathematical constant of gravity! The space that cannot be eluded in the physical realm is thus abolished in the rhetoric of passion.

Johann Gottfried Herder amplifies the metaphor. He defines thought as man's central force, and he grants it a place in the universal equilibrium: "Our soul thinks: such is its central force: — if it were not attracted by another, it would fall indefinitely.... Man gravitates in relation to everything, even in relation to God. Everything gravitates in relation to man: he gives and takes thoughts to and from the universe. He is part of God's thought; a part of God's thought is his thought."[5]

Moreover, sympathy is not the only thing likened to Newtonian attraction. For Hume, who is ever prudent, there is a similarity between attraction and the association of ideas: "Here is a kind of attraction, which in the mental world will be found to have as extraordinary effects as in the natural, and to shew itself in as many and as various forms. Its effects are every where conspicuous; but as to its causes, they are mostly unknown, and must be resolv'd into *original* qualities of human nature, which I pretend not to explain."[6] The formula is adopted in yet other domains. In the preliminary summary he gives of a work on language by the scholar Johann David Michaelis, Jean-Bernard Mérian writes: "Language and men's opinions may be compared to two springs continuously acting upon each other. A diagram or picture in which this action and reaction could be precisely pinpointed would form, so to speak, the general map of the human mind."[7] This time we are entirely within the realm of social life.

We will now turn our attention to such conceptions of social life and history, since these were the privileged fields in which the notion of action/reaction was applied between the eighteenth and the twentieth century. Although we have already examined the life sciences, it will be necessary to consider for a moment how these applications shifted from nature to society.

The equilibrium of nature was a favorite argument of eighteenth-century physico-theology, and it became, almost simultaneously, a common motif in the discourse on political reality.[8] Does not the perpetuation of animal species offer us a glimpse of Providence, despite the war they wage among themselves? How is it that predators do not completely destroy the species they devour? For the ecclesiastic William Derham (1657–1736), everything reveals "a very remarkable act of the Divine providence.... Thus the balance of the animal world, is, throughout all ages, kept even."[9] Although Derham does not speak explicitly of action and reaction to account for this balance, others did so later, at times praising nature's foresight, at times explaining the play of mechanical causes, without invoking final causes. In a note in his *Essay on the Origin of Languages* (completed in 1761), Rousseau speaks of action and reaction among animal species as a generally accepted opinion: "It is said that by a sort of natural action and reaction the various species in the animal realm maintain themselves, in relation to each other, in a perpetual oscillation which keeps them in equilibrium."[10] Through analogy, the couple action/reaction soon became associated with ebb and flow and applied to considerations of world population and collective movements. Rousseau postulates an alternation of migrations in one direction and invasions in the opposite direction:

> Mankind, born in the warm countries, spreads from there to the cold countries; it is in these that it multiplies and later flows back into the warm countries. From this action and reaction come the earth's revolutions and the continual agitation of its inhabitants.[11]

Analogous but more destructive movements are produced in the relations between civilized societies, if one considers them as natural individuals living in competition, outside all contractual juridical obligation:

Some large, others small; some strong, others weak; attacking, resisting, and destroying one another, and in this continual action and
reaction, responsible for more misery and loss of life than if men had
all kept their initial freedom.[12]

Hardly any difference is indicated here between international
relations and the law establishing equilibrium among animal pop-
ulations. It is quite different within states, especially in the state
according to Rousseau's *Social Contract*, where freedom through
law supplants natural independence. In a fundamental situation
examined by Rousseau in *The Social Contract*, the forces that
could be expended against each other are withdrawn from individuals and transferred, by law, to the institution, that is, to the
collective power of the "sovereign." A mechanism is set in place
that no longer has the spontaneity of the competition for life
among species or nations (if it is true, as Locke asserts, that they
live together in a state of nature). The intervention of a legislator,
that is, "a mechanic who invents the machine," becomes necessary. Equality must be ensured by opposing the "force of legislation" to the "force of things." Here Rousseau is not speaking of
weight and counterweight, or of action and reaction. But does it
not suffice that he speaks of a machine? Rousseau also discusses
the "object," or the privileged activity, by which the legislation
is instituted. He asserts that Montesquieu drew attention to the
goals that tend to be served by the various legislations: "The author
of *The Spirit of the Laws* has given large numbers of examples of the
art by which the legislator directs the institution toward each of
these objects."[13]

Now, if we reread Montesquieu, we notice that his thought on
these matters makes use of physical models. Montesquieu mentions action and reaction first to establish the necessary sequence
of causes and effects among natural forces and, from there, to

express the conflicts and imbalances that can set in among social, collective, and individual agents. Beginning in his youthful writings, he argues in terms of mechanical models in order to mark out the sequence of "physical causes." He asserts them very speculatively, but postulates that they could be subjected to rigorous measurement and objective calculation. Hence, in *The Spirit of the Laws*, Montesquieu explains the effects of a cold climate in terms belonging to the language of mechanistic medical science: "People are therefore more vigorous in cold climates. Here the action of the heart and the reaction of the extremities of the fibres are better performed."[14] The formula is applied to the military art, in which brute force is used. In *Considerations on the Causes of the Greatness of the Romans and Their Decline* (1734), Montesquieu justifies his preference for the infantry over the cavalry: "The action of [the cavalry] consists more in its impetuosity and a certain shock; that of [the infantry], in its resistance and a certain immobility; it is more of a reaction than an action."[15] When Montesquieu uses these same models to speak of the play of political forces, he notes that he is borrowing the couple action/reaction from cosmology and physics and using it as an analogy. Such a reminder of the terms' scientific origins clearly demonstrates that this transposed use was still innovative in French, even though the metaphor of the checks and balances had become common in the language of politics. To justify the turbulence of free states, Montesquieu asserts that their agitation is not incompatible with a certain happiness: "[T]here can be union within a state in which people think they see only trouble, a harmony from which happiness results, which is the only true peace. It is like the parts of this universe, eternally bound together by the action of some, and the reaction of others."[16] Yet again, in *The Spirit of the Laws* he privileges physical metaphors, with references to the weights and counterweights of the English government, the image of mutually compensating mechanical springs, the image of inevitable friction, and so on. The ideal of the mixed or temperate constitution, which the jurists find, notably, in Polybius (*History* 6.10), is transcribed into mechanical terms. In Montesquieu's language, the play of action and reaction is therefore no longer descriptive or purely explanatory, but a goal to pursue, a value to assert. The concept of action and reaction intervenes to define good constitutions and the duties legislators must respect:

> That the laws of education ought to be relative to the principle of each government, has been shewn in the preceding book. Now the same may be said of those which the legislator gives to the whole society. This relation of laws to this principle strengthens the several springs of government, and this principle receives from thence, in its turn, a new degree of strength. Thus it is that in physical movements, action is always followed by reaction.[17]

Clearly, we are no longer dealing with a verifiable fact on a par with a natural phenomenon: Montesquieu is defining a task, a norm to be respected. The decisions that regulate the relations of power must proceed from the legislator's will: it is not the cause, but rather the desired result of the action expressed in physical terms. The legislator is a metalworker. This represents an exemplary application of a principle formulated by Francis Bacon: one must obey nature in order to dominate it. The physical law is the same whether one is speaking of nature left to its own devices or nature manipulated by technology. But the design that leads to the machine uses the natural law for a definite purpose. And that is exactly how one defines an art: the art of politics.

To phrase this differently: action/reaction is a given that is de facto omnipresent. If one does not wish to submit to it, one must master it. To submit, according to a providentialist vision of history (which Montesquieu does not share), would be simply to leave it in the hands of God, who carries out his designs for the best: we have but to endure, hope, be patient, and try to understand. In the opposite case, if one believes it possible to *intervene* with a view to ensuring security, tranquillity, and happiness in our own or a community's interests, then there is an action to be undertaken. It is necessary to legislate, that is, to manage human relations while taking account of the natural reactions of individuals, their physical and historical milieus, and the new actions and reactions that will result from the legislation. Thus an instituting authority (a legislator) has the *duty* to foresee as precisely as possible the results of his choices. Montesquieu, always inclined to extend the realm of physical necessity, in no way restricts moral obligations. He recalls the conditions that must inevitably be confronted. He also knows — and this is the only true "historical lesson" — that corruption, "perverse effects," and unmastered actions and reactions can sometimes regain the upper hand. Nature follows its course, but societies are lost: "Under the last emperors, the empire, reduced to a suburb of Constantinople, ended up like the Rhine, which is but a river when it loses itself in the Ocean."[18]

However that may be, well-tempered actions and reactions became almost synonymous with good government. When Edmund Burke praises the ancestral principles of the English monarchy — contrasting them with the political order that the French revolutionary assemblies attempted to set up — he declares that the former were founded on nature. In the same breath, and in a manner that Montesquieu would not have completely disavowed, he reproaches the French for having abandoned their former constitution, meaning their feudal institutions prior to absolutism, since these ensured a better equilibrium:

You possessed . . . all the foundations of a noble and venerable castle. You might have repaired those walls; you might have built on those old foundations. . . . In your old states you possessed that variety of parts corresponding with the various description of which your community was happily composed; you had all that combination, and all that opposition of interests, you had that action and counter-action which, in the natural and political world, from the recipro-cal struggle of discordant powers, draws out the harmony of the universe.[19]

In a burst of confidence that seems premature to us today, Diderot, while resigning himself to seeing societies disappear, believed that the scourges of the past were henceforth behind Europe. He proposed an image of dynamic equilibrium:

Europe, the only continent of the globe on which one should rest one's gaze, seems to have settled too solidly and fixedly to give rise to rapid and surprising revolutions. Its societies are almost equally populated, enlightened, spread out, strong, and jealous. They will crowd each other, they will act and react upon each other; in the midst of this continual fluctuation, some will spread out, others will be compressed, some might disappear. . . . Fanaticism and the spirit of conquest, the two causes of upheaval in this world, have ceased.[20]

This optimistic image of European equilibrium formulated in terms of the dynamics of fluids — according to the model of tides — finds its immediate complement, in terms of the forces at play between solid bodies, in a note that Melchior Grimm added to this text. Rather brutally, Grimm calls for calculation so as not to let oneself be deluded by appearances of equilibrium. Yes, there is always action and reaction in nature, but this does not necessarily result in harmony. A violent and "skillful" man can always seize power in order to exercise a tyrannical domination unless another force is opposed to his:

> The eternal law is forever in force, and it demands that the weak be the prey of the strong. Now, weakness becomes the attribute of peoples when there is a lack of agreement in their wills and in the measures they take. The man who is resolute, enterprising, firm, active, and skillful will subjugate the multitude as surely and as necessarily as a weight of 50 pounds overwhelms a weight of 50 ounces. If he does not succeed, it is because in the opposing party he encountered a man of his caliber who draws the multitude to his side. Then the results conform to the complication of *counterweights acting and reacting upon each other*; but the calculation of these results would always be rigorous if one could know the elements involved. The declamations of the philosophers against slavery, in directing us to survey the whole rest of the globe or the duration of centuries, only confirm good minds in the sad opinion that three quarters of the human race are born with a spirit of servitude.[21]

Grimm's cynical realism stresses that in order to change the course of things, one must be able to foresee the results and thus know how to calculate. Grimm, a friend to sovereign rulers, willingly resigns himself to the idea that a part of mankind will remain enslaved. He seems to admit that in politics, superiority is rigorously ponderable. Putting the forces exercised in the "moral world" into equations is useful in the highest degree. And in this "moral world," there is a force that is equally as universal as that of attraction: interest. Rousseau, who recognizes this, considers the calculation of interest the task of all those who have opted "to live in the world":

> To live in the world one must know how to deal with men, one must know the instruments which give one a hold over them. One must know how to calculate the action and the reaction of particular interests in civil society, and to foresee events so accurately that one is rarely mistaken in one's undertakings, or at least has chosen the best means for succeeding.[22]

This is meant as pedagogical advice, but it is also an avowal of one of the reasons that convinced Rousseau not "to live in the world."

According to the materialist credo preached by Paul Henri d'Holbach, mechanical laws are the same in the infinitely small and the infinitely large, in the swirl of dust and in the planetary orbits. By the same token, why exempt living beings and historical changes? In *The System of Nature* (1770), Holbach extends the vocabulary of physics to the passions. They are "movements of attraction or repulsion by which nature makes man susceptible to the objects that appear useful or harmful to him." In Holbach, one finds most resolutely expressed the principle according to which interest and self-love govern the human world in the same way as attraction rules the great bodies of the universe. In this determinism, which makes everything the cause of everything else, there exists "an immense chain of causes and effects, which flow without ceasing one from the other."[23] To convince his reader, Holbach takes an example first from physics and then from the "moral" realm, that is, from politics. The determinist analogy is imposed most peremptorily:

> In a whirlwind of dust, raised by the impetuous elements, confused as it appears to our eyes; in the most frightful tempest, excited by contrary winds, when the waves roll high as mountains; there is not a single particle of dust, or drop of water, that has been placed by

chance; that has not a sufficient cause for occupying the place where it is found; that does not, in the most rigorous sense of the word, act in the manner in which it ought to act; that is, according to its own peculiar essence, and that of the beings from whom it receives its impulse. A geometrician, who exactly knew the different energies acting in each case, with the properties of the particles moved, could demonstrate that, after the causes given, each particle acted precisely as it ought to act, and that it could not have acted otherwise than it did.

In those terrible convulsions that sometimes agitate political societies, shake their foundations, and frequently produce the overthrow of an empire — there is not a single action, a single word, a single thought, a single will, a single passion in the agents, whether they act as destroyers or as victims, that is not the necessary result of the causes operating; that does not act as of necessity it must act from the peculiar situation these agents occupy in the moral whirlwind. This could be evidently proved by an understanding capacitated to seize and to rate *all the actions and reactions* [italics mine] of the minds and bodies of those who contributed to the revolution.[24]

The image of swirling dust, common to the physical and the moral world, does not merely connect them distantly through a metaphor; it makes it possible to imagine the transition from the physical sphere to the political sphere. Natural causes — climatic or meteorological — modify individuals, and individuals modify institutions and societies:

In fact, if all be connected in nature; if all motion be produced the one from the other, notwithstanding their secret communications frequently elude our sight; we ought to feel convinced that there is no cause, however minute, however remote, that does not sometimes produce the greatest and the most immediate effects on man. It may perhaps be in the arid plains of Libya, that are amassed the first elements of a storm or tempest, which, borne by the winds, approximate our climate, render our atmosphere dense, which operating on the temperament, may influence the passions of a man whose circumstances shall have capacitated him to influence many others, and who shall decide after his will the fate of many nations.

Man, in fact, finds himself in nature, and makes a part of it: he acts according to laws which are peculiar to him; he receives, in a manner more or less distinct, the action, the impulse of the beings who surround him; who themselves act after laws that are peculiar to their essence. It is thus that he is variously modified; but his actions are always the result of his own peculiar energy, and that of the beings who act upon him, and by whom he is modified. This is what gives such variety to his determinations; what frequently produces such contradiction in his thoughts, his opinions, his will, his actions; in short, that motion, whether concealed or visible, by which he is agitated.

Like his friend Diderot, Holbach refers to a living nature that is the totality made up jointly (and unconsciously) of all the parts contained in its core:

> Nature is an active, living whole, whose parts necessarily concur, and that without their own knowledge, to maintain activity, life, and existence. Nature acts and exists necessarily: all that she contains necessarily conspires to perpetuate her active existence.[25]

This idea of totality is less distant than it might seem from the one favored by Romantic thought, at least insofar as the latter becomes attached to a vitalist monism. With Holbach, however, it is an argument against religion, whereas with the Romantics it will be an argument against mechanistic determinism, of which Holbach himself would be the prime example.

When probabilistic mathematics went on to develop new methods of calculation, the Libyan storm imagined by Holbach was categorized as a rationally calculable event, to the point of becoming (much later) the famous beating of a butterfly's wing causing a hurricane.[26] The calculation of probabilities, as it was developed in the eighteenth century, was not restricted to the play of chance and the evaluation of risks. At the end of the eighteenth century, the success of "analysis" in the physical realm seemed to foreshadow analogous successes in a broader field of application, passing from material facts to social ones. The idea of a "social mathematics" based on statistical data was meant to objectify the many different types of circumstances that make up the situation of a country and a population. In the absence of fully demonstrable certitudes, it is important for man's happiness that decisions be based on "probable opinions." In his testamentary work, Condorcet announces an age in which political action, thanks to calculation, would more surely anticipate and attain its goals:

> The application of the calculus of combinations and probabilities to these sciences promises even greater improvement, since it is the only way of achieving results of an almost mathematical exactitude and of assessing the degree of their probability or likelihood. Sometimes, it is true, the evidence upon which these results are based may lead us, without any calculation, at the first glance, to some general truth and teach us whether the effect produced by such-and-such a cause was or was not favourable, but if this evidence cannot be weighed and measured, and if these effects cannot be subjected to precise measurement, then we cannot know exactly how much good or evil they contain; or, again, if the good and evil nearly balance each other, if the difference between them is slight, we cannot pronounce with any certainty to which side the balance really inclines. Without the application of the calculus it would be almost impossi-

ble to choose with any certainty between two combinations that have the same purpose and between which there is no apparent difference in merit.[27]

Condorcet adds that the application of this method is only in its "first elements." "It must open to later generations a source of truly inexhaustible light, like the science of calculus itself and like the number of combinations, relationships and facts that can be subjected to it." It did not take long for these ideas to find an echo. The "ideologue" Constantin-François Volney (1757–1820), who taught a remarkable course on history at the Ecole Normale Supérieure in 1795, wrote: "Knowledge of these physical laws is becoming a necessary element in the science of governing and organizing a social body, and of constituting it in relation to natural motion, which is to say that political legislation is nothing other than the application of the laws of nature."[28] These views became reality under the French Directory; Benjamin Constant and Germaine de Staël proposed such views in their first writings. In a more nuanced manner, their friend Wilhelm von Humboldt, in the short essay "Betrachtungen über die bewegenden Ursachen in der Weltgeschichte" (1818), proposes this way of reading the world's events. One must begin with the "nature of things" before considering the work of freedom and the interpretation of chance:

> The nature of things is determined, either completely or within certain limits; and in the nature of things, one must above all count also the moral nature of man, for man himself, especially if one considers the way in which he acts within a whole and as a mass, maintains himself on certain uniform paths, receives more or less the same impressions, from the same objects, and reacts [zurückwirkt] more or less in the same way. Considered from this point of view, the entire history of the world, in the past and in the future, could be calculated

mathematically, and the perfection of the calculation would depend only on the extent of our familiarity with the determining causes.[29]

Humboldt is a proponent of statistical (particularly demographic) data. In these data, he finds regularities whose consequences are accepted at first:

> Even man's voluntary actions assume the character of nature, which follows a path that always doubles back onto itself, according to uniform laws. The study of this way of explaining world history, through mechanics and (since nothing influences human affairs more than the force of elective moral affinities) through chemistry, is important to the highest degree, especially when it is directed toward a more exact knowledge of laws according to which the isolated components of history, the forces and the reacting agents [*die Kräfte und Reagentien*], act and undergo actions in return [*wirken und Rückwirkungen empfangen*].[30]

Once he has presented this approach to history, however, Humboldt adds that it is doomed to failure if one limits oneself to it alone. He has presented it only preliminarily and, to some extent, as a concession. History does not follow a regular course; human freedom intervenes: innovation comes from great minds, and upheavals are produced by passionate beings. When their undertaking succeeds, something happens of which they themselves had but a vague presentiment. There are therefore two series of causes in history: nature and freedom. One can recognize that which natural necessity (which comes from "masses") forbids to freedom (which comes from "individuality") better than one can recognize the point at which freedom intervenes in nature. Humboldt remarks that these are two orders of causality that "limit themselves reciprocally." Is their relationship exclusive? In a fragment of an older essay titled "Theorie der Bildung des Menschen," Humboldt speaks of an interaction (*Wechselwirkung*) between man and the world:

> To give the greatest possible content to the concept of humanity
> in our person..., through the traces we leave of our living activity,
> such is the ultimate task of our existence. And this task is accomplished only through the joining of our self to the world in the
> most general, most moving, and most free interaction.... What
> man necessarily needs is simply an object that will make possible
> the interaction between his receptivity and his autonomous activity
> [*Selbsttätigkeit*].[31]

In a work from 1797, at the beginning of his stay in Paris, Humboldt assigns to man the vocation of perfecting his personal value. This perfecting can only be accomplished by involving other people. Reason and will must be employed to this end. "Reason seeks its totality in the world and does not know other boundaries than those of the world: will finds its boundaries in the individual and cannot surpass them." But reason and will may find themselves in contradiction with each other. To overcome this contradiction, the individual's march toward his goal must at the same time promote a general progress toward this same goal: "The general interaction of theoretical reason and practical will produces a way of acting in which, with an entirely individual energy, we merely fulfill a single role within a general plan."[32]

Chances of and Obstacles to Progress

Diderot is attached to the precept articulated by Francis Bacon: "Natura non nisi parendo vincitur" (Nature is conquered only by obedience).[33] It is necessary to increase knowledge in order to increase man's power over the natural world. Diderot, as we have seen, was convinced that, on a very large scale, nature perpetuates itself through the active and reactive motion of its parts. Yet he also acknowledged, paradoxically, that the knowledge we have been fortunate enough to acquire also authorizes us to predict that its progress will not be perpetuated indefinitely. In his time, "progress" was still a neutral term, applied as much to self-perfection as to deterioration. Pascal had declared that modern science surpassed that of Antiquity, but he also wrote: "Everything that is perfected by progress is also destroyed by progress."[34] Diderot imagined catastrophic vicissitudes, an inexhaustible fecundity, and new forms of life following great destructions. His certainty about material eternity allowed him to imagine every kind of disaster. The world would survive such disasters without molecules losing their ability to recombine. In the *Encyclopédie* entry titled "Encyclopédie," he defines his great undertaking as an ark of knowledge that could help the people who might survive a new deluge. While hoping to offer his contemporaries the means to perfect their faculties and instruments with his great dictionary, Diderot did not say that nature sets any plan or goal for itself: chance was more closely associated with it. The figure of the world to come is aleatory or cyclic. Having supplanted God, nature promises only an indefinite series of metamorphoses. The divinity's disappearance meant the passing away of finality as well. Providence had vanished without leaving an heir.

Condorcet, for his part, was convinced of the perfectibility of human nature. In his interpretation of history (and its successive eras), he points to the progress of knowledge and — though to a much lesser degree — of morality and social institutions. The accomplishments and improvements seem henceforth irreversible to him: they infallibly announce the progress yet to come. The doctrine of *Sketch for a Historical Picture of the Progress of the Human Mind* is already found in *The Life of M. Turgot* (1786):

M. Turgot...considered an indefinite perfectibility as one of the distinctive qualities of the human race. The effects of this ever growing
perfectibility seemed to him infallible. The invention of printing
undoubtedly advanced its progress, and even made any retrogression
impossible.... He believed, for example, that progress in the physical sciences, in education, in scientific method, and in the discovery
of new methods, would contribute to the perfecting of our organization, making men capable of collecting more ideas in their memories
and multiplying their combinations: he believed that their moral
sense was also capable of being perfected.

According to these principles, all useful truths must end up one
day becoming generally known and adopted by all men. All former
errors must be gradually reduced to nothing and replaced by new
truths. This progress, growing century by century, knows no limit,
or has but an absolutely unassignable one in the current state of our
enlightenment.

He was convinced that the perfection of the social order would
necessarily lead to one no less great in morality; that men would
continuously become better to the extent that they became enlightened. He therefore wished that instead of seeking to bind human
virtues to prejudices or to make them reliant upon enthusiasm or
exaggerated principles, one would limit oneself to convincing men
...that their self-interest should lead them to practice sweet, peace-
ful virtues, and that their happiness is bound up with that of other
men.[35]

In recalling Condorcet's text, which is so important in the history
of the ideas of progress, I would like to draw attention to the expressions designating the obstacles to progress: "errors," "prejudices," and "retrogression."

The idea of progress imposed itself as a result of the success of
scientific thought, in which the triumph of the laws of Newtonian

mechanics played an important role. In fact, it involved an interpretative choice.[36] The developments of scientific knowledge
were considered indications of a much more general perfectibility
that was not limited to science alone. Now it would not be long
before the word "reaction" was borrowed from the already popularized language of the laws of mechanics to designate that which
impedes or opposes progress. To it would be attributed the role
of the term "retrogression" in the text just cited. It was not Condorcet, as far as I know, who introduced this new usage: after the
deaths of Condorcet and Robespierre, new circumstances were
necessary for the progress/reaction antinomy to become established in politics. It was Benjamin Constant's task to establish a
clear opposition between progress and reaction. But to put Constant's observations into perspective, we must reexamine the work
of Kant, especially his writings on human history.

According to Kant, man has the ability to develop his faculties,
and this development allows for the conjecture of a "plan of
nature."[37] Universal history would then be a stage on which progress is played out in a continuous series. Let us suppose that
there is a hidden goal at work without man's being aware of it
(nature acting "through an art hidden to man," *durch eigene, ob-
zwar dem Menschen abgedrungene Kunst*), allowing our species to
pass little by little from the lower to the higher levels of humanity.
(With Hegel, nature's hidden art becomes "the ruse of reason.")
Through conflictual relations such as antagonisms and wars,
states will be forced to establish a new equilibrium (*Gleichge-
wicht*). Just as the struggle between primitive man against adverse
circumstances led to the creation of civil societies, the struggle
among civil societies, whose freedom has remained barbarous
(*barbarische Freiheit*), should lead in the long run, and in the interest of each of them, to an association of states (*Staatenverbindung*),
a federation of peoples (*Völkerbund*), which we are still very far

from attaining. Relations between societies — the jurists of the Enlightenment had often repeated this — remain as independent and as violent as those between men in the state of nature. The principle of association and of submission to a common law, which is the "solution to strife," is supposed to intervene in such a way as to surmount the conflict among sovereign states, just as it intervened at the beginning of human history to appease antagonisms among independent individuals. The threat of war would persist, of course, but it would represent a salutary danger that would keep humanity's strengths ever alert: "But ... not without a principle of the *equality* of their reciprocal *actions and reactions*, lest they [the states] should destroy one another."[38]

Kant was perfectly aware that this sort of thinking proceeded by analogy and in no way implied conclusive arguments. Proof of this is found in a remark in section 90 of *The Critique of Judgement*:

> In the case of two dissimilar things we may admittedly form some conception of one of them by an analogy which it bears to the other, and do so even on the point on which they are dissimilar [*Eben in dem Punkte ihrer Ungleichartigkeit*]; but from that in which they are dissimilar we cannot draw any inference from one to the other on the strength of the analogy — that is, we cannot transfer the mark [*Merkmal*] of the specific difference to the second. Thus on the analogy of the law of the equality of action and reaction in the mutual attraction and repulsion of bodies I am able to picture to my mind the social relations of the members of a commonwealth [*Gemeinschaft*] regulated by civil laws; but I cannot transfer to these relations the former specific modes, that is, physical attraction and repulsion, and ascribe them to the citizens, so as to constitute a system called a state.[39]

Indeed, analogy can be misleading. In mechanics, in action and reaction, and in any application of the parallelogram of forces, the sum of the forces remains equal. This is not the case with a social body. The forces that can be isolated, and between which interactions are thought to be found, are abstractions. Political decisions and protests, dominant tendencies and resistances are not really in mechanical opposition to each other. Innovation and its consequences cannot be evaluated in terms of constituent forces, nor can persuasion and faith, satisfaction and discontent, and so on. Action and reaction are never more than an approximate figure for the likely causes of a society's equilibrium, instability, or blockages.

With regard to the progress of humanity, Kant considers contrary eventualities. He multiplies the questions. Would not conflicts among states lead to arbitrary, entirely precarious equilibriums? "The states, by an Epicurean concourse of efficient causes, should enter by random collisions (like those of small material particles [*wie die kleinen Stäubchen der Materie*]) into all kinds of formations which are again destroyed by new collisions, until they arrive *by chance* at a formation which can survive in its existing form." (One might ask, incidentally, if Kant was thinking of Holbach's swirl of dust.) Might not these conflicts destroy all cultural progress and plunge us back into barbarity? It could be that "nothing at all, or at least nothing rational, will anywhere emerge from all these actions and reactions among men."[40] Failure is therefore always possible.

In all of these hypotheses, the question concerns the orientation of actions and reactions in the endless spectacle of the history of states. These actions and reactions, so constantly evoked by Kant, form the web of history, its empirical reality. "Reflective judgement," as *The Critique of Judgement* applies it to the knowledge of nature and art, allows one to read in this history a universalizable finality, a design, a direction, a superior will that needs our cooperation to be realized.[41] Compared with primitive barbarity, our civilizations, however imperfect, attest to something better (*Verbesserung*). Kant sees this as a reason to hope for more progress, thanks to which contractual bonds will bring closer together all the states belonging to a better-educated humanity. The task of practical reason is therefore to extend to the institutions of human society as a whole the universalizing power of reason that each individual has the potential to use — so that the autonomy of thought, the free exercise of reason and will, and respect for the dignity of others would all be politically guaranteed. One can see in Kant the affirmation of the idea of *a possible direction of history*, which for others soon took on the name "Progress."[42]

For Kant, that which impedes or opposes progress is human violence, the "twisted wood" of which men are made. He observes their "unsocial sociability" (*ungesellige Geselligkeit*), which explains the slowness of the most desired moral and political transformations. History, according to Kant, is the field of action of a nature that gave man the predisposition (*Anlage*) toward progress. Nature thus constituted the human race as an agent responsible for its own destiny. This theory of history, however, merely announces from afar the antithetical couple Progress/Reaction, which will emerge in the language of nineteenth-century ideologies. Kant does not attribute the difficulties of progress to immaturity and prejudices alone: the problem lies in man's very nature.

An important change occurred in the last decades of the eighteenth century. On the one hand, the word "progress" was not used as often in neutral (temporal or spatial) senses as it had been previously. It assumed a new meaning that associated it with the idea of perfectibility.[43] On the other hand, and simultaneously, in political struggles, the resistance to progress-perfectibility was attributed to social groups and political forces, and no longer simply to a "radical evil in man." Once the hypostatized "Progress" (now in the singular, after a long use in the plural) became good, any restrictions placed on it had to be attributed, for the sake of symmetry, to an equally hypostatized antagonist. This function was filled by the word and the concept "reaction," whose semantic expansion throughout the eighteenth century we have just seen. Without losing its previous meanings, the word, charged with a new value, will insinuate itself into the language of political struggle.

Revolution and Reaction

The word "reaction" at first appeared sporadically among the journalists and orators of the French Revolution. Its meaning was completely neutral. It was the riposte, the action in the other direction, of a previously "oppressed" party or a cause under attack, whoever or whatever these may have been. "It is used figuratively for an oppressed party seeking revenge and acting in turn" (*Dictionnaire de l'Académie*, 1798). Is it purely coincidental that the emergence of the lexical couple "revolution/reaction" is more or less contemporary with the polarization of the political arena? Aristocrats and sansculottes, antagonistic clubs and factions, oath-taking and recalcitrant clergy, right and left sides of the Legislative Assembly — oppositions were forming all around. In the language of the time, the opposite of "revolution" was initially "counterrevolution," which became another aspect of "reaction."

This usage was at first incidental. Mirabeau speaks of the "necessity of establishing a sort of reaction against the incurable tendency among bishops and parish priests to bring back the former abuses" (November 27, 1790). He therefore recommended a

322

reaction in order to counter conservative resistance within the clergy. This resistance was called "counterrevolutionary." At the National Convention, orators could use "react" and "reaction" in various ways, depending on their implicit convictions. As long as the word retained a neutral meaning, it was suited to designate abstractly any violence caused by previous violence. However, to the extent that the partisans of the Revolution conceived of it as a founding effort that should not let up, they placed their opponents in the position of having only defensive or vengeful intentions, and thus reactions. In Jean-Paul Marat's vocabulary, reaction is associated with the court and its mercenaries. Thus an appeal from "L'Ami du Peuple," dated August 10, 1792, hails the taking of the Tuileries and the arrest of the royal family and calls upon the patriotic French to remain vigilant:

> I repeat: fear the reaction, for your enemies will not spare you if chance falls their way again. No mercy, then, for you are irrevocably lost if you do not hasten to eliminate the corrupt members of the municipality and the department, all the anti-patriotic justices of the peace and the most gangrenous members of the National Assembly.... No one abhors the shedding of blood more than I. But in order to prevent a flood of it, I urge you to shed a few drops.[44]

The emergence of the modern meaning of "reaction," I would stress, is linked to the advent of the idea of progress in political institutions. It was necessary to have a strictly delimited term to designate the action that goes against this progress (and thus positing two opposing agents) above and beyond the simpler opposition between progression and retrogression (which concerns the direction of the movements of a single subject).

After 9 Thermidor, the winds shifted. This was the moment the modern political meaning of "reaction" truly entered the scene.[45] Initially, however, it was used to designate the "revolutionary" and liberating character of the movement following the death of the "tyrant" Robespierre. The situation was compared to the mechanical effect of a spring suddenly released.[46] In an address to the Society of Jacobins dated 18 Thermidor, we read: "Great events took place in Paris a few days ago; a great revolution has occurred; the tyrant exists no longer, the *patrie* breathes, liberty triumphs.... After such a long compression, one must expect a powerful and proportionate reaction to the evils we have had to deplore; one must grant to sensitivity all that humanity requires."[47] In the use made of it here, one could say that the word preserves a neutral meaning. It expresses a movement in return or, as Bronislaw Baczko says, a *backlash*. The first Thermidorian moment is not antirevolutionary; it is first and foremost anti-Robespierre.

One month later, the word "reaction" designated more specifically the movements hostile to "the people." On 8 Fructidor, year II (August 25, 1794), the Jacobin François-Etienne-Jacques Raisson declared to the Convention: "After each crisis that has occurred since the Revolution, a reaction has been felt; the dangers have been but precarious and short-lived, and until this point the people have made up for lost time; but never has this reaction been felt in such a terrible way as at the present juncture."[48] Measures were first taken against the direct executors of the Committee of Public Safety: rage and rancor rained down upon the Terror's agents and sympathizers. Once the Thermidorian phase, strictly speaking, was past (that is, the phase when Robespierre's clique was the principal target), the situation favored a reversal toward monarchy. Soon royalist opinion was more openly expressed, inciting anti-republican retribution and calling for the restoration of the ancien régime. Sébastien Mercier, a good recorder of events, devotes a chapter in *Nouveau Paris* to the "royal reaction":

"Three quarters and a half of all Parisians have no idea of the appalling royal reaction. After the fall of the scaffolds, it caused more republicans to perish than had been immolated by them. The patriots most exempt from all weaknesses and crimes were incarcerated by the thousands."[49] Clearly, in this new political climate, partisans of the Republic and the representative regime were becoming alarmed. Baczko correctly pointed out the importance of Marie-Joseph Chénier's report dated 29 Vendémiaire, year IV (October 5, 1795), following the royalist uprising of 13 Vendémiaire. It became more and more common for republicans to designate the excesses of the "companies of Jesus," the "companies of the Sun," and royalist "conspirators" by associating them with the word "reaction," usually in the plural. Such is the case, for example, during the troubles that shook the south of France in early 1796, in the message addressed by the Directory to this department's inhabitants:

> Republicans of the Midi, today your happiness lies in your own hands; it lies especially in the sincere forgetting of all the hate, and the full and frank renunciation of all these dreadful projects for revenge, and the reactions that a diabolical spirit nurtures in your midst.[50]

The agents of this reaction were known as "reactors" (*réacteurs*) before the term "reactionary" (*réactionnaire*) was definitively created, with a suffix based on the word "revolutionary" (*révolutionnaire*).[51] At the Council of Five Hundred, the word "reaction" punctuated oratorial flights.[52] On 27 Prairial, year IV, Jean-Lambert Tallien (who bore his share of responsibility for the violent abuses of the Terror) held the floor at great length. *Le Moniteur* dramatized the scene and noted that the word "reaction" provoked an uproar and reopened the debate:

325

Tallien: "I think that the government, for its own safety, should trust only patriots; and yet — and I say this with bitterness — I see that for three months now people have not taken enough precaution against the reaction taking place...."

Until this point, the audience had been listening to Tallien in the greatest silence. With these words, one hundred members arose in a spontaneous movement and addressed heated challenges to the speaker.... A long tumult ensued.

Antoine-Claire Thibaudeau, who replied, used the same vocabulary:

Reaction has been mentioned, and at this word I stood up to answer, certain that one must also speak of reaction if one truly wants to arouse public sentiment, win over upstanding men, and keep the scoundrels in check.[53]

Confusion sets in. Once it had acquired its pejorative meaning, the word "reaction" remained a weapon used by each party to discredit the actions of the other. In an interesting note to his pamphlet *Du fanatisme dans la langue révolutionnaire* (1797), Jean-François de La Harpe, a former follower of Voltaire turned into a defender of persecuted religion, discusses the use of the word "reaction" in the vocabulary of the "faction": with the collective word "faction," he designates a broader group than the Jacobins alone. But at the same time, he notes that the "patriots" were calling for a reaction in the revolutionary sense:

"Reaction" is one of the *revolutionary* words to which the *Faction* has given a convenient and odious meaning. When the assassins were prosecuted after 9 Thermidor, it called this overdue and soon illusory justice by the name *reaction*: and among them this meant that since they had oppressed France, they too would be oppressed; hence the hallowed term, after 13 Vendémiaire, of *oppressed patriot*; and at this same time, the *patriots* cried out in the Assembly for a *republican reaction*, just as there had been a royalist one; for from that point on *republicanism* purified the reaction they had so condemned.[54]

Clearly, the term retained a floating meaning and became more specific only through the addition of qualifiers. La Harpe's lexicological note shows that one could both denounce a reaction, when it came from one's adversary, and give the name "reaction" to the response deemed necessary.[55]

A single example should suffice: that of Joseph de Maistre, who was certainly a theorist of "reaction" (according to the terminology of the republicans and of his later commentators) — although in an unusual way — and who still used this term in its most firmly established physical sense. In 1797, de Maistre, denouncing the excesses of a revolution whose main protagonists were destroying each other, put forward the theory of a revolution in the opposite direction, a *royalist revolution*, which he named "counter-revolution," as did the "patriot" republicans. He gave it little immediate chance of success but considered it ineluctable in the long term. He hoped in particular that events would be left in the hands of Providence. With de Maistre, the rejection of revolutionary innovations was accompanied by a political fatalism that defined itself more specifically as a providentialist quietism. The will of God ("the eternal geometer") would be accomplished sooner or later despite human designs. One needed only to be patient. In the meantime, the Jacobins and the republican armies would do the work — territorial conquests — that would eventually profit the future monarchy. The designs of Providence would be realized with the same inevitability as the laws of nature:

Since the reaction should be equal to the action, do not rush, impatient men, and remember that the length of the suffering itself will usher in a *counter-revolution* of which you still have no idea.[56]

If one attributes regressive value to the prefix *re-* of "revolution," then "counterrevolution" and "reaction" are negations of a negation and thus signal a return to an original state, to divine order. De Maistre does not invite his readers into a "reactive" struggle; he urges them to wait for the inevitable reaction that will take place despite human agitations. At the time he published his book, the word "revolution" was firmly associated with the upheaval that took place beginning in 1789. It had already become a hypostatized entity. This was not yet the case for "reaction," but the word soon evolved into the antonym of "revolution."

Benjamin Constant: "Political Reactions"
For polemical purposes, Benjamin Constant devoted himself to constructing a precise definition of "reaction."[57] In the pamphlet titled *Des réactions politiques* (Floréal, year V, 1797), he elaborates the meaning that would be attached to the word in its modern political use.[58] Constant proposes an analysis of the recent troubles, attempting to ground it in a philosophy of history. He writes as a theorist in order to demand theoretical coherence and rigorous principles from politicians. Lacking a rational theory and principles, as well as a government firmly attached to these principles, individuals, Constant asserts, find themselves at the mercy of the arbitrary, that is, of violence, which inevitably provokes reactions. This is a major theme of this brief work. With the word "arbitrary," Constant designates the terrorist state of emergency.

At the beginning of the pamphlet, Constant proposes a fundamental distinction that will dictate the structure of its development: "There are two sorts of reactions: those exerted over people, and those that have ideas as their object." Whenever one side in a conflict regains power after a defeat, it deals ruthlessly with its adversaries. Such instances of violence involve "reactions against people." The excesses form a chain:

> Reactions against people, which result from a prior action, are the causes of future reactions. The party that was oppressed will oppress in turn; the party that saw itself illegally victimized by the rage it merited, will endeavor to seize control of power once again; and when it triumphs, there are two reasons for excess instead of one: man's natural disposition, which caused him to commit crimes in the first place, and his resentment over the crimes that followed as punishment for his own.[59]

Thus "reactions against people perpetuate revolutions, for they perpetuate the oppression that gave rise to them." In the circumstances in which he is writing, Constant has but one solution to propose: legality, a refusal of the arbitrary. A reaction is thus "the arbitrary used for the purposes of reestablishment." Put more directly: it is the revenge of the monarchists who were the victims of revolutionary arbitrariness. Constant appeals to the government (the Directory); the government alone should punish crimes so that the field is not left open for private vendettas:

> Against [the reactions] that have people as their object, there is but one means, and this is justice. It is necessary for it [the government] to take control of reactions so as not to be carried away by them. The succession of forfeitures can become eternal if one does not hasten to halt their course.[60]

The government, being the sole bearer of legal authority, will protect individuals and defend them from their own violence. By firmly ensuring justice, it will stop the cycle of violence.

"Reactions against ideas" are different: they "make revolutions unfruitful, for they recall the abuses," and "they strike the entire species with stupor."[61] This time, Constant no longer considers reactions something that two adversaries take turns imputing to each other. There is a "march of ideas." Intellectual advancements have taken place during the past century: these should be irreversible. From Condorcet, and undoubtedly from Kant as well, Constant took the notion of perfectibility, making it an element of his own system.[62] Suddenly it is clear that "reactions against ideas" are regressions or "retrogressions." It is also clear that they can only emanate from the partisans of a backward order who desire "*to return*" to "prejudices" (meaning religious orthodoxy) or to "abuses" (meaning the feudal orders and hereditary privileges):

> After great misfortunes overturned many prejudices, [reaction] is bringing these prejudices back without redressing these misfortunes, and reestablishing abuses without picking up the ruins; they are returning man to his shackles, but they are bloody shackles.... It is therefore not enough to have conquered freedom, to have made enlightenment triumph, to have bought these two priceless treasures through great sacrifice, to have brought these sacrifices to an end through great effort; it is still necessary to prevent the retrograde movement — which inevitably follows an excessive impulse — from being prolonged beyond its necessary limits, preparing the reestablishment of all its prejudices, and leaving behind destruction, tears, shame, and blood as vestiges of the desired changes.[63]

What is the origin of this desire to return to the past and reestablish an earlier order? Constant proposes a psychological interpretation, similar to the one used at the time to explain homesickness. Medi-cine saw homesickness as an illness and, based on the Greek, gave it the technical name "nostalgia" (since then, of course, the term has come into common usage). In this way, the term equated intellec-tual and sentimental forms of a yearning for the past. They are both related to the passions, more or less determined by an association of ideas, and based on remembered sensations. Constant remarks:

> These reactions ... are born of the tendency of the human mind to wrap in its regrets everything that surrounded what it misses. Thus in our childhood memories, or in those of a happy time that is no longer, indifferent objects are mixed in with things we held most dear, and the charm of the past attaches itself to every detail; the man who, in the general upheaval, saw the edifice of his personal happiness crumble, thinks he can only resurrect it by re-creating everything that fell with it; even the inconveniences and abuses become precious to him, because they appear to him, from afar, inti-mately bound to the advantages whose loss he laments.[64]

As he would do later in *Adolphe*, Constant proceeds here through aphoristic generalizations. He inserts a general maxim in his argu-ments that applies to the "human mind" as well as to "childhood memories." He universalizes the lesson provided by erroneous conduct, making it into a psychological law. The memories dear to us are closely tied to an entire past world. The problem, ac-cording to Constant, lies in the attempt to restore a past that is out of our reach, that nothing can bring back. Here one finds, if not an excuse for those who foment political reactions, at least an honorable motive that credits the political adversary with an excess of sensitivity but that also attributes a weakness to him, assigning him a pathology.[65] In more modern terminology, this pathology is that of *regression*. The biological evolutionism established during the nineteenth century developed out of the doctrine of perfectibility, which, as it was elaborated in the second half of the eighteenth century, applied at first only to human civilization. Then came the epoch when the biological evolution of species and the maturation of individuals were considered two closely related forms of progress. Regression seeks to evade this imperative: it is a retrograde movement toward a past stage and toward a structure that is less rich — a flight from the complex tasks of adult life. The deprecatory notion of regression goes hand in hand with the reprobation of the archaic (whose defenders, throughout the ages, have never lacked arguments).

"Reaction" thus takes on the pejorative meaning it retains in later political vocabulary. In fact, when Constant speaks of reactions, he uses the abstract term (most often in the plural) to designate adversaries he does not want to mention by name; personal innuendos are concealed within the generality of the discourse. The abstract terms thinly veil the people and parties whom the author is certain the readers will recognize. In rhetoric, this is called antonomasia, in which a name is replaced by a quality specific to the object or person designated. This allowed Constant to exploit the form of the polemical pamphlet as well as that of a theory on the laws of history.

Constant begins with a wholly mechanical definition of reactions. This definition was initially formulated as a universal law on the relations between a people's institutions and its ideas. When a people's institutions are not on the same level as its ideas, revolutions are necessary to transform the institutions. Hegel later implied that the state is ill when individuals cannot recognize themselves in the laws.[66] Constant thought that the structures following the initial changes of the Revolution had a chance of remaining stable as long as they corresponded to generally held opinions. The risk of reactions began once the innovations sur-

332

passed the "level of ideas." Then increasingly voluntaristic measures became necessary. "Because the level is no longer the same,
institutions maintain themselves only through a constant series of
efforts, and because the moment when the tension ceases is also
the moment of a release of energy." Reactions are stimulated by
an excess in the new arrangements. The Revolution, Constant
asserts, went beyond commonly shared "ideas"; without limiting
itself to abolishing privileges, it attacked property. Constant was
alarmed by this threat: he had acquired national property and
frequented wealthy circles. He was not content with saying that
the Revolution had gone too far: he found it necessary to explain
how it had been threatened by a retrogression. This is why, in his
analysis of reaction, Constant uses spatial metaphors and simple
physical models evoking the scale or the spring: what comes before the point of equilibrium, and what goes beyond it; that is,
compression and release.

Constant expresses himself in this fashion because he shares
Condorcet's idea that scientific rigor and political freedom are
closely linked and that calculation and geometric demonstration
represent the main progress of modern thought, culminating in
equality through the law.[67] At the end of his work, Constant
broadly outlines a system in which scientific reason and the Revolution are closely allied in their fight against "retrograde" tendencies. His pamphlet ends with the affirmation of a "system of
principles" and with the assurance that this "progressive and regular system," in completing itself, will express "the supreme will
of nature": it will be "the inevitable effect of the force of things."
Indeed, in its execution, this system will base itself on "political
calculations, akin to the exact sciences in their precision." A proportional equality is established in which revolution is to reaction what reason is to passion: reason is naturally at the service of
political progress, whereas reaction can only be a matter of

passion. Constant declares: "Wherever [rational] demonstrations burst forth in their brilliance, the passions have lost their hold." Through an aphorism, calculating reason is attributed with the ability to predict and disarm the undertakings of unreason. It has not only psychological perspicacity but also offensive and defensive efficacy. Such a show of hope, at so late a date! In 1797, there were insufficient resources to fulfill it. (Are there today?)

During these years, when she was so close to Constant, Germaine de Staël wrote in *De l'influence des passions* (1796):

> Political science might one day acquire geometric proofs.... The organization of a constitution is always based on a fixed set of givens, since every kind of large number leads to ever similar and ever predictable results.... This revolution must end in reasoning.[68]

She went even further in a work that, though almost finished, was not published until 1798:

> The political state must be founded on a demonstrable principle.... Descartes applied algebra to geometry; one must apply calculus to politics.... The passions of men are as subject to calculation as is friction in machines; in a certain number of cases, the return of the same events is certain.... Everything that is true can be measured.... Moral forces are calculated according to laws as positive as physical forces. If we completely understood them, we would be able to predict all of life's events through the chain of cause and effect, just as Newton measured the motion of the earth; and man, the sole repository of this science, would direct the world by means of the most simple actions.[69]

Nothing is gained in trying to block the passions; the projects for liberation must take them into account: "Political freedom must

334

always be calculated according to the positive and indestructible existence of a certain number of passionate beings among the people to be governed."[70] The politician becomes an ingenious mechanic, superior to the crowd. Mme de Staël attributes to him the faculty of anticipating the inevitable reaction and making use of it — "*taking hold*" of it. Thus knowledge of the laws of motion in nature will have prepared the way for a philosophical and political progress that should lead (and this is certainly a dream) to mastery over historical events. By contrast, "the reaction" that "adjusts itself to motion" can only be based on "superstitions."[71]

In the years preceding Napoleon's appearance, Mme de Staël was devoted to an idea that was a pivotal motif of nineteenth-century thought: the antagonism between tendencies of progress and forces of reaction.[72] At the same time, she proposed another idea, which was poorly received by Napoleon but had repercussions throughout the century: the political vocation of the writer who places himself at the service of freedom. Like Constant, she believed not only in the role of those who will later be called "intellectuals" but also in the necessity of their presence in public affairs.

On this point, Constant's argument is interesting, because the function he assigns to the writer initially falls outside the sphere of political power. In *Des réactions politiques*, Constant draws a dividing line between the tasks proper to government and those that are not its concern. When it is a matter of "reactions against people," as mentioned above, it is the government's responsibility to "take hold of the reactions" (a phrase used by Germaine de Staël), that is, to administer justice and legality so as to discourage private vengeance. On the other hand, with regard to "reactions against ideas," the responsibility for the struggle against anti-republican opinions should never rest with the government, which would then be condemned to "an endless task." The defense of republican ideas should fall to the writers, in the free expression of their thoughts: "It is up to the men who direct opin-ions through enlightenment to oppose reactions against ideas. These are the domain of thought alone, and the law should not invade it." The rest of the text can obviously be read as an offer to collaborate with the Directory, but its ideological scope is more general: "The treaty between power and reason is a beautiful one; it is used by enlightened men to say to the trustees of a legitimate power: you safeguard us from any illegal action, and we will safe-guard you from any harmful prejudice. You surround us with the protection of the law, and we will buttress your institutions with the power of opinion." By this we must understand that under a constitutional regime, expressions of "reactions against ideas" ought not to be the object of legal interdiction or censorship. The writer has the right and the duty to intervene as a scientific authority who demonstrates and calculates. In his conclusion, Constant proclaims himself victorious on a few specific points: "Slavery and feudalism are no longer the seeds of war among us. Superstition, in its religious guise, is almost everywhere put on the defensive." Certain moral truths have been acquired once and for all, and these must be propagated in new areas. The struggle against retrograde writers, especially journalists hostile to new institutions, must belong to the writers attached to principles, especially those who know how to use true eloquence against their adversaries' "pathetic declamations": "Let the friends of freedom, those in whom enlightenment shines forth, advance toward these slight phantoms: as soon as they take a step, these phantoms will disappear; then, never letting up in their pursuit, they will cover their vain murmurs with the strong and manly voice of truth." Constant concludes with a new call to battle: "Enlightenment must be spread, the human species must become equal and rise up, and each successive generation engulfed by death must leave at least one brilliant trace on the path of truth."[73]

Germaine de Staël calls this "brilliant trace" by a different name: glory. She invites the writer to embrace it. Why should he refuse to fulfill "the career of public affairs"?

> Nothing does more to animate and regularize intellectual meditations than the hope of making them immediately useful to the human species. When thought can be the precursor of action, when a happy reflection can instantly be transformed into a beneficent institution, what interest will man not take in the development of his intelligence! He no longer fears consuming within himself the torch of reason without ever being able to carry his beacon on the road of active life.[74]

Shortly after expressing — along with Constant — her confidence in a rational and calculating approach to politics, Germaine de Staël adds an important qualification to this idea. Morality and moral feeling, which elude calculation, must serve as points of departure for all political thought. Calculation comes into play only in an auxiliary way. In the chapter of *De la littérature* titled "Philosophy," Mme de Staël condemns the sacrifices demanded during the Revolution in the name of "well-intentioned interest":

> The sacrifice that must be made by the small number to the greater is presented as a mathematical truth: nothing could be more mistaken, even with regard to political arrangements. The effect of these injustices on the state is that it necessarily becomes disorganized.

She goes on to discuss the victims' posthumous victory. But the great phrase she uses here to describe the sequence of useless violence recalls — in a probable allusion to the title of Constant's work — the importance of action and reaction during the Revolution:

From action to reaction, from one act of vengeance to another, the victims who have been immolated under the pretext of the common good are reborn from their ashes, they rise from their exile; and those who would have remained obscure if justice had remained on their side are given a name, a power from the very persecutions of their enemies.... Politics is subjected to calculation, since, in always applying itself to men as a mass, it is based on a general combination and is therefore abstract; but morality, having as its goal the particular conservation of the rights and happiness of each man, is necessary to force politics to respect, in its general combinations, the happiness of individuals. Morality should direct our calculations, and our calculations should direct politics.... The moral sciences are susceptible only to the calculation of probabilities, and this calculation can only be based on a large number of facts, from which one can draw an approximate result.

When it sets its sights on the "happiness of the multitude," political science can consider probabilities a "certitude," but its general rules are not applicable when it comes to "each man in particular," "each fact," or "each circumstance." By considering the individual, morality invites us to make room for feeling:

> Only in feeling can one find the living and constant source that each day renews itself for each man in each moment. Morality is the only human thought that needs a regulator other than the calculation of reason.[75]

Mme de Staël goes even further. She recognizes that innovation in history can result from "strong passions" and even from the "crimes" often associated with them:

> Although strong passions lead to crimes indifference would never have caused, there are circumstances in history in which these pas-

sions are necessary in order to revive the mainsprings of society. Reason, with the help of centuries, takes hold of some of the effects of these great movements; but certain ideas are revealed by passions and would be unknown without them. Violent jolts are necessary to expose the mind to entirely new objects; these are earthquakes and subterranean fires that show men the riches time alone could not have revealed.[76]

The theorist of revolutionary violence Georges Sorel quotes these lines; he is grateful to Mme de Staël for having proclaimed "the creative mission of violence." She developed this argument on the "fanaticism inspired by the Christian religion" in a passage speaking of the Reformation that insists on the ultimately "salutary" influence "of the Gospel on morality."[77] The calculations of reason thus take a subordinate position.

Constitutional guarantees, representatives elected by the nation, freedom of the press — all individual freedoms — Constant never ceases calling for such things. He seeks to defend these goals during the Hundred Days by proposing to Napoleon an "additional act to the constitutions of the empire." Through journalism and parliamentary eloquence, he defends them yet again after the Bourbons' return. What characterizes this moment of combative liberalism is that the locus of the confrontation is alternately the book, the newspaper, and the parliamentary tribune (or, secondarily, political banquets). In the Chamber and in his articles, Constant avoids using the word "reaction" for fear of causing unnecessary agitation. At Charles X's accession in 1824, he becomes alarmed at the catastrophic consequences to which ultraroyalist legitimism would lead.[78] He intensifies his criticisms against a power that is seeking again to become absolute, that places itself above the law, and that ends up governing by decree. He expresses no desire, however, for a republican government,

under which the conflicts would become exacerbated. (The events
of 1848, and the coup d'état of 1851, confirmed these fears.) The
freedoms he calls for are fully compatible with a constitutional
monarchy, which would be an "imperceptible republic." He sometimes mentions the "working class" (he is one of the first to use
the term) in the hope that it would soon receive the right to vote,
thanks to "the development of its intelligence . . . as precious discoveries begin to replace man's muscular might with the forces of
material nature." He never ceases including the legal protection of
property in his system of freedoms, but he foresees its "inevitable
dissemination."[79] He offers proof of his "system of perfectibility"
by recalling the obstacles that had been successively overcome and
that marked the stages of historical evolution. In his last writings,
Constant, admitting his weariness and sadness only a few days
before his death, extends this view of history into the future,
declaring that a good number of contemporary institutions would
appear corrupt to future generations, for "the perfectibility of the
human race is nothing other than the tendency toward equality."[80]
Indeed, his confidence in the "march of ideas" and in the movement of civilization anticipates inevitable *resistances*, periods of
decadence and retreat. But he believes in "reactions" (favorable
this time) and is convinced that despite "accidental setbacks," a
new epoch has begun. He calls it "the epoch of legal conventions":

> The majority of the human race . . . always advances at a more or less
> rapid pace. If sometimes, for an instant, it seems to regress, it is in
> order immediately to react against the powerless obstacle it soon
> overcomes. . . . The human mind is too enlightened to allow itself to
> be long governed by power or ruse, but not enough to govern itself
> by reason alone. It needs something that is both more reasonable
> than power and less abstract than reason. Thus the need for legal
> conventions, a sort of shared and appropriate reason, the median

product of all individual reasons, more imperfect than that of some, more perfect than that of many others. . . . These conventions are not natural or immutable; they are artificial, susceptible to change, and created to replace still little known truths, to come to the aid of temporary needs; they are, consequently, in need of amendment, improvement, and especially restraint as these truths are uncovered or as these needs become modified.[81]

After the days of July 1830, in his last speeches and articles, Constant becomes alarmed by the measures taken by the new regime, which was too indifferent to the people's needs, too repressive of public opinion.[82]

Does the human spirit only need legal conventions? Constant changed course in his work on religion, undertaken at the age of eighteen, completed and published late in life. He had begun by dreaming of a great, erudite history in the style of Edward Gibbon that would have provided solid material for a radical critique of Christianity. His book, as first published in 1824, is instead an apology for religious *sentiment* and for the Christian faith, above and beyond dogmas and imposed practices. From his initial project, Constant retains only his critique of dogmatic forms and clerical institutions. His thought on religion (remarkably studied by Henri Gouhier) belongs to the current of liberal Protestantism.[83]

In an 1811 letter to his friend Claude Hochet, Constant said he was "withdrawing into religious ideas," and added: "I certainly did it in very good faith, for each step backward cost me dearly."[84] An unusual turnabout, seen by Constant as a return, almost as a "reaction," but finally accounted for as a fairer evaluation of the growth of the "circle of civilization." Because religion is "progressive," one must recognize its importance. Together with many of his generation, Constant had begun by denouncing "prejudices," but in the final version of his book religion is greeted as a force

341

that slowly stimulated progress in customs and manners. The revelation made to Moses, and the rise of Christianity in the ancient world, were a "revolution," an advent of freedom and equality in which the "inner perfectibility" of the human being manifested itself. This step forward led to the abolition of slavery. Without religion, the progress of knowledge and intelligence would be in vain: men would remain captives to personal interest.

In his critique of Mme de Staël, Chateaubriand set up an opposition between faith in perfectibility and faith in Jesus Christ. He had hoped to see Mme de Staël "take her place beneath the banner of religion." But it was Constant who came back to religion, although in doing so he accepted only the "sentiment" proper to it. With the idea of a "progressive religion," he did not need to repudiate perfectibility. Chateaubriand was familiar with the letter to Hochet mentioned above, and he included a passage from it in one of his writings. For his part, he came around to the idea of the progressive perfection of civilization, but without crediting human nature alone for it: he attributes it to revelation and religious faith. His view of Roman history is opposed to that of Gibbon, who saw Christianity as one cause of the Roman Empire's decline. For Chateaubriand, Christianity's victory was the advent of freedom, and the vain endeavors of Julian the Apostate against the Christian cult had been nothing more than "the reactionary movement of paganism."[85] Clearly, Chateaubriand is seeking to establish a parallel between eighteenth-century materialists and Julian the Apostate, whom they had made a hero. Thus reaction changes sides according to one's view of the direction of history or the orientation of progress. Here we can keenly grasp the way in which a polemical term, created for the revolutionary cause, comes to be used for an apology of the faith and the culture that the Revolution had sought to supplant. The questions are no longer: Has humanity made progress? Is a revolution necessary?

Everyone is in agreement. So the questions become: What is true progress? What will be the source of the true revolution? Chateaubriand adopts the perspective of progress in order to celebrate Christian revelation and the renewed spread of faith. Thus we see a new category — the collective progress of humanity — replacing the traditional idea of the succession of the four empires and the hope of the Second Coming. In proposing a general view of the epoch at the conclusion of his *Mémoires d'outre-tombe*, Chateaubriand declares that the Christian idea "is the future of the world," for it contains not only the idea of the unity of God, and that of charity, but also the principles of freedom, equality, and fraternity, which still await realization. "Do you think that the Christian idea is but the human idea in progress? I agree." But this evolution will not be the outcome of humanly predictable forces. It is vain to think that the present evil will result in good solely through action and reaction:

> The present world, the world without consecrated authority, seems poised between two impossibilities: the impossibility of the past and the impossibility of the future. Do not think, as some imagine, that if we are experiencing ills in the present, good will be reborn from evil; human nature, disturbed at its source, does not proceed along such lines; for example, excessive freedom leads to despotism; but excessive tyranny leads only to tyranny; by degrading us, this tyranny transforms us into slaves and makes us incapable of independence.... To assert that a reaction is in principle always followed by a contrary reaction is to go beyond experience: facts are completely logical only for God, whose justice has all of Eternity in which to act.[86]

If there is a logic (and a dialectic), it is not within our reach. "The vision of justice is the pleasure of God alone," as Arthur Rimbaud wrote some years later.[87]

343

In and Around the Communist Manifesto

Characteristically, the use of "reaction" and its derivative "reactionary" against the ultraroyalists of the restored monarchy in France, then against the "conservative" powers, remained a favorite element of the language of the "left" during the nineteenth century. These terms are inseparable from the long rereading and reinterpretation of the revolutionary period. At the same time, they were used in assessments of present conflicts and future stakes. In the postrevolutionary political world, where parties occupied the symbolic space between the right and the left, the discourse of the extremes showed a predilection for antinomic terminology. On the right, the antinomy is that of order and anarchy. On the left, the opposition revolution/reaction, or progress/reaction, corresponds to the opposition between the working class and the exploiting class.

The word "reaction" becomes banal and commonplace from this moment on.[88] At times it retained its former neutral meaning, but in general it was marked by its tie to postrevolutionary circumstances. Within the European "left" of the nineteenth century, the hoped-for forms of democratic progress — such as equal rights and the dignity of work — became the reference points for evaluating a politics or an intellectual tendency. They indicated the direction of a "march" or a "movement" of history. Social doctrines hold out various fields of application for the word "reaction." This pejorative term stigmatizes certain people: those who as a group profit from social inequality. It also stigmatizes ideas, especially opinions tending to reestablish "feudal" prerogatives or the temporal influence of a clergy at the service of absolutism. Thus Sainte-Beuve (though very reserved about the Revolution) sees a "monarchic, religious, and literary reaction" emerge by 1800: "Bonaparte favored this movement because he would profit from it."[89] He speaks in the same way of the excessive hold — and

344

the unpopularity — of clerical power (the congregation) between 1821 and 1828: it was a "fatal reaction."[90] In his *Cours de philosophie positive*, Auguste Comte speaks of the "retrograde reaction" in discussing Bonaparte's "theological and military restoration."[91] In all these cases, one notes an implicit reminder of the Thermidorian crisis and the White Terror. This was the primal scene that haunted all political uses of the word "reaction." How could one forget the final pages of Jules Michelet's *History of the French Revolution* (1853)? These pages attribute to the dying Robespierre "a bitter sense of the reaction that was coming." Soon after the tyrant's execution, it is suddenly unleashed: "A reaction that from the outset was violent and immense had begun at that very moment." For Michelet, who made the people the hero of his work, the reaction marked the end of the history of the French Revolution: "There is no need to recount what followed: the blind reaction sweeping through the Assembly, from which it would barely recover in Vendémiaire." In addition, words that assumed their meaning during the Revolution and in relation to it — such as "reaction" — become, in Michelet, tools for interpreting history as a whole, including that preceding the Revolution and that of the Revolution in relation to the epoch preceding it. We read in the introduction to *History of the French Revolution*: "The revolution is nothing but the tardy reaction of justice against the government of favor and the religion of grace."[92] A perfectly legitimate procedure, since all interpretation starts from the present and uses the experience and tools of the present. In 1799, when Constant published his pamphlet *Des suites de la contre-Révolution de 1660 en Angleterre*, he not only established a parallel with the present situation regarding incriminatory deeds, but he used the word "counterrevolutionary," which did not appear in French until 1790.

In 1865, Edgar Quinet is no less eloquent than Michelet. The twentieth book of *La Révolution* is titled "La Réaction":

By turns passive and enraged, Reaction, as if certain of its success, knows how to postpone its claims. It does not proclaim its goal from afar, but takes steps day by day. If you want to go backward, a thousand paths will open: those who take this path find an easy way that they were not aware of; they alone seem to have profited from the experience. Prudent, well informed, aged by a century in a few years, they will not lose themselves through an excess of victory.... Reaction is in its essence a product of fear; and fear drives man to flee beyond all the known limits of servitude; he is assuaged only by political and civil death.[93]

Reaction is thus the *aggressive* face of that which has no future. With his sense for concise and vivid images, Victor Hugo notes: "Agony can lash out. In political language, this is called reaction.... A reaction: a boat going upstream, which does not, however, prevent the river from flowing downstream."[94]

One objective of golden-mean liberalism was to make the overly radical alternative between progress and reaction more flexible. Thus Charles de Rémusat argued for another vocabulary:

Historical fatalism is ready to justify the errors of every epoch — by referring to them as necessary transitions — and to make progress out of decadence itself. It will tell you that everything must be balanced, and will look to Newton's Principles for a rule in mechanics on the equality of the reaction to the action, a discovery very apt for explaining all excesses, while postponing indefinitely the moment of true equilibrium. But ultimately, metaphor for metaphor, another idea should be borrowed from mechanics: the resultant of forces. Just as two opposing forces find a median direction, which is a marvelous law that makes the planets move in space and boats on the waves, there could be, in modern society, not two extreme limits between which it would eternally oscillate, but rather two seemingly opposite forces that must become united in one common and powerful impulse.[95]

In fact, Newton's third law in no way suggests the political use that was made of it; in a strict sense, political excesses themselves could be analyzed in terms of the composition of forces. Rémusat, who prefers equilibrium, hoped to disqualify the political use of the word "reaction" and politely dismiss it. He did not succeed.

"Reactionary" (constructed, we recall, on the model of "revolutionary") is a partisan word used only polemically or disparagingly. Its use is widespread, to say the least. Those who use it announce themselves as enemies of reaction or, in positive terms, as supporters of indispensable reforms or revolution. The term is also used by historians, who, when they judge conflicting forces after the fact, effortlessly assess their respective merits. They know which side won out in the long run, how history has evolved, which new ideas established a "historical breakthrough."[96] They are capable of discerning — from their present point of view, which is valid only for the present — attitudes that were obsolete, without a future, in short, reactionary, which is to say vainly opposed to inevitable evolutions. Here a temptation arises to qualify as reactionary what did not succeed, what was defeated, and thus to confuse change with progress, triumphant necessity with real "advance."

Consider the most typical use of the words "reaction" and "reactionary" in the nineteenth century: the one found in Karl Marx's *Communist Manifesto* (1848). In distinguishing the bourgeoisie from the reactionaries, Marx notes a difference: the "reactionaries" have not yet accepted the reign of the bourgeoisie. They are the last representatives of — or are nostalgic for — a social order prior to the bourgeois revolution:

The bourgeoisie has through its exploitation of the world market given a cosmopolitan character to production and consumption in every country. To the great chagrin of the reactionaries, it has drawn from under the feet of industry the national ground on which it stood. All old-established national industries have been destroyed or are daily being destroyed.

But the reactionary attitude, according to Marx, can reach the middle class, dispossessed as it is by "Modern Industry":

> They are therefore not revolutionary, but conservative. Nay more, they are reactionary, for they try to roll back the wheel of history. If by chance they are revolutionary, they are so only in view of their impending transfer into the proletariat, they thus defend not their present, but their future interests, they desert their own standpoint to place themselves at that of the proletariat.[97]

Only the proletariat is revolutionary. In Marx's view, disappointed members of the middle class find themselves on the dividing line between revolution and reaction. The same is true for the lumpen proletariat: "The 'dangerous class,' the social scum, that passively rotting mass thrown off by the lowest layers of the old society may, here and there, be swept into the movement by a proletarian revolution; its conditions of life, however, prepare it far more for the part of a bribed tool of reactionary intrigue."[98]

It would appear that the *Manifesto*'s strategy consists in posing an alternative, with no middle ground, between the proletarian revolution, which conforms to the "march of modern history," and reaction. One section of the *Manifesto* examines "socialist and communist literature" and leads to the same alternative. Marx first identifies a socialism that is immediately and globally

348

described as "reactionary." This category has three components: "feudal socialism," "petit-bourgeois socialism," and "German socialism." Next Marx identifies a literature of "bourgeois social-ism" (which he associates with Pierre-Joseph Proudhon), which is discredited because it denies class antagonisms and the necessity of political change. Last, he casts a glance at "critical-utopian socialism and communism." These, according to Marx, are prema-ture viewpoints, doctrines whose disciples end up forming "reac-tionary sects" or movements that "sink into the category of the reactionary [or] conservative socialists." The impasse is complete. The conclusion of the *Manifesto* addresses Germany in particular. In this country, the bourgeoisie must bring down the "reactionary classes" before being itself overturned by the proletariat. "[T]he bourgeois revolution in Germany will be but the prelude to an immediately following proletariat revolution."[99] In the *Manifesto*'s rhetoric, which, as we know, was very effective, the proletarian revolution is the only prospect for the future, because the new means of production render any other social organization obso-lete and unacceptable. With omnipresent reaction prohibiting a nonviolent outcome, the revolutionary clash will occur "neces-sarily," and readers are invited to consider it the only reasonable option. "Reactionary" and "conservative" become almost synony-mous, for there is little difference between the obstacle that op-poses motion through its inertia and that which opposes it by a counter-motion: a clash is inevitable in either case.

Marx's goal was to demonstrate that there was no way out except by the path proposed in the *Manifesto*. The word "reac-tion" therefore serves, *a contrario*, to legitimize the coming to consciousness (today we would call it the "intellectual construc-tion") of the radicality of "the antagonism between bourgeoisie and proletariat." The claim of scientific rigor plays an important role here, especially since an entire aspect of economic science can be treated mathematically. In the method adopted, the struggle among different social strata appears both as the object of an objective statement (of an "analysis") and as the motive force behind a call to liberating action. Thus, since the struggle already exists, it is urgent to organize it and make it more decisive. Fact (determined by a whole prior history) is translated into duty (with a view to determining the history to come). As a historian, Marx interprets the preceding transformations of human societies as "political progress." The organizer of a movement, he invites us to direct revolutionary action toward the consequences already arising from prior history as he interprets it. This is an application to history of Newton's first two laws of motion.

Whereas Condorcet, in a utopian mode, saw "the human race, emancipated from its shackles, released from the empire of fate and from that of the enemies of its progress, advancing with a firm and sure step along the path of truth," Marx set his sights on the present, and what he found there was reaction.[100] It was certainly real, since the means of production did not belong to the proletariat. Marx needed this enemy not only to wind up the springs of the struggle and mobilize the supporters of his theory but also to fight more effectively against rival theories and competing socialisms and, if need be, to accuse these other socialisms, or the dissidents within his own movement, of being consciously or unconsciously reactionary. He gave his followers an argument that allowed them to condemn not only the existing order but also everything within the revolutionary movement that deviated from the path he had traced out. It is the secular argument of religious reformers and church militants: whoever is not with me is against me. Marxist thought distinguished between two types of ideologies: those that are intrinsically reactionary in their explicit content, that is, those on the extreme right that appeal to models of the past; and those that play a functionally reactionary role, that is, those that, even on the left, play "the game of reaction" because of the power relations in a given circumstance.[101] These distinctions, which Lenin used in turn, make it possible to extend the grievances against reaction according to the "necessities of action" and as dictated by strategic decisions and tactical opportunities. The inverse notion was defended as well, according to which certain national movements, although of bourgeois inspiration, "work" in the interests of the revolution and can therefore be supported temporarily as objective allies. As in any collective action, designating an adversary plays a central role. In this type of argument, the adversary is not only anyone who professes reactionary ideas but also anyone who does not combat reaction properly. In this way, one can categorize as reactionary those who embrace forms of politics that one wishes to discredit. As a result, the ostracizing party can close ranks and radicalize its activity.[102] In a caricature of this process, literary movements in the twentieth century operated according to the same model.

This tendency among rival revolutionary groups to exchange accusations of reaction cannot be attributed to Marx alone. Pierre-Joseph Proudhon took it one step further: reaction, or a party that seeks to preserve or reestablish past institutions, presents less of a danger than corrupt democrats who betray the revolution they claim to support. From his prison in the Conciergerie, Proudhon writes, on January 7, 1851:

> I warn you that we shall return to the world as journalists only to mercilessly strap the false brothers who increasingly mislead and dishonor the Republic and bury the Revolution. The reaction is no longer but a shadow; if there is a danger somewhere, it is no longer among the old parties; it is among the revolutionaries, at the heart of the democracy.[103]

Certainly, moral sense — a sense of what is due to the dignity of individuals — allows us quite generally to distinguish what conforms to justice from what is "reactionary."[104] But is this common sense so widespread? Recall that in their use of force the tyrannies of the twentieth century all tried to pass themselves off as revolutions and that they sought, systematically or incidentally, to discredit their opponents by treating them as reactionaries. An abused word is often the first to be spoken. I will cite only one example. The "Horst-Wessel-Lied" — the war hymn of the German National Socialists — salutes the dead partisans: "The comrades, shot down by the Red Front and the Reaction, march in spirit in our ranks."[105] Activism wants to be not only a movement but a revolution, for being revolutionary means combating reaction, all the way to the ultimate sacrifice.

Strength Versus Reaction: Nietzsche and The Genealogy of Morals

As we have seen, whether we are dealing with a partisan of parliamentary freedoms (in a property-holding parliament) like Constant or with a legitimist like Chateaubriand, one conviction is held in common: human history has been the theater of moral progress. This progress has not yet reached its term, so the values it has established must be protected. There has been disagreement, as my examples have shown, in defining the moment when decisive "progress" first took place. Was it when Christianity prevailed? Is it during the revolutionary struggles of the present? Will it be in the future? A few Romantics hoped to unify all these assertions and temporal horizons.

The omnipresence in the nineteenth century of various ideologies of progress resounds in Nietzsche's exasperation with this widespread intoxication. His hostility toward Christianity is matched only by his sarcasm toward the revolutionary spirit, whose archetype he sees in Rousseau.[106] Nietzsche's hammer blows spare neither the socialism emerging from the French Revolution nor the ideas defended by Constant, Chateaubriand, and Lamennais, which affirmed in various ways a common conviction concerning the links between progress and the rise of Christianity. Nietzsche's critique — his overturning of values — takes on aspects of a systematic inversion. There is no turning back, no possible restoration of the past, because the decadence is irreversible:

> We physiologists, at least, know this.... [I]t's no use: one *must* go forward, that is to say, further, step by step, into decadence (this is *my* definition of modern "progress"). One can hinder this development, and in this way block up the degeneration, gather it up, make it more vehement and sudden: more than that one cannot do.[107]

Is this prognosis irrevocable? Could there not be, despite everything, a "true" progress, another sort of progress? How might one define it? In fragments from the 1880s, we read: "Progress? the strengthening of the type, the aptitude for great will: all the rest is misunderstanding, danger."[108] Nietzsche is speaking as a moralist when he discusses *decadence* but as a physiologist when he diagnoses *degeneration* or when he hopes for "the strengthening of the type." From this twofold stance, and in a hybrid language, *On the Genealogy of Morals* lengthily considers "active" and "reactive" attitudes. Nietzsche usually keeps to the adjectives "active" and "reactive," without hypostatizing action and reaction. When he does use the word "reaction," it is in a physiological rather than a political sense, though he associates the physiological image of reaction with the moral notion of *ressentiment*. (How significant the use of the prefix *re-* is here!)

The forces of reaction are manifested among the adepts of moral improvement and religious asceticism and among the partisans of

353

revolutionary egalitarianism, all of whom oppose "noble" strength, claiming to resist it. Their morality is that of slaves:

> The slave revolt in morality begins when *ressentiment* itself becomes creative and gives birth to values: the *ressentiment* of natures that are denied the true reaction, that of deeds, and compensate themselves with an imaginary revenge. While every noble morality develops from a triumphant affirmation of itself, slave morality from the outset says No to what is "outside," what is "different," what is "not itself"; and *this* No is its creative deed. This inversion of the value-positing eye — this *need* to direct one's view outward instead of back to oneself — is of the essence of *ressentiment*: in order to exist, slave morality always first needs a hostile external world; it needs, physiologically speaking, external stimuli in order to act at all — its action is fundamentally reaction.
>
> The reverse is the case with the noble mode of valuation: it acts and grows spontaneously, it seeks its opposite only so as to affirm itself more gratefully and triumphantly.[109]

Nietzsche attempts to correct the contemporary physiology of adaptation in order to transform it into a physiology of the dominating will. He proposes a metaphysiology that will set contemporary intellectuals right and that does not hesitate to take sides. It is in this way, we may recall, that he adopts the dynamics of Ruggero Giuseppe Boscovich, for whom strength supplants matter, over that of Robert Mayer, considered a narrow "specialist" because his principle of the conservation of energy remains too attached to the concept of matter.[110] Nietzsche introduces the concept of the "will to power" by articulating it in a critique of Herbert Spencer's ideas on evolution. At this point in Nietzsche's text, the notions of activity and reactivity are most clearly opposed:

The "evolution" of a thing, a custom, an organ is thus by no means its progress [*progressus*] toward a goal, even less a logical progress [*progressus*] by the shortest route and with the smallest expenditure of force — but a succession of more or less profound, more or less mutually independent processes of subduing, plus the resistances they encounter, the attempts at transformation for the purpose of defense and reaction, and the results of successful counteractions....

It is not too much to say that even a partial *diminution of utility*, an atrophying and degeneration, a loss of meaning and purposiveness — in short, death — is among the conditions of an actual progress [*progressus*], which always appears in the shape of a will and way to *greater power* and is always carried through at the expense of numerous smaller powers. The magnitude of "progress" [*Fortschritt*] can even be measured by the mass of things that had to be sacrificed to it; mankind in the mass sacrificed to the prosperity of a single *stronger* species of man — that *would* be progress [*Fortschritt*].[111]

Nietzsche's argument continues with a critique of the "democratic idiosyncrasy" that he calls "*misarchism*." By this he means opposition to the will to power. This, he declares, has "robbed [life] of a fundamental concept, that of *activity*":

Under the influence of the above-mentioned idiosyncrasy, one places instead "adaptation" in the foreground, that is to say, an activity of the second rank, a mere reactivity; indeed, life itself has been defined as a more and more efficient inner adaptation to external conditions (Herbert Spencer). Thus the essence of life, its *will to power*, is ignored; one overlooks the essential priority of the spontaneous, aggressive, expansive, form-giving forces that give new interpretations and directions, although "adaptation" follows only after this; the dominant role of the highest functionaries within the organism itself in which the will to life appears active and form-giving is denied.[112]

Although the natural sciences are not exempt from Nietzsche's criticism, he uses their terminology and its derivatives, and their mythology (health, illness, race, degeneration, reaction), to reinforce his moral critique of the era and of the individuals and powers of the day. Physicochemical reactions form the texture of all reality: health is a matter of defensive reaction; illness, too, involves a reaction that is not well executed or well oriented. Nietzsche transports the term "reaction," which functions so well in discussions of causality, into the realm of values. Scientists use it to *explain* the succession of physical causes; Nietzsche, taking a more global, more "physiognomic" approach, turns to it in order to *understand*. Listening to Nietzsche's vocabulary, one notes the extent to which he invests an entire philosophy of nature with psychic value, the better to interpret in physiological terms the phenomena of the contemporary world. The genealogy of morals, according to Nietzsche, is in fact a psychophysiology and psychopathology of moral feeling (such as bad conscience, asceticism, fear of God, compassion for the humiliated and the wronged). This leads Nietzsche to elaborate a very dubious psychology of peoples and races, notably of the "Jewish race" responsible for a "poison" transmitted to Christianity and to humanitarian egalitarianism.

In another respect, this psychophysiology subscribes to the model of "reaction time" used in scientific laboratories.[113] In particular, note the great distinction Nietzsche makes: on the one hand, there are primary and rapid reactions, immediately liquidated (physiological terminology), of "noble" individuals (moral terminology); on the other hand, there are secondary and slow reactions, the long-nurtured and deferred revenge of weak individuals (physiological terminology), that is, of slaves in revolt (moral terminology). The man of *ressentiment* "understands how to keep silent, how not to forget, how to wait, how to be provisionally self-deprecating and humble." And "[r]essentiment itself, if it should appear in the noble man, consummates and exhausts itself in an immediate reaction."[114] In Nietzsche, action and reaction have nothing of the Kantian "relation" or "community." They are engaged in a conflict with unequal weapons in which, as Christianity has spread, the weak and the slaves have won out over the strong: asceticism, the reactive attitude par excellence, has triumphed.

I have already noted that the opposition between rapid reaction and the reactivity of "the lower order" is quite close to the opposition between abreaction and neurotic repression in Freud and Breuer's *Studies on Hysteria*. In Nietzsche, the dueling forces are presented in a language similar to that used by Freud in speaking of drives.

Nietzsche's argumentation is extremely mobile, which means that his excesses are always contradicted or compensated for, to the great satisfaction of his commentators. *On the Genealogy of Morals*, which begins by implicating the Jews in the "slave revolt" and its repercussions in the contemporary world, goes on to direct the same accusation at anarchists and anti-Semites. Among the latter, "reactive feelings" have "always bloomed, in hidden places, like the violet, though with a different odor":

> And as like must always produce like, it causes us no surprise to see a repetition in such circles of attempts often made before ... to sanctify *revenge* under the name of *justice* — as if justice were at bottom merely a further development of the feeling of being aggrieved — and to rehabilitate not only revenge but all *reactive* affects in general.... The active, aggressive, arrogant man is still a hundred steps closer to justice than the reactive man; for he has absolutely no need to take a false and prejudiced view of the object before him in the way the reactive man does and is bound to do. For that reason the aggressive

man, as the stronger, nobler, more courageous, has in fact also had at all times a *freer* eye, a *better* conscience on his side: conversely, one can see who has the invention of the "bad conscience" on his conscience — the man of *ressentiment!* [115]

Thus we see Nietzsche transferring to the realms of behavior and character a term that acquired scientific legitimacy when applied to natural phenomena and the study of reflexes. Of course, Nietzsche also uses it more neutrally, with less concern for "characterization" and accusation. He speaks of reaction simply to designate the antagonism, the consequence, or the adverse effect that may result from any given deed. The word is also given a demystifying turn. Consider, for example, this remark from *Human, All Too Human* (*The Wanderer and His Shadow*):

> *Reaction against machine-culture.* — The machine, itself a product of the highest mental energies, sets in motion in those who serve it almost nothing but the lower, non-intellectual energies. It thereby releases a vast quantity of energy in general that would otherwise lie dormant, it is true; but it provides no instigation to enhancement, to improvement, to becoming an artist. It makes men *active* and *uniform* — but in the long run this engenders a reaction [*Gegenwirkung*], a despairing boredom of the soul, which teaches them to long for idleness in all its varieties. [116]

The growth of available mechanical energy has as its counterpart (or backlash) the degeneration of human energy and therefore passivity. Nietzsche considers the boredom produced by submission to machines an action in return. Here again (and this time perhaps for better reasons), he denounces the illusion of progress and uses the word "reaction" to convince us that his critique is well founded: non-progress (Nietzsche does not yet use the word "regression," as would Freud) is the inevitable reaction provoked by the increase of mechanical resources. This intuition has lost none of its relevance.

On the Contemporary Vocabulary

Reaction, which Nietzsche saw as an enemy to combat (when it is *ressentiment*, moralism, asceticism, or nihilism), nonetheless became acceptable, so long as it was reassumed by the will to power. Through the very intensity of negation — and therefore of a supplementary reaction — reactive nihilism could be overcome. Nietzsche's thought, mobile and provocative, risks the most unexpected reversals. Revalorizations follow devalorizations... Nietzsche's manipulation of the notion of reaction is exemplary of the *singular* appropriations to which the term "reaction" lent itself and will continue to lend itself. It is rare, however, to see it today in the sense Nietzsche gave it.

In its common meaning, "reaction" has penetrated everywhere. Being a term from general physics, the word was destined for diffusion. It was introduced through a metaphoric breaking and entering into many areas, and it took different forms as these areas developed. Over the course of two centuries, it has infiltrated chemistry, medicine, biology, psychology, politics, and historical thought. Like the word "energy," it is easy to manipulate. It has been widely used not only in Western adaptations of Eastern wisdom and religions but also in sectarian doctrines — some of which claim to teach good reactions, others of which invite us to overcome our enslavement to reactive behavior in order to gain access to a superior "spiritual" independence.[117] New Age patter rustles with "reactions" and "interactions." But when it is refined, disciplined, and reduced to an auxiliary role, the term becomes part of the most serious specialized languages when these need a password (in physics, systems theory, and so on). It is not out of its element in common language, where it inconspicuously adds a rational and dynamic accent. The term is omnipresent in the press, both written and spoken. It would be an endless task to enumerate its occurrences, all of which recapitulate its past meanings, at times reviving them. It is a color almost never lacking in the palette of contemporary language. The word "reaction" has the twofold advantage of designating relation and being *anaphoric*, implying a connection with an antecedent. That which reacts is never isolated. This is what I meant when I spoke before of the "secondariness" implicit in the notion of reaction.

I would like to conclude by noting some important features of this modern usage.[118]

In discussing the history of the French Revolution, I demonstrated how a lexical usage, by slowly becoming more specific, became a rather precise interpretative schema that could be reused in new circumstances. But we also saw that this deciphering tool, in order to work, had to be subordinated to a larger interpretative code: that of progress. The word "reaction" was a synthetic expression for attitudes that run contrary to a recognition of the individual's freedom and dignity. Soon, having become a collective singular, the term designated the personified ensemble of these attitudes and their representatives. The same holds true for Nietzsche, for whom the motif of the "man of reaction" (or the "man of *ressentiment*") has its place in a broader conceptual framework applied to deciphering the history of European thought beginning with its Greek and Jewish origins: this code allows him to decipher signs of degeneration and decadence. We can see that the word "reaction," and the couple action/reaction, make up subunits within more developed interpretative systems or discourses that have nothing in common with each other. They are partial components or, if one prefers, modular elements that can be inserted into the most complex codes, each time adjusted accordingly. They occur in many different types of discourse: the accusation, the excuse, the injunction.

These terms occur in accusatory discourse, which is quite widespread today. On the one hand, this is because there really is a reactionary refusal that deserves to be denounced. But on the other hand, the widespread tendency to present oneself as a victim makes it necessary to stigmatize the perpetrators of the wrong one believes one has suffered. In everyday language, "reaction" designates what is against oneself. The reaction is the deed of an unjust adversary, either quite real or simply presumed. We have become accustomed to calling reaction the power that sets us back when we want the best for the world. Nothing prevents us from attributing the same name to that which hinders man's most egocentric pleasures. When we find a rule governing human relations outworn or obsolete (and thus reactionary), it is often because it is a bad rule or simply because it is a rule.

Things are very different in the discourse of the excuse. Defensive pleas also speak of reaction, but in a completely different sense of the term. This sense comes from the way in which the word "reaction" is used in the language of psychological explanation and comprehension. This use likewise stems from a good intention: it satisfies the expectations of a society anxious to see the rules of responsibility and justice applied, for it can extenuate the punishment incurred by those who act in a state of limited responsibility. Since it was necessary to evaluate individuals' capacity and legal responsibility, modern psychiatry developed the study of "pathological reactions"; this includes the study of mental states that limit the aptitude for rational decisions. A reprehensible act, if it is the culmination of a compelling determinism, is no longer attributable to the will. Therefore, extenuating responsibility — highlighting the *circumstances* determining the reaction — sets aside the motive for condemnation.[119] The same argument is common in everyday quarrels, historical debates, and various appeals to indulgence and pardon. Since reaction only occurs in a given situation or circumstance, it becomes an effect, and, as Pangloss says in *Candide*, there is no effect without a cause. Whatever share of responsibility one may attribute to an antecedent or to circumstances can apparently be subtracted from the charges against the accused. In this case, reaction becomes nothing more than the ineluctable product of supplemental external causes. When an aggressor caught in the act appears in court, the defense usually pleads (not without success) a disadvantaged childhood, long-standing complexes, or police provocation: the accused *simply* reacted. From playground scuffles to international litigation, the excuse is always the same: "They started it." The *re-* of "reaction" exculpates by inculpating the acts of others. Certainly, the intelligibility of an event requires that its context and necessary conditions be taken into account. The event did not arise out of nothing. But does understanding all mean forgiving all? Pardon belongs to a different category from understanding. Circumstances and antecedents make it possible to explain and even to understand reasonable decisions as well as criminal choices. In any case, establishing causal necessity in no way permits one to prejudge the ethical basis of an action. If rational effort makes it possible to grasp the causal necessity underlying a reaction, it does not follow that this reaction itself is reasonable and justified. The thought that surmises the possibility and *genesis* of an act involves a certain rationality, as does the thought that judges the *meaning* and *value* of this act; but these are not the *same* rationality. In its current usage, the word "reason" is notoriously charged with multiple meanings. Even if it is the basis of intelligibility, it is not the basis of legitimacy. (Psychology has accustomed us to this: it seeks to understand irrational impulses rationally.) There are many opportunities to play on words here, and arguments for the defense are not short on subterfuge when they seek to reduce the responsibility of an individual who "reacted." Considering provocation an admissible excuse or alibi for reaction, these arguments attempt to demonstrate that the reaction is the prolongation of an act attributable to a prior actor; by the same token, they present the basis of intelligibility (de facto) as if it were at the same time a legitimation (de jure).

In a note in *The Passing of an Illusion: The Idea of Communism in the Twentieth Century*, François Furet discusses twentieth-century tyrannies and expresses his interest in the explanatory perspective proposed by Ernst Nolte, who sees them as a concatenation of reactions. According to this approach, "the victory of Russian Bolshevism in October 1917" was "the point of departure for a chain 'reaction' by which Italian fascism first, Nazism later, appear as responses to the communist threat, modeled on the revolutionary and dictatorial mode of communism." Now, although he acknowledges this theory of the genesis of Nazism, Furet is wary of any confusion — which he finds unacceptable — between a search for origins and the extenuation of responsibility: "This type of interpretation can lead, if not to a justification, at least to a partial exoneration of Nazism, as the recent debate on the subject among German historians has shown."[120] What Furet presents as a possibility seems to me to be a fact.

After accusatory and exonerative discourse, there is a third type of discourse to which the word "reaction" belongs: the call to action. There are many examples of this. Why not examine one proposed by one of the interlocutors in the dialogue just mentioned? In this exchange of letters, after somewhat hesitantly acknowledging a difference in interpretation, and after moving back and forth between accusatory and exonerative discourse in the past, the interlocutors perceive the present duty with uneasiness and melancholy. Furet discusses this duty by calling for reaction. This time, the question of reaction is posed with regard to the historian's *attitude* and decision. Like any historian, he confronts his own biographical situation:

> Here we are enclosed in a single horizon of history, pulled toward the standardization of the world and the alienation of the individual from the economy, condemned to slow the effects without having a hold on their causes. History appears all the more sovereign as we lose the illusion of governing it. But as always, the historian *must react* against what seems inevitable at the time he writes; he knows too well that these kinds of collective givens are ephemeral. The forces at work toward the universalization of the world are so powerful that they trigger sequences of events and situations incompatible with the idea of the laws of history, *a fortiori* of possible prediction. Understanding and explaining the past is already difficult enough.[121]

The historian must react! Here reaction is not a tool of explanation. The word indicates only the task, the spurring of a resistance and the invention of a response. To react is to act spontaneously. Presented in this way, reaction is the movement — once changes that cannot be mastered have been acknowledged, once the weight of what appears to be an established fact has been recognized — that does not resign itself. Knowing only its opposition, without yet knowing how to manifest this opposition or how to overcome the enormous adversity of the unjust and the inexplicable, it does not consent to having things remain as they stand.

The historian must react: this is an injunction, but it remains indeterminate; it is a warning in the face of a perceived danger, but it comes with no theoretical assurance, no promise of success. It is above all spoken personally, by a reacting individual confronted with impersonal "forces," because it is necessary to respond to

364

them, even if from a position of ignorance. The historian sets to work not knowing what he will discover at the end of his personal reaction; he merely hopes that it will be an admissible response between a past whose meaning is still not sufficiently clear and a future that remains hidden. Reacting through his activity, he will perhaps have a sense of making progress on the day when he can discern, among currently opaque facts, relations of concomitance or causality, actions and reactions, systematic interactions ... He will thus have used the energy of his personal reaction (an act of resistance and freedom) to propose a sense to be read in facts that have ceased to be obscure, a sense that illuminates itself in objectivity — though we would know that it appeared only because the historian decided to react, in the first person. Through the play of words, a circularity takes shape between the reacting subject and the intelligible side of the objective world, where causality will take on all the forms of action and reaction.

To continue along these lines: philosophy, according to a direction it once followed — phenomenology, existential analysis — devoted a great deal of attention to describing a few fundamental feelings: dread (Søren Kierkegaard), care (Martin Heidegger), melancholic depression and maniacal euphoria (Ludwig Binswanger), disgust (Aurel Kolnai), nausea (Jean-Paul Sartre), fatigue (Emmanuel Lévinas), and so on.[122] To be sure, such studies examined human experience in a way that sought to be concrete and grounded in lived experience. What has nonetheless remained imprecise is the role played, from the beginning, by the preexisting names and meanings given to the phenomena under observation. Nuances and variations of the experience in question were often interrogated only because they had an assigned place in the word's semantic field and because it was necessary to account for related words, for synonyms or antonyms, based on a "central" meaning assumed to be stable and in principle universalizable. But a language's specificities leave their traces in experience itself. It is difficult to escape the spectrum of meanings imposed by a natural language's lexicon. Do phenomenological analyses of affects rejoin the affects themselves at their source? Don't they at the same time follow preexisting linguistic networks? An appeal to experience, to the immediacy of the specific experience in question, was not lacking, but rarely was it clearly acknowledged that this experience was maintained and guided by linguistic relationships. The analysis did not want to diminish any of the emotive phenomena's iridescence, but what the analysis differentiated was so often preconceived and preconditioned by language that it ought to have assigned its findings as much to vocabulary as to original lived experiences. I mention as a reminder the arbitrary aggression implicit in declaring that the language in which or on which one works is the language of authentic revelation or of the only valid philosophical thought: Greek, Hebrew, German, and so on.

What I have developed in this work belongs to an expanded semantic history, not phenomenology. Without losing sight of the phenomena preceding the theoretical attention that captures them, I have directed my gaze to the language in which these phenomena were described. No doubt each human being undergoes the bodily experiences of effort, resistance, shock, and contact with the things that oppose him. I have noted the attention that Maine de Biran gave to this; one of the words he used was "reaction." I have not followed him in his observation of what he called the "original impulse [*fait primitif*]." Had I chosen to refer to this experience, it would have been necessary to pass through many other words, calling upon a great many other linguistic vestiges and examining other prefixes (the *ob-* in Latin that produces "opposition," "objection," "object," and so forth; the *contra-* that produces "counteract," "counterattack," "counterweight," and so on). The totality I chose is nothing other than a word's various

366

transformations. On this technical word, such as it was conveyed by the discourse of physics and science, the sources are silent: "reaction" is an orphaned word. "Action" and "reaction" (once the collateral meanings of "action" are subtracted) are word tools, abstract entities that are easily manipulated.[123] In popular science, they served for a long time as substitutes for calculation. The scientific success of these terms diffused them and later mixed them in with the vocabulary of lived experience. As we have seen, the Romantic treatment of "action" and "reaction" was an attempt to re-enchant the world through terms that had contributed to its disenchantment. Paul Valéry, observing his own mind, waxed ironic about a "metaphysical drive" whose illusion seized him for a moment: "I caught myself in the act — in the process of *asking* myself the deep... meaning of action and reaction, this principle drawn by Newton from experience! As if this relation between q[uantities] of motion was already closer to I know not what *secrets* than any experience from which one can deduce it."[124] There is nothing to seek in the "depths" of the word "reaction."

According to the most acceptable genealogy, primary emotions precede and determine words; but words — ever since they came into being for us in time immemorial and ever since we have been subject to their mutable authority — precede and determine secondary emotions. We live within social bonds and within speech, and we hardly know anything other than secondary emotions. Rare are the moments in which we have the impression of returning to this side of words and regaining access to a preverbal experience — in pleasure, pain, or poetry. "Action and reaction" belong to the intellectual lexicon, to the thought that objectifies emotion, not to emotion itself, however derivative it may be.

It is therefore a word through which the desire to know attempted to explain the law of the material world (Newton), to

understand and make understood what contributes to the production of the form of living beings (Aristotle) and what keeps
them alive (Bichat). When we attribute reaction to a singular subject (him, you, or me), this shifter word allows one to evoke, by
naming and defining them, the affective, so-called primal reactions (which are most often negative: disgust, spite, envy, anger,
jealousy, and so on). In the subjective order, the field of the reactive unfolds broadly, and, once any given reaction is named and
categorized as such, it gains a sense of objectivity, almost to the
point of becoming confused with the phenomena of that physics
of life known as physiology. The measurements of physiology
have sometimes intertwined with explorations that attempt to
probe the *depths* of psychic life. When, at the beginning of the
twentieth century, Eugen Bleuler and Carl Gustav Jung studied
verbal associations, they patiently measured *reaction times* with a
chronometer, while the words they obtained from their patients
led them to the psychological *complex*. In more recent usage, the
field of application of the word "reaction" extends to all human
relations, from the immediate relation with the living environment to the relation with the sum of what the individual believes
he knows about the world — from the sensory space to the hori-
zon that reason strives for, from the intimate to the most general
sphere. Whether we are talking about the unconscious movement
that contracts the pupil in bright light, the emotions stimulated
by an encounter with a person, an insult, an overwhelming piece
of news, or, finally, the ambition that brings us to challenge the
present through thought or work, the word that comes to mind is
"reaction." Aesthetics, works of art, and philosophies have been
attributed with a reactive gesture at their very origin. In his preface to the second edition of *The Interpretation of Dreams*, Freud
remarks: "This book has a further subjective significance for me
personally — a significance which I grasped only after I had com-

pleted it. It was, I found, a portion of my own self-analysis, my reaction to my father's death — that is to say, to the most important event, the most poignant loss, of a man's life." Later he declared that his essay "On Narcissism: An Introduction" (1915) marked his "reaction to Alfred Adler." Charles-Ferdinand Ramuz, in recalling the beginning of his literary works, sees them not as merely an opposition to what he had been taught in school but as an apprenticeship to things, to the shock things provoke and the reaction that results: "We suffocated in our schoolrooms; we gasped toward the open air. It seemed to us that health returned when we found ourselves again before things. An immediate contact with things, shock and reaction: that was the whole story.... It was necessary for us to create our rhetoric on the spot, including our grammar, even our syntax — and, once the shock had been received, we had nothing in mind other than to restore it as such." In a prefatory note from 1920 for a novel dated 1907, Joseph Conrad writes: "The origin of *The Secret Agent*: subject, treatment, artistic purpose and every other motive that may induce an author to take up his pen, can, I believe, be traced to a period of mental and emotional reaction." In a note in which he recapitulates his life, Valéry places his work under the sign of reaction: "My development 'in depth' was a reaction against the tyranny of literary and other credulity." At the beginning of the twentieth century, Georg Simmel proposed a general definition of the philosophical enterprise: "One can designate the philosopher, perhaps, as someone who possesses the organ capable of receiving the totality of being and reacting to it."[125] This certainly entails much more than "defining oneself through opposition," a saying that has become common in French.[126] The various texts I have just cited all indicate a point of departure and designate it as a reaction. The reaction signals a beginning: a revolt, the composition of a book, the discovery of a style, a thought, a form of knowledge. According to this later use of the term, "reaction" marks the inaugural and causal moment in the history of an individual life, and of the life of a group as well. While implying a prior situation (its negative aspect), the word applies to an originary decision, to what Sartre would call a "situated choice."

Previously, in Balzac (*Louis Lambert*) and in Nietzsche, the word "reaction" bore the stigma of secondariness: reaction was worth less than spiritual action (Balzac) or spontaneous will (Nietzsche). Earlier still, reaction concerned matter, not people. In the beginning, it was almost synonymous with "passion"; it was tied to the object that undergoes... It was produced in the body, impersonally. It was located, reflected upon, and calculated in order to describe, through analysis, the relations between masses in motion. With this concept that was elevated to the status of a law, it became possible to predict these motions, to master them when they were on a human scale, and to exert a power over things. At the same time, in pursuing these analyses in all accessible realms, in multiplying the fields and types of these impersonal reactions, one penetrated the order of the living being, in which one witnessed the workings of mechanical chains of cause and effect. Cerebral activity and thought, to which it was of course necessary to grant a higher degree of complexity, were no less determinate than physical systems. Things among things, they relayed the chain of causes that had produced them. Thus impersonal reaction took possession of this territory in which it had been believed an immaterial subject was entrenched — the self, the subject, the mind. Nietzsche believed that henceforth one should say "it thinks," the way one says "it rains" or "it snows."[127] One might be fascinated or, on the contrary, horrified by this decomposition, this fragmentation, this anonymity.

Here a repossession and a relaunching take place. I have called attention to Valéry's words at the end of his life: "I am a reaction to what I am." This is much more than a neutral statement; an obstinate desire commands this *activation* of the word "reaction." In the face of death, the thought that had consented to be merely an effect affirms that it is also a cause. As long as thought keeps vigil, the "I am" that reacts detaches itself from the "I am" that is no longer, and in declaring its difference, it traces out a mark that will survive. Within the confines of what happens, a decision, always and never the last, takes over from a state of facts.

In each case, this decision was also primary. The objective knowledge that claims to trace consciousness to its origins (biological, neurological), and that appears to dispossess it, must recognize itself as the product of a decision and as the bearer of future decisions: it cannot reverse the choice that produced it. This tentative freedom discovers that it was itself — through its interpretation of the world — that set out to discover its origins, to the point of hoping to see itself being born. At the end of the causal chain we try to reconstruct — that is where our existence must lie. We hope to find the causes that made us live, and then made us emerge from animality and respond to the challenges of the external world through calculation and reason. But it is first of all we ourselves who have set out in search of our origins. We are the origin of our search for the origin. The circle closes, and another action begins.

Notes

PREFACE

1. Erich Auerbach to Martin Hellweg, Istanbul, May 22, 1939, *Briefe an Martin Hellweg, 1939–1950*, ed. Martin Vialon (Tübingen: Francke, 1997), pp. 57–58.

2. Honoré de Balzac, "Louis Lambert," in *Seraphita*, trans. Clara Bell (London: Dent, 1913), pp. 160–62.

3. On the history of this search for a founding language, see Maurice Olender, *The Languages of Paradise: Race, Religion, and Philosophy in the Nineteenth Century*, trans. Arthur Goldhammer (Cambridge, MA: Harvard University Press, 1992).

4. See Maurice Merleau-Ponty, "Sur la phénoménologie du langage," in *Eloge de la philosophie* (Paris: Gallimard, 1963), pp. 83–111, and the commentary by Karlheinz Stierle, "Historische Semantik und die Geschichtlichkeit der Bedeutung," in Reinhart Koselleck (ed.), *Historische Semantik und Begriffsgeschichte* (Stuttgart: Klett-Cotta, 1978), pp. 154–89; see also, in the same collection, the studies by Horst Günther (pp. 102–120) and H.U. Gumbrecht (pp. 75–101); see also the bibliography in Dietrich Busse, *Historische Semantik. Analyse eines Programms* (Stuttgart: Klett-Cotta, 1987).

5. This is a reference to Kant's "Table of Categories" in *Critique of Pure Reason*, in which "action" and "reaction" are included under the broader heading "relation." — TRANS.

6. Michel Bréal, *Semantics: Studies in the Science of Meaning*, trans. Nina Cust (London: Heinemann, 1900), p. 139. [Trans. modified.]

7. Any inquiries into the history of French words should include: Paul Imbs and Bernard Quemada, eds., *Trésor de la langue française: Dictionnaire de la langue du XIXe et du XXe siècle*, 16 vols. (Paris: CNRS and Gallimard, 1971–1994); Alain Rey, ed., *Dictionnaire historique de la langue française* (Paris: Le Robert, 1992 and 1998). See Alain Rey, *"Révolution": Histoire d'un mot* (Paris: Gallimard, 1989).

CHAPTER ONE: A WORD FROM PHYSICS

1. Alfred Ernout and Antoine Meillet, *Dictionnaire étymologique de la langue latine*, 2nd ed. (Paris: Klincksieck, 1939), pp. 25–29.

2. The word *reactio* appeared around 960 in *Il Chronicon di Benedetto, monaco de S. Andrea di Soratte*, ed. Giuseppe Zucchetti (Rome: Istituto Storico Italiano, 1920), p. 147, 11Z. It appears in reference to reacting against the Saracens: "Ceperunt reagere Sarracenis consilium." I wish to thank the editors of *Thesaurus linguae latinae* (Munich) for providing me with this information. The Forcellini dictionary notes the presence of the verb *reagere* in the fabulist Avienus (around 400 C.E.). It was, in fact, a misreading of the manuscript and was deleted by the current editors. The words *retroagere* and *retroactio* were part of classical Latin. They were maintained, in unstable uses. Their modern use has been revived only in cybernetic language, mainly by Norbert Wiener. The term *reactio* is not found in Albert Blaise, *Dictionnaire latin-français des auteurs chrétiens*, rev. Henri Chirat (Turnhout: Brepols, 1993).

3. These quotations are from *The Complete Works of Aristotle: The Revised Oxford Translation*, 2 vols., ed. Jonathan Barnes (Princeton, NJ: Princeton University Press, 1984).

4. Aristotle, *Metaphysics* 12.7.1072a, *Complete Works*, vol. 2, p. 1694.

5. *Ibid.* 7.1072b8–9, p. 1694.

6. *Ibid.* 1072b14–15, p. 1695.

7. Aristotle, *On Generation and Corruption* 2.337a, and *Complete Works* 336b, vol. 1, pp. 551–52.

8. Aristotle, *Generation of Animals* 1.18.724b5, p. 1125.

9. Aristotle, *Categories* 14, p. 23.

10. Aristotle, *Generation of Animals* 4.3.768b. The Greek text does not explicitly attribute a motion in return to a moved object, which is why the word *reactio* did not appear in the Latin, medieval, and Renaissance translations of this Aristotelian passage. For the lines cited here, William of Moerbeke (1215–1286) gives this Latin equivalent: "Universaliter movens preter primum contramovetur aliquo motu, ut propellens contrapellitur aliqualiter et retunditur tundens: aliquando autem et totaliter passum est magis quam fecit et infrigidatum est calefaciens, calefactum est infrigidans, aliquando autem nihil fecit, quandoque autem minus quam sit passum"; see *De generatione animalium: Translatio Guillelmi de Moerbeka*, ed. H.J. Drossaart Lulofs, Aristotles latinus, 17, 2 (Leiden: E.J. Brill, 1966), pp. 130–31. This passage from the *Generation of Animals* was cited regularly, on the subjects of both action and passion, or reaction, by medieval and Renaissance scholars.

11. On Aristotelian "hereditary kinetics," see Erna Lesky, *Die Zeugungs- und Vererbungslehren der Antike und ihr Nachwirken* (Mainz: Akademie der Wissenschaften in der Literatur, 1950), pp. 148–58. For Lesky, material that has received the formative impulse exerts a reaction (*Gegenwirkung, Rückwirkung*), and the author sees in this the first occurrence in which an active force is attributed to the mother (pp. 152–53). Aristotle does not use the substantive *antikinesis*, which would have prefigured *reactio*. But *antikinesis* is used by his commentator Simplicius in the sixth century C.E. (commentary on *De caelo* 366.8 and 395.29; commentary on *Physics* 677.20).

12. Aristotle, *On Generation and Corruption* 1.7.322b, p. 527.

13. Aristotle, *Metaphysics* 10.4.1055a, *Complete Works*, vol. 2, p. 1666; *On Memory* 2.453a, vol. 1, p. 720.

14. These examples are from the *Opera omnia* (Monasterii Westfalorum: In Aedibus Aschendorff, 1982–) published in Münster, vol. 12, pp. 117 and 123; vol. 4, 1, p. 163. It is generally agreed that Albertus Magnus had as his principal source *De animalibus* by Michael Scot, reprinted around 1210 in Toledo and based on the Arab text of *Historia animalium*, from *De partibus animalium* and *De generatione*

animalium. He might also have used some of Petrus Hispanus's manuscripts commenting on these works of Aristotle. See Aristotle, *De animalibus*. Scot's *Arabic-Latin Translation, Part Three, Books XV–XIX: Generation of Animals*, ed. Aafke M.I. van Oppenraaij (Leiden: E.J. Brill, 1992), 4.3.768b28, pp. ix and 179. See as well S.D. Wingate, *The Mediaeval Latin Versions of the Aristotelian Scientific Corpus, with Special Reference to the Biological Works* (London: Courier, 1931). The words *reagere* and *reactio* do not appear in the Latin of Scot. See Charles H. Lohr, *Commentateurs latins d'Aristote au Moyen Age: Bibliographie de la littérature secondaire récente* (Fribourg and Paris: Editions Universitaires and Editions du Cerf, 1988).

15. Albertus Magnus, *Quaestiones super De animalibus* 15.Q.20 and 2.Q.17–19.

16. Albertus Magnus, *Physica*, bk. 3, tract 1, cap. 7.

17. Gerardus Johannes Vossius (1577–1649), *De vitiis sermonis* 4.20. Cited as sole example by Charles Du Fresne Du Cange, "Reagere," in *Glossarium ad scriptores mediae et infimae latinitatis* (Paris, 1734), vol. 5. One can verify this purist disapproval of the word *reactio* in the French-Latin dictionaries. Whereas the word *réaction* was well established in French, François Noël's *Dictionnaire français-latin*, in its late edition of 1850, gave as its Latin equivalent the word *repulsus*, masculine substantive. For the word *réagir* ("said of a body acting on another from which it has received an action"), four Latin equivalents are proposed: *repellere, repercutere, acceptum motum reddere, reciproca vi agere*.

18. Aristotle, *Physics* 3.201a and 8.254b, *Complete Works*, vol. 1, pp. 343 and 425; Thomas Aquinas affirms, "Omne quod movetur ab alio movetur" (*In physicorum* 7.1). See Eric Weil, "Quelques remarques sur le sens et l'intention de la métaphysique aristotélienne," in *Essais et conférences*, 2 vols. (Paris: Plon, 1970), vol. 1, pp. 81–105; Anneliese Maier, *Zwischen Philosophie und Mechanik* (Rome: Storia e Letteratura, 1958); James A. Weisheipl, O.P., "The Principle *Omne quod movetur ab alio movetur* in Medieval Physics," *Isis* 56 (1965), pp. 26–45.

19. Aristotle, *Physics* 2.192b, p. 329. The complete proposition from Thomas Aquinas is: "Natura est principium motus et quietis in eo in quo est primo et per se et non secundum accidens" (Nature is the principle of motion and of rest for the thing in which it resides immediately and essentially and not by accident) (*In physicorum* 1).

20. Aristotle, *On Generation and Corruption* 1.7.322b–324b, pp. 527–30.

21. I will recall a few of the propositions that are relevant to our purposes from this chapter of *On Generation and Corruption* 323b29–324a5: "But since only those things which either involve a contrariety or are contraries — and not any things selected at random — are such as to suffer action and to act, agent and patient must be alike (i.e. identical) in kind and yet unlike (i.e. contrary) in species. (For by nature body is affected by body, flavour by flavour, colour by colour, and so in general what belongs to any kind by a member of the same kind — the reason being that contraries are in every case within a single identical kind, and it is contraries which reciprocally act and suffer action.) Hence agent and patient must be in one sense identical, but in another sense other than (i.e. unlike) one another" (*Complete Works*, vol. 1, p. 529).

22. Swineshead's altered and simplified name — Suisset — gave rise to many mistakes in the reprintings and citations of his writings up to the beginning of the seventeenth century.

23. An account of these debates can be found in Christopher Lewis, *The Merton Tradition and Kinematics in Late Sixteenth and Early Seventeenth Century Italy* (Padua: Antenore, 1980), esp. pp. 19–32. See as well the general account by Edith Dudley Sylla, in Norman Kretzmann, Anthony Kenny, and Jan Pinborg (eds.), *Cambridge History of Later Medieval Philosophy* (Cambridge, UK: Cambridge University Press, 1982), pp. 540–63. One should pay attention to the varieties of occasions in which an event — be it material or metaphoric — has called for an interpretation involving a reaction: percussion, impact, collision, clash, shock. In French, the word *choc* can be used in all these instances.

24. Albert of Saxony and Marsilius of Inghen both commented on Aristotle's *De generatione et corruptione*. Their commentary has often been added to Aegidius Romanus's older commentary; new editions of their work were still appearing in the sixteenth century. See the collection *In Aristotelis libros de Generatione commentaria* (Venice, 1567).

25. Alain de Libera, *La Philosophie médiévale* (Paris: PUF, 1993), p. 443.

26. According to Anneliese Maier, the writings from Galileo's youth attest to his familiarity with Scholastic physics, notably that of the Parisian doctors. He

mentions the *intensio et remissio formarum*, the *mixtio*, the *reactio*, and so on. Therefore, it can be claimed that Galileo did not radically break with his predecessors. See Anneliese Maier, "Galilei und die scholastische Impetustheorie," in *On the Threshold of Exact Science: Selected Writings of Anneliese Maier on Late Medieval Natural Philosophy*, ed. and trans. Steven D. Sargent (Philadelphia: University of Pennsylvania Press, 1982), pp. 103–123. This thesis was put forth by Pierre Duhem (1861–1916) in his study long ago. William A. Wallace takes up the same theme of scientific continuity, with other arguments, in *Prelude to Galileo: Essays on Medieval and Sixteenth-Century Sources of Galileo's Thought* (Dordrecht: Reidel, 1981). On this point, Alexandre Koyré expresses the opposite opinion, notably in *Etudes d'histoire de la pensée scientifique* (Paris: PUF, 1966), pp. 147–75.

27. Aristotle, *Parts of Animals* 2.648b, *Complete Works*, vol. 1, p. 1010.

28. See Gaston Bachelard, *Etude sur l'evolution d'un problème de physique: La Propagation thermique dans les solides* (Paris: Vrin, 1928). For a philosophical description of the transformations of scientific language, see Jürgen Mittelstrass, *Neuzeit und Aufklärung. Studien zur Entstehung der neuzeitlichen Wissenschaft und Philosophie* (Berlin and New York: W. de Gruyter, 1970); I. Bernard Cohen, *Revolution in Science* (Cambridge, MA: Harvard University Press, 1985).

29. See Owsei Temkin, *Galenism: Rise and Decline of a Medical Philosophy* (Ithaca, NY: Cornell University Press, 1973).

30. On Marliani, see Marshall Clagett, *Giovanni Marliani and Late Medieval Physics* (New York: Columbia University Press, 1941), in particular pp. 40ff. On the school of Padua, see John H. Randall Jr., *The School of Padua and the Emergence of Modern Science* (Padua: Antenore, 1961); Giuseppe Saitta, *Il pensiero italiano nell'umanesimo e nel rinascimento*, 2 vols. (Bologna: C. Zuffi, 1949–1951), vol. 2, pp. 249–323; and Eugenio Garin, *La filosofia: Storia dei generi letterari italiani*, 2 vols. (Milan: Vallardi, 1947), vol. 1, pp. 338–52, and vol. 2, pp. 1–65. On Pomponazzi, see Bruno Nardi, *Studi su Pietro Pomponazzi* (Florence: Le Monnier, 1965); *De intentione et remissione* and *De reactione* were Pomponazzi's first published works (1514–1515). On Zabarella, see Charles B. Schmitt, "Experience and Experiment: A Comparison of Zabarella's View with Galileo's in *De*

motu," *Studies in the Renaissance* 16 (1969), pp. 80–138; and Antonino Poppi, *La dottrina della scienza in Giacomo Zabarella* (Padua: Antenore, 1972). Zabarella's *Liber de reactione* (1585) was part of the collection *De rebus naturalibus* (Padua, 1589).

31. Nicole d'Oresme's work on degrees of qualities — *De latitudine formarum* — is today considered one of the most important of the fourteenth century. See Marshall Clagett (ed.), *Tractatus de configurationibus qualitatum et motuum*, in *Nicole Oresme and the Medieval Geometry of Qualities and Motions* (Madison: University of Wisconsin Press, 1968).

32. Saitta, *Il pensiero italiano*, vol. 2, p. 390.

33. Zabarella, *Liber de reactione* (Cologne, 1602), col. 452.

34. *Ibid.*, col. 451.

35. See, among others, John L. Heilbron, *Elements of Early Modern Physics* (Berkeley: University of California Press, 1982), pp. 1–65; see also Dino Buzzetti, "Matematica e logica nel Medioevo: Sul concetto di misura," *Dianoia* 1 (Bologna, 1996), pp. 61–76.

36. Johannes Magirus is interesting, for his book *Physiologiae peripateticae libri sex* (1597) was studied by Newton at the beginning of his university years.

37. Rudolphus Goclenius the Elder (1547–1628), *Lexicon philosophicum* (Frankfurt, 1613). Complete text: "Reaction is in some way an action of the patient, in return and reciprocated, by which it resists the agent (it exerts force in the opposite direction against the agent) and changes it at the same time as it is changed by it. As a result, one may say, in a way, that the agent is passive and that the patient acts. And 'repassion' is a 'reciprocated' passion. These terms are understood sometimes in a broad sense and sometimes in a strict sense. In a broad sense when, without having made any distinction between agent and patient, one says that both react and that both are 'reacted upon.' In the strict and proper sense when one gives the name 'agent' to what, in action, is the principal, triumphant element and the name 'patient' to the other element. This, in fact, is how reaction is attributed to the patient and 'repassion' to the agent. Just as the latter is called 'agent' only insofar as it is the principal element, so the other is called 'reagent' because it is in some way weaker; inversely, the latter is

called 'patient' while the principal agent is called 'repatient' instead of 'patient.' This is why reacting properly means acting secondarily, and being reacted upon means being acted upon secondarily." In a subsidiary schematic formula, without any further explication, Goclenius then subdivides reaction into "reactio physikē" and "reactio pneumatikē, ut in potentia cognoscente," that is, "natural reaction" and "spiritual reaction, as in cognitive power." Are we dealing here with a distinction between reaction *ex parte objecti* and reaction *ex parte subjecti*? If so, it would be an important step in the history of the meanings of the term. We can see the complications that arise for those who seek purely verbal explanations in this area. The distinction between "reaction" and "repassion" is correct but will not pass into ordinary language, though it will be perfectly translated into the language of mechanics and its calculations.

This definition should be supplemented by that of Johannes Micraelius (1597–1658), *Lexicon philosophicum terminorum philosophis usitata* (Jena, 1653). Under *actio*, we read: "We call that action 'mutual' by which the agent is 'reacted upon' through physical contact, and this action is referred to as 'reaction' and 'repassion.' Thus heat is 'reacted upon' by ice. We speak of non-mutual action when the agent is not 'reacted upon' because it acts only through virtual contact. Thus the sun is not in any way 'reacted upon' by the air on which it acts."

38. Ernout and Meillet in *Dictionnaire étymologique de la langue latine*, pp. 853–54, note that "from re- there derives an adjective *recus*, which is part of *reciprocus*."

39. Jean Gabriel Boivin, *Philosophia Scoti* (Paris: Tertia Pars, 1690), pp. 431–32: "Action is a sort of victory, by which the agent breaks the action of the patient and prevails over it; in this conflict between agent and patient, the agent 're-suffers' that which was undergone by the patient: one must therefore acknowledge that there exist an action and a 're-passion.' Next, one might imagine that a combination of elements is given with which to make a compound; but in the compound the elements become altered, and the alteration can only be accomplished through reaction, since, of course, an element is tempered by the reaction of its opposite, which indicates that the qualities of the compound are found not in the sum (or the extreme) but in the mean. It must therefore be

granted that there is a reaction and a 're-passion.' Finally, experience teaches that snow, when compressed in the hand, chills the hand and is warmed by this same hand ... and that a white-hot iron, plunged into cold water, will heat it, while the iron's heat is lessened by the water's cold.... The reaction, however, is nothing but a reciprocal action, or an action of the object acted upon, by which the latter acts on the agent." The case of "reaction" intervening in a mixture or compound becomes a resource for the language of the next century's chemists.

40. Heilbron, *Elements of Early Modern Physics*, pp. 11–22.

41. *Ibid.*, p. 18.

42. Jean Perréal, *La Complainte de nature à l'alchimiste errant*. The text (attributed at the time to Jean de Meung) was published in the appendixes of the *Roman de la rose* in the Dominique-Martin Méon edition, 4 vols. (Paris, 1813). The passage takes up lines 460–67 of the poem. On Perréal, see André Vernet, *Etudes médiévales* (Paris: Institut d'Etudes Augustiniennes, 1981), pp. 416–54. For a recent account of alchemical studies, see *Le crisi dell'alchimia*, Micrologus, no. 3 (Brepols, 1995). The words "reaction" and "react" do not appear in Danièle Jacquart and Claude Thomasset, *Lexique de la langue scientifique* (Paris: Klincksieck, 1997).

43. Here, by way of example, is a passage from René de Ceriziers, *Le Philosophe françois*, 2 vols. (Paris, 1644), vol. 1, pp. 80–81: "Those who assure us that an Agent suffers nothing from the Patient, by which I mean the subject upon which it acts, deny the experience of the senses and the force of reason. Who does not know that from boiling water and cold water, one obtains lukewarm water, which occurs as much because the cold is warmed by the hot as because the hot is chilled by the cold? Who does not know that the hand melts snow and the snow chills the hand? Who does not know that the stomach does not only alter food but that food acts upon the stomach by impressing its own accidents upon it? Truly, those who reject reaction (such is what one calls the mutual combat of Causes) doubt the power of Compounds, into which the Elements can enter only by virtue of the reciprocal weakening of their qualities. Without it, Medicine would not be able to create remedies, since their power comes from the fact that the virtue of one simple is tempered by the virtue of

another. Although this opinion cannot be contradicted, Richard Swineshead, who is called the Calculator or Reckoner in the School, nevertheless maintains that two Agents suffer in their mutual effort but that they suffer in different parts of their subject. For example (he says), an iron 2 feet in length, the first part of which has 6 degrees of heat, and the second part of which has 3, acts upon 2 feet of water, one-half of which has 6 degrees of cold, and the other, 3 degrees; but in such a way that the 6 degrees of heat act on the part of water that has only 3 degrees of cold, and that the part of the water that has 6 acts on the half of the iron that has only 3 degrees of heat."

44. Giordano Bruno, *The Expulsion of the Triumphant Beast*, trans. Arthur D. Imerti (Lincoln: University of Nebraska Press, 1964), p. 91. Contrariety — the opposition of contraries or opposites — is a logical category faithfully mentioned by the Scholastics and their heirs. See Scipion Dupleix, *La Physique* (Paris, 1640), bk. 3, ch. 4; reprinted in the series Corpus des oeuvres de philosophie en langue française (Paris; Fayard, 1990), pp. 189–90: "Action always presupposes passion, because these are relative things that are related not only to each other but also each one to itself; and I would go even further and say that these two mean the same thing, though they are seen from different points of view."

45. Cited by the *Oxford English Dictionary*. The same dictionary notes a nice metaphoric use in *Religio medici* (1642) by Sir Thomas Browne: "It is the method of Charity to suffer without reaction" (1, no. 5). The material fact is transposed into the spiritual order.

46. The word "reaction" is not found in Galileo's vocabulary. See Maria Luisa Altieri Biagi, *Galileo e la terminologia tecnico-scientifica* (Florence: Olschki, 1965). The important term for Galileo is "moment."

47. Eric Mendoza (ed.), *Reflections on the Motive Power of Fire by Sadi Carnot, and Other Papers on the Second Law of Thermodynamics by E. Clapeyron and R. Clausius* (New York, 1960).

48. Isaac Newton, "Axioms, or Laws of Motion," in *Mathematical Principles of Natural Philosophy*, 2 vols., ed. Florian Cajori (New York: Greenwood, 1962), vol. 1, pp. 13–14. In the French edition of this book, this quotation was taken from the translation by Pierre-Louis Moreau de Maupertuis in his *Examen*

philosophique de la preuve de l'existence de Dieu employée dans "L'Essai de cosmologie," in *Oeuvres* (Hildesheim and New York: Olms, 1974), vol. 1, p. 411. Maupertuis goes on to argue: "In the idea we have of the body, we find only a perfect indifference to motion and rest: neither its extent nor its impenetrability allows one to see that it must resist or react; even less that its reaction must be equal to action: each body could by reason of its mass have a certain degree of reaction beyond which it could not go: to find the origin of reaction, one must look at inertia; this priority of the body we can discover only through experience" (*ibid.,* p. 414). Maupertuis, an admirer of Newton, was answering objections made by French scholars who remained attached to Cartesian models. He advised Emilie du Châtelet in her translation of Newton, *Les Principes mathématiques,* which appeared in 1756. Newton's example of the pressed stone that presses back corresponds to the above-mentioned passage in Aristotle. It is an intermediate example, which shows a continuity between the old and the new physics, at least in terms of the familiar image, though not in terms of its interpretation.

49. See Georges Gusdorf's summary in *Les sciences humaines et la pensée occidentale,* vol. 2, *Les Origines des sciences humaines* (Paris: Payot, 1967), p. 453: "The vitalist analogy prevents the constitution of a physics as a taking possession of material reality. . . . Modern science was born with Galileo, whose thought is free of all hylozoism." See also Paolo Rossi, *The Birth of Modern Science,* trans. Cynthia De Nardi Ipsen (Oxford: Blackwell, 2001).

50. Descartes considered matter and extension as one and the same substance, and the physics he developed deductively is based on the transmission of motion and the conservation of the quantity of motion. He takes resistance into account but — to my knowledge — never uses the word "reaction." See, for example, the formulation of rule 42 of *Principles of Philosophy.* At every moment, God renews the laws he has established: "For all places are filled with body, and at the same time the motion of every body is rectilinear in tendency [rule 39]; so clearly, when God first created the world, he must not only have assigned various motions to its various parts, but also have caused their mutual impulses and the transference of motion from one to another; and since he now preserves motion by the same activity and according to the same laws, as when he created

it, he does not preserve it as a constant inherent property of given pieces of matter, but as something passing from one piece to another as they collide." In René Descartes, *Philosophical Writings*, trans. Elizabeth Anscombe and Peter Thomas Geach (London: Nelson, 1954), p. 219.

51. Richard S. Westfall, "The Culmination of the Scientific Revolution: Isaac Newton," in Paul Theerman and Adele F. Seeff (eds.), *Action and Reaction: Proceedings of a Symposium to Commemorate the Tercentenary of Newton's "Principia"* (Newark: University of Delaware Press, 1993), p. 37; Richard S. Westfall, *Never at Rest: A Biography of Newton* (Cambridge, UK: Cambridge University Press, 1980), p. 420; John Herivel, *The Background to Newton's "Principia"* (Oxford: Clarendon Press, 1965).

52. In chapter 7 of *Liber de reactione* (1585), Zabarella, who was associated with the Paduan tradition, treated separately the question of local motion: he then examined the questions of impact (*pellere* and *premi*), pressure (*premere* and *imprimi*), impulse or effort (*conatus*), which find their solution in conformity with the Aristotelian doctrine. Zabarella does not recognize the common principles that allow for the unification of these problems. See Schmitt, "Experience and Experiment," and articles cited above, note 30. Local motion, the falling of bodies, and impact will give rise to the quantified formulas that nascent modern science considered the sole base for an effective knowledge of nature.

53. Newton, *Mathematical Principles*, vol. 2, p. 545.

54. Isaac Newton, *Correspondence*, ed. H.W. Turnbull (Cambridge, UK: Cambridge University Press, 1961), vol. 3, *1688–1694*, pp. 253–54. See also François de Gandt, *Force et géometrie* (Lille: ANRT, 1987).

55. Colin Maclaurin, *An Account of Sir Isaac Newton's Philosophical Discoveries* (London, 1748), bk. 2, ch. 2, pp. 152–56; bk. 4, ch. 9, p. 408.

56. G.W. Leibniz, "Principles of Nature and of Grace," in *Philosophical Papers and Letters*, trans. Leroy E. Loemker (Dordrecht: Reidel, 1969), pp. 636–37.

57. G.W. Leibniz, "Examen des principes de Malebranche," in *Recueil de diverses pièces sur la philosophie, la religion naturelle, l'histoire, les mathématiques, etc. par Mrs Leibniz, Clarke, Newton, et autres auteurs célèbres*, 2 vols. (Amsterdam, 1740), vol. 2, p. 524.

58. *Ibid.*, p. 525.

59. Immanuel Kant, *The One Possible Basis for a Demonstration of the Existence of God* (1763), 2.7.3.

60. Jules Vuillemin, in *Physique et métaphysique kantiennes* (Paris: PUF, 1955), writes: "The Kantian theory of knowledge is the first consequential and truly philosophical theory of knowledge without God" (pp. 258–59).

61. Immanuel Kant, *Metaphysical Foundations of Natural Science*, trans. James Ellington (Indianapolis: Bobbs-Merrill, 1985), ch. 3, prop. 4, n. 2, p. 110. See also Michel Puech, *Kant et la causalité* (Paris: Vrin, 1990), pp. 390–94.

62. Vuillemin, *Physique et métaphysique kantiennes*, pp. 316 and 355.

63. Kant, *Metaphysical Foundations of Natural Science*, ch. 3. This aspect of Kant's thought was criticized by Arthur Schopenhauer in *The World as Will and Idea*, trans. R.B. Haldane and John Kemp (London: Routledge and Kegan Paul, 1964), vol. 2, pp. 1–159.

64. Kant, *Metaphysical Foundations of Natural Science*, pp. 105–106.

65. Vuillemin, *Physique et métaphysique kantiennes*, p. 299. Jakob Friedrich Fries (1773–1843), in *Die mathematische Naturphilosophie nach philosophischer Methode bearbeitet* (Heidelberg, 1822), secs. 98–104, attempts to limit himself to the calculable, but his "pure doctrine of motion" (*reine Bewegungslehre*) includes mythic elements that prefigure the Freudian opposition between life and death drives.

Precise calculation by engineers applies just as much to the work done by the "animated motors" (man, horse) as to that done by inanimate forces (water, steam). A glance at *Traité de mécanique industrielle*, 2nd ed. (Liège, 1844), by Jean Victor Poncelet (1788–1867) reveals some of the ways in which the laws of mechanics were applied during the Industrial Revolution. Recalling Newton's third law, Poncelet writes: "It is inconceivable to us that a force would exert an action without giving rise, at that very instant, to an equally and directly opposed resistance" (p. 33). A translation into economics soon follows: "One distinctive feature of mechanical work is that, when money is paid for the exercise of force, it is mechanical work that is being paid for, and its value, its monetary price, increases in precise proportion to its quantity" (p. 44).

66. Newton kept most of his theories on the natures of "small bodies" to himself, in particular those on living bodies. He could not find a way to apply to them the laws he had fixed in the purity of numbers. The *Opticks* and especially the chemical manuscripts that came to light in the twentieth century reveal a Newton trying to find, on the level of particles, a complement to the laws of gravitation and the mechanics of solid bodies. His disciples John Keill (1671–1721) and John Freind (1675–1728) formulated some very schematic propositions on this subject.

On the very unusual Georges-Louis Le Sage (1724–1803), see Pierre Prevost, *Notice de la vie et des écrits de George-Louis Le Sage* (Geneva, 1805), and the note written by Pierre Speziali in Charles P. Enz (ed.), *Physica Genevensis* (Geneva: Georg, 1997), pp. 41–44. Le Sage is the author of *Essai de chimie méchanique* (Geneva, 1761).

67. Ruggero Giuseppe Boscovich, *A Theory of Natural Philosophy* (Cambridge, MA: MIT Press, 1966), p. 20: "If the matter is worked back to the genuine and simplest natural principles, it will be found that everything depends on the composition of the forces with which the particles of matter act upon one another; and from these forces, as a matter of fact, all phenomena of Nature take their origin." In sections 265 and 266, Boscovich admits either repulsion or attraction, depending on the distances, between the points of unextended matter. See Mirko D. Grmek's "La Méthodologie de Boscovich," *Revue d'histoire des sciences* 49, no. 4 (Oct.–Dec. 1996), pp. 379–400.

68. Friedrich Nietzsche, *Beyond Good and Evil*, trans. Walter Kaufmann (New York: Vintage Books, 1966), p. 20. Nietzsche speaks highly of Boscovich in a letter to Peter Gast dated March 20, 1882. James Clerk Maxwell, *Proceedings of the Royal Institution of Great Britain* (London, 1873–1875), vol. 7, pp. 48–49, and James Clerk Maxwell, *Matter and Motion* (London, 1876; repr., New York: Dover, 1991).

69. See Bas C. Van Fraassen, *Laws and Symmetry* (Oxford: Clarendon Press, 1989). In modern mechanics, Walter Noll's axiom, which corresponds to Euler's laws of motion, has a general principle of action and reaction as corollary: "The forces and torques exerted by separate bodies on each other are pairwise equili-

brated." Cited by Clifford A. Truesdell, *An Idiot's Fugitive Essays on Science* (New York: Springer, 1984), p. 546.

70. A neo-vitalist of the twentieth century, Hans Driesch, declared, in *Die Philosophie des Organischen*, that "Kant's third category is in fact a category of organic life." Cited by Viktor von Weizsäcker, who takes up this idea in *Der Gastaltkreis*, 4th ed. (Stuttgart: Thieme, 1950), pp. 131–32, n.10. For Weizsäcker, the action and reaction of the organism and its environment (*Wechselwirkung*) are simultaneous as opposed to successive.

71. Alan Sokal and Jean Bricmont, *Fashionable Nonsense: Postmodern Intellectuals' Abuse of Science* (New York: Picador USA, 1998). On the years preceding the French Revolution, see Robert Darnton, *Mesmerism and the End of the Enlightenment in France* (Cambridge, MA: Harvard University Press, 1986).

72. John Wesley, *Works* (1872), vol. 5, p. 232.

73. John Turberville Needham, *Nouvelles Observations microscopiques*, trans. Louis Anne Lavirotte (Paris, 1750), sec. 37, p. 322, sec. 46, p. 381; pp. 389 and 340. Needham also sees an opposition between positive and negative in action/reaction. Here one is at the source of the idea of compensation, which will be upheld by the authors of optimist systems, such as Antoine de La Salle and Pierre-Hyacinthe Azaïs. On Needham, see Jacques Roger, *The Life Sciences in Eighteenth-Century French Thought*, ed. Keith R. Benson, trans. Robert Ellrich (Stanford, CA: Stanford University Press, 1997), pp. 399–420. Needham sees activity everywhere: "The last power in Nature is that of resistance to motion, an attribute sensibly distributed in each material combination that falls before our senses: Does not this power produce sensible impressions? Does it not counterbalance and surmount the motor activity? Is not a resistant mass an essentially reacting one? Can this be extended into as real and as positive an activity as that of motion itself, although by nature contrary and producing opposite effects? Do not the two ideas of solidity and resistance exclude that of inactivity in the most direct sense?" (*Nouvelles Observations microscopiques*, sec. 46, p. 435). But no sooner has the notion of activity been posited than it becomes a secret weapon with which to withdraw the material sub-foundations from the universe: the active and immediate agents must "necessarily resolve themselves into

individual Beings, uncombined, simple, and immaterial" (*ibid.*, pp. 445–46).

A distinction had been made in the Middle Ages between the concepts of resistance and reaction, but they had always been studied conjointly.

74. Jean-Louis Carra's work appeared in 1773 and was reprinted for the third time in 1791. Darnton, in *Mesmerism*, notes that Carra almost sparked a "Mesmerist revolution" around 1785. Carra belonged to a group of Girondist deputies arrested on May 31, 1793, and executed in the autumn of that year. Jean-Louis Carra, *Système de la raison, ou le prophète philosophe* (Paris, 1791), pp. 27–28.

75. This pulsating image of action/reaction is found in many Romantic texts. I will return to it later in Chapter Six, "Dead World, Beating Hearts."

76. Franz Anton Mesmer, "On the Discovery of Animal Magnetism," in *Mesmerism*, trans. George Bloch (Los Altos, CA: William Kaufman Inc., 1980), pp. 46 and 67.

77. Cited by Odo Marquard, *Farewell to Matters of Principle: Philosophical Studies*, trans. Robert M. Wallace (New York: Oxford University Press, 1989), p. 43. See also Paul Bénichou, *Le Temps des prophètes* (Paris: Gallimard, 1977), pp. 227–29. For La Salle and Azaïs, see Jean Svagelski, *L'Idée de compensation en France, 1750–1850*, preface by François Dagognet (Lyon: L'Hermès, 1981).

78. Antoine de La Salle, *La Balance naturelle*, 2 vols. (Paris, 1788), vol. 1, p. 133.

79. *Ibid.*, vol. 2, p. 1.

80. *Ibid.*, vol. 2, p. 74.

CHAPTER TWO: DIDEROT AND THE CHEMISTS

1. Diderot admired the chemist Guillaume François Rouelle, whose experiments he followed. See Jean-Claude Guédon, "Chimie et matérialisme: La Stratégie anti-newtonienne de Diderot," *Dix-huitième siècle* 11 (1979).

2. Denis Diderot, *Oeuvres complètes*, 15 vols., intro. Roger Lewinter (Paris: Club Français du Livre, 1969–1973), vol. 10, p. 79.

3. Denis Diderot, article "Encyclopédie" in *Encyclopédie*, in *Oeuvres complètes*, vol. 2, p. 408.

4. Denis Diderot, *Notes on Painting*, in *Diderot on Art*, 2 vols., trans. John Goodman (New Haven, CT: Yale University Press, 1995), vol. 1, p. 215.

5. Italics mine. Denis Diderot, *Lettre sur les sourds et muets* (1751), in *Oeuvres complètes*, vol. 2, p. 582. In Diderot's time, the image of ferment was already in use to designate popular emotion, and it became more and more frequent in characterizations of public agitations. Diderot mentions "a secret movement of ferment within the city" at the end of Nero's reign (*Oeuvres complètes*, vol. 12, p. 619). Hence in *The Barber of Seville* (2.8), Beaumarchais has someone say to Bazile, "Start a nasty rumor, that's right, and as it ferments, have it spread by those in the know." See Michel Delon, *L'Idée d'énergie au tournant des Lumières, 1770–1820* (Paris: PUF, 1988).

6. Denis Diderot, *Mémoires sur différents sujets de mathématiques* (1748), in *Oeuvres complètes*, vol. 2, p. 129. See Aram Vartanian, "Diderot et Newton," in Claude Blanckaert, Jean-Louis Fischer, and Roselyne Rey (eds.), *Nature, histoire, société: Essais en hommage à Jacques Roger* (Paris: Klincksieck, 1995), pp. 61–77.

7. Denis Diderot, *De l'interprétation de la nature* (1753), 40, in *Oeuvres complètes*, vol. 2, pp. 747–48.

8. Diderot, *Mémoires sur différents sujets de mathématiques*, p. 114.

9. The first comparisons of this sort are ancient and are found in Plato. In the *Phaedo* (85e and 86a–d), Simmias compares the relationship between the soul and the body to the strings of a lyre and harmony.

10. Diderot, *De l'interprétation de la nature*, 36, pp. 738–44.

11. Diderot to Voltaire, Feb. 19, 1758, *Oeuvres complètes*, vol. 3, p. 630. Almost sixty years later, Goethe deplored the victory of mathematics: "Phenomena have been killed and embalmed with numbers and signs; the scientific coffin has been painted with multicolored figures representing the experiments that have consigned to earth all that is unmeasurable and eternal in the singular being." Letter to Christoph Ludwig Friedrich Schulz, Nov. 24, 1817, *Gedenkausgabe der Werke. Briefe und Gespräche*, 24 vols., ed. Ernst Beutler (Zurich: Artemis, 1950), vol. 21, p. 250.

12. On the question of motion as essential to matter, see Delon, *L'Idée d'énergie au tournant des Lumières, 1770–1820*, pp. 157–206.

13. Denis Diderot, "Philosophic Principles on Matter and Motion," in *Diderot, Interpreter of Nature: Selected Writings*, trans. Jean Stewart and Jonathan Kemp (New York: International Publishers, 1963), pp. 128–29. [Trans. modified.] Lester G. Crocker has shown that Diderot's argument in this work owes a great deal to John Toland's *Letters to Serena* (London, 1704). On Toland, see Paolo Casini, *L'universo-macchina: Origini della filosofia newtoniana* (Bari: Laterza, 1969), pp. 205–237.

14. Jean-Jacques Rousseau, *Emile*, trans. Barbara Foxley (London: Everyman, 1992), bk. 4, pp. 282–83.

15. Diderot, "Philosophic Principles on Matter and Motion," p. 129. [Trans. modified.] As we will see in Chapter Three, "Life Reacting," this thesis had been upheld in the preceding century by the English physician Francis Glisson.

16. Charles Daremberg, *Histoire de la médecine et des sciences médicales*, 2 vols. (Paris: Baillière, 1870), vol. 2, p. 815.

17. Diderot, "Philosophic Principles on Matter and Motion," p. 131.

18. Jean Le Rond d'Alembert, *Traité de dynamique*, 2 vols. (Paris: Gauthier Villars, 1921), vol. 1, pp. xxvi–xxvii.

19. Denis Diderot, *D'Alembert's Dream*, in *Rameau's Nephew and Other Works*, trans. Ralph H. Bowen (Garden City, NY: Doubleday, 1956), p. 114. [Trans. modified.]

20. *Ibid.*, pp. 121–24. [Trans. modified.]

21. *Ibid.*, pp. 129–30. [Trans. modified.]

22. *Ibid.*, p. 165. Today we would speak in terms of "interaction" and "interdependence," but these terms did not enter the intellectual vocabulary until much later. In Chapter Four, I shall devote a few remarks to their history. Let me merely note for now that their use here would be anachronistic. Diderot keeps repeating the following definition of animal life: "The animal body is a system of actions and reactions; actions and reactions affect the forms of the viscera, the membranes" (*Eléments de physiologie*, in *Oeuvres complètes*, vol. 12, p. 683). "Can you really believe that in a machine such as man, in which all the organs act and react upon each other, one part, either solid or fluid, could be tainted without bringing harm to the others?"; see *Réfutation suivie de l'ouvrage*

d'Helvétius intitulé "L'Homme," in *Oeuvres philosophiques*, ed. Paul Vernière (Paris: Garnier, 1967), p. 612.

23. The importance of the diaphragm was discussed by Théophile de Bordeu himself in *Recherches anatomiques sur la position des glandes* (1752). Another physician influenced by Montpellier, Louis de La Caze, developed a rather complete theory out of it in *Specimen novi medicinae conspectus* (1749) and in *Idée de l'homme physique et moral* (1755; repr. 1798). Thus we read in chapter 8, article 5: "We are confident in asserting that there is a principal and perpetual commerce of action and reaction between the head and the center of phrenic forces; that consequently the action of one is transmitted to the other at the same instant that it is determined." Diderot's text should be compared with the articles in this work treating sleep (ch. 6) and "the excretion of seminal fluid" (ch. 8, art. 5). La Caze's *Idée de l'homme physique et moral* is a breviary of action and reaction. See Jacques Roger, *Les Sciences de la vie dans la pensée française au XVIIIe siècle* (Paris: Albin Michel, 1993), pp. 636–39.

24. Denis Diderot, *Rameau's Nephew*, in *Rameau's Nephew and Other Works*, pp. 8–9. [Trans. modified.]

25. Before Lavoisier, chemistry still used the notion of menstruum (a masculine substantive of alchemical origin), which designates dissolving substances capable of separating mixtures and aggregates.

26. Denis Diderot, "Fragments," in *Oeuvres complètes*, vol. 13, p. 913.

27. The same is true for Rousseau: puberty and its dangers are announced, for Emile, by a "dull ferment," compared to the roaring of the sea (*Oeuvres complètes*, vol. 4, p. 490). We remember that in the medicine of Descartes, fertilization begins with fermentation.

28. See Gaston Bachelard, "La Pâte," in *La Terre et les rêveries de la volonté* (Paris: José Corti, 1948), pp. 74–104.

29. Diderot, *Rameau's Nephew*, p. 73. [Trans. modified.]

30. *Ibid.*, p. 79. [Trans. modified.]

31. Diderot, *D'Alembert's Dream*, p. 98. [Trans. modified.]

32. Diderot, entries in the *Encyclopédie*, in *Oeuvres complètes*, vol. 14, pp. 863–92, esp. pp. 882–86.

33. These latter two terms were invented by van Helmont: "blas" is related to breath and "blast" and was his term "for a supposed 'flatus' or influence of the stars, producing changes of weather" (*OED*); "gas" was formed from the Greek word "chaos" and designated "an occult principle supposed by van Helmont to be contained in all bodies, and regarded by him as an ultra-rarefied condition of water" (*OED*); the "archeus" was "the immaterial principle supposed by the Paracelsians to produce and preside over the activities of the animal and vegetable economy; vital force" (*OED*).

34. Diderot, entries in the *Encyclopédie*, pp. 889–90. See Jean Fabre, "Diderot et les théosophes," in *Lumières et romantisme* (Paris: Klincksieck, 1963), pp. 57–83; Jacques Chouillet, *La Formation des idées esthétiques de Diderot* (Paris: Armand Colin, 1973).

35. Diderot, *Réfutation suivie de l'ouvrage d'Helvétius intitulé "L'Homme,"* p. 534.

36. Aristotle, *Problems* 5.30, *The Complete Works of Aristotle: The Revised Oxford Translation*, 2 vols., ed. Jonathan Barnes (Princeton, NJ: Princeton University Press, 1984), vol. 2, pp. 1498–1502. See the classic work by Raymond Klibansky, Erwin Panofsky, and Fritz Saxl, *Saturn and Melancholy* (London: Nelson, 1964).

37. Bartolomeo Castelli, "Orgao," in *Lexicon medicum graeco-latinum* (Geneva, 1746), p. 547. The first editions of this dictionary, based on the vocabulary of Hippocrates and Galen, date from the beginning of the seventeenth century. Revised and corrected, it was reprinted in various locations until 1755. Its author, who was active in Messina, died there in 1607.

38. The word "orgasm" was treated differently by Louis de Jaucourt in the *Encyclopédie*. The interpretation there pertains no longer to the humors but to the solids, and the proposed meaning does not apply at all to normal physiology; it is a uniquely pathological term describing a morbid state that can become "terrifying": orgasm is given as a quasi synonym of "hysteria" and is related to states in which life is gravely threatened. Its synonyms are "irritability," "violent oscillation," "mobility," "twitching."

39. Diderot, *Eléments de physiologie*, p. 799.

40. Diderot, *Réfutation suivie de l'ouvrage d'Helvétius intitulé "L'Homme,"* pp. 595–98.

41. *Ibid.*, p. 597.

42. Diderot, *Eléments de physiologie*, pp. 652 and 653.

43. *Ibid.*, p. 699.

44. *Ibid.* pp. 699, 700, 698, 796, 795.

45. Diderot, *Réfutation suivie de l'ouvrage d'Helvétius intitulé "L'Homme,"* pp. 490–92.

46. *Ibid.*, p. 557.

47. *Ibid.*, p. 558.

48. The word *espèce* (species) was used in eighteenth-century French to designate a person both singular and morally despicable.

49. Diderot, *Réfutation suivie de l'ouvrage d'Helvétius intitulé "L'Homme,"* p. 577.

50. *Ibid.*, p. 521. The same terms are used in the debate at the beginning of *Rameau's Nephew*.

51. Diderot, *Réfutation suivie de l'ouvrage d'Helvétius intitulé "L'Homme,"* p. 522. See Roland Mortier, *L'Originalité: Une Nouvelle Catégorie esthétique au siècle des Lumières* (Geneva: Droz, 1982).

52. The English translation of Freind's *Praelectiones chymicae, Chymical Lectures*, appeared in London in 1712. The work was preceded by nine lemmas. Lemmas 4 through 9 merely beg the question of attraction among particles: "Datur vis attractrix, seu omnes materiae partes a se invicem trahuntur."

53. Denis Diderot, "Réflexions sur une difficulté proposée contre la manière dont les newtoniens expliquent la cohésion des corps, et les autres phénomènes, qui s'y rapportent," printed in *Journal de Trévoux* (April 1762), *Oeuvres complètes*, vol. 5, pp. 9–18.

54. Isaac Newton, *Opticks* (New York: Dover, 1952), p. 397. On these different points, see Hélène Metzger, *Newton, Stahl, Boerhaave et la doctrine chimique* (Paris: Félix Alcan, 1930; repr. 1974); Betty Jo Teeter Dobbs, *The Janus Face of Genius: The Role of Alchemy in Newton's Thought* (Cambridge, UK: Cambridge University Press, 1991); Paolo Casini, "Newton, Diderot et la vulgate de l'atomisme,"

Dix-huitième siècle 24 (1992), pp. 29–37; Arthur Donovan, "Newton and Lavoisier — From Chemistry as a Branch of Philosophy to Chemistry as a Positive Science," in Paul Theerman and Adele F. Seeff (eds.), *Action and Reaction: Proceedings of a Symposium to Commemorate the Tercentenary of Newton's "Principia"* (Newark: University of Delaware Press, 1993), pp. 255–76. More generally, see James R. Partington, *A History of Chemistry* (London: Macmillan, 1961–1970).

55. Jean Piveteau (ed.), *Oeuvres philosophiques de Buffon* (Paris: PUF, 1954), pp. 39–41.

56. Maurice P. Crosland, in *Historical Studies in the Language of Chemistry* (1962; repr., New York: Dover, 1978), does not mention when the word "reaction" appeared in the language of chemistry. This absence does not lessen the merit of his excellent work. We must conclude that the word "reaction" did not play a major role in chemistry. The matter seems so unimportant to most historians that they readily use this term anachronistically in speaking of the operations of a chemistry in which this term never appeared.

57. Venel, taking up a familiar idea, named the effects of these operations "diacretic" and "syncretic": "The former is also known by many chemists as analysis, decomposition, corruption, solution, destruction; and the latter as mixture, generation, synthesis, combination, coagulation, and even confusion by a few" ("Chemistry" entry in the *Encyclopédie*). A Latin precept summarized all chemistry as *solve et coagula*.

58. Johann-Joachim Becher, *Physica subterranea*, ed. Georg Ernst Stahl (Leipzig, 1738), *Supplementum II, Theses chymicae*, pp. 361–69. Becher was a major influence on the vitalist physician Georg Ernst Stahl (1660–1732). Stahl, who was deeply interested in chemistry, edited Becher's *Physica Subterranea* in 1702, to which he added an outline of his own system, titled *Specimen beccherianum*, in which he defended the idea of the phlogiston (an incorrect explanation of combustion).

59. Torbern Bergman, *Opuscules chymiques et physiques*, 2 vols., trans. Louis-Bernard Guyton de Morveau (Dijon, 1780), vol. 1, p. 97. This is not the first appearance of the word *réactif* (reagent) in French. Ferdinand Brunot, in *Histoire de la langue française des origines à 1900, tome VI: Le XVIIIe siècle*, 4 vols., ed.

Alain François (Paris: Armand Colin, 1930–1933), 2nd pt., 1, p. 1314, cites a use by Father Louis-Bertrand Castel in *L'Optique des couleurs*. Guyton de Morveau uses this term in a precise way. Twenty years later, it appeared in Antoine François de Fourcroy's *Système des connaissances chimiques*, 10 vols. (Paris, 1800), vol. 1, sec. 1, art. 5 ("On the Separation of the Principles of Bodies, or Chemical Analysis"): "We can admit... four types of analysis: mechanical analysis, spontaneous or natural analysis, analysis through fire, and analysis through reagents.... Analysis through reagents is obtained by placing the compound one wishes to analyze in contact with a more or less numerous series of other bodies, which react upon it in such a way as to favor the separation of its principles. The only limits to this method lie in the genius and insights of the chemist; he can use any bodies in nature, all the products of his art: in his hands, everything becomes a reagent, provided he understands clearly and has determined beforehand the mode of reaction that the bodies he is using might produce on the body he wishes to analyze. One might say, in comparing the preceding method of analysis by fire to this one, that they overlap, since fire is a true reagent" (p. 57). Fourcroy also speaks of "general reactions that take place between metals and acids" (p. cx). He is therefore an important figure, for he was one of the scholars who established the new chemical nomenclature.

60. This restricted use persisted. In the lexicon at the end of Melchior Esslinger's French translation of Jöns Jakob Berzelius's *Traité de chimie*, 8 vols. (Paris, 1830–1833), *réagir* (to react) is defined as follows: "Said in speaking of a substance when that substance has the ability to produce a determinate phenomenon when combined with another substance, by means of which one can recognize one or the other of them. The production of this phenomenon is called a reaction" (vol. 8, p. 308).

61. Torbern Bergman, *Disquisitio de attractionibus electivis*, Nova Acta Regiae Societatis Upsalensis (1775), vol. 2, p. 159. As Guyton de Morveau notes, we find in Bergman the argument put forth by Buffon. It is necessary to take the particles' (hypothetical) shape into account: "The relationship between these bodies that are brought together is very different, for the shape and placement not only of the whole but also of the parts greatly modify the effects of the attraction."

62. In his *Eloge de M. Bergman*, Condorcet confirms Guyton de Morveau's judgment and salutes the progress toward a formalized and mathematized scientific expression in Bergman's tables of affinities. These constitute the point at which chemistry "is most tied to physics and should one day be united with the mathematical sciences," for, he adds pertinently, "the moment is approaching when the alphabetical language will not be sufficiently quick, rich, or precise to respond to the needs of the sciences and to follow their progress"; see *Oeuvres de Condorcet*, published by Arthur Condorcet O'Connor and François Arago (Paris, 1847), vol. 3, pp. 151–53. Here we find ourselves at the origin of a separation of languages, one result of which was that establishing the formula for a reaction and speaking or writing the word "reaction" could no longer be the same thing.

63. Louis-Bernard Guyton de Morveau, *Elémens de chymie théorique et pratique*, 3 vols. (Dijon, 1777), vol. 2, pp. vi–vii. To illustrate the rift between physicists and chemists, a note from Guyton de Morveau refers to the entry on menstruum in the *Encyclopédie* (written by Venel), in which recourse to "mechanical laws" was criticized. In the new chemistry, the menstruum would be replaced by the solvent.

64. Guyton de Morveau, *Elémens de chymie*, p. viii. Here we recognize the four figures from Goethe's novel *Elective Affinities*: Charlotte, Edward, the Captain, and Ottilie. On the affinities, see the long entry on affinity (also by Guyton de Morveau) in the first volume of the Chymie series in the *Encyclopédie méthodique* (Paris: Panckoucke, 1786). In volume 2 (1792), Guyton de Morveau wrote the very interesting entry on attraction.

65. Claude-Louis Berthollet, *Essai de statique chimique* (Paris: Didot, 1803), pp. 1–2.

66. The same expression was used by Fourcroy as early as "Discours préliminaire" of his *Système des connaissances chimiques*.

67. Berthollet, *Essai de statique chimique*, pp. 1–4. Laplace clearly presented his principles on the equilibrium of a system of bodies in book 1, chapter 3, of *Celestial Mechanics*, trans. Nathaniel Bowditch (New York: Chelsea, 1966), vol. 1, pp. 71–89. The views he develops in book 12, "De l'attraction et de la répulsion des sphères et des lois de l'équilibre et des mouvements des fluides élas-

tiques" (1825), vol. 5, pp. 87–144, gave rise to many exchanges of ideas with his longtime friend Berthollet.

68. Satish C. Kapoor, entry on Berthollet, in Charles C. Gillispie (ed.), *Dictionary of Scientific Biography* (New York: Scribner, 1970), vol. 1. See also Gillispie's long article on Laplace in vol. 18 (the supplement) of this same dictionary.

69. Hans Christian Ørsted, *Recherches sur l'identité des forces chimiques et électriques*, trans. Marcel de Serres (Paris, 1813), pp. 4–5.

70. *Ibid.*, p. 248.

71. Among the recent books on this issue is Martin Rees, *Before the Beginning: Our Universe and Others* (London: Simon and Schuster, 1997. On this work, see the review by Stephen Weinberg, "Before the Big Bang," *New York Review of Books*, June 12, 1997). For a general view of the history of Newtonianism, see Simon Schaffer, "Newtonianism," in Robert Olby et al. (eds.), *Companion to the History of Modern Science* (London: Routledge, 1990), pp. 610–26.

72. Wilhelm Ostwald, *Der Werdegang einer Wissenschaft* (Leipzig, 1908).

73. Wilhelm Ostwald, "Elfte Vorlesung. Klassiker und Romantiker," in *Grosse Männer* (Leipzig, 1909), pp. 371–88. Ostwald claims that the "speed of the mind's reaction" is a "scientifically established" given (p. 371). Shortly thereafter, the formula becomes "the tempo of the spiritual pulse" (p. 373). Ostwald, who had ideas on universal energetics, developed these ideas also in the area of psychic energetics. He discussed them in a series of lectures, dedicated to Ernst Mach, under the title *Vorlesungen über Naturphilosophie* (Leipzig, 1902), in which chapters 17 to 20 treat excitation, reaction, memory, consciousness and the unconscious, will, and so on. Ostwald's considerations are more or less contemporary with the neurophysiological research of Louis Lapicque (1866–1952) on the duration of the stimulating current and on chronaxie.

CHAPTER THREE: LIFE REACTING

1. Robert James, *A Medicinal Dictionary, Including Physic, Surgery, Anatomy, Chymistry, and Botany*, 3 vols. (London, 1743–1745). The French title is *Dictionnaire universel de médecine, traduit de l'anglais de M. James par Mrs. Diderot,*

Eidous et Toussaint, 6 vols. (Paris, 1746–1748). Mark Twain called it "a majestic literary fossil." See Arthur M. Wilson, *Diderot* (New York: Oxford University Press, 1972), pp. 52–53.

2. Joseph Capuron, *Nouveau Dictionnaire de médecine, de chirurgie, de physique* (Paris, 1806).

3. See René Descartes, *Discourse on Method*, pt. 5. He went into more detail in the treatise *The Passions of the Soul* (1649) and in the posthumously published *Man* (1664).

4. René Descartes, *The Passions of the Soul*, in *The Philosophical Works of Descartes*, ed. Elizabeth S. Haldane and G.R.T. Ross (Cambridge, UK: Cambridge University Press, 1979), p. 332.

5. Text included in *Philosophical Works of Descartes*, p. 65.

6. Thomas Hobbes, *Elements of Philosophy* (1655), pt. 3, chap. 22, 19, in *The English Works*, ed. William Molesworth (London, 1839), vol. 1, p. 348: "Action and reaction proceed in the same line, but from opposite terms. For seeing reaction is nothing but endeavor in the patient to restore itself to that situation from which it was forced by the agent: the endeavor or motion of both the agent and patient or reagent will be propagated between the same terms; yet so, as in action the term, from which, is in reaction the term to which." These ideas are the starting point for Hobbes's entire philosophy. They are outlined in the fourth part of *De corpore*, ch. 25, in the first part of *Leviathan*, in *De homine*, as well as in *De natura humana*. Hobbes's psychology has been very well summarized, though long ago, in Arthur Hannequin, "La Philosophie de Hobbes," in *Etudes d'histoire des sciences et d'histoire de la philosophie*, 2 vols. (Paris, 1908), vol. 1, pp. 162–208.

7. Hobbes, *Elements of Philosophy*, p. 391.

8. Hannequin, "La Philosophie de Hobbes," p. 172.

9. Thomas Hobbes, *Human Nature*, ch. 2, sec. 8, in *English Works*, vol. 4, pp. 6–7. Hobbes uses several terms almost interchangeably: "resistance," "counterpressure," "antitypia," "endeavor" (in *Leviathan*, pt. 1, ch. 1, for example). During the next century, these mechanical conjectures were supplanted by references to Newton. Newton's *Opticks*, translated into French in 1722, had a great influ-

ence. He proposed another model of explanation. In fact, Queries 12 and 24, which deal with visual perceptions and the nerves, discuss the continuous propagation of vibrations.

10. Hobbes, *Elements of Philosophy*, pt. 4, ch. 25, 4.

11. Hannequin, "La Philosophie de Hobbes," p. 173. On Hobbes's early philosophy, see also Frithiof Brandt, *Thomas Hobbes' Mechanical Conception of Nature* (Copenhagen, 1928); Yves-Charles Zarka, *La Décision métaphysique de Hobbes* (Paris: Vrin, 1987); and Yves-Charles Zarka (ed.), *Hobbes et son vocabulaire* (Paris: Vrin, 1992).

12. Hannequin, "La Philosophie de Hobbes," p. 173.

13. Henry More, *Immortalitas animae* (1659), bk. 2, chs. 1 and 2, in *Opera philosophica*, 4 vols. (London, 1679), vol. 2, pp. 327–35. On Henry More, see G.R. Cragg, *The Cambridge Platonists* (New York: Oxford University Press, 1968), as well as Sarah Hutton (ed.), *Henry More (1614–1687) Tercentenary Studies* (Dordrecht: Kluwer Academic Publishers, 1989).

14. See *Philosophical Works of Descartes*, vol. 2, p. 62.

15. *Ibid.*, p. 65.

16. Hannequin, "La Philosophie de Hobbes," p. 157: "Conatum esse motum per spatium et tempus minus quam quod datur, id est determinatur, sive ex positione vel numero assignatur, id est, per punctum" (*De corpore*, ch. 15, 2). According to Yves-Charles Zarka's, interpretation, "the *conatus* is the motion carried out in a space and a time that are less than any definable space or time. It is an instantaneous motion, carried out at a point in time and a point in space.... For Hobbes, however, the *conatus* is not characterized by virtual or evanescent motion; the infinitely small does not yet have the differential status it will have in the physics elaborated by Leibniz" (Zarka, *La Décision métaphysique de Hobbes*, p. 205).

17. Francis Glisson, *Anatomia hepatis* (Amsterdam, 1665), pp. 368–69. In translating this passage into French in his *Histoire de la médecine* (Paris, 1870), Charles Daremberg renders *iisdem vindicari* as *réagir* (to react). He projected the vocabulary of the nineteenth century onto the Latin of the seventeenth century. He certainly respected the meaning, but Glisson did not use *reagere*, which had

not yet been admitted into medical Latin. People once speculated on Glisson's influence on the young Leibniz, who traveled to London in 1675. See Victor Cousin, *Histoire générale de la philosophie*, 4th ed. (Paris, 1829), p. 497; and Henri Marion, "Francis Glisson," *Revue philosophique de la France et de l'étranger* 14 (July 1882), pp. 121–55. The importance of the notion of effort (*conatus*) for Spinoza is well known, yet his vocabulary did not include *reagere* or *reactio*.

18. In *De rachitide*, it is a question of the irritation of the heart and the arteries, which combine to incite the pumping of the blood. This irritation can be provoked from either the outside or the inside (see the 3rd ed., Leiden, 1671, pp. 94–106). In *Tractatus de ventriculo et intestinis* (London, 1677), chapter 7 is titled "De irritabilitate fibrarum." See Owsei Temkin, "The Roots of Glisson's Doctrine of Irritation," in *The Double Face of Janus* (Baltimore: Johns Hopkins University Press, 1977), pp. 290–316. Temkin demonstrates that Glisson's thought is part of a medical tradition going back to Galen. See also the entry on Glisson, written by Temkin, in Charles C. Gillispie (ed.), *Dictionary of Scientific Biography* (New York: Scribner, 1972), vol. 5.

19. Albrecht von Haller, "First Discourse," in *A Dissertation on the Sensible and Irritable Parts of Animals* (London: J. Nourse, 1755), p. 7. The "First Discourse" places Haller's discovery of irritability on an equal footing with Newton's discovery of gravitation. The comparison is found again in Charles Bonnet, who "admits" irritability "the way the Newtonian admits attraction, which is to say as a true fact whose cause may well remain unknown to him, without his being any less certain as to the consequences"; see Charles Bonnet, *Oeuvres* (Neuchâtel, 1783), vol. 15, pp. 82–83. Haller introduces a subdivision. Irritability, in his opinion, is the property of a fiber capable of contracting under the effect of various types of mechanical, thermal, chemical, or electrical agents. Haller does not see the action of the nerve as being exclusive in this regard. Innervation, he believes, is indispensable only for the sensitive parts capable of experiencing pain. Haller takes an inventory of the parts of the animal body — irritable and non-irritable, or sensitive and insensitive — and attempts to evaluate the degrees of irritability and sensitivity. As Georges Canguilhem has demonstrated in *La Formation du concept de réflexe aux XVIIe et XVIIIe siècles* (Paris:

PUF, 1955), Haller's investigations are not concerned with "involuntary" motions (which are actually "reflexes"). Robert Whytt (1714–1766) studied them systematically in the same epoch and described them in *An Essay on the Vital and Other Involuntary Motions of Animals* (Edinburgh, 1751).

20. Glisson, *De ventriculo*, ch. 5, nos. 12–17.

21. In *De motu musculari* (1670), Thomas Willis spoke of *motus reflexus*. He is acquainted with the ideas of the iatrochemists. But he does not use the word "irritability" and has no recourse to the word "reaction." Canguilhem saw Willis as the true founder of the concept of reflex. This proves that initially the reflex could have been conceived, of course, through the notion of excitation ("stimulus," which is found in Giorgio Baglivi and which Whytt uses constantly) but not through that of reaction, which will not come into the language of reflex physiology until much later. In his research into the prehistory of the reflex, Canguilhem never turned his attention to the notion of reaction. In truth, the word "reaction" does not appear either in Haller's essay (see above) or in Whytt's (see above). For Whytt, the phenomena provoked by the stimuli seem to have as their principle "the mind," or a "sentient principle." Yet, he declares, as for knowing "the intimate structure of a muscular fibre, or the precise manner in which the nervous influence acts upon it, when it produces its contradiction, ... [t]hese are questions which we have wholly avoided." *An Essay on the Vital and Other Involuntary Motions of Animals*, in *The Works of Robert Whytt*, vol. 1 (Edinburgh, 1768), p. 172.

22. Francis Glisson, *Tractatus de natura substantiae energetica, seu, De vita naturae* (London, 1672), ch. 7, p. 90.

23. Francisco Suárez, *Disputationes metaphysicae* (1597; repr. Hildesheim: Olms, 1965), vol. 2, disp. 48, "De actione," 6, 10. Disputatio 49 is titled "De passione." The word "reaction" does not appear there.

24. Glisson, *Tractatus de natura substantiae energetica, seu, De vita naturae*, ch. 20, 17, p. 273.

25. *Ibid.*, ch. 20, 17, p. 274.

26. *Ibid.*, ch. 19, 9. See Jacques Roger, *Les Sciences de la vie dans la pensée française du XVIIe siècle* (Paris: Armand Colin, 1963; repr. 1993), pp. 614–82, esp. p. 641.

27. On La Caze, see note 23, Chapter Two.

28. The Latin expression was used by Boerhaave in his lectures given between 1730 and 1735, which were not published until 1761, in Leiden, under the title *Praelectiones academicae de morbis nervorum*. He concluded a long development on motor and sensory innervation, and on the non-sensory organs (heart and liver), with the following formula: "Homo simplex in vitalitate, duplex in humanitate." It was not a question of the duality between body and soul but a first outline of the distinction made later by Xavier Bichat regarding animal versus organic life. This expression echoes Maine de Biran's commentaries, in particular in *Mémoire sur la décomposition de la pensée* (1805). See François Azouvi, *Maine de Biran: La Science de l'homme* (Paris: Vrin, 1995), pp. 21–34; and François Azouvi, "Homo duplex," *Gesnerus* 42, fasc. 3/4 (1985), pp. 229–44.

29. Thomas Willis, in particular in *The Anatomy of the Brain and Nerves* (Montreal: McGill University Press, 1965) and *Two Discourses Concerning the Soul of Brutes* (Gainesville, FL: Scholars Facsimiles and Reprints, 1971).

30. After research in Ewald Hering's laboratory, Henry Pickering Bowditch (1840–1911) formulated the "law of all or none" in 1871: provided a certain minimal threshold of intensity is reached, all excitations will produce identical reactions. The law applies primarily to the heart but covers other systems as well.

31. Buffon, "Discours sur la nature des animaux," *Histoire naturelle* (1753), vol. 4, in *Oeuvres complètes* (Paris: Duménel, 1836), vol. 4, pp. 364–65.

32. *Ibid.*, p. 365.

33. *Ibid.*, p. 365.

34. *Ibid.*, p. 366.

35. Italics mine. Note that here Buffon opposes one "action" to another without using the word "reaction." It is nonetheless clear that what he calls the "action of the animal" here corresponds exactly to what he had previously called "reaction."

36. *Ibid.*, p. 367.

37. *Ibid.*, p. 381.

38. *Ibid.*, p. 384.

39. *Ibid.*, p. 374.

40. *Ibid.*, p. 381.

41. *Ibid.*, p. 385. For the context of this judgment on love, see Robert Mauzi, "Le Problème des passions," in *L'Idée du bonheur dans la littérature et la pensée françaises au XVIIIe siècle* (Paris: Armand Colin, 1967), pp. 450–51 and 468–69.

42. See Mauzi, *Idée du bonheur*, p. 125, n.4, for an "exact division of the roles between the body...and the soul" as a condition for happiness; and *ibid.*, pp. 348–49.

43. Buffon, *Histoire naturelle*, vol. 4, p. 383.

44. *Ibid.*, p. 382.

45. *Le physique* and *le moral* (the physical and the moral): this pair of adjectives made into nouns appeared in French during the first half of the eighteenth century with Abbé Du Bos. In *Réflexions critiques sur la poésie et sur la peinture*, 2 vols. (Paris, 1719), vol. 2, sec. 19, p. 292, we read: "It is the physical that gives the moral its law."

46. Charles Bonnet, *Essai de psychologie* (London, 1755), ch. 46. Bonnet is in epistolary correspondence with all the thinkers of Europe. He corresponded amicably with Albrecht von Haller, whose treatise *A Dissertation on the Sensible and Irritable Parts of Animals* experimentally explores muscular contraction (due to irritability) and sensations (which come from sensibility). Their shared ideas were presented in Johann Gottfried Herder, *Vom Erkennen und Empfinden der menschlichen Seele* (1774–1778), in which, to define human nature, various antitheses are brought to light and resolved in terms of reciprocity (expansion and concentration, flux and reflux, excitation and sensibility, and so on). Herder makes note of "mechanical" phenomena in the desire to go beyond them. In us, God married thought to sensory life.

47. Charles Bonnet, *Essai de psychologie*, in *Collection complète des oeuvres* (Neuchâtel, 1783), vol. 17, ch. 1, pp. 5–6.

48. *Ibid.*, ch. 7, pp. 16–17.

49. *Ibid.*, ch. 36, p. 105.

50. *Ibid.*, ch. 37, p. 106.

51. *Ibid.*, ch. 41, p. 133.

52. Condillac, *La Logique/Logic*, trans. W.R. Albury (New York: Abaris

Books, 1980), pt. 1, ch. 9, p. 175. Dreams, according to Condillac, can be explained by the image of the musician, who "lets his fingers move as if at random" over the keyboard (p. 181). In the first chapter of *The Interpretation of Dreams* (1909), a chapter that reviews the scientific literature on dreams, Freud speaks disparagingly of this "very old comparison," without mentioning Condillac's use of it.

53. Bonnet, *Essai de psychologie*, ch. 42, p. 136.

54. Jean-Jacques Rousseau, "Fragments divers," in *Oeuvres complètes* (Paris: Gallimard, 1961), vol. 2, p. 1323. The project of a "morals of sensibility" (which he calls *morale sensitive*) that occupied Rousseau in 1756 takes the "previous impressions from external objects" into account. His basic claim is that "everything acts on our machine." Rousseau insists on "physical causes," whose knowledge would allow one "to compel the animal economy to support the moral order." The project was conceived in the footsteps of "Buffon's Discours sur la nature des animaux," which dates from 1749. On closer examination, one sees that in this passage from the *Confessions*, the schema of action and reaction and that of cause and effect are similar. *Confessions*, trans. J.M. Cohen (Harmondsworth, UK: Penguin, 1953), bk. 9, p. 381. [Trans. modified.]

55. *Corps-esprit-monde* (body-spirit-world): the triad was used by Paul Valéry in many notes for his *Cahiers*. This ternary system allowed him to multiply various relations and avoid the pitfalls of strict dualism.

56. Buffon, *Histoire naturelle*, vol. 4, p. 387.

57. Jean-François Féraud, *Dictionnaire critique de la langue française* (Paris, 1788).

58. William Cullen, *First Lines of the Practice of Physick*, 2nd ed. (Edinburgh, 1778), 1, 1, 3, sec. 59, pp. 127 and 450. In David Gaub's *Institutiones pathologiae medicinalis* (Leiden, 1763), one reads that destructive forces would make life unlikely were it not for the faculties and forces favoring reparation (secs. 633–49, under the title "Vires naturae medicatrices").

59. On Cullen's works and teachings in chemistry, see Arthur Donovan, *Philosophical Chemistry in the Scottish Enlightenment* (Edinburgh: Edinburgh University Press, 1975).

60. Brown's theory is recorded in *Elementa medicinae* (Edinburgh, 1780). Brown's doctrine found supporters among Schelling's disciples; one of the most active was the physician Andreas Röschlaub, the author of *Untersuchungen über Pathogenie*, 3 vols. (Frankfurt, 1800); Giovanni Rasori (1767–1837), his Italian translator, was very popular in "high society." His influence is still perceptible in François Broussais, who deserves credit for his insistence on inflammatory alterations in the viscera.

61. Novalis, *Gesammelte Werke*, 5 vols., ed. Carl Seelig (Herrliberg and Zurich: Bühl, 1945), vol. 4, *Fragmente der letzten Jahre*, no. 2973 ("Mühe und Pein haben eine angenehme Reaktion; daher scheinen sie den Menschen so verdienstlich und wohltätig") and no. 2795 ("Die Idee der Reaktionen ist eine echte historische Idee"), p. 279.

62. Samuel Hahnemann, *Organon of Homeopathic Medicine* (New York: William Radde, 1849), p. 99 and pt. 1, nos. 128–48. The first edition of *Organon of Homeopathic Medicine* appeared in German in 1810. Its main points have been summarized by August Bier in *Homöopathie und harmonische Ordnung der Heilkunde*, ed. Oswald Schlegel (Stuttgart: Hippokrates, 1949), pp. 116–45. Other key words — synthetic interpretations of the enigma of reality — followed. The beginning of the twentieth century is full of them. I cite, for example: "universal struggle" (Félix Le Dantec) or the hypostatized "memory" of Richard Semon in *Die Mneme* (Leipzig, 1906), who speaks of the sequence of stimulus/reaction leading to the engram. According to Semon, who was unfamiliar with cellular biology, a conserving memory counterbalances changes in "organic development."

63. See Elizabeth Haigh, *Bichat and the Medical Theory of the Eighteenth Century* (London: Wellcome Institute for the History of Medicine, 1984). On vitalist thought from the middle of the eighteenth century, see the writings collected in Guido Cimino and François Duchesneau (eds.), *Vitalisms: From Haller to the Cell Theory* (Florence: Olschki, 1997).

64. Xavier Bichat, *Physiological Researches on Life and Death*, trans. F. Gold (New York: Arno Press, 1977), pt. 1, ch. 1, intro. The bibliography of studies on Bichat is considerable. See Philippe Huneman, *Bichat, la vie et la mort* (Paris: PUF, 1998).

65. Bichat, *Physiological Researches on Life and Death*, pt. 1, ch. 7, sec. 5: "The organic contractility can never be separated from the sensibility of the same species; the re-action of the excreting tubes is immediately connected with the action, which the secreted fluids exercise on them: the contraction of the heart must necessarily succeed the flow of the blood into it. But authors have by no means separated these two things, either in their considerations or their language. Irritability denotes at the same time the sensation stimulated in the organ from the contact of bodies, and the contraction of the organ re-acting upon its stimuli" (pp. 103–104). Sec. 6: "It is true, that in this respect the muscles occupy the first rank in the scale of the animal solids; they possess the maximum organic contractility; but every living organ re-acts as they do, though in a manner less apparent, upon the stimulus that is artificially applied to them, or on the fluid, which in the natural way is carried to it" (p. 116 [trans. modified]).

66. *Ibid.*, pt. 1, ch. 6, no. 3. [Trans. modified.] Bichat also considers the sympathies and reactions that take place among various visceral organs or between them and the skin. Other vitalist authors—Paul-Joseph Barthez (1734–1806) from Montpellier, in particular — never spoke of reaction, even while developing a doctrine of the vital force and unity of the organism in terms of the "sympathetic influence of each organ on the whole living system," as well as the "sensitive attention" of such organs. Barthez's disciples attacked the "solidism" of Bichat and Pierre-Jean-Georges Cabanis (according to which all diseases were attributed to morbid changes in solid parts of the body). Certainly solidism, which favors the role "of the increased or diminished action of the organs," could allow for reactions between organs. Barthez spoke of "vital resistance," but this is referred to a "vital unity" that reigns over the entire organism. Illness would be the result of a modification of this vital power. See Jacques Lordat, *Exposition de la doctrine médicale de P.-J. Barthez* (Montpellier, 1818), pp. 210–33 and 284–94. Within the morphological perspective of comparative anatomy, Georges Cuvier asserts the interdependence of the parts of the animal organism: "Any organized being forms a whole, a unique and closed system, whose parts mutually correspond and proceed toward the same definitive action through reciprocal reaction. None of these parts can modify itself without thereby mod-

ifying the others, and thus each of them taken separately gives an indication of the state of all the others"; see Cuvier, *Discours sur les révolutions de la surface du globe* (1800; Paris, 1851), p. 62.

67. Bichat, *Physiological Researches on Life and Death*, pt. 1, ch. 6, no. 4.

68. *Ibid.*, pt. 1, ch. 6, no. 4.

69. *Ibid.*, pt. 1, ch. 6, no. 4.

70. *Ibid.*, pt. 1, ch. 7, no. 1. [Trans. modified.]

71. One of the first people to contradict Bichat was his cousin Matthieu François Régis Buisson (1776–1804), who takes up Louis de Bonald's definition of man: "An intelligence served by organs." See M.-F.-R. Buisson, *De la division la plus naturelle des phénomènes physiologiques* (Paris: Brosson, 1802), pp. 46–74.

72. Capuron, *Nouveau Dictionnaire de médecine, de chirurgie, de physique.* Capuron's definition is also used by J.-L. Hanin in *Vocabulaire médical* (Paris, 1811). It appears again in the first edition of Pierre-Hubert Nysten, *Dictionnaire de médecine*, with which Emile Littré associated his name many years later, eventually reworking it and publishing it under his name alone.

73. Claude Bernard, *Introduction à l'étude de la médecine expérimentale* (Paris, 1865), 2, 1, secs. 6 and 7.

74. *Ibid.*, 2, 1, sec. 6.

75. *Ibid.*, 2, 1, sec. 6.

76. *Ibid.*, 2, 1, sec. 6 and 2, 2, sec. 2.

77. *Ibid.*, 2, 1, sec. 4.

78. Claude Bernard, *Leçons sur les phénomènes de la vie communs aux animaux et aux végétaux* (Paris, 1878; repr., Paris: Vrin, 1966, with a preface by Georges Canguilhem); repr. in *Etudes d'histoire et de philosophie des sciences* (Paris: Vrin, 1983), pp. 156–62. In the first lecture of *Leçons sur les effets des substances toxiques et médicamenteuses* (1857), Bernard, in paying homage to his mentor François Magendie, mentions the period in which "medicine and physiology in France were dominated exclusively by the anatomico-vitalist ideas of Bichat, which at the time were reactions against the iatro-mechanical or chemical theories of Borelli, Sylvius De le Boë, Boerhaave, and so on. M. Magendie necessarily developed an aversion to all theories and all systems."

79. Bernard, *Leçons sur les phénomènes de la vie*, pp. 7–8 (1966 ed.). In these lectures, Bernard does not create an opposition between plant life and animal life. However, the physiologist Moritz Schiff, who taught at Geneva, does. Schiff restricts the sphere in which reaction is expressed to animal life: "There exists ... in the animal a reciprocal reaction of all parts, in which one part responds to the irritation of another. This reciprocal unity gives the animal a kind of individuality that is lacking in the plant"; see Moritz Schiff, *Recueil des mémoires physiologiques*, 4 vols. (Lausanne, 1895), vol. 1, p. 464.

80. Bernard, *Leçons sur les phénomènes de la vie*, p. 242.

81. Bernard, *Leçons sur les effets des substances toxiques et médicamenteuses*, 5, p. 52.

82. Bernard, *Leçons sur les phénomènes de la vie*, p. 242.

83. *Ibid.*, p. 288.

84. *Ibid.*, p. 288.

85. I cannot review here the history of the exploration of the nervous system. My research into semantic history intersects with the history of several other disciplines but is not to be confused with them. Further examination of nineteenth-century physiological texts would show that the word "reaction" was used abundantly, but never as anything other than a preliminary instrument. Only rarely is it included in the indexes of subjects treated. One should note, however, its presence in the "Table alphabétique et analytique des matières contenues dans les oeuvres de Claude Bernard," comp. Roger de la Coudraie, in *L'Oeuvre de Claude Bernard*, with an intro. by Mathias Duval (Paris, 1881).

86. Claude Bernard, *Leçons sur la physiologie et la pathologie du système nerveux* (Paris, 1858), pp. 339–40.

87. On Ludwig, see Heinz Schröer, *Carl Ludwig, Begründer der messenden Experimentalphysiologie* (Stuttgart, 1967).

88. See Canguilhem, *Formation du concept de réflexe aux XVIIe et XVIIIe siècles*; E.G. Liddell, *The Discovery of Reflexes* (Oxford: Clarendon Press, 1960); Edwin Clarke and L.S. Jacyna, *Nineteenth-Century Origins of Neuroscientific Concepts* (Berkeley: University of California Press, 1987); Marcel Gauchet, *L'Inconscient cérébral* (Paris: Seuil, 1992).

89. See Jean Delacour, *Le Cerveau et l'esprit* (Paris: PUF, 1995).

90. The fundamental text on immunity by Elie Metchnikoff, *Immunity in Infective Diseases*, trans. F.G. Binnie (1901; New York: Johnson Reprint Corp., 1968), speaks in particular of "struggle" and "defense" when discussing "inflammatory reaction" (p. 572) or "phagocytic reaction" (p. 580). In one historian's account, the word "reaction" becomes more than an implication and becomes more frequent. See Anne-Marie Moulin, *Le Dernier Langage de la médecine: Histoire de l'immunologie de Pasteur au sida* (Paris: PUF, 1991). Moulin points out similarities between the immune response and the reflex arc (pp. 369–76). In the conclusion, she writes: "The idea of an organism integrating the endocrine, nervous, or immune interactions is really as close as possible to the biological solution of the problem of the relations between the soul and the body. The 'great system' of contemporary biology rehabilitates the obscure findings and the long historical experience of physicians" (p. 421). I will have occasion to comment further on the appearance of "interaction" in recent vocabulary.

91. Friedrich Nietzsche, *Beyond Good and Evil*, trans. Walter Kaufmann (New York: Vintage Books, 1966), no. 17, p. 24.

92. Gauchet, *Inconscient cérébral*, p. 12.

93. Alexandre Herzen, *Physiologie de la volonté* (Paris, 1874), pp. 96–97. My emphasis on the repeated use of "reactions." Alexandre Herzen was the son of the Russian philosopher Aleksandr Ivanovich Herzen (1812–1870). He taught physiology at the University of Lausanne. On Griesinger, see Gauchet, *Inconscient cérébral*, pp. 48–55.

94. Herzen, *Physiologie de la volonté*, p. 129.

95. *Ibid.*, p. 133.

96. *Ibid.*, pp. 133–34.

97. *Ibid.*, p. 134.

98. Nietzsche knew Olga Herzen, the physiologist's sister, and it is very possible that he took an interest in *Physiologie de la volonté*, the second chapter of which treats "vital force."

99. Anton Chekhov, *Ward Number Six and Other Stories*, trans. Ronald Hingley (New York: Oxford University Press, 1998), pp. 47–49.

CHAPTER FOUR: REACTIVE PATHOLOGIES

1. See Marta Fattori with Luigi Bianchi (eds.), *Lessico filosofico dei secoli XVII e XVIII: Sezione latina* (Rome: Ateneo, 1992–1999), vol. 1, 1–4. The "Anthropologia" entry refers to Christian Wolff's *Discursus praeliminaris* (1728), in which anthropology is defined as a "tractatio physica de homine in specie." Otto Casmann, in *Psychologia anthropologica sive animae humanae doctrina* (1594–1596), defined *anthropologia* as a "doctrina humanae naturae."

2. See Odo Marquard, "Zur Geschichte des philosophischen Begriffs 'Anthropologie' seit dem Ende des 18. Jahrhunderts," *Collegium philosophicum* (1965), pp. 209–239. The author notes that in the seventeenth and eighteenth centuries, the anthropological project in France took the more fashionable form of a literature of moralists.

3. See Odo Marquard, "Anthropologie" in Joachim Ritter (ed.), *Historisches Wörterbuch der Philosophie* (Basel: B. Schwabe, 1971), vol. 1. There one finds a list of the authors who published works of medical and philosophical anthropology between 1790 and 1856.

4. Pierre-Jean-Georges Cabanis, *On the Relations Between the Physical and Moral Aspects of Man*, 2 vols., trans. Margaret Duggan Saidi (Baltimore: Johns Hopkins University Press, 1981), 2nd memoir, sec. 8, p. 120.

5. *Ibid.*, 11th memoir, sec. 1, pp. 647–48, and sec. 4, p. 654 (italics mine).

6. In Cabanis, the difference between periphery and center is also considered within the theory of circulatory disorders accompanying fevers. The febrile state begins with the pulse becoming "progressively weaker": "But by a constant law of the animal economy, the more remarkable is this forcing into the interior; this concentration of all the forces in the main nervous centers, the more acute and prompt is the subsequent reaction" (*ibid.*, 7th memoir, sec. 7, pp. 336–37).

7. One should compare Cabanis's pages to Freud's essay *Instincts and Their Vicissitudes*, in *The Standard Edition of the Complete Psychological Works of Sigmund Freud*, trans. James Strachey (London: Hogarth Press, 1953), vol. 14, p. 111. See the following chapter on "abreaction."

8. Cabanis, *On the Relations Between the Physical and Moral Aspects of Man*, 2nd memoir, "The Physiological History of the Sensations," sec. 6, pp. 112–13.

9. Of course, Cabanis was familiar with the experiments of Haller, Lazzaro Spallanzani, and Alessandro Volta. But he was an armchair physiologist, as was Anthelme Richerand after him.

10. Cabanis, *On the Relations Between the Physical and Moral Aspects of Man*, 2nd memoir, sec. 6, p. 112. For a discussion of Cabanis's thought, see Sergio Moravia, *Il pensiero degli idéologues* (Florence: La Nuova Italia, 1974); M.S. Staum, *Cabanis: Enlightenment and Medical Philosophy in the French Revolution* (Princeton, NJ: Princeton University Press, 1980); François Azouvi, *Maine de Biran: La Science de l'homme* (Paris: Vrin, 1995); and François Azouvi, "Le vitalisme de Maine de Biran," in Guido Cimino and François Duchesneau (eds.), *Vitalisms: From Haller to the Cell Theory* (Florence: Olschki, 1997), pp. 111–25.

11. See my analysis of "imaginary fluids" in *La Relation critique* (Paris: Gallimard, 1970), pp. 196–213.

12. Cabanis, *On the Relations Between the Physical and Moral Aspects of Man*, 3rd memoir, sec. 2, p. 138.

13. *Ibid.*, p. 136.

14. *Ibid.*, p. 139.

15. In Germany, at almost the same moment, a conflict arose between those who imputed madness to a failing of the soul (the *Psychiker*) and those who saw it as the result of a bodily ailment (the *Somatiker*). The one who insisted most on the responsibility of the soul, Johann Christian Heinroth (1773–1843), formed a compound word, "psychicosomatic," (Schmorak's "psychic-somatic") in *Textbook of Disturbances of Mental Life*, trans. J. Schmorak (Baltimore: Johns Hopkins University Press, 1975), vol. 2, sec. 313, p. 260.

16. Cabanis, in his tenth memoir (*On the Relations Between the Physical and Moral Aspects of Man*, pt. 2, sec. 10, p. 561), mentions the role Destutt de Tracy attributed to the sensation of effort, especially with regard to the "consciousness of a feeling I." This was a starting point for Maine de Biran.

17. Maine de Biran, *Essai sur les fondements de la psychologie*, in *Oeuvres choisies*, intro. Henri Gouhier (Paris: Aubier, 1942), p. 87. In a passage from his journal dated June 12, 1815, Maine de Biran contrasts "the free and spontaneous action" of the individual exercising his rights and "the reaction of society that

creates duties"; see *Journal*, 3 vols., ed. Henry Gouhier (Neuchâtel, La Baconnière, 1954), vol. 1, p. 87.

18. Maine de Biran, *De l'aperception immédiate*, ed. Yves Radrizzani (Paris: Vrin, 1995), pp. 114–15.

19. Emile Vacherot, *La Science et la conscience* (Paris, 1870), p. 9.

20. A graduate of the University of Montpellier, Jean-François Delpit, along with Maine de Biran, founded the Medical Society of Bergerac in 1806. See Maine de Biran, *Journal*; and Maine de Biran, *Discours à la société médicale de Bergerac*, ed. François Azouvi (Paris: Vrin, 1984). Balzac's father owned a copy of *Dictionnaire des sciences médicales*, which came out in 1819, and the novelist had studied this work. See Moïse Le Yaouanc, *Nosographie de l'humanité balzacienne* (Paris: Maloine, 1959).

21. Bricheteau (1789–1861) was a physician at the Necker hospital and became a member of the Academy of Medicine. The quotations are taken from the "Reaction" entry in *Encyclopédie méthodique*, Medicine series (Paris: Agasse, 1827), vol. 12.

22. Bricheteau specifies: "If an organ such as the stomach or the brain becomes severely injured or disorganized in its parts, aside from the local affliction, there will occur — following a strong reaction — accidents in a multitude of other organs, resulting in a fever, difficulty breathing, trouble with the functioning of the liver, the kidneys, the intestines, and so on. Would you like to create a reaction that benefits the whole economy? Administer an emetic whose action will react on the brain, or else apply mustard plasters to the feet, with the aim of obtaining the same result. The multiple sympathies of the organs sometimes give rise to double reactions or reflected reactions." As we see, the justifications of therapy remain verbal, and "reaction" and "sympathy" are the fashionable words of this science.

23. Jean-François Delpit, "Reaction," in *Le Dictionnaire des sciences médicales* (Paris, 1820), vol. 47.

24. *Ibid.*

25. On Bernheim's role in the history of modern psychiatry, see Henry F. Ellenberger, *The Discovery of the Unconscious* (New York: Basic Books, 1970), pp.

85–89; Elisabeth Roudinesco, *Histoire de la psychanalyse en France*, 2 vols. (Paris: Seuil, 1986), vol. 1, pp. 53–59 (repr., Paris: Fayard, 1994).

26. Amédée Dechambre (ed.), *Dictionnaire encyclopédique des sciences médicales* (Paris: Asselin, 1875), vol. 81, pp. 583–90.

27. Italics mine. The word *fonctionnel* appeared in the French medical vocabulary around 1830. It was followed by the word *fonctionnalisme*, which did not last. See Louis Fleury, *Traité thérapeutique et clinique d'hydrothérapie* (Paris, 1866), p. 333: "It is again due to the call of functionalism — pardon the term, which I'm contrasting to organicism — that research, vivisection, and experiments came into being which, at the present moment, have as their object the nervous system of the great sympathetic nerve."

28. Over the course of his career, Bernheim was no less obliged to defend himself against those who accused him of making suggestion into a panacea. No, he protested, suggestion does not cure tuberculosis. But it can help tubercular patients to sleep better, eat better, and so on, and in this way may be useful to them.

29. Hippolyte Bernheim, *Die Suggestion und ihre Heilwirkung. Autorisierte deutsche Ausgabe von Dr. Sigm. Freud* (Leipzig and Vienna: Deuticke, 1888), pp. 409–410. Freud also translated *Hypnotisme, suggestion, psychothérapie: Etudes nouvelles* (Paris, 1891), under the title *Neue Studien über Hypnotismus, Suggestion und Psychotherapie* (Leipzig and Vienna: Deuticke, 1892).

30. François Leuret, *Du traitement moral de la folie* (Paris, 1840).

31. Thomas Laycock, *A Treatise on the Nervous Diseases of Women* (London, 1840); Jean-Martin Charcot, *Lectures on the Diseases of the Nervous System* (1872–1873), trans. and ed. George Sigerson (1881; repr., New York: Hafner, 1962).

32. Hippolyte Bernheim, *L'Hystérie* (Paris: Doin, 1913), pp. 3, 73, 74.

33. *Ibid.*, p. 240.

34. *Ibid.*, p. 242.

35. Hippolyte Bernheim, *De la suggestion et de ses applications à la thérapeutique*, 3rd ed. (Paris, 1891), ch. 8, p. 198.

36. Bernheim, *Hystérie*, pp. 244–45.

37. Sigmund Freud, "Preface to the Translation of Bernheim's Suggestions," in *Complete Psychological Works*, vol. 1, pp. 83–84. In *Studies on Hysteria*, with regard to the stories of Frau Emmy von N. and Miss Lucy R., Freud contests the favorite theses of the Nancy school, which asserted that "everything is in the suggestion" (Bernheim) and that the hypnotic state could be produced in a large proportion of cases (Liébeault).

38. Sigmund Freud, *On Aphasia*, trans. E. Stengel (London: International Universities Press, 1953). Freud's conclusion maintains a functional perspective: "It appears to us, however, that the significance of the factor of localization for aphasia has been overrated, and that we should be well advised once again to concern ourselves with the functional states of the apparatus of speech" (p. 105).

39. In his first notebooks, Paul Valéry remains in the grips of the same dichotomy. Freud's German editors note, with regard to *Project for a Scientific Psychology*, that "the accent is placed on the influence of the environment on the organism, and on the organism's reaction in response to it.... The internal forces are therefore nothing more than secondary reactions on external forces"; see *Nachtragsband*, in *Gesammelte Werke*, ed. Angela Richards and Ilse Grubrich-Simitis (Frankfurt: Fischer, 1987), p. 118.

40. Sigmund Freud, *An Autobiographical Study*, in *Complete Psychological Works*, vol. 20, p. 22. In this text, Freud declares that the term "psychoanalysis" has taken the place formerly occupied by "catharsis."

41. See Jean Dubois et al., *Dictionnaire de linguistique* (Paris: Larousse, 1973), pp. 294–95.

42. Friedrich Nietzsche, *The Birth of Tragedy and The Case of Wagner*, trans. Walter Kaufmann (New York: Vintage Books, 1967), no. 22, p. 132. Nietzsche was inclined to prefer the medical meaning, concerning the individual's health in the broadest possible sense. See Mathias Luserke (ed.), *Die aristotelische Katharsis. Dokumente ihrer Deutung im 19. und 20. Jahrhundert* (Darmstadt: Wissenschaftliche Buchgesellschaft, 1991).

43. See Jakob Bernays, *Zwei Abhandlungen über die aristotelische Theorie des Drama* (Berlin, 1880). Bernays's remarkable works spurred a debate among specialists of his time. See Albrecht Hirschmüller's remarks in *The Life and Work*

of Josef Breuer: Physiology and Psychoanalysis (New York: New York University Press, 1989), pp. 155–59.

44. André Dacier, cited in the "Purger" entry in *Dictionnaire de Trévoux* (1752).

45. R.P. Pierre Brumoy, *Le Théâtre des Grecs*, 6 vols. (Amsterdam, 1733), vol. 1, pp. 70–71.

46. Hence in Bartolomeo Castelli's *Lexicon medicum* (Venice, 1607; Geneva: de Tournes, 1746), *catharsis* refers to *purgatio*; *catharticus* to *purgans*. The entry on *purgatio* is of particular interest: it differentiates between a purging that takes place naturally and a purging stimulated by artificial means, such as drugs or clysters. In German, the remedies that stimulate intestinal evacuation are the *Abführmittel* (means of evacuation). The terms are defined more or less the same way in the nineteenth-century medical dictionaries. In his *Dictionnaire de médecine* (1810, and many subsequent editions), Pierre-Hubert Nysten writes the following entry on catharsis: "This word expresses any natural or artificial evacuation by any means whatsoever." He mentions a "cathartin," which is the active principle of senna. The meaning of the adjective "cathartic" is specified in the following way: "This term sometimes designates purgatives in general, sometimes purgatives that are stronger than the various laxatives but less active than drastic purgatives." Nysten's *Dictionnaire de médecine* was absorbed into that of Emile Littré and Charles-Philippe Robin. The definitions just cited were still found in the (posthumous) seventeenth edition (1893) of Littré's *Dictionnaire de médecine*! This edition gives synonyms in German, *kathartisch*; English, "cathartic;" and Italian, *catartico*. In the passage by Freud cited above (p. 410, n.7), it is less a matter of "quota of affect" (or "quantum d'affect," an expression proposed by certain French translators) than a "sum [*montant*] of affect" (*Affektbetrag*), and less a question of "discharge" than of "bringing to evacuation": "wo er zur Abfuhr gelangen konnte (abreagieren)" (*Gesammelte Werke*, vol. 14, p. 47). *Betrag*, translated in English as "quota," designates primarily a sum of money. The French translation as *quantum* (which has nothing to do with quantum theory in physics) is typical of some translators' attempts to make Freud's language more technical. In an article that Freud wrote in French, he himself gives "valeur affective" for the

French equivalent of *Affektbetrag* (see "Quelques considérations pour une étude comparative des paralysies motrices organiques et hystérique," translated as "Some Points for a Comparative Study of Organic and Hysterical Motor Paralyses," in *Complete Psychological Works*, vol. 1, p. 171, and n.5).

47. Once one admits a "predisposition to hysteria," a single symptom would clearly be the exception: one would expect to see not one foreign body but a series of foreign bodies, more or less related to each other; for each of them, an expenditure of abreaction could take place in a partial manner, in installments, over a long period of time — such that the notion of the "foreign body" itself would become inappropriate.

48. Friedrich Nietzsche, *On the Genealogy of Morals*, trans. Walter Kaufmann (New York: Vintage Books, 1969), p. 39. See Reinhard Gasser, *Nietzsche und Freud* (Berlin: W. de Gruyter, 1997).

49. Sigmund Freud, "Remembering, Repeating, and Working Through," in *Complete Psychological Works*, vol. 12, pp. 135–36.

50. Jean Laplanche and J.-B. Pontalis, "Abreaction," in *The Language of Psycho-Analysis*, trans. Donald Nicholson-Smith (New York: Norton, 1973), p. 1.

51. On the terms "reaction formation" and "negative therapeutic reaction," see *ibid.*

52. The reference is to the "female currents" and the "male currents." See *The Complete Letters of Sigmund Freud to Wilhelm Fliess*, trans. and ed. Jeffrey Moussaieff Masson (Cambridge, MA: Belknap Press, 1985), letter no. 270, Aug. 7, 1901, p. 448. This letter definitively marks the distance Freud had placed between himself and Fliess. After the publication of *The Interpretation of Dreams* (which appeared at the end of 1899, dated 1900), Freud seems to have been concerned not to disappoint Fliess, who upheld the notion of a permanent bisexuality in all individuals and who claimed this point as his own in a way that was not open to dispute. In this letter of August 7, 1901, addressed to "Dear William," Freud redefined their roles. In their exchange of ideas, it was he, Freud, who had been the first to propose sexuality as a solution to the problem of neurosis; Fliess had added bisexuality to it. In other words, in this letter that divides up their respective claims regarding their "discoveries," and that attempts — improbably

— to map out the course of a common labor, Freud agrees "for the moment" to read repression, his own idea, from the perspective of bisexuality, an idea dear to Fliess, on the condition that a "reaction" has intervened. It was a final attempt to wed the two theories: repression, in each sex, would be the representative of the opposite sex. Once the divorce had taken place, the idea would be brought up but expressly rejected by Freud, along with Alfred Adler's "masculine protest," in the essay "A Child Is Being Beaten" (1919).

53. See Ernst Kris's remarks in the third part of his introduction to the first (incomplete) edition of the correspondence between Freud and Fliess (1950). I am quoting from the complete Sigmund Freud, *Briefe an Wilhelm Fliess*, ed. Jeffrey Moussaieff Masson and Michael Schröter (Frankfurt: Fischer, 1986), p. 543. Kris's essay was published in English in Sigmund Freud, *The Origins of Psycho-Analysis: Letters to Wilhelm Fliess, Drafts and Notes, 1887–1902*, ed. Marie Bonaparte, Anna Freud, and Ernst Kris, trans. Eric Mosbacher and James Strachey (New York: Basic Books, 1954). — TRANS.

54. See the quotation from Cabanis in note 6 of this chapter.

55. Wilhelm Griesinger, *Mental Pathology and Therapeutics*, intro. Erwin H. Ackerknecht (1867; New York: Hafner, 1965), p. 63. One notes the notion of a "complexus of ideas" here, which long precedes the use of this term by Freud and Jung. One of Griesinger's earliest works is titled "Ueber psychische Reflexaktionen," *Archiv für physiologische Heilkunde* 2 (1843), pp. 76–104. Laplanche and Pontalis's *Language of Psycho-Analysis* mentions a prior use of the word "repression" by Johann Friedrich Herbart.

56. See Hans Reichenbach, *Experience and Prediction* (1938; repr., Chicago: University of Chicago Press, 1970). From the perspective of logical empiricism, the author estimates that reaction language, which notes simply the stimulus and the response, is the only legitimate one in the absence of an in-depth physiological understanding of intracerebral phenomena. He points out that Freud constructed psychoanalysis entirely "in stimulus and reaction language" (or the *concreta*) by introducing "internal states" (or the *illata*), which can lead to "deep insights" (pp. 246–47).

57. See Marcel Gauchet, *L'Inconscient cérébral* (Paris: Seuil, 1992). The

extrapolation of physiological theories of the medullary functioning of the nerves led to the notion of an "unconscious cerebration" (pp. 30–32).

58. Sigmund Freud, "Some Points for a Comparative Study of Organic and Hysterical Motor Paralyses," in *Complete Psychological Works*, vol. 1, pp. 168–71. [Trans. modified.]

59. Sigmund Freud, "On the Psychical Mechanism of Hysterical Phenomena," in *Complete Psychological Works*, vol. 3, p. 28.

60. Sigmund Freud, "Sketches for the 'Preliminary Communication' of 1893," sec. C, "On the Theory of Hysterical Attacks," in *Complete Psychological Works*, vol. 1, p. 154. See also Josef Breuer and Sigmund Freud, "On the Psychical Mechanism of Hysterical Phenomena: Preliminary Communication (1893)," in *Complete Psychological Works*, vol. 2, pp. 3–17.

61. The distant literary reference for *Leidensgeschichte* is clearly Goethe's *Sorrows of Young Werther*. The stimulus-response and reflex-arc models remained very present in Freud's thought as terms of comparison. Most notably, it is the point of departure in *Instincts and Their Viscissitudes* (1915). To define the fundamental concept of drive (instinct in *Complete Psychological Works*), Freud begins with a comparison to, and a distinction from, motor reflex: "[Physiology] has given us the concept of a 'stimulus' [*Reiz*] and the pattern of the reflex arc, according to which a stimulus applied to a living tissue (nervous substance) from the outside is evacuated [*abgeführt*] by action to the outside" (*Complete Psychological Works*, vol. 14, p. 118; trans. modified). But the motor-reflex model is used to recognize what deviates from it. As for the drives, Freud continues, one is no longer in the presence of the law of externally originated excitation, in which the evacuation takes place through immediate reaction. The instinctual excitation continually forms from within the individual and cannot find a univocal motor issue, such as flight in the animal. The drives are never exhausted in a single response. As for the sexual drive, in humans the search for satisfaction is capable of modification: it produces a history, a "vicissitude" or literally a "destiny" (*Schicksal*), according to the goal, the object, and the obstacles encountered. In the deferred action of the instinct, biographical facts become psychological behaviors.

62. Sigmund Freud, "The Neuro-Psychoses of Defence," in *Complete Psychological Works*, vol. 3, pp. 46–47.

63. Here I am using the opposition set up by Ferdinand de Saussure, although it is not entirely adequate.

64. Breuer and Freud, "Preliminary Communication," p. 17; this passage is repeated by Freud in the last chapter of *Studies on Hysteria*, in *Complete Psychological Works*, vol. 2, p. 255. On the relationship between Freud and Breuer, see Hirschmüller, *Life and Work of Josef Breuer*, pp. 183–93; see also Albrecht Hirschmüller, "La Genèse de la 'Communication préliminaire,' of Breuer and Freud," in André Haynal (ed.), *La Psychanalyse, cents ans déjà* (Geneva: Georg, 1996), pp. 24–47; Marcel Gauchet and Gladys Swain, *Le Vrai Charcot* (Paris: Calmann-Lévy, 1997); Mark S. Micale, *Approaching Hysteria: Disease and Its Interpretations* (Princeton, NJ: Princeton University Press, 1995).

65. See Ilse Grubrich-Simitis, *Zurück zu Freuds Texten. Stumme Dokumente sprechen machen* (Frankfurt: Fischer, 1993).

66. See Paul Ricoeur, *Freud and Philosophy: An Essay on Interpretation*, trans. Denis Savage (New Haven, CT: Yale University Press, 1970); and Paul Ricoeur, *Time and Narrative*, trans. Kathleen McLaughlin and David Pellaner (Chicago: University of Chicago Press, 1984).

67. Freud, *Autobiographical Study*, p. 16.

68. Freud and Breuer, *Studies on Hysteria*, pp. 160–61. These remarks are found at the beginning of the "Discussion" of Freud's study of Fräulein Elisabeth von R.

69. *Ibid.*, p. 265. On Freud the writer, see the works by Marthe Robert and Lydia Flem.

70. Etienne-Eugène Azam (1822–1899), author of *Etude sur les actions réflexes du cerveau* (1864), devoted himself primarily to the study of "dual consciousness." He attracted the attention of Théodule Ribot, Charcot and Pierre Janet. See his *Hypnotisme et double conscience* (Paris, 1893), which includes a preface by Charcot and letters of Charcot, Paul Bert, and Ribot.

71. The opposition between the clinical "tableau" found in Charcot and the Freudian "novel" was brought up by Michel de Certeau in *Histoire et psychanalyse entre science et fiction* (Paris: Gallimard, 1987), pp. 121–25.

72. On the "detective" aspect of Freudian investigation, see Michael Shepherd, *Sherlock Holmes and the Case of Dr. Freud* (London: Tavistock, 1985).

73. Sigmund Freud, *Five Lectures on Psycho-Analysis* (1909), in *Complete Psychological Works*, vol. 11, p. 16. The emotional traumas that Breuer and his patient discussed were recent, never more than a year old. The originary affect of Anna O. (Bertha Pappenheim) was never sought either in childhood or in sexuality. Freud knew she had not been cured and thought he could do better, for other patients, in returning to "precocious seduction." Then, alarmed at eliciting so many allegations of this sort, he challenged his own idea and substituted the Oedipal fantasy for it. In the authority situation created by the therapeutic relationship, every search for the past, whether real or phantasmic, risks leading to induced fabulations. The better the theoretical story is articulated, the more chance it has of finding its confirmation in the cases studied. But the more one relies on a preconceived theory, the more one risks finding only what one is looking for! One must learn to allow oneself to be surprised and not to know what one is looking for. I am convinced that, fortunately, the best psychoanalysts learned this from experience. If the case of Anna O. has paled, it is not because historians have become relativistic but because long-lost documents have revealed all that was left out of the narrations — henceforth recognized as myths — of Breuer, Freud, Ernest Jones, and others. See in particular the works of Ellenberger and Hirschmüller cited above.

74. Sándor Ferenczi, "Introjection and Transference," *First Contributions to Psycho-Analysis* (1909; London, 1952), ch. 2.

75. Freud, *Five Lectures on Psycho-Analysis*, 5th lecture.

76. Carl Jung (ed.), *Diagnostische Assoziationsstudien. Beiträge zur experimentellen Psychopathologie*, 2 vols. (Leipzig: A. Barth, 1906–1910), vol. 1, pp. 1–6. Freud was aware of these studies, and his first letter to Jung, in April 1906, mentions this. See *The Freud/Jung Letters*, trans. Ralph Manheim (Princeton, NJ: Princeton University Press, 1974), pp. 3–4. Bleuler created and first adopted the word "schizophrenia," proposed in his work *Dementia Praecox* (New York: International Universities Press, 1950). The first of the fundamental symptoms he observed in this illness was a disturbance of associations — that is, dissociation.

77. Jung, *Diagnostische Assoziationsstudien*.

78. Carl Gustav Jung, "Psychoanalysis and Association Experiments," in *Experimental Researches*, trans. Leopold Stein (Princeton, NJ: Princeton University Press, 1973), pp. 288–318.

79. See also Sigmund Freud, *Psycho-Analysis and the Establishment of the Facts in Legal Proceedings*, in *Complete Psychological Works*, vol. 9, pp. 97–115.

80. Sigmund Freud, *Introductory Lectures on Psycho-Analysis*, in *Complete Psychological Works*, vol. 15, p. 110.

81. Jung, "Psychoanalysis and Association Experiments," pp. 316–17. [Trans. modified.]

82. For example, in Richard von Krafft-Ebing's *Lehrbuch der Psychiatrie*, 4th ed. (Stuttgart, 1890), "psychic causes" are listed among "accessory and occasional causes." The author insists: "We are still a long way from madness," as, unilaterally, the playwrights and novelists would have one believe (pp. 185 and 240–41). Krafft-Ebing, of course, did not overlook the sexual domain. His *Psychopathia Sexualis* (1886) saw twelve editions.

83. I found this use of the word in a work by Karl Jaspers dating from 1913 to characterize Freud's doctrine, which developed as "a certain reaction to the extreme tendencies that recent somatic research had been following." See Karl Jaspers, *Gesammelte Schriften zur Psychopathologie* (Berlin: Springer, 1963), p. 337.

84. A student of Auguste Forel at the Zurich hospital of Burghölzli, Adolf Meyer pursued a career of psychiatry in the United States, principally at Johns Hopkins University in Baltimore. His main influence was through teaching.

85. Henri Ey, "La Notion de 'réaction' en psychopathologie," *Confrontations psychiatriques* 12 (1974), pp. 43–62.

86. Adolf Meyer, *The Collected Papers*, 4 vols., ed. Eunice Winters (Baltimore: Johns Hopkins University Press, 1951), vol. 2, p. 598. Later, especially during the 1950s in France, American psychiatry and psychoanalysis were reproached for fostering social conformism (with the ideal of the well-adjusted personality). It is true that in distinguishing between adjusted and maladjusted reactions Meyer introduced a normative criterion. But for Meyer, it was important to suggest to

his students and peers an interpretation of the problems raised by psychiatric practice that was not exclusively somatic and ahistorical. Hence, in his approach to his cases, he introduced biographical and social considerations. George Herbert Mead (1863–1931) was Meyer's contemporary. Mead's description of personal identity (Self) distinguished between the functions of the I and the Me: whereas the I is the bearer of innovative resources, the Me is constructed according to social models. By the constant interaction of the I and the me, the individual, formed in and by society, modifies his environment by responding to it. Jürgen Habermas gave a great deal of attention to Mead's thought. See George Herbert Mead, *Mind, Self, and Society*, ed. Charles William Morris (Chicago: University of Chicago Press, 1934). When Jean Piaget declares himself an "interactionist," it is to highlight the active quality of the process of accommodation, which represents an important step in the formation of the individual. Accommodation modifies the response to the other, as opposed to assimilation, in which the child reduces what he perceives of external reality to his preexisting mental structure. See Jean Piaget, *The Child's Construction of Reality*, trans. Margaret Cook (London: Routledge and Paul, 1955).

87. Meyer, *Collected Papers*, pp. 602–603.

88. *Ibid.*, p. 601.

89. Robert Sommer, *Diagnostik der Geisteskrankheiten* (Vienna and Leipzig: Urban and Schwartzenberg, 1894), pp. 126–27. This German psychiatrist was in contact with Meyer, who often invited him to teach at the hospital of Johns Hopkins University.

90. Sommer speaks of "psychogenic natures" (*ibid.*, pp. 154–55) and cites Kraepelin on this score: "We may perhaps consider as characteristic of all hysterical mental disturbances the extraordinary facility and speed with which psychological states effectively manifest themselves in a multitude of somatic reactions, whether we are speaking of anesthesias or paraesthesias, expressive movements, paralyses, contractions, or abnormal secretions"; see Emil Kraepelin, *Psychiatrie* (Leipzig: Abel, 1889), p. 428. Kraepelin did not immediately accept the notion of psychogenesis, but ended up using it to designate all disorders in which one might consider the symptoms to be translating mental events,

under the influence of a particular predisposition (qualified as degenerative in the fifth edition of his major treatise). The best clinical study on psychogenic mental diseases has been written by the Danish psychiatrist August Wimmer. See August Wimmer, *Psychogenic Psychoses*, ed. and trans. Johan Schioldann (Retterstol: Adelaide Academic Press, 2002). In his discussions which took place in 1946 at Ey's clinic in Bonneval, a debate arose between the theses of psychogenesis (Lacan) and those of organodynamism, whose program was articulated by Henri Ey, citing the integrative theory of John Hughlings Jackson. Mental illness is really only explainable in terms of deficient integration: "Were we to follow Lacan in his conception of psychogenesis, there would no longer be any psychiatry.... I repudiate all psychogenesis, all psychic causality of mental disturbances, I believe that psychogenesis defines the plane of normal psychic activity. I regret the infinite extension of the domain of neuroses considered as psychogenic reactions." Ey tempered this overly radical negation: "What we find to be the common denominator of all psychogenic factors is that they constitute intentional and significant reactions.... Our life of relationships is nothing more than an infinite psychogenic series of purposive acts capable of assuring our adjustment to reality and of realizing our destinies." See Lucien Bonnafé, Henri Ey, S. Follin, Jacques Lacan, and Julien Rouart, *Le Problème de la psychogenèse des névroses et des psychoses* (Paris: Desclée de Bouwer, 1950). In his *Traité de psychiatrie of 1960*, Ey recommends imagining normal life from the perspective of "psycho-sociogenesis." Noting the trouble stirred up by the concept of psychogenesis, Sir Aubrey Lewis, in 1972, suggested that the word be "decently buried." See Aubrey Lewis, "Psychogenic: A Word and Its Mutations," in *The Later Papers of Sir Aubrey Lewis* (Oxford: Oxford University Press, 1979), pp. 185–91.

91. The typical literary example of homesickness is found in Johanna Spyri's novel *Heidi* (1880).

92. Jaspers, *Gesammelte Schriften zur Psychopathologie*, p. 79.

93. Karl Jaspers, *General Psychopathology*, trans. J. Hoenig (Manchester, UK: Manchester University Press, 1963), pp. 42 and 462.

94. *Ibid.*, p. 53.

95. See also Karl Jaspers, "Kausale und 'verständliche' Zusammenhänge zwischen Schicksal und Psychose bei der Dementia praecox (Schizophrenie)" (1913), in *Gesammelte Schriften zur Psychopathologie*, pp. 329–412.

96. See Wilhelm Dilthey, *The Formation of the Historical World in the Human Sciences*, ed. Rudolf A. Makkreel and Frithjof Rodi (Princeton, NJ: Princeton University Press, 2002); Wilhem Dilthey, *Introduction to the Human Sciences*, trans. Ramon J. Betanzos (Detroit: Wayne State University Press, 1988); and Wilhelm Dilthey, *Hermeneutics and the Study of History*, ed. Rudolf A. Makkreel and Frithjof Rodi (Princeton, NJ: Princeton University Press, 1996).

97. Jaspers, *Gesammelte Schriften zur Psychopathologie*, p. 329. See also, in the same collection, the 1912 study "Die phänomenologische Forschungsrichtung in der Psychopathologie," pp. 314–28.

98. Jaspers, *General Psychopathology*, p. 305. [Trans. modified.] See in particular the first chapter of part 2, no. 5, "Meaningful Psychic Connections." It is, notably, a question of the "hermeneutic circle" (p. 356; trans. modified). On this problem, see Paul Ricoeur, "The Task of Hermeneutics," in *From Text to Action*, trans. Kathleen Blamey and John B. Thompson (Evanston, IL: Northwestern University Press, 1991), pp. 53–74). Ricoeur returns to these issues in Jean-Pierre Changeux and Paul Ricoeur, *What Makes Us Think? A Neuroscientist and a Philosopher Argue About Ethics, Human Nature, and the Brain*, trans. M.B. DeBevoise (Princeton, NJ: Princeton University Press, 2000), pp. 125–33.

99. Jaspers, *General Psychopathology*, p. 453. [Trans. modified.] Jaspers notes a little further on that "causal relations do not run only one way, but take reciprocal effect; they extend in this circular fashion so that they either build life up or as 'circuli vitiosi' foster a process of destruction" (p. 454).

100. At the beginning of part 4 ("The Conception of the Psychic Life as a Whole"), Jaspers warns against the simplifying totalities that emerge from the "mistaken enthusiasm" that "tends to start from the whole as something fully known," and "then proceeds to accommodate all the particulars within this framework" (*ibid.*, pp. 558–59).

101. Jaspers, *General Psychopathology*, pp. 460 and 549.

102. *Ibid.*, p. 457.

103. *Ibid.*, p. 461.

104. *Ibid.*, p. 462.

105. *Ibid.*, pp. 347–54.

106. *Ibid.*, p. 462.

107. *Ibid.*, p. 777.

108. See Martin Heidegger and Karl Jaspers, *Briefwechsel* 1920–1963 (Frankfurt am Main: Klostermann, 1990).

109. Jaspers, *General Psychopathology*, p. 307.

110. *Ibid.*, pp. 364–66.

111. *Ibid.*, p. 366.

112. *Ibid.*, pp. 364–66 and 773–75. Jaspers emphasizes the similarities, and especially the differences, between Nietzsche's aphorisms and Freud's historicized systematization. It is common knowledge that in the 1880s Freud might have come in contact with the thought of the author of *Zarathustra* through his friend Josef Paneth, who visited Nietzsche in Italy many times. On Nietzsche and Freud, see Odo Marquard, *Transzentdentaler Idealismus, romantische Naturphilosophie, Psychoanalyse* (Cologne: Verlag für Philosophie Jürgen Dinter, 1987), pp. 441–44; and Rolf Peter Warsitz, *Zwischen Verstehen und Erklären: Widerständige Erfahrung der Psychoanalyse bei Karl Jaspers, Jürgen Habermas, und Jacques Lacan* (Wurzburg: Königshausen and Neumann, 1990).

113. Jaspers, *General Psychopathology*, pp. 383–85. [Trans. modified.]

114. *Ibid.*, p. 384. [Trans. modified.]

115. *Ibid.*, p. 385.

116. One title should be cited: Hans Selye, *The Physiology and Pathology of Exposure to Stress: A Treatise Based on the Concept of the General Adaptation Syndrome and the Diseases of Adaptation* (Montreal: Acta, 1950). The complete title is as long as those of seventeenth-century Latin treatises. Stress challenges the regulatory mechanism and creates pathological mechanisms. Selye writes: "The expression 'systematic stress' is used ... to denote a condition in which — due to function or damage — extensive regions of the body deviate from their normal resting state.... The term 'alarming stimulus' has been employed to denote any agent capable of eliciting first an alarm-reaction and, if its action is prolonged,

the entire general-adaptation syndrome.... The alarm-reaction (A-R) is defined as the sum of all non-specific phenomena elicited by sudden exposure to stimuli, which affect large portions of the body and to which the organism is quantitatively or qualitatively not adapted. Some of these phenomena are merely passive and represent signs of damage or 'shock'; others are manifestations of active defense against damage" (pp. 9–10). See also the works of the physiologist Walter Cannon, who summarized his theory in *The Wisdom of the Body*, 2nd ed. (New York: Norton, 1939.

117. Jaspers, *General Psychopathology*, pp. 384–92.

118. *Ibid.*, pp. 453–54.

119. *Ibid.*, p. 456. [Trans. modified.]

120. Jaspers, *Gesammelte Schriften zur Psychopathologie*, p. 329.

121. Jaspers, *General Psychopathology*, p. 325. [Trans. modified.]

122. *Ibid.*, p. 327. [Trans. modified.] For the question at issue here, the pertinent passages of *General Psychopathology* (1948) are found in part 2, "Meaningful Psychic Connections," pp. 302–446, as well as on pp. 756–79.

123. In his great book on the organism, the neurologist Kurt Goldstein, (1878–1965) considers the major activities ("reflection, thinking, feeling, or doing") as resulting from different types of reactions. The complete development of the human individual depends on the integration and centering of all of these reactions into a "whole that is adequate to the nature of the organism and the human environment." See Kurt Goldstein, *The Organism* (New York: Zone Books, 1995), pp. 247 and 248. In French, *La Structure de l'organisme*, trans. E. Burckhardt and Jean Kuntz (Paris: Gallimard, 1951): "Actions and reactions have meaning only to the extent that phenomena, considered abstractly, are resubmerged into the totality that, alone, is truly real" (p. 272 of the French ed.); Maurice Merleau-Ponty, *The Structure of Behavior*, trans. Alden L. Fisher (Boston: Beacon Press, 1963).

124. Was the objectivizing, analytic approach, with its tendency toward fragmentation, complicit in the crimes of Nazi medicine? This claim has been made. But, as it happens, the authorities under Hitler had long been ardent proponents of "holistic" medicine, complete with totality, doctrines inspired by

Paracelsus, phytotherapy, and so on. See Anne Harrington, *Reenchanted Science: Holism in German Culture from Wilhelm II to Hitler* (Princeton, NJ: Princeton University Press, 1996).

125. Changeux and Ricoeur, *What Makes Us Think?*, pp. 125–26.

126. Helmuth Plessner, *Lachen und Weinen* (Arnhem, 1941). As Harald Weinrich aptly notes in his preface to the French translation: "In both cases, one is led by a plurality of mutually incompatible meanings toward a limit where reason is no longer capable of exercising control over behavior. It is in these limit situations that one 'bursts out' laughing or 'breaks down' in tears. The body responds in place of the soul, and in this substitution it asserts itself as an integral part of the human condition." On the contestation of physiological reductionism, we may recall the text by Max Scheler (1874–1928), *Formalism in Ethics and Non-formal Ethics of Values*, trans. Manfred S. Frings and Roger L. Funk (Evanston, IL: Northwestern University Press, 1973).

127. Ludwig Wittgenstein, *Philosophical Occasions, 1912–1951*, bilingual German-English ed., ed. James C. Klagge and Alfred Nordmann (Indianapolis: Hackett, 1993), pp. 372–73.

[410] Wir reagieren auf die Ursache.

Etwas "Ursache nennen", ist ähnlich, wie zeigen und sagen: "Der ist Schuld!"

See also Ludwig Wittgenstein, *Remarks on the Philosophy of Psychology*, trans. G.E.H. Anscombe (Chicago: University of Chicago Press, 1980), vol. 1, nos. 912–17, pp. 160–63. For Wittgenstein, there are "primitive" reactions, which are "pre-linguistic."

128. Jan Frederik Niermeyer, *Mediae latinitatis lexicon minus*, 2nd ed. (Leiden: Brill, 1993).

129. See Kant's essay *De mundi sensibilis atque intelligibilis forma et principiis*, sec. 16, in *Kant's Inaugural Dissertation of 1770*, trans. William J. Eckoff (New York: AMS Press, 1970).

130. Leo Spitzer, "Les Théories de la stylistique," *Français moderne* 20 (1952), pp. 160–68.

131. Ferdinand de Saussure, *Course in General Linguistics*, trans. Wade Baskin

(London: Fontana/Collins, 1974), pt. 4, ch. 4, sec. 1, p. 205. The notion of "co-action" appears today in ecological research. See Hubert Greppin et al., *The Co-action Between Living Systems and the Planet* (Geneva: University of Geneva Press, 1998).

Chapter Five: Raphael, Louis, Balthazar

1. Honoré de Balzac, "Louis Lambert," in *Seraphita*, trans. Clara Bell (London: Dent, 1913), pp. 201.

2. Italics mine. *Ibid.*, pp. 160–62.

3. Honoré de Balzac, "Les Proscrits," in *La Comédie humaine* 12 vols. (Paris: Gallimard, 1980), vol. 11, p. 550.

4. Honoré de Balzac, "The Quest for the Absolute," in *The Country Doctor, The Quest for the Absolute, and Other Stories*," trans. Ellen Marriage (Philadelphia: Gebbie, 1899), p. 20.

5. Honoré de Balzac, *The Splendors and Miseries of Courtesans*, trans. Ellery Sedgwick (Philadelphia: George Barrie and Son, 1896), p. 19.

6. *Ibid.*, p. 392.

7. Honoré de Balzac, "The Secrets of the Princess of Cadignan," in *The Harlot's Progress, The Hated Son, and Other Stories*, trans. James Waring and John Rudd (Philadelphia: Gebbie, 1899), p. 416.

8. Honoré de Balzac, "Le Cousin Pons," in *Comédie humaine* (1971), vol. 7, p. 483.

9. Honoré de Balzac, "Pierette," in *Comédie humaine* (1970), vol. 4, p. 421.

10. Honoré de Balzac, "The Country Doctor," in *The Country Doctor, The Quest for the Absolute and Other Stories*, p. 48.

11. Honoré de Balzac, "The Seamy Side of History," in *A Woman of Thirty and The Seamy Side of History, and Other Stories*, trans. Ellen Marriage and Clara Bell (Philadelphia: Gebbie, 1899), p. 145.

12. Honoré de Balzac, *Lettres à Madame Hanska*, 2 vols., ed. Roger Pierrot (Paris: Robert Laffont, 1990), vol. 2, p. 909. I shall return to the political meaning of the word "reaction" in the last chapter of this book.

13. Honoré de Balzac, *The Wild Ass's Skin*, trans. Herbert J. Hunt (Harmondsworth, UK: Penguin, 1977), pp. 32–33. [Trans. modified.]

14. *Ibid.*, p. 32. [Trans. modified.] On the semantic history of the word "milieu," see Leo Spitzer's thorough study "*Milieu* and *Ambiance*," in *Essays in Historical Semantics* (New York: Vanni, 1948).

15. Balzac, *Wild Ass's Skin*, p. 204.

16. Balzac, "Seraphita," in *Seraphita*, p. 63.

17. Balzac, *Wild Ass's Skin*, pp. 229–39.

18. *Ibid.*, p. 237.

19. Joseph-Claude-Anthelme Récamier (1774–1852) is the least known of the trio. He was a remarkable teacher at the Hôtel-Dieu. Attentive to observable facts, he invented the speculum and systematized the practice of autopsies. He was known for his generosity and piety and was critical of Broussais and his circle. In the first volume of his *Mémoires d'un bourgeois de Paris* (1853), Louis-Désiré Véron wrote: "More than once, whether by bleeding or by provoking a violent reaction, he succeeded in resuscitating his patients" (p. 322).

20. Balzac, *Wild Ass's Skin*, pp. 248–50.

21. See above. See Moïse Le Yaouanc, *Nosographie de l'humanité balzacienne* (Paris: Maloine, 1959).

22. Balzac, "Louis Lambert," p. 203.

23. Regarding what Balzac might have known about Schelling, through his friend Barchou de Penhoën, see Arlette Michel, "A propos de Barchou de Penhoën," *Année balzacienne* (1969), pp. 147–63. See also Madeleine Fargeaud, *Balzac et "La Recherche de l'absolu"* (Paris: Hachette, 1968).

24. Balzac, "Proscrits," p. 542.

25. Balzac, preface to *Le Livre mystique*, in *Comédie humaine*, vol. 11, p. 503; Balzac, "Proscrits," p. 541.

26. Balzac, "Louis Lambert," p. 215.

27. In an earlier draft Balzac had written, "The whole of our physical actions, movements, and speech constitute the reaction" (*Comédie humaine*, vol. 9, p. 1534).

28. Balzac, "Louis Lambert," pp. 203–204. As recent editions have shown,

Balzac drafted several versions of this doctrinal statement. There is no reason to believe that he was familiar with the theory of the imagination formulated by Charles Victor de Bonstetten in "De la réaction des idées," in *Recherches sur la nature et les lois de l'imagination*, 2 vols. (Geneva: Paschoud, 1807), vol. 2, sec. 3, p. 1. After analyzing sentiments and ideas, the author proposes explaining "the reaction of ideas." Ideas, like sentiments, influence the organs; therefore, one must also consider "the reaction of the organs on sentiments and ideas."

29. Balzac, "Louis Lambert," p. 190.

30. *Ibid.*, pp. 204–206.

31. *Ibid.*, p. 208. We later read: "Lambert was led to believe that the collected ideas to which we give the name of feelings may very possibly be the material outcome of some fluid which is generated in all men, more or less abundantly, according to the way in which their organs absorb, from the medium in which they live, the elementary atoms that produce it" (p. 263). These ideas are offered to explain the "total abolition of physical life," as found in catalepsy.

32. *Ibid.*, p. 223.

33. This is "the grief of a poor child pining for the glorious sunshine, the dews of the valley, and liberty" (*ibid.*, p. 187).

34. *Ibid.*, pp. 180, 186, 177, 189, 180.

35. *Ibid.*, pp. 186, 178, 215–16.

36. *Ibid.*, p. 277. The theory of motion is discussed by Planchette in *The Wild Ass's Skin*, pp. 229–39, and by Laurent Ruggieri in *Sur Catherine de Médicis* (*Comédie humaine*, vol. 11, pp. 429–35). On the role of the will and resistance in Balzac's thought, see Georges Poulet's fine studies in *The Interior Distance*, trans. Elliot Coleman (Baltimore: Johns Hopkins University Press, 1959), pp. 97–152, as well as in *The Metamorphoses of the Circle*, trans. Carley Dawson and Elliot Coleman (Baltimore: Johns Hopkins University Press, 1967); Per Nykrog, *La Pensée de Balzac* (Copenhagen: Munskaard, 1966); Claude Duchet (ed.), *Balzac et "La Peau de chagrin"* (Paris: CDU-SEDES, 1979); Max Andréoli, *Le Système balzacien: Essai de description synchronique*, 2 vols. (Lille: Atelier National de

Reproduction des Thèses, Lille III; Lille and Paris: Aux Amateurs de Livres, 1984).

37. Balzac, "Louis Lambert," p. 231–32. The image of the unknown flower was evoked by Thomas Gray in his famous "Elegy Written in a Country Churchyard" and reworked by Baudelaire in "Le Guignon" (*Les Fleurs du Mal*, poem XI):

Mainte fleur épanche à regret

Son parfum doux comme un secret

Dans les solitudes profondes.

[Many a flower regretfully releases

Its scent, sweet as a secret,

Into the deepest solitudes.]

38. Balzac, "Louis Lambert," p. 236.

39. *Ibid.*, pp. 211, 246, 249, 262.

40. Balzac alludes to this by periphrasis, referring to "the operation to which Origen believed he owed his talents" (*ibid.*, p. 264).

41. *Ibid.*, p. 250.

42. *Ibid.*, p. 264.

43. *Ibid.*, pp. 267–68. In a letter to Valéry, André Gide describes his admiration of Balzac's novel: "I reread it every year. For me, it is enormous. I even find that it is well written. Nothing has staggered me like that vision of Louis Lambert in the dark room, nothing — not even Poe, I believe — and yet!..."; (see "Valéry-Gide Correspondence," in *The Collected Works of Paul Valéry*, ed. Jackson Mathews (Princeton, NJ: Princeton University Press, 1975), vol. 15, p. 125. Three years later Valéry wrote: "To look for similar figures in the sciences, the group Poe-Balzac is like the group Laplace-Ampère-Poisson, etc." (*ibid.*, p. 162). Valéry even ventured to compare "Louis Lambert" to Descartes's *Discourse on Method*, in terms of their autobiographical nature, but to Balzac's disadvantage: "I require theory to be better than mere faking, as in *Louis Lambert*" (*ibid.*, p. 161).

44. Balzac, "Louis Lambert," pp. 268–69.

45. *Ibid.*, pp. 200 and 177.

46. *Ibid.*, p. 262.

47. The narrator magnifies his subject by confessing his own insufficiency: "Such are the meditations which I have with great difficulty cast in a form adapted to our understanding" (*ibid.*, p. 276).

48. Balzac, "Quest for the Absolute," p. 200. The Absolute is the name given to a primitive element common to all substances and from which they would have been produced by "the action of some unknown force, no longer exerted." Here we recognize the alchemists' hypothetical *materia prima*. From the perspective of more recent chemists, Claes is seeking the single element of which all substances would be compounds. The "quest" for the Absolute represents a radical analytic decomposition, with the aim of constituting a "science of a single element," thanks to which, in the hands of the chemist and through synthesis, the activity that created all organic and inorganic bodies would be revived (*ibid.*, pp. 74–76).

49. *Ibid.*, p. 39. [Trans. modified.]

50. *Ibid.*, p. 219. [Trans. modified.]

51. *Ibid.*, pp. 221–22. [Trans. modified.]

52. *Ibid.*, p. 76.

53. On this story, see Gladys Swain, *Dialogue avec l'insensé*, preface by Marcel Gauchet (Paris: Gallimard, 1994), pp. 149–66. "Adieu," in Balzac, *La Comédie humaine*, vol. 10, pp. 1012–13.

54. Jean-François Delpit, "Reaction," in *Dictionnaire des sciences médicales* (Paris, 1819), vol. 47. (See above, pp. 162ff.)

55. Balzac, *Wild Ass's Skin*, pp. 281–82. [Trans. modified.] On Balzac and the psychiatric literature of his time, see Juan Rigoli, *Lire le délire: Aliénisme, rhétorique et littérature en France au XIXe siècle* (Paris: Fayard, 2001).

CHAPTER SIX: DEAD WORLD, BEATING HEARTS

1. Senancour, *Rêveries sur la nature primitive de l'homme* (Paris, 1802), "Première rêverie," pp. 31–32.

2. *Ibid.*, pp. 28–33.

3. *Ibid.*, p. 38.

4. Senancour, *Obermann*, trans. J. Anthony Barnes (London: Walter Scott Publishing Co., Ltd., 1922), vol. 2, p. 266.

5. *Ibid.*, p. 163. In his fine work *Senancour* (Paris: José Corti, 1965), Marcel Raymond compared these statements with Mallarmé's verse: "Quand du stérile hiver a resplendi l'ennui" (When from sterile winter boredom shone forth) (p. 116).

6. Senancour, *Obermann*, p. 255. [Trans. modified.]

7. *Ibid.*, p. 252. Albert Camus recalls this sentence in *The Rebel*.

8. Johann Wolfgang von Goethe, "Principes de philosophie zoologique discutés en Mars 1830 au sein de l'Académie Royale de Sciences par Mr. Geoffroy de Saint-Hilaire," in *Sämtliche Werke in sechs Bänden* (Stuttgart: Cotta, 1863), vol. 6, p. 612.

9. *Ibid.,* p. 612.

10. Samuel Taylor Coleridge, *Biographia Literaria* (1817) (Oxford: Oxford University Press, 1985), ch. 10, pp. 239, 308, 310.

11. Johann Wolfgang von Goethe, *Problem und Erwiederung*, in *Sämtliche Werke*, vol. 6, p. 584.

12. Johann Wolfgang von Goethe, *Contributions to Optics*, in *Goethe's Color Theory*, ed. Rupprecht Matthaei (New York: Van Nostrand Reinhold, 1971), p. 20. [Trans. modified.] See Georg Simmel, *Goethe* (Leipzig, 1913); Frederick Amrine, Francis J. Zucker, and Harvey Wheeler (eds.), *Goethe and the Sciences* (Dordrecht: Reidel, 1987); Jean Lacoste, *Goethe: Science et philosophie* (Paris: PUF, 1997).

13. Johann Wolfgang von Goethe, "The Experiment as Mediator Between Object and Subject," in *Scientific Studies*, ed. and trans. Douglas Miller (New York: Suhrkamp, 1988), pp. 15–16. [Trans. modified.]

14. *Goethe's Theory of Colors*, trans. Charles Lock Eastlake (London: Cass, 1967), sec. 739, pp. 293–94.

15. In fact, the Apostle Paul's words, in which the Latin *movemur* corresponds to the Greek *kinoumetha*, echo a line from Aratus's *Phaenomena* (2.6). Goethe knew and admired Aratus's poem. Newton was familiar with both the apostle and the pagan poet. See Betty Jo Teeter Dobbs, *The Janus Face of Genius: The Role of Alchemy in Newton's Thought* (Cambridge, UK: Cambridge University Press, 1991), pp. 193–207. In a letter written to John Thelwall, dated December 17, 1796, Coleridge used the words of Paul and Aratus to define Christianity:

"The religion which Christ taught is simply, first, that there is an omnipresent Father of infinite power, wisdom, and goodness, in whom we all of us move and have our being; and, secondly, that when we appear to men to die we do not utterly perish; see *The Letters of Samuel Taylor Coleridge*, ed. Kathleen Raine (London: Grey Walls Press, 1950), p. 76. The same reference to Paul's discourse before the Areopagus is found in "Les Proscrits," in the mouth of Sigier, and in "Seraphita," in the mouth of the pastor Becker expounding on Swedenborg's thought. See Honoré de Balzac, *La Comédie humaine*, 12 vols. (Paris: Gallimard, 1980), vol. 11, pp. 543 and 781.

16. Johann Wolfgang von Goethe, "Analysis and Synthesis," in *Scientific Studies*, p. 49. See also Goethe's writing on the influence of recent philosophy ("The Influence of Modern Philosophy," in *Scientific Studies*, p. 28).

17. William Wordsworth, *The Poems*, 2 vols., ed. John O. Hayden (New York: Penguin, 1977), vol. 1, pp. 879–80.

18. See M.H. Abrams's comments in *Natural Supernaturalism* (New York: Norton, 1973); he cites these lines on pp. 278–80.

19. John Keats, *Lamia*, pt. 2, ll. 229–37.

20. Novalis, *Die Christenheit oder Europa*, in *Gesammelte Werke*, 5 vols., ed. Carl Seelig (Zurich: Bühl, 1945), vol. 5, pp. 22–23.

21. John Keats to John Hamilton Reynolds, May 3, 1818, *Letters*, ed. M.B. Forman (Oxford: Oxford University Press, 1947), p. 142.

22. Keats to Reynolds, Aug. 25, 1819, in *ibid.*, p. 374.

23. Novalis, *Christenheit oder Europa*, esp. pp. 26–30.

24. *Plutarch's Moralia*, ed. H. Cherniss and W.C. Helmbold (Cambridge, MA: Harvard University Press, 1960), vol. 12, pp. 92–93.

25. Marsilio Ficino, *Liber de arte chemica*, ch. 8, in Jean-Jacques Manget, *Bibliotheca chemicae curiosae*, 2 vols. (Geneva, 1702), vol. 2, p. 175. It is a question not of the center of the world but of the central orb of the seven planetary spheres encircling Earth. Ficino's cosmology is not heliocentric. After the Copernican revolution, William Harvey could more legitimately compare the centrality of the heart to that of the sun, while continuing to affirm the centrality of the monarch as their analogical equivalent. See the dedication to the king

in *De motu cordis et sanguinis* (1628). My remarks here are added to those of Georges Poulet in *The Metamorphoses of the Circle*, trans. Carley Dawson and Elliot Coleman (Baltimore: Johns Hopkins University Press, 1967). On the verbal expression of pulsation, see Harald Weinrich, *Le Temps, le pouls, les tempes* (Paris: College de France, 1999). See also Neil Hertz, "George Eliot's Pulse," *Differences* 6, no. 1 (1994).

26. See Antoine Faivre, *Philosophie de la nature: Physique sacrée et théosophie, XVIIIe et XIXe siècles* (Paris: Albin Michel, 1996). On contemporary versions of this idea, see Stephen Toulmin, *The Return to Cosmology: Postmodern Science and the Theology of Nature* (Berkeley: University of California Press, 1982).

27. Between 1820 and 1827, Victor Cousin published the work of Proclus in Paris (in six volumes, with J.-M. Eberhart and Firmin Didot).

28. G.W.F. Hegel, *Vorlesungen über die Geschichte der Philosophie*, Introduction, A, 2, c, in *Werke in zwanzig Bänden*, 20 vols. (Frankfurt: Suhrkamp, 1971), vol. 1, p. 47.

29. G.W.F. Hegel, *Logic*, trans. William Wallace (Oxford: Oxford University Press, 1975), secs. 91–108. See also *Encyclopedia of Philosophical Sciences* (1817), secs. 91–108; *Encyclopedia of Philosophical Sciences* (1830), secs. 142–59 and 354; see also *Science de la logique* (1831), pt. 1, bk. 2, sec. 3, ch. 3, "Das absolute Verhaltris." In this work, the heartbeat is treated in section 354, in the tripartite schema characteristic of Hegel's thought.

30. F.W.J. Schelling, *The Ages of the World*, trans. Jason M. Wirth (Albany: State University of New York Press, 2000), p. 11. On Schelling and the philosophy of nature, see the collection of studies published by Ludwig Hasler (ed.), *Schelling, seine Bedeutung für eine Philosophie der Natur und der Geschichte* (Stuttgart: Frommann-Holzboog, 1981).

31. Schelling, *Ages of the World*, pp. 20–21. Compare the texts cited above, Chapter One.

32. Karl Löwith, *Nietzsche's Philosophy of the Eternal Recurrence of the Same*, trans. J. Harvey Lomax (Berkeley: University of California Press, 1978), p. 148. See also Ernst Bloch, *Das Materialismusproblem, seine Geschichte und Substanz* (Frankfurt: Suhrkamp, 1972), pp. 216–29.

33. F.W.J. Schelling, *Erster Entwurf eines Systems der Naturphilosophie*, in *Ausgewählte Werke. Schriften von 1700–1801* (repr., Darmstadt: Wissenschaftlichte Buchgesellschaft, 1975), p. 125.

34. Colin Maclaurin, *An Account of Sir Isaac Newton's Philosophical Discoveries* (London, 1748), bk. 4, ch. 9, p. 408 (the theological version of the hypothesis); Immanuel Kant, *Universal Natural History and Theory of the Heavens* (1755), trans. W. Hastie (Ann Arbor: University of Michigan Press, 1969); Pierre-Simon Laplace, *Exposition du système du monde* (Paris, 1796).

35. Gershom Scholem, *On the Kabbalah and Its Symbolism*, trans. Ralph Manheim (New York: Schocken Books, 1996), p. 110; Gershom Scholem, *Major Trends in Jewish Mysticism* (New York: Schocken Books, 1946), pp. 260–64.

36. F.W.J. Schelling, *Einleitung zu dem Entwurf eines Systems der Naturphilosophie*, in *Ausgewählte Werke*, p. 306. See also F.W.J. Schelling, *Ideas for a Philosophy of Nature*, trans. Errol E. Harris and Peter Heath (Cambridge, UK: Cambridge University Press, 1988), pp. 81–82. On "quality" as a "reciprocal limitation" of attraction and repulsion, see Xavier Tilliette, *Schelling, une philosophie en devenir*, 2 vols., 2nd ed. (Paris: Vrin, 1992), vol. 1, pp. 160–84.

37. Friedrich Hölderlin, too, gives an important role to reaction. See "On the Difference of Poetic Modes," in *Essays and Letters on Theory*, ed. Thomas Pfau (Albany: State University of New York Press, 1988), pp. 83–88.

38. Heinrich Heine, *Religion and Philosophy in Germany*, trans. John Snodgrass (New York: State University of New York Press, 1986), pp. 148–49. [Trans. modified.]

39. *Ibid.*, pp. 151–52.

40. *Ibid.*, p. 155. [Trans. modified.]

41. Gotthilf Heinrich Schubert, *Fünfte Vorlesung, Das Weltgebäude*, in *Ansichten von der Nachtseite der Naturwissenschaft* (repr., Darmstadt: Wissenschaftlichte Buchgesellschaft, 1967), pp. 141–51; Gotthilf Heinrich Schubert, *Geschichte der Seele*, 2 vols., 4th ed. (Stuttgart, 1850), vol. 2, nos. 30–31, pp. 148–79. Albert Béguin devotes a chapter to Schubert in *L'Ame romantique et le rêve*, 2 vols. (Marseilles: Cahiers du Sud, 1937).

42. Hans Christian Ørsted, *Der Geist in der Natur*, 2 vols., trans. K.L. Kannegiesser (Leipzig, 1854), vol. 2, pp. 199–200.

43. Carl Gustav Carus, *Psyche: On the Development of the Soul*, trans. Renata Welch (New York: Spring Publications, 1970), pp. 33–34. The opening sentence of this work is remarkable: "The key to an understanding of the nature of the conscious life of the soul lies in the sphere of the unconscious." Carus means, of course, an unconscious that is both cosmic and organic.

44. *Ibid.*, p. 34; see also pp. 126–27 of the German edition, *Psyche* (1846; new ed., 1860; repr. Darmstadt: Wissenschaftlichte Buchgesellschaft, 1964), where it is a question of the formation of the soul in animals. This is but one example among a multitude of expressions of the same intuition. I will limit myself to noting the passages that the physiologist Karl Friedrich Burdach devotes to the correspondences between the universe and the organic world in his popular work *Der Mensch* (Stuttgart, 1837): "In this chain, everything is reciprocally end and means at the same time, so much so that in a constant circulation the product of life reacts upon life" (secs. 543–48, pp. 621–25); the harmony commands both the relationship between the parts of the organism and the relationship between organic life and the outside world (sec. 568, pp. 651–52).

45. Carl Gustav Carus, *Vergleichende Psychologie oder Geschichte der Seele in der Reihenfolge der Thierwelt* (Vienna, 1866), pp. 3–14.

46. Adolf Trendelenburg, *Logische Untersuchungen*, 2 vols. (Berlin, 1840), vol. 1, ch. 4, "Die Bewegung," pp. 110–22.

47. *Ibid.*, ch. 7, "Kategorien aus der Bewegung," p. 308. Trendelenburg asks which act of thought corresponds to the action and reaction observed in nature. He discusses Kant, who places the category of relation (in which action and reaction are inscribed) in relation to disjunctive judgment (see note 63, p. 385 in Chapter One).

48. *Ibid.*, pp. 314 and 317.

49. Quoted in *ibid.*, p. 308 and n.2. "Surrhoia gar mia, sumpnoia panta, panta sumpathea." See Hippocrates, *Selected Works*, 4 vols., trans. W.H.S. Jones (Cambridge, MA: Harvard University Press, 1957–1959), vol. 1, pp. 350–51. See

Victor Hugo, *Oeuvres poétiques*, ed. Francis Bouvet (Paris: Pauvert, 1961), *L'Ane*, pt. 10, entitled "Réaction de la création sur l'homme," verses 2272–78.

50. Félix Ravaisson, *De l'habitude*, ed. Jean Baruzi (Paris: Félix Alcan, 1927), p. 12.

51. *Ibid.*, pp. 14–16. In a note, Ravaisson refers to Buffon and his *Discours sur la nature des animaux*. The reference is certainly to the passage cited in Chapter Three, p. 116, where a weak excitation causes a violent response, comparable to the explosion of a barrel of gunpowder.

52. Ravaisson, *De l'habitude*, p. 16.

53. *Ibid.*, pp. 59–62.

54. Johann Wolfgang von Goethe, *Faust*, trans. Walter Kaufmann (New York: Anchor Books, 1963), p. 427.

55. Maurice de Guérin, "Méditation sur la mort de Marie," in *Oeuvres complètes*, 2 vols. (Paris: Les Belles Lettres, 1947), vol. 1, pp. 248–49.

56. Cited by Abrams in *Natural Supernaturalism*, p. 435.

57. Honoré de Balzac, "Seraphita," in *Seraphita, A Daughter of Eve, and Other Stories*, trans. Clara Bell and R.S. Scott (Philadelphia: Gebbie, 1899), p. 149. [Trans. modified.]

58. Gottfried Keller, "Ein Tagewerk," in *Gesammelte Gedichte* (Zurich: Rascher, 1918), p. 69.

59. Poe's point of departure had been imagined by others before him. Thus, curiously, Joseph Joubert, in 1800, writes, "Only one grain of matter was needed to create the world"; see *The Notebooks of Joseph Joubert*, trans. Paul Auster (San Francisco: North Point Press, 1983), p. 58; also see the chapter Poulet devotes to Poe in *Metamorphoses of the Circle*.

60. Allusion is made to this in the study and bibliography by David Van Leer in *Romanticism and the Sciences*, ed. Andrew Cunningham and Nicholas Jardine (Cambridge, UK: Cambridge University Press, 1990). See also Edward H. Davidson, *Poe: A Critical Study* (Cambridge, MA: Harvard University Press, 1969), pp. 223–51; and Joan Dayan, *Fables of Mind: Inquiries into Poe's Fiction* (Oxford: Oxford University Press, 1987). See Hélène Tuzet, *Le Cosmos et l'imagination* (Paris: José Corti, 1965).

61. Edgar Allan Poe, *Eureka*, in *The Works*, 10 vols. (Chicago: Stone and Kimball, 1896), vol. 9, p. 4.

62. *Ibid.*, p. 25.

63. *Ibid.*, pp. 16 and 124–25. Poe could have read the word "consistency" in an author he cites, Auguste Comte. Comte speaks of the "mathematical consistency" one can give to Laplace's theory of the formation of the solar system; see Auguste Comte, "Twenty-seventh Lecture," in *Cours de philosophie positive* (Paris: Editions Anthropos, n.d.), vol. 2, p. 291. Here it is only a question of calculations that might consolidate the cosmogonic hypothesis. Comte includes no poetic considerations, and the cycle of condensation and expansion that Poe assigns to the entire universe is limited in Comte to the solar system. The perpetual cycle that Comte imagines nevertheless resembles that of *Eureka*: "We know ... that by the mere continuous resistance of the general environment, our world must, in the long run, inevitably reunite with the solar mass from which it emanated, until a new dilation of this mass occurs in the immensity of future times, to organize, in the same fashion, a new world, destined to provide an analogous career" (p. 297). Auguste Blanqui took the conviction of the repetitive nature of the cosmological cycles to the limits of absurdity in his strange essay *L'Eternité par les astres* (1872; repr., Paris: Slatkine, 1996).

64. Poe, *Eureka*, p. 41.

65. *Ibid.*, pp. 28 and 53. In "Allgemeine Deduktion des dynamischen Prozesser oder der Kategorien der Physik," originally published in *Zeitschrift für speculative Physik* 1 (1800), Schelling assigned to science "the sole task of constructing matter." In the fifth paragraph of this short text, he wants to begin "from the point where the opposition of forces, in the ideal subject of nature, would appear necessary for this construction.... Let us simply remark again that we will call one of the forces — that which goes toward the outside — the *expansive* force, and that which should be thought of as moving toward the inside of nature, we will call the *retarding* or *attractive* force. The former, considered in and of itself, is a pure act of producing [*ein reines Produzieren*], in which nothing can be distinguished absolutely, while the other is what brings division [*Entzweiung*] in this general identity and is thus the first condition of effective

production"; see F.W.J. Schelling, *Werke*, 3 vols., ed. Otto Weiss (Leipzig: Fritz Eckardt, 1907), vol. 1, p. 743. These general principles, in this case, apply to magnetism, electricity, and "chemical processes."

66. Poe, *Eureka*, p. 31.

67. *Ibid.*, p. 66.

68. *Ibid.*, p. 129. See Eveline Pinto, *Edgar Poe et l'art inventeur* (Paris: Klincksieck, 1983), pp. 271–338.

69. Poe, *Eureka*, pp. 130–31.

70. *Ibid.*, p. 132.

71. *Ibid.*, p. 134.

72. James Lawler, *Edgar Poe et les poètes français, suivi d'une conférence inédite de Paul Valéry* (Paris: Julliard, 1989), p. 105.

73. Edgar Allan Poe, "The Island of the Fay," in *Works*, vol. 2, pp. 84–91. This marvelous tale is the story of the perpetual return of a supernatural being.

74. Paul Valéry writes, "Poe's universe is formed on a plan the profound symmetry of which is present, to some degree, in the inner structure of our minds. Hence the poetic instinct should lead us blindly to the truth"; see "On Poe's 'Eureka,'" in *The Collected Works of Paul Valéry*, ed. Jackson Mathews (Princeton, NJ: Princeton University Press, 1956), vol. 8, p. 164. As we know, the cosmogonic myth in *Eureka* was taken up on very serious foundations beginning in the early part of the twentieth century, but without its anthropomorphic component. In 1931, Georges Lemaître (from the Louvain observatory) summed up in the following terms his astrophysical observations, which were supported by Arthur Eddington: "Originally the whole mass of the Universe existed in the form of a single atom; the radius of the Universe, while not strictly nil, was relatively very small. The whole Universe is the result of the disintegration of this primitive atom. One can demonstrate that the radius of space must grow. Certain fragments, having retained their products of disintegration, formed the constellations of stars or the stars of all mass." (See James Jeans, Georges Lemaître, W. De Sitter, Arthur Eddington, Edward Arthur Milne, and Robert Andrew Millikan, *Discussion sur l'évolution de l'univers,* trans. Paul Couderc (Paris: Albin Michel, 1933), pp. 15–22.

75. Edgar Allan Poe, "The Tell-Tale Heart," in *Works*, vol. 2, p. 61.

76. Charles Baudelaire, *Baudelaire on Poe*, ed. and trans. Lois Hyslop and Francis E. Hyslop (Carrolltown, PA: Carroll Press, 1952), p. 84.

77. Poe, *Eureka*, p. 137.

78. Charles Baudelaire, "Mon Coeur mis à nu," in *Oeuvres complètes*, ed. Claude Pichois, 2 vols. (Paris: Gallimard, 1975–1976), vol. 1, p. 676. See the texts by Emerson that Baudelaire transcribed in English, edited and annotated by Claude Pichois, pp. 673–75 of this same volume.

79. Stéphane Mallarmé, *Collected Poems*, trans. Henry Weinfield (Berkeley: University of California Press, 1984), pp. 44–45.

80. Poe, *Eureka*, pp. 93–94.

81. Mallarmé, *Collected Poems*, pp. 124–45. Yves Bonnefoy, "La Poétique de Mallarmé," in *Le Nuage rouge* (Paris: Mercure de France, 1977), p. 204.

82. Stéphane Mallarmé, *Poésie*, ed. Bertrand Marchal, preface by Yves Bonnefoy (Paris: Gallimard, 1992), p. 239.

83. Mallarmé, *Collected Poems*, p. 34.

84. *Ibid.*, "When the shadow menaced with its fatal law," p. 66.

85. Mallarmé, "Hérodiade," in *Collected Poems*, p. 34.

86. See Pierre Brunel, in *Paul Claudel: Quelques influences formatrices*, Revue des Lettres Modernes, 1st ser. (Paris, 1964); Lawler, *Edgar Poe et les poètes français*.

87. Paul Claudel, *Art poétique* (Paris: Mercure de France, 1907); I am citing from later editions augmented with prefatory material: 12th ed. (Paris, 1929), p. 95.

88. *Ibid.*, pp. 98–99.

89. *Ibid.*, pp. 46–49.

90. Paul Valéry, "On Poe's 'Eureka,'" p. 164.

91. Paul Valéry, "Au sujet d'Eurêka," in *Oeuvres*, 2 vols. (Paris: Gallimard, 1962), vol. 1, pp. 864–65.

92. Paul Valéry, *Cahiers*, 2 vols., ed. Judith Robinson (Paris: Gallimard, 1974), vol. 1, p. 313. See also vol. 1, p. 237, and vol. 2, pp. 755–57. The notion of return (symbolized in the last notebooks by the letters *RE*) fascinated and

tormented Valéry. His Faust is a "victim of the eternal Return" (vol. 2, p. 1345). Valéry's exasperation is not unlike the horror Poe's hero faces with the unstoppable beating of the telltale heart. Valéry speaks of "cyclosis," probably based on the idea of "neurosis."

93. *Ibid.*, vol. 1, p. 237.

94. *Ibid.*, vol. 1, p. 954. We find the same idea in Ernst Mach: "When ... we apply abstract concepts to a fact, the fact merely acts upon us as an impulse to a sensational activity, which introduces new sensational elements, which in their turn may determine the subsequent course of our thought in harmony with the fact. By this activity we enrich and extend the fact, which before was too meagre for us.... The concept of the physicist is a definite reaction-activity [*Reaktionstätigkeit*], which enriches a fact with new sensational elements"; see Ernst Mach, *The Analysis of Sensations*, trans. C.M. Williams (New York: Dover, 1959), p. 323. Cognitive reaction, according to Mach, appears more as an adjunction than an interpretation. In 1957, Jean Piaget denounced this "sensorial theory of the origin of scientific knowledge" as a myth.

95. Valéry, *Cahiers*, vol. 1, p. 213.

96. Paul Valéry, "Sketches for a Portrait of Monsieur Teste," in *The Collected Works of Paul Valéry*, vol. 6, *Monsieur Teste*, trans. Jackson Mathews (Princeton, NJ: Princeton University Press, 1973). Mach wrote: "Thought is only one reaction among others" (*Analysis of Sensations*, p. 323).

97. Valéry, "Sketches for a Portrait of Monsieur Teste," p. 68 and Valéry, *Cahiers*, vol. 2, p. 293.

98. Valéry, *Cahiers*, vol. 2, p. 1356. See also the notes regrouped in pp. 277–333, where Valéry defines the relation and the difference between the "me" and the personality. For example: "The *pure Me* is comparable to an ever instantaneous fact — like the center of a mass. *Consciousness* is comparable to the equality of action and reaction" (p. 322).

99. *Collected Works of Paul Valéry*, vol. 1, *Poems*, trans. James R. Lawler, p. 215.

100. Valéry, *Cahiers*, vol. 2, p. 329. Variation on the same theme: "The I is what 'responds' or can respond to anything; or what is common to all responses" (*ibid.*, p. 313).

101. Marcel Gauchet, *L'Inconscient cérébral* (Paris: Seuil, 1992), pp. 153–70.

102. Valéry, *Cahiers*, vol. 1, p. 42; *Collected Works of Paul Valéry*, vol. 14, *Analects*, trans. Stuart Gilbert, p. 407. Stated peremptorily, "For there is no man in man, no *me* in *me*" (*ibid.*, p. 662).

103. Valéry takes this requirement very far: "The analysis of the meaning of words used in psychology must itself be a part of psychology — and thus these meanings themselves cannot be used as instruments" (*Cahiers*, vol. 1, p. 784).

104. *Ibid.*, p. 791.

105. Paul Valéry, *Analects*, p. 286 (italics mine —TRANS.); and Valéry, *Cahiers*, vol. 1, p. 806.

106. Valéry, *Cahiers*, vol. 1, pp. 859–60, 784, 1046.

107. *Ibid.*, vol. 2, pp. 295–96; and Paul Valèry, *Cahiers*, 29 vols. (Paris: CNRS, 1957–1961), vol. 16, p. 45.

108. Valéry, *Cahiers*, vol. 1, p. 843.

109. Lawler has pointed this out in *Edgar Poe et les poètes français*, p. 63.

110. Valéry, *Cahiers*, vol. 1, p. 832.

111. *Ibid.*, vol. 2, pp. 295 and 297. In another formula, the same note affirms that "the Me must play the role of zero in the writing of the All."

112. Valéry, "Sketches for a Portrait of Monsieur Teste."

113. *Collected Works of Paul Valéry*, vol. 1, *Poems*, trans. David Paul, pp. 85, 87, 97. [Trans. modified.]

114. *Ibid.*, pp. 103 and 105. [Trans. modified.]

115. Eugenio Montale, *The Occasions*, trans. William Arrowsmith (New York: Norton, 1987), p. 97. In his commentary on this poem, Dante Isella speaks of a "search backward: for the mystery of the pulsing blood in the veins of the beloved woman during the primordial times of the great cosmic upheavals"; see Eugenio Montale, *Le Occasioni*, ed. Dante Isella (Turin: Einaudi, 1996), p. 150. The commentator traces this motif back to Giacomo Leopardi and Giovanni Pascoli.

116. I have been focusing on a few images of pulsation. It goes without saying that there are other literary uses of "reaction." A text from Francis Ponge's *Le Peintre à l'étude* (1948), "Matter and Memory," speaks of the lithographic stone.

The stone "reacts on the expression.... Is it precisely the fact that it reacts that makes it capable of memory?" See Francis Ponge, *Oeuvres complètes*, ed. Bernard Beugnot (Paris: Gallimard, 1999), vol. 1, pp. 118–19.

117. Paul Klee, *On Modern Art*, trans. Robert Findlay (London: Faber and Faber, 1948), pp. 49–51.

CHAPTER SEVEN: REACTION AND PROGRESS

1. George Berkeley, "Moral Attraction," *Guardian*, Aug. 5, 1713. See *Works*, 4 vols., ed. A.C. Fraser (Oxford, 1901), vol. 4, pp. 186–90. On Berkeley's spiritualist interpretation of Newton's physics, see Paolo Casini, *L'universo-macchina: Origini della filosofia newtoniana* (Bari: Laterza, 1969), pp. 239–74. Berkeley's Newtonian politics have been discussed by I. Bernard Cohen in *Interactions* (Cambridge, MA: MIT Press, 1994).

2. Francis Hutcheson, *An Inquiry into the Original of Our Ideas of Beauty and Virtue* (London, 1738), pt. 2, 5, 2, pp. 221–22.

3. This generalization could be legitimized by Query 31 of Newton's *Opticks* (New York: Dover, 1952): "It's well known, that bodies act one upon another by the attraction of gravity, magnetism, and electricity; and these instances shew the tenor and course of nature, and make it not improbable but that there may be more attractive powers than these. For nature is very consonant and conformable to her self" (p. 376). I cited another passage of this famous text, in relation to Diderot and chemistry, on pp. 92–93, and on p. 393, note 54.

4. Jean-Jacques Rousseau, *Julie; or, The New Heloise*, pt. 2, letter 15, in *The Collected Writings of Rousseau*, trans. Philip Stewart and Jean Vadré (Hanover, NH: University Press of New England, 1977), vol. 6, p. 195.

5. Johann Gottfried Herder, *Grundsätze der Philosophie*, in *Sämtliche Werke*, 33 vols., ed. Bernhard Suphan, Carl Redlich, and Reinhold Steig (Berlin, 1877–1913) (repr., Hildesheim: Olms, 1967–1968), vol. 32, p. 229.

6. David Hume, "Of the Connexion or Association of Ideas," in *A Treatise of Human Nature*, ed. L.A. Selby-Bigge (1739; Oxford: Oxford University Press, 1978), bk. 1, pt. 1, sec. 4, pp. 12–13.

7. Johann David Michaelis, *De l'influence des opinions sur le langage et du langage sur les opinions: Dissertation qui a remporté le prix de l'Académie Royale des Sciences et Belles-Lettres de Prusse en 1759*, trans. André Pierre Le Guay de Prémontval and Jean-Bernard Mérian (Bremen, 1762; repr., Stuttgart, 1974), p. 177.

8. See Otto Mayr, *Authority, Liberty, and Automatic Machinery in Early Modern Europe* (Baltimore: Johns Hopkins University Press, 1986).

9. William Derham, "Of the Balance of Animals," in *Physico-Theology* (London, 1798), pp. 257–59.

10. Jean-Jacques Rousseau, *Essay on the Origin of Languages*, in *Collected Writings of Rousseau*, vol. 7, p. 305. [Trans. modified.] While Rousseau is probably referring to Buffon, one must remember that the idea of "oscillation" was advanced by a number of authors, notably Father Louis-Bertrand Castel in his curious *Traité de physique sur la pesanteur universelle des corps*, 2 vols. (Paris, 1724). There we read, "Weight is a system of falling, condensation, and collapse, whereas Reaction, which causes the return of substances, is a system like lightness, transport, dilation, and elevation" (vol. 1, p. 499). The author even ventures to claim that "in the Earth" there is a "Reaction that pushes all the parts of the center back toward the Circumference" (vol. 1, p. 516). According to Castel, God first established a nature that was materially regular but that tended toward self-destruction through weight. The "hand of God" fortunately disturbed this equilibrium by creating a spiritual counter-nature, namely, man. Hence, through the cultivation of the earth, the construction of dams, and so on, man's action corrects and overcomes that of nature (vol. 1, pp. 508–532). On the equilibrium of nature, see Carl von Linné, *L'Equilibre de la nature,* trans. Bernard Jasmin (Paris: Vrin, 1972); Antonio Di Meo, "'Révolution' et 'equilibre': Science et histoire des sciences au XVIIIe siècle," in Pierre Louis, Jacques Roger, and Martine Groult, *Transfert de vocabulaire dans les sciences* (Paris: CNRS, 1988), pp. 113–24; see Antonello La Vergata, *L'equilibrio e la guerra della natura: Dalla teologia naturale al darwinismo* (Naples: Morano, 1990), which includes an extensive bibliography.

11. Rousseau, *Essay on the Origin of Languages*, p. 305.

12. Jean-Jacques Rousseau, *Emile; or, On Education*, trans. Allan Bloom (New York: Basic Books, 1979), bk. 5, p. 466.

13. Jean-Jacques Rousseau, *Social Contract*, bk. 2, ch. 11, in *Collected Writings of Rousseau*, vol. 4, p. 163. In his *Letter to d'Alembert*, Rousseau is again close to Montesquieu when he discusses the relation between customs and laws. Customs are more important: "If sometimes the laws influence morals [manners], it is when the laws draw their force from them. Then they return to morals [manners] this same force by a sort of reaction well known to real statesmen"; see *Politics and the Arts: Letter to M. d'Alembert on the Theater*, trans. Allan Bloom (Ithaca, NY: Cornell University Press, 1968), p. 66.

14. Montesquieu, *The Spirit of the Laws*, trans. David Wallace Carrithers (Berkeley: University of California Press, 1977), bk. 14, ch. 2, pp. 243–44.

15. Montesquieu, *Considerations on the Causes of the Greatness of the Romans and Their Decline*, trans. David Lowenthal (Indianapolis: Hackett, 1999), ch. 18.

16. *Ibid.*, ch. 9. Unlike Voltaire, Montesquieu is far from convinced by the Newtonians' cause. See Jean Ehrard, *Esprit des mots: Montesquieu en lui-même et parmi les siens* (Geneva: Droz, 1998), pp. 195–211, as well as Jean Ehrard, *L'Idée de nature en France dans la première moitié du XVIIIe siècle* (1963; repr., Paris: Albin Michel, 1994), pp. 132ff.

17. Montesquieu, *Spirit of the Laws*, bk. 5, ch. 1, p. 132.

18. Montesquieu, *Considerations on the Causes of the Greatness of the Romans and Their Decline*, ch. 23.

19. Edmund Burke, *Reflections on the French Revolution*, 5th ed. (London, 1790), pp. 50–51.

20. Denis Diderot, *Fragments politiques*, in *Oeuvres complètes*, 15 vols., intro. Roger Lewinter (Paris: Club Français du Livre, 1969–1973), vol. 10, pp. 77–79. Melchior Grimm's commentary is at the bottom of these pages. The same image is found in Rousseau in *L'Extrait du projet de paix perpétuelle de Monsieur l'abbé de Saint-Pierre* (1761): "There is an action and a reaction among the European powers which, without entirely displacing them, keeps them in a continual agitation; and their efforts are always in vain and always being reborn, like the sea's waves, ceaselessly agitating the surface without ever changing its level; in a similar way, the peoples of Europe incessantly devastated, with no real profit for the sovereigns" (*Oeuvres complètes*, vol. 3, p. 572). The eighteenth century was a time of

international equilibrium in Europe, as Wilhelm von Humboldt affirmed in 1818: "Between the death of Louis XIV and the French Revolution, . . . the power of the states became a sort of mechanism, communicated progressively to them as a whole, placing them in a certain equilibrium . . . and one can almost prove that it was impossible for an individual man, however exceptional he may have been, to rise up to dominate the world"; see Wilhelm von Humboldt, "Betrachtungen über die bewegenden Ursachen in der Weltgeschichte," in *Werke in fünf Bänden*, vol. 1, *Schriften zur Anthropologie und Geschichte* (Stuttgart: Cotta, 1960), p. 580.

21. From Denis Diderot, *Fragments échappés du portefeuille d'un philosophe*, sec. 8, in *Oeuvres complètes*, vol. 10, p. 78, n.21.

22. Rousseau, *Emile; or, On Education*, bk. 4, p. 244.

23. Paul Henri Holbach, *Système de la nature*, 2 vols. (London, 1770), vol. 1, p. 147.

24. *Ibid.*, pp. 41–42. The theory of a sovereign knowledge is from Leibniz; in the next century, the physician and physiologist Hermann Helmholtz gave it the hypothetical name "spirit of Laplace," in reference to a famous passage from Laplace, *Philosophical Essay on Probabilities*, trans. Andrew I. Dale (New York: Springer, 1995), p. 2: "We ought then to consider the present state of the universe as the effect of its previous state and as the cause of that which is to follow. An intelligence that, at a given instant, could comprehend all the forces by which nature is animated and the respective situation of the beings that make it up, if moreover it were vast enough to submit these data to analysis, would encompass in the same formula the movements of the greatest bodies of the universe and those of the lightest atoms. For such an intelligence nothing would be uncertain, and the future, like the past, would be open to its eyes. The human mind affords, in the perfection that it has been able to give to astronomy, a feeble likeness to this intelligence."

25. Holbach, *System of Nature*, pp. 42 and 43.

26. Henri Poincaré, *Théorie des tourbillons* (Paris, 1893).

27. Condorcet, *Sketch for a Historical Picture of the Progress of the Human Mind*, trans. June Barraclough (London: Weidenfield and Nicolson, 1955), pp.

190–91. A naive variation of this quantification is found in Jeremy Bentham's "moral arithmetic" and "calculations of pleasures and pains" (*An Introduction to the Principles of Morals and Legislation*). For an overview of social mathematics, see Georges Gusdorf, *La Conscience révolutionnaire: Les Idéologues* (Paris: Payot, 1978). On Condorcet, see Keith Michael Baker, *Condorcet: From Natural Philosophy to Social Mathematics* (Chicago: University of Chicago Press, 1975), as well as Bronislaw Baczko, *Job, mon ami* (Paris: Gallimard, 1977), pp. 354–90; Lorraine Daston, *Classical Probability and the Enlightenment* (Princeton, NJ: Princeton University Press, 1988).

28. Constantin-François Volney, *Leçons d'histoire*, in *Oeuvres* (Paris, 1876), p. 587.

29. Humboldt, "Betrachtungen über die bewegenden Ursachen in der Weltgeschichte," p. 579.

30. *Ibid.*, p. 580. Humboldt stayed in Paris from 1797 to 1801: he spent time with ideologues and frequented Mme de Staël's salon. The interactions discussed by Humboldt find their mediator in language. See the works of Ernst Cassirer, Hans Aarsleff, Jean Quillien, and Jürgen Trabant on Humboldt's linguistic theory.

31. Wilhelm von Humboldt, "Theorie der Bildung des Menschen," in *Werke in fünf Bänden*, vol. 1, pp. 235–37.

32. Wilhelm von Humboldt, *Ueber den Geist der Menschheit* (1797), nos. 7 and 8, in *Werke in fünf Bänden*, vol. 1, pp. 507–508.

33. Francis Bacon, *The New Organon*, ed. Lisa Jardine and Michael Silverthorne (Cambridge, UK: Cambridge University Press, 2000), p. 33.

34. Blaise Pascal, *Préface sur le traité du vide*, in *Oeuvres complètes*, 4 vols., ed. Jean Mesnard (Paris: Desclée de Brouwer, 1970), vol. 2, pp. 777–85; Blaise Pascal, *Pensées*, ed. Philippe Sellier (Paris: Gallimard, 1986), no. 643, p. 322.

35. Condorcet, *The Life of M. Turgot, Comptroller General* (London: J. Johnson, 1787).

36. See Eric Weil, "Qu'est-ce qu'une 'percée' en histoire?" in *Philosophie et réalité* (Paris: Beauchesne, 1982), p. 222.

37. I am summarizing Immanuel Kant's "Seventh and Eighth Propositions"

of the "Idea for a Universal History with a Cosmopolitan Purpose," in *Political Writings*, 2nd ed., ed. Hans Reiss (Cambridge, UK: Cambridge University Press, 1991). See Eric Weil, *Problèmes kantiens* (Paris: Vrin, 1963), esp. pp. 109–141.

38. Kant, "Seventh and Eighth Propositions," p. 49. [Trans. modified.] At the beginning of Carl von Clausewitz's work *On War*, one finds a very developed idea of action and reaction. War must be considered in relation to politics as an "organic whole" (8, 6). See Raymond Aron, *Clausewitz, Philosopher of War*, trans. Christine Booker and Norman Stone (Englewood Cliffs, NJ: Prentice-Hall, 1985); Hervé Guineret, *Clausewitz et la guerre* (Paris: PUF, 1999).

39. Immanuel Kant, *The Critique of Judgement*, trans. James Creed Meredith (Oxford: Clarendon Press, 1973), pp. 136–37.

40. Kant, *Political Writings*, p. 48.

41. "If, however, only the particular is given and the universal has to be found for it, then the judgement is simply reflective" (Kant, *Critique of Judgement*, p. 18).

42. Reinhart Koselleck, in his entry "Fortschritt," in Otto Brunner, Werner Conze, and Reinhart Koselleck, *Geschichtliche Grundbegriffe* (Stuttgart: Klett-Cotta, 1975), vol. 2, pp. 384–90, notes that eighteenth-century writers, including Condorcet, used the plural in speaking of arts, sciences, and "progresses," whereas nineteenth-century writers hypostatized Art, Science, and Progress, often giving them sacred value.

43. This was the time when, simultaneously, part of the neutral meaning of "progress" was delegated to the word "evolution," which designated a succession of favorable or unfavorable events. People continued nonetheless to use "progress" to designate the quantitative or intensive growth of phenomena, including those that are harmful. One speaks of the progress of an illness, the progress of corruption, and so on.

44. "L'Ami du peuple aux français patriotes," in Jean-Paul Marat, *Oeuvres* (Brussels: Pôle Nord, 1995), vol. 7, p. 4162.

45. At about the same time, another lexical innovation was the political meaning of the adjective "conservative."

46. The physics of reaction also applies to elastic bodies if a coefficient is

taken into account. The metaphor of the mechanical spring is of considerable importance. On the one hand, it is an operative physical model (notably for muscular movement). On the other hand, it is a term that is easily carried over into the vocabulary of inner motivation, the terms "motive" and "motivation" being themselves no more than figures of motion (*motus*). Furthermore, it is an image that makes it possible to represent the forces set into play in political life. In his political vocabulary, Rousseau associates "springs" (*ressorts*) with "reaction": "No human art could prevent the sudden action of the strong against the weak; but it can provide the weak with the means [*ressorts*] of reaction"; see Rousseau, *Political Writings*, trans. Frederick Watkins (Madison: University of Wisconsin Press, 1986), p. 243. [Trans. modified.] In the language of the 1790s, the semantic couples "to compress/to release," "compression/release" were used frequently, especially in politics.

47. Bronislaw Baczko, *Ending the Terror: The French Revolution After Robespierre*, trans. Michael Petheram (Cambridge, UK: Cambridge University Press, 1994), pp. 243–58. [Trans. modified.] See Raymonde Monnier, "Un Mot nouveau en politique: *Réaction* sous Thermidor," in *Dictionnaire des usages sociopolitiques (1770–1815)*, no. 6, *Notions pratiques* (Paris: INaLF, 1998); Jean-Clément Martin, *Contre-révolution: Révolution et nation en France, 1789–1799* (Paris: Seuil, 1998).

48. Cited by Ferdinand Brunot, *Histoire de la langue française* (Paris, 1937), vol. 9, 2, p. 844. Another example, which Bronislaw Baczko very kindly pointed out to me: on 8 Germinal, year IV, Jean-Baptiste Mailhe addressed the council of Five Hundred: "Can it come as any surprise that 9 Thermidor, which, very simply, should be for the throne of anarchy what August 10 was for the throne of royalty, was slowly sidetracked from its restorative goal and presented as the principle of a bloody and arbitrary reaction; or that this principle was preached by the same societies and often the same men who had actively figured in preceding scenes?" (repr. from *Moniteur* 28 [Paris, 1863], p. 89).

49. Sébastien Mercier, *Le Nouveau Paris*, ed. Jean-Claude Bonnet (Paris: Mercure de France, 1994), pp. 573–74. In its first political uses, the word "reaction" was always accompanied by a qualifying epithet, such as "royal" in this case.

50. Reprinted from *Moniteur* 28 (21 Germinal, year IV [April 10, 1796]), p. 165.

51. In Emmanuel de Las Cases, *Mémorial de Sainte-Hélène: Journal of the Private Life and Conversations of the Emperor Napoleon at St. Helena* (London: H. Colburn, 1823), Oct. 9–10, 1816, Napoleon treats the words "reactors," "counter-revolution," and "old feudalists" as synonyms.

52. I'd like to cite Baczko's analysis: "There were several reactions in what people were now sometimes calling the *Thermidorian reaction*. There was an anti-Jacobin and anti-terrorist reaction, a backlash of public opinion calling for the reparation of the evils and sufferings undergone during the Terror, and which appealed to 'justice as the order of the day.' There was a reaction which, often driven by the will to revenge, identified the Revolution with the Terror and its consequences and so put back into question the Revolution's principles themselves. The reaction then took the form of a denial of the principles of 1789, or, in another variation, of again discussing whether a Republic was inappropriate, as a form of government, in a large country.... There was also a reaction in the domain of ideas when the 'publicists,' freshly converted to Catholicism, denied and condemned with the zeal of the neophyte the enlightened mind which they had favored just the day before" (*Ending the Terror*, p. 248; trans. modified). The expression "Thermidorian reaction" was used by Gracchus Babeuf.

53. Reprinted from *Moniteur* 28 (June 15, 1796), p. 321.

54. Jean-François de La Harpe, *Du fanatisme dans la langue révolutionnaire* (Paris, year V [1797]), pp. 90–91. Throughout his text, La Harpe uses italics to underscore the neologisms he considers "barbarous." In another note from this text, pp. 29–30, La Harpe sharply criticizes Benjamin Constant and his pamphlet *De la force du gouvernement actuel de la France et de la nécessité de s'y rallier* (May 1796), which approved the measures taken by the Directory after the crushing of the royalist riot of 13 Vendémiaire.

55. For a long time, the same was true for the word "revolution." I will not summarize here a history that has often been recounted. See Karl-Heinz Bender, *Revolutionen. Die Entstehung des politischen Revolutionsbegriffes in Frankreich*

(Munich: Fink, 1977); and in particular Alain Rey, *"Revolution": Histoire d'un mot* (Paris: Gallimard, 1989).

56. Joseph de Maistre, "Conjectures on the Ways of Providence in the French Revolution," in *Considerations on France*, trans. Richard Lebrun (Montreal: McGill University Press, 1974). The association of "reaction" and "counter-revolution" is very clear in the thought of Germaine de Staël. She writes to Pierre-Louis Roederer on April 15, 1797: "If we come up with an idea of reaction like this one, or rather one that is like it except in name, has the counter-revolution not already been completed?" See Mme de Staël, *Des circonstances actuelles qui peuvent terminer la révolution et des principes qui doivent fonder la république en France* (1798), critical ed. by Lucia Omacini (Geneva: Droz, 1979), p. xxix.

57. Constant's pamphlet in favor of the Directory violently displeased de Maistre, who had replied with *Considerations on France*.

58. See Benjamin Constant, *Political Writings*, trans. Biancamaria Fontana (Cambridge, UK: Cambridge University Press, 1988). The expression Constant uses in his title (which he probably did not invent) seems to have become formulaic. In Balzac's *L'Envers de l'histoire contemporaine*, one reads this sentence by the former public prosecutor Bourlac, now fallen on hard times: "I am one of the thousand victims of the *political reactions*"; see *La Comédie humaine*, 12 vols. (Paris: Gallimard, 1977), vol. 8, p. 341.

59. Benjamin Constant, *De la force du gouvernement actuel de la France et de la nécessité de s'y rallier. Des réactions politiques. Des effects de la terreur* (Paris: Flammarion, 1988), p. 96.

60. *Ibid.*, pp. 96, 150, 101. The implication is obvious: it is a matter of punishing the former terrorists.

61. *Ibid.* It is a question here of humanity as a species. Kant speaks of *Gattung*. Constant was familiar with Kant's recent writings. *Des réactions politiques* contains a polemic against Kant's categorical imperative, in particular against the absolute interdiction against lying, even to save a friend sought by evildoers. Kant later took the trouble to respond. On the debates stimulated by the concept of perfectibility, see two excellent works: Sergio Moravia, *Il tramonto del-*

l'illuminismo (Bari: Laterza, 1968); and Ernst Behler, *Unendliche Perfektibilität. Europäische Romantik und Französische Revolution* (Paderborn: Schöningh, 1989).

62. The word "perfectibility" is a neologism first used by Rousseau in *Discours sur l'inégalité* (1755). Constant included a piece titled "De la perfectibilité de l'espèce humaine" in his *Mélanges de littérature et de politique* (1829). This explains why it is not difficult for him, under the restoration, to make a case for "civilization" and "legal conventions" rather than for the "revolution" he defended in his pamphlets of 1797. Perfectibility is the common denominator.

63. Constant, *Des réactions politiques*, pp. 98–99. This theme was taken up by Constant again in his brief essay *Des suites de la contre-Révolution de 1660 en Angleterre* (1799). It warns the French of the consequences of a return to monarchy by recounting the abuses that took place in England when Charles II came to the throne and punished the republicans: "When the monarchy rises again, the judges of the king must perish" (p. 20). Constant uses the word "counterrevolution" but not "reaction."

64. Constant, *Des réactions politiques*, p. 99.

65. See Patrick Tort, "Progrès," in *Dictionnaire du darwinisme et de l'évolution*, 3 vols., ed. Patrick Tort (Paris: PUF, 1997), vol. 3, pp. 3568–72.

66. See Eric Weil, "Hegel et le concept de la Révolution," in *Philosophie et réalité*, vol. 2, pp. 127–45; Joachim Ritter, *Hegel and the French Revolution*, trans. Richard Dien Winfield (Cambridge, MA: MIT Press, 1982).

67. The opponents of the Revolution, beginning with Edmund Burke, mocked the new legislators' use of the ruler and compass and their disregard for the realities that make the social body a living being.

68. Mme de Staël, *De l'influence des passions sur le bonheur des individus et des nations* (Lausanne, 1796), pp. 13 and 28.

69. Mme de Staël, *Des circonstances actuelles qui peuvent terminer la révolution et des principes qui doivent fonder la république en France*, ed. Lucia Omacini (Geneva: Droz, 1979), pp. 26, 27, 305, 338. Mme de Staël adds that, with the exception of a small number of free individuals, "the human species can be calculated like a chemical experiment" (pp. 317–18).

70. Mme de Staël, *De l'influence des passions*, p. 16.

71. Mme de Staël, *Des circonstances actuelles*, pp. 339 and 66.

72. On the history of the idea of progress, aside from the classic works of Jules Delvaille (1910) and John Bagnell Bury (1924) and the contributions of Christian Meier and Reinhart Koselleck to the great dictionary *Geschichtliche Grundbegriffe* (see note 42 above), see Joachim Ritter, "Fortschritt," in *Historisches Wörterbuch der Philosophie*, 10 vols., ed. Joachim Ritter (Basel: B. Schwabe, 1972), vol. 2, cols. 1032–59; and Jochen Schlobach, "Progrès," in *Dictionnaire européen des Lumières*, ed. Michel Delon (Paris: PUF, 1997), pp. 905–909. See also Peter J. Bowler, *The Invention of Progress: The Victorians and the Past* (Oxford: Blackwell, 1990).

73. Benjamin Constant, *Des réactions politiques*, pp. 107 and 151. In *De la littérature*, 2 vols. (Paris, 1800), Germaine de Staël also defines the writer's political function. While celebrating scientific thought and its rigorous demonstrations, she nonetheless reserves a dominant role for "moral ideas" and enthusiasm. She calls upon both the energies of devotion and the calculations whose effectiveness had been proved by Newton. The reign of eloquence has not ended. "But if moral truths can one day be demonstrated, and if the language that must express them should achieve a mathematical precision, what will become of eloquence?" (vol. 2, ch. 8, pp. 276–77). The answer is reassuring: "Since everything that has to do with virtue comes from another source, having a principle other than that of reason, eloquence will always reign in the empire it must possess." She even reaches a paradoxical conclusion: "One might say that everything that is eloquent is true" (p. 278). "Enlightenment and morality, morality and enlightenment help each other mutually" (*ibid.*, ch. 9, p. 293). With regard to this work, Chateaubriand, in *Lettre à M. de Fontanes sur la 2ème édition de l'ouvrage de Mme de Staël* (1801), focuses entirely on the theory of perfectibility, which he challenges: "Has the human race taken a step toward moral science? No; it has advanced in the physical sciences alone.... Every writer who refuses to believe in God, the author of the universe,... banishes the infinite from his works.... He no longer sees anything noble in nature. Everything takes place through the impure methods of corruption and regeneration.... Hence, everything is disenchanted; everything is exposed by the skeptic.... What is

essentially lacking in your work is eloquence. Now, there is no eloquence without religion"; see *Oeuvres complètes*, 16 vols. (Paris: Krabbe, 1852), vol. 3, pp. 154 and 162–63.

74. Mme de Staël, *De la littérature*, vol. 2, 3, pp. 138–39.

75. *Ibid.*, vol. 2, 6, pp. 221–25.

76. *Ibid.*, vol. 1, 8, pp. 239–40.

77. Georges Sorel, *The Illusions of Progress*, trans. John Stanley and Charlotte Stanley (Berkeley: University of California Press, 1969), pp. 129–30.

78. He hardly used the word "reaction" in writings after 1800. In his articles from 1829 to 1830, he designates the ultraroyalists in speaking of the "counterrevolutionary faction." Charles X and his last ministry wanted "to govern against an entire people." See Benjamin Constant, *Recueil d'articles, 1829–1830*, ed. Ephraïm Harpaz (Paris: Champion, 1992), pp. 327, 328, 346.

79. Benjamin Constant, *Ecrits et discours politiques*, 2 vols., ed. Pozzo di Borgo (Paris: Pauvert, 1964), vol. 2, pp. 134 and 142.

80. Constant, "De la perfectibilité de l'espèce humaine," p. 407. This motif will be examined in Tocqueville's American research.

81. *Ibid.*, pp. 408–413.

82. These speeches were delivered on August 7 and September 6, 1830. See Stephen Holmes, *Benjamin Constant and the Making of Modern Liberalism* (New Haven, CT: Yale University Press, 1984).

83. See Henri Gouhier, *Benjamin Constant* (Paris: Desclée de Brouwer, 1967).

84. Benjamin Constant and Mme de Staël, *Lettres à un ami* (Neuchâtel, 1948), Oct. 11, 1811, pp. 194–95. Cited in part by Chateaubriand, *Etudes, ou, Discours historiques sur la chute de l'empire romain*, in *Oeuvres complètes*, vol. 10, p. 75.

85. Chateaubriand, *Etudes*, p. 86.

86. Chateaubriand, *Mémoires d'outre-tombe*, 4 vols., ed. Maurice Levaillant (Paris: Flammarion, 1950), vol. 4, pt. 4, bk. 12, 6, p. 585.

87. Arthur Rimbaud, *A Season in Hell*, in *Complete Works, Selected Letters*, trans. Wallace Fowlie (Chicago: University of Chicago Press, 1966), p. 209.

88. See Jean Dubois, *Le Vocabulaire politique et social en France de 1869 à*

1872: A travers les oeuvres des écrivains, les revues et les journaux (Paris: Larousse, 1962). See in particular the remarks on the role of antonymy in the semantic unity of words from the political and the social vocabulary and pp. 398–400.

89. Charles-Augustin Sainte-Beuve, "Madame de Staël," in *Portraits de femmes* (1844), ed. Gérald Antoine (Paris: Gallimard, 1998), p. 162. One notes that Napoleon did not stop speaking the language of Condorcet when he addressed himself to the learned. To the report presented in 1808 by the "Class in physical sciences and mathematics" at the Institut not in use at the time (directed by Cuvier), he replied: "I wanted to listen to you about the progress of the human mind in recent times, so that the things you will tell me might be heard by all nations and silence our century's detractors, who, in seeking to make the human mind regress, appear to have taken as their goal to extinguish it"; see *Rapport historique sur le progrès des sciences naturelles depuis 1789, et sur l'état actuel* (Paris, 1810), p. 395.

90. Charles-Augustin Sainte-Beuve, "Le Père Lacordaire," in *Nouveaux Lundis*, 3rd ed. (Paris, 1881), vol. 4, p. 423.

91. Auguste Comte, "Fifty-seventh Lecture," in *Cours de philosophie positive* (1830), 6 vols. (Paris, 1908), vol. 6, p. 298.

92. Jules Michelet, *Histoire de la Révolution française* (1847–1853), 2 vols., ed. Gérard Walter (Paris: Gallimard, 1962), vol. 2, bk. 21, chs. 9 and 10, pp. 986–90.

Jules Michelet, *History of the French Revolution*, trans. Charles Cocks, ed. Gordon Wright (Chicago: University of Chicago Press, 1967), p. 27. Nothing, in fact, prevents the use of new terms for circumstances predating their adoption. Historians have used the expressions "noble reaction" and "aristocratic reaction" for the nobility's resistance to attempts at reforming the administration preceding the Revolution. These "reactions" therefore preceded the appearance of the political meaning of the word "reaction." Provided they recognize the languages of the past, historians have the right to use the language of the present. The most scrupulous history is disciplined anachronism. There is no reason to renounce applying contemporary forms of knowledge to the past, as long as distance and differences are taken into consideration.

93. Edgar Quinet, *La Révolution*, 2 vols. (Paris, 1865), vol. 2, pp. 384–85.

94. Cited by Robert Carlier et al. (eds.) in *Dictionnaire des citations françaises* (Paris: Larousse, 1977), p. 276, Victor Hugo, "Le Tas de pierres," in *Oeuvres complètes*, 4 vols., ed. Francis Bouvet (Paris: Pauvert, 1963), *Oeuvres dramatiques et critiques complètes*, p. 1550. In Hugo's imagination, progress is also associated with the image of the beating heart: "Each beat of the heart signifies: progress"; see *Oeuvres complètes, Politique* (Paris: Robert Laffont, 1985), p. 1070.

95. Charles de Rémusat, *Passé et présent*, 2 vols. (Paris, 1847), vol. 1, p. 35. On the preceding page, Rémusat assigns to spirit the task of fighting "against materialism when it attacks in the forms of anarchy and when it defends itself with the weapons of reaction."

96. Weil, "Qu'est-ce qu'une 'percée' en histoire?," pp. 193–223.

97. Karl Marx and Friedrich Engels, *The Communist Manifesto*, ed. John E. Toews (Boston: Bedford/St. Martin's, 1999), pp. 69 and 75. [Trans. modified.] In *The German Ideology*, Marx was particularly critical of Max Stirner (1806–1856), who, after his resounding book *Der Einzige und sein Eigentum* (1844), wrote *Geschichte der Reaktion* (1852), in which he approves of the repression of the 1848 revolution in Germany as a healthy reaction. See Max Stirner, *Geschichte der Reaktion* (repr., Aalen: Scientia, 1967), pt. 2, pp. 19–20.

98. Karl Marx, *Birth of the Communist Manifesto with text of the Manifesto*, ed. Dirk J. Struik (New York: International Publishers, 1971), p. 100.

99. *Ibid.*, p. 125.

100. Condorcet, *Sketch for a Historical Picture of the Progress of the Human Mind*, p. 201.

101. See Andrzej Walicki, *A History of Russian Thought from the Enlightenment to Marxism*, trans. Hilda Andrews-Rusiecka (Stanford, CA: Stanford University Press, 1979), ch. 14, pp. 290–91. See also Leszek Kolakowski, *Main Currents of Marxism*, 3 vols., trans. Paul Stephen Falla (Oxford: Clarendon Press, 1975–1978).

102. I have focused on the fate of "reaction" without dwelling on the semantic variations of "action" and related terms: "to act," "agent," "actor/ actress," "to agitate," "agitation," "agitator," "activity," "activist." These are also very revealing. On these terms, one can consult historical dictionaries of language.

457

103. Pierre-Joseph Proudhon, *Philosophie du progrès*, intro. and notes by Théodore Ruyssen (Paris: Marcel Rivière, 1946), pp. 102–103, n.5.

104. See Albert O. Hirschman, *The Rhetoric of Reaction: Perversity, Futility, Jeopardy* (Cambridge, MA: Harvard University Press, 1991).

105. Cited by Reinhart Koselleck in his "Revolution" entry in *Geschichtliche Grundbegriffe*, vol. 5, pp. 689–788, esp. p. 760: "Kameraden, die Rot-Front und Reaktion erschossen, marschier'n im Geist in unseren Reihen mit."

106. Paul Valéry, a careful reader of Nietzsche, sometimes thinks as he does about democracy. One finds, in a notebook of 1918–1919, the following remark containing Nietzsche's theory of *ressentiment*: "The vice of the democratic state is that it is born not from a study of the problem of social functioning, considered in itself, but from a *reaction*, a negation of a prior state, a desire to efface, which is exaggerated in F[rance] by envy, *invidia*, etc."; see Paul Valéry, *Cahiers*, 2 vols., ed. Judith Robinson (Paris: Gallimard, 1974), vol. 2, p. 1461. [We have retained Nietzsche's use of the French term *ressentiment* in *The Genealogy of Morals*. *Ressentiment*, even more clearly than the English "resentment," suggests a "re-feeling" or a "feeling-again." — TRANS.]

107. Friedrich Nietzsche, *Twilight of the Idols*, trans. Richard Polt (Indianapolis: Hackett, 1997), p. 78.

108. Friedrich Nietzsche, *Werke*, 4 vols., ed. Karl Schlechta (Munich: Hanser, 1954–1956), vol. 3, *Fragmente aus dem Nachlass der Achtzigerjahre*, p. 779. The same idea is found in *On the Genealogy of Morals*, trans. Walter Kaufmann (New York: Vintage Books, 1969), pp. 76–79.

109. Nietzsche, *On the Genealogy of Morals*, pp. 36–37.

110. Friedrich Nietzsche to Peter Gast, March 21, 1882. See Alwin Mittasch, *Friedrich Nietzsche als Naturphilosoph* (Stuttgart: Kröner, 1952).

111. Nietzsche, *On the Genealogy of Morals*, pp. 77–78. [Trans. modified.] These pages are a celebration of violence. One cannot escape the sense of unease they produce by looking for statements that might qualify them in other parts of the work or by underscoring their author's pathetic solitude. Nietzsche, at this moment, was not howling with the wolves, but the wolves did echo him.

112. *Ibid.*, pp. 78–79.

113. Nietzsche was an avid reader of *Revue philosophique*, edited by Théodule Ribot. Studies of scientific psychology occupied a considerable part of it.

114. Nietzsche, *On the Genealogy of Morals*, pp. 38 and 39. Nietzsche does not, however, fear the rhetoric of *we* and *moving onward*. In a remark in *Human, All Too Human* (1, sec. 26), titled "Reaction as progress," he considers Schopenhauer's reaction against the Enlightenment beneficial in terms of his celebration of "Christianity and its Asiatic relations." In doing justice to this outmoded ideal, he served the cause of the Enlightenment: "Only after this great *triumph of justice*, only after we have corrected the mode of historical interpretation introduced by the Age of Enlightenment on so essential a point as this, may we bear the banner of the Enlightenment — the banner bearing the three names Petrarch, Erasmus, Voltaire — further onward. Out of reaction we have created progress" (pp. 25–26). The same idea occurs in *Daybreak*, bk. 3, sec. 197, where one finds an invitation to make the Enlightenment "progress" by converting reaction to its advantage; see Friedrich Nietzsche, *Daybreak*, trans. R.J. Hollingdale (Cambridge, UK: Cambridge University Press, 1982), pp. 117–18. See Paul Widmer, "Die 'Reaktion' als Opfer der Fortschrittskrise," *Neue Zürcher Zeitung*, June 29–30, 1985, pp. 65–66.

115. *Ibid.,* pp. 73–75. The role of the notion of reaction in Nietzsche's thought is demonstrated by Gilles Deleuze in *Nietzsche and Philosophy*, trans. Hugh Tomlinson (New York: Columbia University Press, 1983).

116. Friedrich Nietzsche, *Human, All Too Human*, trans. R.J. Hollingdale (Cambridge, UK: Cambridge University Press, 1986), pp. 366–67. [Trans. modified.]

117. After reading a book by René Guénon about Hindu doctrines, Simone Weil wrote in one of her notebooks in 1941: "The limit — and consequently the action and reaction, the ruptures of the equilibriums compensating one another, the relationships, the condition — is the law of the manifest world." See Simone Weil, *Oeuvres complètes*, ed. André Devaux and Florence de Lussy (Paris: Gallimard, 1997), vol. 6, *Cahiers*, 2, p. 75 and n.90.

118. See Mark Lilla, "A Tale of Two Reactions," *New York Review of Books*, May 14, 1998, pp. 4–7.

119. See the study by Tony Honoré, "Being Responsible and Being a Victim of Circumstance," *Proceedings of the British Academy, 97, 1997, Lectures and Memoirs* (London and New York, 1998), pp. 169–87.

120. These two quotations are taken from François Furet and Ernst Nolte, *Fascism and Communism*, trans. Katherine Golsan (Lincoln: University of Nebraska Press, 1998), p. 2. In the epistolary exchange, Furet introduces nuances: "I think you insist too much on the 'reactive' character of fascism to communism, that is, on the posterior character of its appearance in chronological order and on its being shaped by the precedent of October. I myself see two potential figures of modern democracy in both movements, which arise from the same history" (p. 19). Furet prefers the theory of a common origin, marked by certain similar traits, to that of the reactive filiation of one revolution with the other. The German historian to whom Furet addresses his remarks develops all the auxiliary arguments of revisionism, though not revisionism itself.

121. *Ibid.*, pp. 90–91. Italics mine.

122. Aurel Kolnai, "Der Ekel," *Jahrbuch für Philosophie und Phänomenologische Forschung* (1929); Emmanuel Lévinas, *Existence and Existents*, trans. Alphonso Lingis (The Hague: Nijhoff, 1978).

123. The semantic scope of "action" is great, with its military, juridical, and rhetorical meanings. The word "reaction," because it mirrors "action," benefits from its partner's range of associations.

124. Valéry, *Cahiers*, vol. 1, p. 566.

125. Sigmund Freud, *The Standard Edition of The Complete Psychological Works of Sigmund Freud*, trans. James Strachey (London, Hogarth Press, 1953), vol. 4, p. xxvi. Charles-Ferdinand Ramuz, *Raison d'être*, in *Oeuvres complètes*, 5 vols. (Lausanne: Rencontre, 1967), vol. 2, pp. 604–605; Joseph Conrad, *The Secret Agent* (New York: Doubleday Anchor Books, 1953), p. 9; Valéry, *Cahiers*, vol. 1, p. 1148. Georg Simmel, *Hauptprobleme der Philosophie* (Berlin: Göschen, 1913), p. 12: "Man kann den Philosophen vielleicht als denjenigen bezeichnen, der das aufnehmende und reagierende Organ für die Ganzheit des Seins hat." The category of interaction (*Wechselwirkung*) was important in Simmel's sociological works. In an autobiographical work, he declares that he has extended it

"progressively, to the point of making it a general, all-encompassing metaphysical principle" (*Anfang einer unvollendeten Selbstdarstellung*), cited by Helmut Bachmaier and Thomas Rentsch in the entry on Simmel in *Metzler Philosophen Lexikon*, ed. Bernd Lutz and Norbert Retlich (Stuttgart: Metzler, 1995), p. 830. See Raymond Boudon, *Etudes sur les sociologues classiques* (Paris: PUF, 1998), pp. 165–218.

126. One finds this expression linked to the idea of reaction in Paul Bourget, who refers to the classics: "When our personality is forming, the first expression of its soul is a reaction. To what, if not to the things surrounding us? Classical philosophy had this saying . . . : the self defines itself through opposition"; see Paul Bourget, *Au service de l'ordre* (Paris: Plon), 1912). I cite from Paul Dupré, *Encyclopédie des citations françaises* (Paris: Trévise, 1959), p. 149, no. 2987.

127. Friedrich Nietzsche, *Beyond Good and Evil*, trans. Walter Kaufmann (New York: Vintage Books, 1966), p. 24. The idea is also found in Georg Christoph Lichtenberg (1742–1799).

Index

Designed by Bruce Mau
Typeset by Archetype
Printed and bound by Maple-Vail on Sebago acid-free paper